SHORT-TERM
DYNAMIC
PSYCHOTHERAPY

"Freud discovered the unconscious; Davanloo has discovered how to use it therapeutically."

—David Malan, M.D.

Eminently Sensible

"There is little doubt, and it is abundantly clear from several of the book's chapters, that in both theoretical and clinical terms, the application of a more active role on the part of the psychoanalytically oriented therapist in order to make treatment more effective and more efficient is eminently sensible. In one sense the wheel has turned full circle. We know that early psychoanalytic therapies, as conducted by Freud, were of relatively brief duration. Much later, Freud became aware, as is obvious from his essay, 'Analysis Terminable and Interminable,' that treatment could be much extended, indeed it could continue indefinitely if its goals became unduly ambitious—not the resolution of symptoms and the acquisition of insight alone, but the attainment of 'absolute psychical normality.'

"The major contribution of the proponents of short-term dynamic psychotherapy is the notion that with suitable selection criteria and specified therapeutic techniques, the approach is both feasible and potentially valuable. The snag is how to identify accurately these criteria and techniques. In Part II of the book, four of the best known figures in the field—Davanloo, Malan, Sifneos, and Marmor—all addressed themselves to the question of suitability. In commenting on each other's selection criteria they reveal some important differences among themselves. A similar observation can be made about their treatment techniques. . . . Short-term dynamic psychotherapists are engaged in free and open discussion about their clinical cases; moreover, they place a strong emphasis on showing their video-taped interviews to one another. This process of constructive collaboration is well captured in this volume. Psychiatrists eager to know more about the current state of short-term dynamic psychotherapy will find this book both interesting and useful."

—Sidney Bloch, M.D.
The British Journal of Psychiatry

SHORT-TERM DYNAMIC PSYCHOTHERAPY

edited by
Habib Davanloo, M.D.

1992

𝒜

JASON ARONSON INC.
Northvale, New Jersey
London

ISBN: 0-87668-418-5 (hardcover)
ISBN: 0-87668-301-4 (softcover)

Library of Congress Catalog Number: 80-67986

Manufactured in the United States of America. Jason Aronson Inc. offers books and cassettes. For information and catalog write to Jason Aronson Inc., 230 Livingston Street, Northvale, New Jersey 07647.

Contents

Part II
SELECTION OF PATIENTS

Part III
THE FAMILY

Part IV
CRISIS INTERVENTION

Introduction

During recent years Short-Term Dynamic Psychotherapy has gained a great deal of popularity. Many factors have contributed to this. One of the most important factors is the growing number of systematic research projects which have given scientific validity to Short-Term Dynamic Psychotherapy. Along with this, the imminence of some form of universal health insurance limiting coverage to 20-30 sessions is putting pressure on psychotherapists to find a shorter and more efficient form of psychotherapy. The first two international symposia (Montreal 1975, Montreal 1976) brought together the work of David Malan (Tavistock), Peter Sifneos (Harvard), and myself (McGill). Encouraged by the overwhelming enthusiasm generated at these large gatherings, I set up the Third International Symposium in Los Angeles (November 1977), co-sponsored by the Institute of Short-Term Dynamic Psychotherapy of the

Department of Psychiatry of The Montreal General Hospital and McGill University; The Department of Psychiatry of the University of Southern California; and the Psychiatric Service of Beth Israel Hospital of Harvard Medical School. With its faculty expanded to more than fifty, the symposium brought together nearly one thousand psychiatrists, psychoanalysts, psychologists, and other mental health professionals from various parts of the world. This five-day audiovisual symposium, which included a number of evening workshops, covered a wide range of topics: evaluation, selection of patients, technique, outcome evaluation, research, and teaching and supervision. A great deal of discussion was generated around the similarities and differences in the work of Sifneos, Malan, and myself. Also brought into focus were the contributions of many other workers, including Judd Marmor (USC), Saul Brown (UCLA), Hans Strupp (Vanderbilt), Samuel Eisenstein (UCLA), Mardi Horowitz (University of California, San Francisco), Manuel Straker (UCLA), Jorge de la Torre (Houston), Joseph Zaiden (New York), Roland Pierloot and his collaborators (Louvain, Belgium), Daniel Luminet (Liege, Belgium), and Pierre Schneider (Lausanne).

In addition to these three international events, we have presented in the past decade many audiovisual symposia at national and regional levels; these are in ever increasing demand, which further indicates that the psychotherapeutic community is becoming more and more interested in this mode of therapy. Can we say that the overwhelming response of the seventies is an indication that the psychoanalytic community, which reacted with such hostility in the 1940s to the Alexander group, has changed its position? At any rate, these systematic research projects and audiovisual symposia have had considerable impact on Short-Term Dynamic Psychotherapy throughout the world. As Malan, in his *Individual Psychotherapy and the Science of Psychodynamics* (1979), says, "Anyone who has seen these tapes cannot fail to be convinced both of the effectiveness of dynamic psychotherapy and the truth of basic psychodynamic theory." The ongoing systematic work which has been presented and discussed at many symposia in the 1970s has greatly challenged the validity of certain traditional psychoanalytic ideas.

1. That psychotherapeutic results achieved by a limited number of interviews are superficial and temporary, and that the results achieved by a more prolonged therapy are profound and lasting is a

view that is not supported. The view that the depth of a therapy is proportionate to its length and the frequency of the sessions is not valid. These researches have demonstrated that impressive psychotherapeutic results have been achieved with a limited number of interviews, and they are neither superficial nor temporary; rather, they are profound and lasting. At the same time, the claim that psychoanalysis as distinguished from other forms of dynamic psychotherapy produces profound reconstructive personality changes has not been proved by any systematic research.

2. That brief dynamic psychotherapy is effective only in mild neurotic conditions of recent onset is not supported by any of our research; a large proportion of our patients with whom we have had successful results have suffered from psychoneurotic disorders of many years' duration.

3. That prolonging the course of a therapy on the grounds that this eventually breaks through the patient's resistance is not validated. We have been able to demonstrate time and again, by treating highly resistant patients who had suffered from severe neurotic psychopathology, that it is not necessary to prolong the course of the therapy. One can achieve results with a specific technique within a short period of time—a technique based entirely on psychoanalytic principles that does not react to the increasing resistance of the patient with increasing passivity on the part of the therapist.

4. That short-term psychotherapy is the second-best alternative is a myth. All of our work proves that it is the psychotherapeutic choice for a certain group of patients suffering from psychoneurotic disorders. The limits of this group have not been fully explored.

Our own three systematic researches indicate that a spectrum of patients can be treated in Short-Term Dynamic Psychotherapy. At one end of the spectrum is a healthier group of patients suffering from circumscribed problems based on an uncomplicated unresolved oedipal conflict, who are by and large highy responsive and highly motivated. At the other end of the spectrum are patients who are highly resistant and have suffered from long-standing psychoneurotic disorders and characterological problems—patients quite unresponsive to psychoanalysis and behavior therapy. The technical requirements for these patients and for those patients who suffer from incapacitating phobic and obsessional disorders differ from patients at the other end of the spectrum.

It is obvious that there is a variety of psychotherapeutic interventions of short duration based on psychoanalytic principles.

In this volume we attempt to demonstrate some of the principles of Short-Term Dynamic Psychotherapy, bringing together the contributions of a number of workers in the field, and their theoretical and clinical perspectives. This volume is primarily clinical, focusing on the characteristics of patients, characteristics of technique, and technique of outcome evaluation. We have made extensive use of actual clinical interviews and present many verbatim clinical vignettes to demonstrate, as explicitly as possible, the technical requirements.

A number of the chapters are based on the proceedings of the Third International Symposium. Part I focuses on the historical perspective and some current developments in the field. Chapter 1 is the Franz Alexander Memorial Lecture presented by Judd Marmor at that symposium. Part II focuses primarily on the evaluation and selection of patients, and in the chapter on trial therapy I have outlined some of the technical requirements of the initial interview by presenting the transcript of an initial interview with an analysis of the techniques and content. In that chapter David Malan collaborated with me in the analysis of technique, for which I express my gratitude. In Part V the basic principles and techniques of the follow-up interview of a patient who had been treated by one of our trainees is presented to demonstrate the technical requirements in outcome evaluation of the follow-up interview.

I wish to express my deep appreciation to all those patients who have so generously cooperated in allowing us to record their treatment audiovisually; they have made a major contribution to our research, to the understanding of the psychotherapeutic process and outcome, to teaching and supervision, and most of all to the scientific validity of Short-Term Dynamic Psychotherapy. I am grateful to all of them for allowing their actual clinical interviews to be published. I want to reassure them and our readers that great care was taken to protect their confidentiality, while not making changes in the essential facts.

My gratitude to my wife, Doris, who put a great deal of time, energy, and thought into the preparation of this manuscript and who also made major contributions to the organization of the Third International Symposium.

To my colleagues Saul Brown, Sam Eisenstein, David Malan, Judd Marmor, Katherina Marmor, Bert Moll, John Nemiah, Peter Sifneos, Manny Straker, and Joe Zaiden, I express my thanks for their contributions to the organization of the Third International Symposium and their comments and suggestions about my own work in Short-Term Dynamic Psychotherapy. Our deep appreciation goes to Sybil Straker, who so graciously helped us in the organization of the symposium.

To Alan Mann, Psychiatrist-in-Chief of the Department of Psychiatry at Montreal General, I am greatly appreciative for cordial and continued support and interest in my work. To Maurice Dongier, Chairman of the Department of Psychiatry at McGill, I am grateful for warm encouragement and continued interest in my pursuits.

My grateful thanks goes to Mr. Peter Kirby, our previous Media Director, who so dedicatedly contributed to the Third International Symposium. I am especially grateful to Mr. Jack Root, President, Audio-Visual Headquarters Corporation, Los Angeles, and his collaborators for the magnificent audiovisual operation of the Third Symposium and the recording of the proceedings, which have been used in part in the preparation of this book. I am grateful as well to Mr. Richard Zurowski, our present Media Director, who has so generously given up many of his weekends for the editing and preparation of the videotapes. And last, but certainly not least, I am grateful to Mrs. Ciel Pilosof of Los Angeles, for her excellent organizational contributions, and to Ms. Margaret Barnes, Ms. Holly Bush, Ms. Patricia Deslauriers, Ms. Diane Lund, and Ms. Jacqueline Pichette, who on their own free time have all helped me a great deal, not only in the organization of the Third Symposium but also in the preparation of the manuscript of this book.

The purpose of this volume is to bring together some of the major work being carried out in centers throughout the world. A number of research projects have been carried out in the past two decades which are presently being analyzed for publication, and there are centers currently engaged in clinical research in this field. It is our hope that the projected series of publications, of which this volume is the first, will bring together the contributions of those interested and further augment the scientific validity of Short-Term Dynamic Psychotherapy.

H.D.

Part I

History

1

Historical Roots

JUDD MARMOR, M.D.

We are living in the midst of a major psychotherapeutic revolution in this second half of the twentieth century. New therapies of all kinds have emerged in astounding numbers, some scientifically based, others reverting to the magical, mystical, and religious forms that were the precursors of scientific psychotherapy. Additionally, the imminence of some form of national health insurance is putting psychotherapists under great pressure to find shorter and more efficient techniques of therapy or else be excluded from the program for fiscal reasons. In consequence, various forms of group therapy, behavioral therapy, and family therapy, techniques that can be used with a significant proportion of the patient population, may be emerging more strongly in the years ahead. The fact is, however, that the vast majority of American psychiatrists are still heavily commit-

Franz Alexander Memorial Lecture, Third International Symposium on Short-Term Dynamic Psychotherapy, Los Angeles, California.

ted to a one-to-one model of dynamic psychotherapy. It is in this area, therefore, that we can anticipate the greatest pressure to achieve briefer techniques.

FREUD AND BRIEF THERAPY

Brief dynamic psychotherapy is rooted in the psychoanalytic tradition. Its fundamental insights and basic theoretical principles, including a heavy emphasis on interpretation of the transference, would not have been possible if not for the epochal discoveries of Sigmund Freud.

It is interesting to note that the earliest psychoanalytic treatments conducted by Freud tended to be of relatively short duration. Bruno Walter (1946) has written of his successful treatment by Freud in six sessions in 1906, and Ernest Jones reports that Gustav Mahler was relieved of an impotence problem in four sessions with Freud in 1908 (Jones 1955, pp. 79-80). As the goals of psychoanalysis became more ambitious, however, and its theoretical superstructure grew more complex, analytic treatments began to increase in length to such an extent that Freud in his later years pessimistically concluded that some of them were becoming interminable (Freud 1937).

FERENCZI AND ACTIVE THERAPY

Many of the early analysts were aware of this trend, and were troubled by it, but the first psychoanalytic pioneer to explore modifications in psychoanalytic technique for the purpose of shortening the length of the classical analysis was Sandor Ferenczi, who around 1918 began to experiment with a technique that he called "active therapy." (A few years later another early pioneer, Wilhelm Stekel, adopted a similar course.) Ferenczi claimed that in so doing he was merely following Freud's lead, and referred to statements that Freud had made at the Budapest International Congress in 1918, suggesting that in certain cases of phobias or obsessional neurosis it might be necessary, in order to advance the therapy, to institute active measures to induce the patient to face the phobia or anxiety. Ferenczi also pointed out that the employment of active therapy is in fact inherent in the psychoanalytic process itself: whenever an interpretation is given it constitutes an active interference with the patient's psychic activity at that moment and facilitates the appearance of thoughts that might otherwise have remained unconscious.

In the years that followed, Ferenczi continued to experiment with various types of activity in the psychoanalytic situation, some indulgent, others prohibitive. He admitted in his articles on the subject that some of these techniques were successful and others not. One of the more interesting examples of unsuccessful activity was Ferenczi's effort to offer himself to his patients as a loving parent-surrogate. This was intended as a reparative measure for the rejections and traumas they may have suffered from their actual parents. These reparative efforts on the part of Ferenczi included hugging, kissing, and nonerotic fondling of his patients. When Freud heard of this, he wrote Ferenczi a famous letter (Jones 1957, pp. 163-164) in which he took a very dim view of these activities and predicted prophetically that they would eventually lead to greater excesses on the part of other therapists. Ferenczi subsequently abandoned these techniques but never gave up his efforts to pursue a more active type of analytic therapy.

OTTO RANK AND WILL THERAPY

It was not accidental that these efforts should have brought Ferenczi into collaboration with Otto Rank, who had been pursuing similar efforts independently. For several years they worked closely together on evolving various modifications of technique, culminating in 1924 in their publication of a seminal volume entitled *The Development of Psychoanalysis* (Ferenczi and Rank 1925).

In some ways Otto Rank may well be the most important theoretical precursor of the brief dynamic psychotherapy movement. Unfortunately, his complex and turgid style of writing made him difficult to read. Had he possessed Freud's lucid and persuasive style, his influence would undoubtedly have been much greater. Rank's concept of the birth trauma, although biologically dubious, laid the groundwork for the subsequent recognition of the predominant importance in personality development of the pregenital years and the mother-child relationship. At that period in the history of the psychoanalytic movement the primary emphasis in psychoanalytic theory was on the oedipal period with its attendant castration anxieties. Freud's psychoanalytic contemporaries therefore vig-

orously attacked Rank's views because they were correctly perceived as threatening the central fulcrum of Freud's theories. It is
unfortunate that this issue of disloyalty to Freud has cast so heavy a
shadow over Rank's achievements. Looking back, however, from
the vantage point of more recent knowledge concerning the importance of preoedipal relationships in personality development, as well
as the nuclear importance of separation and individuation in emotional maturation, we can now see that Rank was the prime theoretical precursor of these developments without in any way denigrating
the creative contributions of people like René Spitz, Margaret Mahler, and John Bowlby.

Over the years, Rank himself began to play down the psychological importance of the birth trauma per se. He recognized that the
issue of separation and individuation was really the core problem,
and he made its working through the central focus of his psychotherapeutic method. It is not surprising, therefore, that it was he who
first emphasized the importance of setting a time limit to the analytic
process in order to achieve an earlier therapeutic focus on the
problem of separation. Actually, Freud was the first analyst to
employ the technique of setting a time limit. In "From the History of
an Infantile Neurosis" (1918) he recognized its usefulness, but he
never made it a cardinal issue in his therapeutic approach. Rank,
however, considered it central not only to the therapeutic work but
to the process of adaptation and maturation in all areas of human
existence. Thus, at a very early point in Rankian therapy the analytic
work became centered on the anxieties and conflicts around separation and termination. This is a technique which Dr. James Mann
(1973) has in recent years made the cardinal point of his approach to
time-limited psychotherapy, but he makes only a brief and passing
reference to the work of Rank in his book.

It is interesting also in the light of current developments to take a
second look at Rank's concept of "will-therapy" (1947). Rank emphasized the idea of mobilizing the patient's "will" in the therapeutic
process and claimed that by so doing he was able to shorten therapy.
If we were to substitute for the word *will* the more modern term
motivation to change, we would find that Rank was stressing something that has been emphasized by all modern theorists of dynamic
psychotherapy, namely, the overwhelming importance of a strong
motivation to change on the part of the patient in achieving a

favorable therapeutic outcome as well as in making possible briefer approaches to psychotherapy.

For example, four of the seven criteria for motivation to change utilized by Sifneos (1972) employ the concept of "willingness": willingness to actively participate in the treatment situation, willingness to understand oneself, willingness to change, and willingness to make reasonable sacrifices in terms of time and fees. What is willingness in this context but the ability to mobilize one's will toward a particular objective?

Ferenczi and Rank also emphasized the importance of utilizing here-and-now transference interpretations in the therapeutic process. Without denying the importance of past material, they placed a greater stress on current events and reactions and their reflections in the transference situation than did most other psychoanalytic theoreticians of their day. They advocated an emphasis upon the emotional experiences of the patient in the transference relationship rather than upon the recovery of memories and intellectual reconstructions that characterized long-term psychoanalytic approaches.

FRANZ ALEXANDER AND THE CORRECTIVE EMOTIONAL EXPERIENCE

When, some twenty years later, Alexander and French came out with their seminal volume on psychoanalytic therapy (1946), they were quick to admit that their work was "a continuation and realization of ideas first proposed by Ferenczi and Rank." The work of Alexander and French stands on its own merits, however. Their volume was the culmination of seven years of prior research and investigation into the development of shorter approaches to psychotherapy that had been carried on at the Chicago Institute of Psychoanalysis. Alexander, who was the prime mover in this research, had for years been puzzled by what he called the "baffling discrepancy" between the length and intensity of psychoanalytic treatment and the degree of therapeutic success. He began the study by questioning the validity of certain traditional psychoanalytic dogmas: (1) that the depth of therapy is necessarily proportionate to the length of treatment and frequency of interviews; (2) that therapeutic results achieved by a relatively small number of interviews are necessarily superficial and temporary, while results of more prolonged therapy are necessarily more stable and profound; and (3) that prolongation of an analysis is justified on the grounds that eventually the patient's resistance would be overcome and the desired therapeutic results achieved. The first and most important principle introduced by Alexander, that of flexibility, seems commonplace today, but it was revolutionary in an era dominated by the conviction that the standard psychoanalytic method was the optimum method of therapy for most neurotic patients. Alexander insisted that in psychotherapy as in all medical therapy the physician should adapt his technique to the needs of the patient. "Only the nature of the individual case," he said, "could determine which technique is best suited to bring about the curative processes." In the search for flexible approaches Alexander and his colleagues experimented with the frequency of interviews, the optional use of the chair or couch, interruptions of long or short duration preparatory to termination, and the combination of psychotherapy with drug or other therapy. They also sought to learn how to control and manipulate the transference relationship so as to fit the particular psychodynamics of each case.

Alexander was the first to point out that in many instances daily interviews prove to be antitherapeutic because they gratify the patient's dependent needs more than is desirable. He questioned the therapeutic value of promoting regression and argued that it should be "a general principle in all psychotherapy to attempt to check this regressive tendency from the very beginning of the treatment"; this was a technique strongly advocated by Sandor Rado (1956) also. As one way of heightening the emotional intensity of interviews with patients Alexander recommended consciously manipulating the frequency of visits. He felt that this was an effective way of controlling the transference relationship, limiting regression, preventing the development of overdependency on the therapist, and fostering autonomy. He also advocated interruptions of treatment as another way of increasing the emotional intensity and efficiency of the therapeutic process. By virtue of their ability to test the patient's capacity for self-reliance and more effective coping with his life situation, interruptions could also be used as a preparatory indicator, enabling both therapist and the patient to arrive at a mutually agreed-upon termination point.

Perhaps Alexander's best known contribution to the theory of psychotherapy and one that is uniquely associated with his name is the concept of the corrective emotional experience. He defined this as reexposing the patient under more favorable circumstances to emotional situations that he could not handle in the past. One of the most significant aspects of the psychotherapeutic process, in Alexander's view, is the difference between the original conflict situation and the therapeutic situation. "Because the therapist's attitude [in this context] is different from that of the authoritative person of the past, he gives the patient an opportunity to face again and again, under more favorable circumstances, those emotional situations which were formerly unbearable and to deal with them in a manner different from the old . . . " (Alexander and French 1946). This can be accomplished, Alexander insisted, only through actual experience in the patient's relationship to the therapist; intellectual insight alone is not sufficent.

Alexander asserted that, in order to know what new emotional experiences are necessary to achieve the therapeutic results, the therapist must understand not only the patient's psychodynamics but also the genetic development of his difficulties. In this respect his technique differs decisively from that of Rank. The more precise this understanding, the more adequately the therapist can provide the proper corrective experience. Alexander felt that the therapist's reactions, therefore, had to be planned on the basis of these dynamic insights.

Although Alexander's views were violently attacked by most classical psychoanalysts of that day, the principles that he elucidated have by now become part of the daily working equipment of almost every psychiatrist and psychoanalyst. It is fair to say that Alexander more than any other modern psychoanalyst is responsible for leading the way toward the application of psychoanalytic principles to short-term dynamic psychotherapy.

It is worth noting that Alexander and French's book on psycho-analytic therapy was published in 1946, just after the end of World War II. One of the many historical changes wrought by that war was an increased awareness of the value of psychoanalytically oriented psychiatry as demonstrated by the contributions that it had been able to make through the treatment of mental and emotional disturbances in combat soldiers. As a result of this increased awareness, there was a quantum leap in the popularity of psychoanalysis and of psycho-analytically oriented therapies. The demand for such treatments increased enormously, and analysts who prior to the war found themselves hard put to fill their schedules, now found themselves swamped with more patients than they had time for. A natural consequence of this growing demand was an increased tendency of psychoanalysts to see their patients one, two, and three times a week instead of four and five, although the length of therapy continued to be relatively extended for the most part.

RECENT WORK

In more recent years as the demand for psychotherapy has widened to encompass greater and greater segments of the population and with national health insurance hovering in the background, the pressures to clarify our theories and sharpen our skills in the application of psychodynamic theory to even shorter forms of psychotherapy have increased. A number of psychoanalysts, both here and abroad, have responded to this challenge by picking up where Alexander and French left off. Balint, Malan, and their colleagues at the Tavistock Clinic in London, Wolberg at the Postgraduate Center for Mental Health in New York, Mann and Sifneos in Boston, and Davanloo and Straker in Montreal, among others, are some of the individuals who have contributed or are contributing significantly to this movement. The first two International Symposia on Short-Term Dynamic Psychotherapy in Montreal (1975, 1976) and the third International Symposium (Los Angels 1977) are reflections of this growing interest.

I shall not attempt at this time to delineate the specific contributions' of this more recent group. David Malan has reviewed them superbly in his excellent new book *The Frontier of Brief Psychotherapy* (1976). Aspects of both the theory and practice of short-term techniques are still in a state of flux, but there is no disagreement among these workers about the efficacy and validity of the general approach.

There are still individuals in the psychoanalytic movement who view the development of short-term techniques of dynamic psychotherapy as a regrettable debasement of the pure gold of psychoanalysis and as a process which can only achieve superficial or transitory results, if any at all. This book will present a different perspective about these techniques, which, to quote Barten (1971), constitute "innovative, pragmatic developing approaches which may change our conception of the nature, objectives, possiblities, and limitations of psychotherapy."

Actually, a major reason for the pessimism about short-term techniques was the fact that classical psychoanalysts have tended to think of personality as a closed system. Merely to modify part of it, therefore, leaves the rest untouched and can only signify continued or recurrent difficulties within the system later on. To really achieve a permanent or lasting change, nothing less than a total "working through" of all unconscious repression and conflict is necessary. Anything less means incomplete therapy. Hence the disparagement of "transference cures" or a "flight into health." If, however, we conceive of personality in modern, open-system terms, then modifying a focal area of conflict *can* lead to an alteration of the entire system, with positive feedback both from within through improved self-esteem and from without through improved interpersonal relationships. Consequently, even a brief intervention in suitable cases *is* capable of stimulating long-term personality changes. How to evaluate, select, and treat such cases is the purpose of this book.

Freud's historic discoveries opened vast frontiers of understanding for all of us about the nature of the human unconscious and about the developmental vicissitudes of personality and psychopathology, but the technique that he evolved was designed primarily for research into the unknown mysteries of the human mind and only secondarily for therapy. Today, thanks to all that we have learned from that research and all that has followed from it, it has become possible to focus more directly on the techniques of therapy alone and to develop new approaches based on psychoanalytic understanding that, for selected cases, are more efficient and very possibly more effective than standard, long-term, classical psychoanalysis. In this sense, the movement toward briefer forms of dynamic psychotherapy, which this book epitomizes, is an historical trend of the first magnitude and points to the direction in which the rational psychotherapies of the future will be moving.

References

Alexander, F., and French, T. (1946). *Psychoanalytic Therapy*. New York: Ronald Press.

Barten, H. H. (1971). *Brief Therapies*. New York: Behavioral Publications.
Ferenczi, S., and Rank, O. (1925). *The Development of Psychoanalysis*. New York: Nervous and Mental Disease Publishing Co.
Freud, S. (1918). From the history of an infantile neurosis. *Standard Edition* 17:7-122.
——— (1937). Analysis terminable and interminable. *Standard Edition* 23:216-253.
Jones, E. (1955). *The Life and Work of Sigmund Freud*. Vol. 2. New York: Basic Books.
——— (1957). *The Life and Work of Sigmund Freud*. Vol. 3. New York: Basic Books.
Malan, D. (1976). *The Frontier of Brief Psychotherapy*. New York: Plenum.
Mann, J. (1973). *Time-Limited Psychotherapy*. Cambridge: Harvard University Press.
Rado, S. (1956). Recent advances in psychoanalytic therapy. In *Psychoanalysis of Behavior*. New York: Grune and Stratton.
Rank. O. (1947). *Will Therapy*. New York: Knopf.
Sifneos, P. (1972). *Short-Term Psychotherapy and Emotional Crisis*. Cambridge: Harvard University Press.
Walter, B. (1946). *Theme and Variation*. New York: Knopf.

2

The Most Important Development
in Psychotherapy Since the
Discovery of the Unconscious

DAVID H. MALAN, M.D.

It needs to be stated categorically that in the early part of this century Freud unwittingly took a wrong turning which led to disastrous consequences for the future of psychotherapy. This was to react to increasing resistance with increased passivity—eventually adopting the technique of free association on the part of the patient, and the role of "passive sounding board," free-floating attention, and infinite patience on the part of the therapist.

The consequences have been strenuously ignored or denied by generations of analysts and dynamic psychotherapists, but are there for all to see. The most obvious effect has been an enormous increase in the duration of treatment—from a few weeks or months to many years. A less obvious development is that the method has become, to say the least, of doubtful therapeutic effectiveness, a matter which has received little attention or proper investigation. A further practical consequence is the inability of most psychotherapeutic agencies to provide sufficient service; with most vacancies filled by long-term patients, there is little available for new patients who come seeking relief from their suffering. There is, then, a hidden disillusion with this method of treatment, one consequence of which may be called the "flight into training," a maneuver in which experienced staff give up practicing therapy to concentrate on teaching others to practice it, entirely ignoring the fact that the methods taught have never been shown to be effective.

In private practice the situation is slightly different: here at least, experienced therapists go on practicing psychotherapy, but patient and therapist collude in believing that one day in the distant future the problems will all be properly resolved and the patient will leave able to lead a healthy life—the only trouble being that this future is always about two years away, awaiting the working through of yet another overdetermination.

EARLIER ATTEMPTS TO REMEDY THE SITUATION

Any such attempt must involve the development of a brief method of treatment which is both widely applicable and effective. All workers who have made such attempts have realized that passivity in the therapist must be replaced by activity in some form. Chief of the early workers in this field were Ferenczi and Rank (1925) and Alexander and French (1946). Both attempts foundered on uncertain therapeutic results on the one hand, and on hostility to modifications of the classical analytic technique on the other, the latter from Freud himself.

LATER ATTEMPTS

The literature is full of writings on methods of brief psychotherapy which are claimed to be effective with certain patients, but systematic work with published evidence has never been very much part of the scene. Therefore only two series of publications will be mentioned, those of Sifneos from Boston and those of the Balint team, working at the Tavistock Clinic in London.

Sifneos (1972, 1979) has shown without question that there exists a type of patient suffering from circumscribed problems based on the male or female oedipus complex, who can be substantially helped in a maximum of fifteen sessions. He calls the method Short-Term

Anxiety-Provoking Psychotherapy (STAPP). It is entirely psycho-analytic in orientation, employing interpretation as its main therapeutic tool and making extensive use of the transference. An essential selection criterion is that the patients must show themselves on initial evaluation to be highly motivated and responsive. Sifneos (5) writes that such patients may make up as many as 25 percent of those referred to his unit at the Beth Israel Hospital in Boston; but he has also agreed (personal communication) that this must be an extremely biased figure resulting from patterns of referral to a unit known to specialize in this kind of work. Certainly these patients cannot represent more than a very small proportion of the general psychotherapeutic population.

The Balint team (Malan 1963, 1976a, 1976b) has shown that in addition to the STAPP patient there exist other categories of patients in whom long-standing character problems can be substantially relieved in a maximum of forty sessions. But, once more, the method is entirely dependent on high motivation and responsiveness in the patient. The result is that the patients with whom this type of therapy is attempted represent fewer than 10 percent of those referred to the Tavistock Clinic—and since by no means all such therapies are successful, patients who are actually suitable are even fewer.

The importance of the work of the Boston and Tavistock groups is therefore more theoretical than practical. The two groups have shown without any possibility of doubt, and have substantiated their findings by long follow-up, that brief methods can be effective and that long-term therapy is not always necessary nor necessarily the treatment of choice. But these methods can make very little impact on the operation of psychotherapeutic services in general.

WHERE TO GO FROM HERE?

The result of all the foregoing is that dynamic psychotherapists may be forgiven for being in a state of bewildered despair. We see daily proof that Freud's insights into human beings are essentially correct, and we have a highly refined technique for handling the moment-to-moment interaction with our patients, the principles of which have been thoroughly worked out by clinical work spanning generations. Yet are we to believe that these insights, and the techniques based on them, have little practical relevance to the problem of human mental

suffering? Are we to abandon the field to methods of therapy that
ignore these insights, such as behavior therapy, or to methods that are
used without professional responsiblity and are in danger of becoming cults, like the encounter movement?

A WISH-FULFILLMENT FANTASY

The following is a fantasy that seems so unrealistic that I have never
allowed myself to indulge in it.

A method of brief psychotherapy is developed that is based
entirely on psychoanalytic principles, and with which many analysts
therefore feel comfortable; it is applicable to a high proportion of the
psychotherapeutic population; therapeutic effects begin to appear
within the first few sessions, and the whole neurosis disappears, so
that termination comes smoothly within ten to thirty sessions and
often within fifteen; at termination no trace of the original disturbances remains and long follow-up shows that this position is maintained; finally, certain adverse phenomena that bedevil ordinary
dynamic therapy, such as intense sexualized or dependent transference, acting out, and difficulties over termination, do not become
a problem.

THREE INTERNATIONAL SYMPOSIA

In March 1975 Davanloo set up the first of three International
Symposia on Short-Term Dynamic Psychotherapy. On the whole he
maintained a low profile, and it is certain that no one present realized
the significance of what they were seeing. Indeed, the reaction of the
participants (including myself) to his technique was generally hostile, since it seemed on superficial acquaintance that in some way his
patients were being hounded and persecuted. The fact that under
this relentless pressure some of his patients gave up their secrets,
recovered within about twenty sessions (not merely improved), and
left with profound gratitude could at first be dismissed as instances
of those happy therapeutic miracles that come to all of us on a few
occasions during the course of a lifetime. And yet, as I collaborated
more and more with Davanloo during many other audiovisual
presentations at symposia, including the Second International Symposium in Montreal in 1976 and the Third International Symposium

in Los Angeles in 1977, it gradually became clear to me over several years that what I was witnessing was something very different.

Here was a true research worker in the field of psychotherapy who had become profoundly guilty and dissatisfied at the way in which, under the classical psychoanalytic technique, his patients went on year after year without substantial improvement. In consequence he began a nearly twenty-year series of experiments, working single-handed, in his own private office as well as in the Outpatient Psychiatric Department of The Montreal General Hospital. Publishing nothing before he was ready, and—like Freud in the 1890s—secure in the knowledge that there was not the slightest probability that anyone else in the world might anticipate him, he began to audiotape and shortly thereafter to videotape every session, playing the tapes over and over again in order to see which ingredients in his technique seemed to lead to progress and which to failure. When he thought he had identified an important factor, he would systematically employ it in his next half-dozen cases. Inevitably the result was a progressive reversal of the trend toward passivity set up originally by Freud. He gradually came to see that when a particular subject made a patient resistant and uncomfortable, the correct response was not to become passive and wait for further developments but to challenge the defenses more and more forcefully. Moreover, this inevitably aroused anger in the patient, which he would then try to conceal and avoid in the characteristic ways he employed in his life outside the consulting room. All this would be brought into the open as soon as it occurred, as would any other manifestation of transference. An important principle of this technique is that Davanloo uses a special kind of focused interview but adheres strictly to three fundamental psychoanalytic principles: releasing the patient's hidden feelings by actively working on and interpreting *resistance,* paying strict attention to the *transference* relationship, and linking this to both *current* and *past* relationships. During this he is constantly watching for feedback. In the initial stages feedback consists of increased resistance, but as soon as the core problem is touched on the patient almost invariably experiences relief and hope, which is reflected in an increased willingness to collaborate, i.e. an increase in motivation and the therapeutic alliance. When this appears, the therapist can really be sure that his approach is correct.

The result of this long-drawn-out process is that time and again, in Davanloo's own words, "to my amazement I began to see the neurosis *dissolve before my eyes.*" The patient would go out into the world transformed from a crippled, beaten, severely self-destructive individual into an effective human being, able to form real relationships, deal with difficulties, and achieve satisfaction and fulfillment wherever it was to be found. Moreover, repeated observation has demonstrated that the adverse phenomena mentioned above, such as intense sexualized and dependent transference and acting out, do not occur. This is clearly because all forms of transference are brought out into the open the moment any trace of them appears.

Davanloo has treated more than one-hundred fifty patients in this way, and in follow-ups of up to five years no patient who had recovered at termination has ever been observed to relapse. Here it should be added that as he began to identify the effective ingredients in his technique he began to be able to shorten his therapies. A few years ago they tended to last for ten to thirty sessions with an upper limit of forty; now they usually last for ten to fifteen sessions with an upper limit of twenty-five. Moreover, because of his way of challenging defenses, the technique is applicable even to some of our most resistant patients, who have suffered from symptoms and crippling character problems for many years. His estimate is that it is applicable to about 30-35 percent of the patients presenting themselves at the Community Mental Health Center of The Montreal General Hospital.

Only recently has he begun to publish this work. A publication already in print is *Basic Principles and Techniques in Short-Term Dynamic Psychotherapy* (1978). In preparation is *The Relentless Healer: Short-Term Dynamic Psychotherapy of Phobic and Obsessional Neuroses,* which consists of the detailed analyses of verbatim transcripts of two amazingly successful therapies, in which the effective ingredients become patently obvious.

As the reader will see, I am thus stating as a sober truth that there has occurred a twentieth-century miracle: the wish-fulfillment fantasy described above has come true.

THE EVIDENCE

The reader's reaction may well be that the present author, who once had the reputation of being an objective seeker of truth, has fallen under the influence of a charismatic personality and has completely lost touch with reality. After all, psychotic breakdown is not unknown in the later stages of an analyst's career: Ferenczi himself is an example. How might the world be convinced otherwise?

The first answer is that under certain conditions it is possible to prove the effectiveness of a method of therapy beyond all reasonable doubt without the use of a control series. These conditions are as follows.

1. The patients chosen have suffered from crippling symptoms and other severe disturbances (e.g., behavior patterns such as passivity, and grossly unsatisfactory human relations) for many years, even for one or two decades.

2. In some of these patients, years of psychoanalytic and/or behavior therapy have failed to produce improvement.

3. The patients are taken into treatment, begin to show major improvements within the first few weeks, and show complete recovery after, say, fifteen weeks (the ratio of twenty years to fifteen weeks is nearly seventy).

4. No relapse occurs during a follow-up period of many years.

All these conditions have been fulfilled in Davanloo's work.

Moreover, the evidence does not end there. The following conditions also apply.

5. In patient after patient it can be demonstrated that improvement begins immediately following certain types of events in therapy, particularly the open acknowledgment of hostility in the transference, followed by an interpretation linking patterns in the transference relationship with similar patterns in current and past relationships. Davanloo refers to this as a T-C-P interpretation and has demonstrated time and again, with audiovisual proof, the impact of such interpretations on the patient, both during therapy and in the initial interview itself.

6. The connection between the symptoms, on the one hand, and past events and situations, on the other, can be clearly inferred. An example is a patient whose symptoms crystallized around *fear of falling* and who suffered from severe phobic and obsessional symptomatology of many years' duration, while the major event in his childhood had been that his father, whom he had helped to exclude

from the relation with his mother, had *fallen to his death* down a flight of steps.

7. During therapy the buried feelings about the early events are de-repressed and experienced with such intensity as to leave no conceivable doubt of their significance (this particular patient put his head in his hands and sobbed, "I *robbed* him, I robbed him of his rightful place in the home").

8. From that point on, the patient's improvement rapidly becomes total.

I call conditions six to eight the fulfillment of "Koch's postulates" in psychotherapy, by analogy with the conditions which prove that a given disease is caused by a particular bacterium.

In such circumstances even the most determined skeptic would be hard put to maintain that the improvements were due to "spontaneous remission," which just happened to occur during a period when, by coincidence, the patient was also having psychotherapy.

The almost unbelievable fact is that not only has Davanloo already done all this, but that his therapies and follow-up interviews are available on videotape so that no one can possibly fail to be convinced of the genuineness of his results. It is because I have seen many of these tapes that I am writing with such conviction now.

I am not the only colleague to have seen these tapes. They have been shown not only at the three International Symposia I have mentioned, but at many workshops and symposia throughout the North American continent and in Europe. They have repeatedly demonstrated without question that this technique can cure within a few months even patients suffering from longstanding phobic and obsessional disorders. They have already had considerable impact on psychotherapy throughout the world. As I wrote in a recent publication (Malan 1976b), "I am convinced that Davanloo's work is destined to go much further and to revolutionize both the practice and the scientific status of dynamic psychotherapy within the next ten years. . . . Anyone who has seen these tapes cannot fail to be convinced both of the effectiveness of dynamic psychotherapy and the truth of basic psychodynamic theory."

RESEARCH PROJECT: A CONTROLLED STUDY

The usual trouble with trying to devise a controlled study of dynamic psychotherapy is the impossibility of keeping the control patients untreated for as long as scientific validity requires. A repeated finding in controlled studies is that the treated patients show an advantage over the controls at termination, but that this is steadily eroded, to the point at which the difference is no longer significant, during the follow-up period. Equally, in our own uncontrolled studies of brief psychotherapy (Malan 1963, Sifneos 1973, 1979) improvement was only partial at termination, and many important changes—representing both improvement and relapse—occurred during the next few years. This means that for a meaningful comparison any series of control patients must be kept untreated for many years—which is obviously impossible on practical and unacceptable on ethical grounds.

However, the unique qualities of the method developed by Davanloo—in which patients begin to show improvement within the first few sessions, have recovered by the end of therapy lasting a few months, and show no relapse during a prolonged follow-up period— render a "waiting-list control" design not merely practicable but the design of choice. First of all, only patients who have shown "character problems" lasting for many years are chosen for the study. Then the patients are divided randomly into two groups, one of which (the experimentals) are taken into treatment at once, while the other (controls) wait for a period equal to the duration of the treatment of the experimentals, and then are themselves taken into treatment.

The predictions are obvious:

1. That a high proportion of the experimentals will show major improvement by termination
2. That none of the controls will show such improvement
3. That a high proportion of the controls will show major improvement at the termination of their therapy
4. That most (all?) improvements will be maintained at further follow-up

An application for a research grant for a study based on this design is in preparation.

THE CONSEQUENCES

Because the effectiveness of Davanloo's technique has already been demonstrated beyond reasonable doubt, it is possible to write with confidence of the consequences that would follow if the proposed study were to give a strongly positive result and the method of therapy therefore became generally adopted. These consequences fall under the following headings:

Practical

The operation of psychotherapeutic agencies. Instead of having therapeutic vacancies chronically blocked by long-term patients who fail to improve, it would be possible to offer a service in which a high proportion of patients were given effective help.

The operation of mental health services. The authorities in charge of allocating money to mental health services would know that they were spending wisely and actually making a contribution to mental health.

Morale. The improvement in morale of the therapists delivering the service could not help being dramatic. When asked the previously embarrassing question of how long treatment should last and what benefits are likely, they would be able to give an optimistic and accurate forecast based firmly on experience.

Scientific

The first consequence would of course be the validation of a method of therapy. In addition to this, the fulfillment of "Koch's postulates" completely validates aspects of psychodynamic theory as laid down by Freud—e.g., the origin of symptoms in conflict, the fact that such conflict often originates in childhood, the existence of "the unconscious," defense mechanisms, the "the return of the repressed," etc. In other words, psychodynamics would at last achieve its rightful place as a science. This in turn would have an effect on morale and on psychotherapists' public relations. Hitherto we have all been in the position of "knowing" we are in possession of important truths, yet of being unable to demonstrate them to skeptics with either tangible evidence or therapeutic effects.

Humanitarian

Not "last but not least," but last for emphasis, because clearly it is the most important. The chronic misery caused by psychoneurotic illness is less dramatic and obvious, perhaps, than that caused by many chronic physical illnesses, but no less real. The value of possessing a method of therapy that will reliably and permanently replace such misery by happiness, creativeness, and fulfillment does not need underlining.

These consequences would surely justify the title of the present article. In summary: Freud discovered the unconscious; Davanloo has discovered how to use it therapeutically.

References

Alexander, F., and French T.M. (1946). *Psychoanalytic Therapy*. New York: Ronald Press.

Davanloo, H. (1978). *Basic Principles and Techniques in Short-Term Dynamic Psychotherapy*. New York: Spectrum Publications.

———— (1979). Techniques of short-term dynamic psychotherapy. *The Psychiatric Clinics of North America* 2(1).

———— (in preparation). *The Relentless Healer: Short-Term Dynamic Psychotherapy of Phobic and Obsessional Neuroses*.

Ferenczi S., and Rank O. (1925). *The Development of Psychoanalysis*. Nervous and Mental Disease Monographs, No. 40.

Malan, D.H. (1963). *A Study of Brief Psychotherapy*. London: Tavistock Publications. Reprinted by Plenum Press, 1975.

———— (1976a). *The Frontier of Brief Psychotherapy*. New York: Plenum Press.

———— (1976b) *Toward the Validation of Dynamic Psychotherapy*. New York: Plenum Press.

———— (1979). *Individual Psychotherapy and the Science of Psychodynamics*. London: Butterworths.

Sifneos P.E. (1972). *Short-Term Psychotherapy and Emotional Crisis*. Cambridge: Harvard University Press.

———— (1973). An overview of a psychiatric clinic population. *American Journal of Psychiatry* 130:1032-1036.

———— (1979). *Short-Term Dynamic Psychotherapy*. New York: Plenum Press.

3

The Contributions of
Franz Alexander

SAMUEL EISENSTEIN, M.D.

Brief psychotherapy was born at the same time Freud renounced hypnosis as an effective technique of treatment. All of the cases he treated during and immediately after the Breuer period were brief psychotherapies, the first such case being that of Frau Emmy von N. It was during the period of her treatment that Freud moved from the cathartic to the free association method. While many date the beginnings of psychoanalysis in general from this point, we can with greater specificity and assurance establish it as the beginning of brief psychotherapy. It is on free association, after all, that all workers in the field of brief psychotherapy base their work.

In treating Frau Emmy, Freud learned that the therapeutic effect was due to the personal relationship between patient and therapist; today this insight is the most valuable tool in the brief psychotherapy armamentarium. The briefest of brief psychotherapies Freud treated at this time was the one he described in the most charming chapter of *Studies on Hysteria*—the case of Katarina, the moving story of an eighteen-year-old maid who worked in an Alpine inn where Freud was vacationing. Learning he was a doctor, she followed him on his daily hike and there on an Alpine knoll sat down with him and poured out her heart, telling him about her anxieties and sufferings. That was the only time he met her, and yet he was able to help her and relieve her suffering.

It is not very unusual today for workers in brief psychotherapy to have the opportunity to see a patient only once in consultation; if the combination of patient-therapist is optimal, a good deal of insight is achieved and suffering is relieved. The period described above was the "prehistory" of psychoanalysis, but even years later, when Freud had developed the psychoanalytic technique, he still had occasion to treat patients in brief psychotherapy. The most memorable cases are those of Gustav Mahler, whom he treated on a four-hour walk through the streets of Leyden. He was able to help Mahler, who, according to Freud, swiftly understood what psychoanalysis was all about. This remark of Freud confirms what modern workers in the field of psychoanalysis and of brief psychotherapies require of patients if that treatment is to be successful—namely, the ability to have insight into one's own conflicts.

Another brief psychotherapy conducted by Freud was that of Bruno Walter, the famous conductor. He had six sessions of therapy with Freud and considered the treatment successful. It is perhaps somewhat ironic that Freud, who claimed to be tone deaf and who didn't much care for music, should have treated and helped such prominent men of music as Mahler and Bruno Walter.

FERENCZI AND RANK

As psychoanalysis became more institutionalized and more structured, it became longer and eventually assumed the structure it has at present. It is still an essential and suitable form of treatment for many patients, as well as for students of psychoanalysis. However, almost from the beginning workers in the field attempted to adapt psychoanalysis to brief psychotherapy. The most notable attempts were those of Ferenczi and Rank.

It was Ferenczi who introduced the "active" technique. In the book he jointly published with Otto Rank, *The Development of Psychoanalysis* (1925), the two authors describe their new technique of what one could today call brief psychotherapy. While Ferenczi withdrew from the active technique following criticisms by many of his colleagues, including Freud, for Otto Rank this book involved a departure from classic psychoanalysis. There was merit to their work and some of their contributions are to be found at the basis of modern psychoanalysis. The concept of transference as the most important aspect of therapy and the idea of acting out in therapy, although previously mentioned by Freud and others, were for the first time underscored (Eisenstein 1966).

As psychoanalysis has progressed through the years there have been continuous attempts to apply these principles to brief psychotherapy. Ferenczi and Rank stressed in their attempts at brief psychotherapy that it was not necessary to probe in detail every patient's genetic past. They felt more attention should be paid to the patient's present life and claimed that the purpose of psychoanalysis was to "substitute, by means of the technique, affective factors of experience for intellectual processes." This is in many respects an anticipation of Franz Alexander's "corrective emotional experience." Otto Rank ought to be credited with stressing the preoedipal importance of child development; the great importance of the mother-child relationship in modern psychoanalysis had in Otto Rank an early pioneer. Even his much criticized *Trauma of Birth* was originally accepted by Freud and Jones. There is actually evidence that Freud himself may have mentioned that concept to Rank in 1909. However, Rank took over that concept and constructed around it an entirely new theory that repudiated the oedipus complex and postulated radical new changes in theory and technique.

Both Ferenczi and Rank borrowed from Freud the setting of a time limit to therapy. Freud used it in the analysis of the Wolfman in 1912, published in 1918 as "From the History of an Infantile Neurosis." This technical parameter was later adopted by Franz Alexander and is employed today by almost all therapists doing brief psychotherapy.

FREE ASSOCIATION AND TRANSFERENCE

While some attempts at shortening therapy were often radical departures from classical psychoanalytic concepts, Franz Alexander's contributions to brief psychotherapy lay in applying the basic insights gained from psychoanalysis to brief psychotherapy. He felt that uncovering unconscious material occurs in classic psychoanalytic treatment as well as in other forms of therapy, be they supportive or brief. Any time the ego becomes stronger in therapy it acquires the ability to recognize unconscious material that emerges. He very likely meant that an increase in ego strength facilitates the ability of the patient to deal with unconscious material with diminished anxiety and with greater tolerance for ego dystonic impulses.

He felt that two basic psychoanalytic principles are at work here. One is free association, the other the transference. He shared with other analytic workers the view that these take place in therapy independent of the length of the therapy or the position of the patient, on the couch or sitting up. Alexander did not stress in his writings the importance of the working alliance in brief therapy, but those familiar with his work recognize that establishing a favorable working alliance and keeping it at an optimum level was one of the most important aspects of his technique. He felt that the patient's past attitudes toward the parents will develop in relation to the therapist, no matter what kind of therapy is involved, provided the therapist is objective, empathic, and nonjudgmental.

In the first years the child learns to control dangerous impulses if it wants to avoid conflict with the parents and with authority figures, and this is how the weak ego of the child suppresses impulses. In therapy, the patient is confronted for the first time in adult life with the fact that this method of dealing with impulses is no longer needed. The therapist encourages this attitude and allows the patient to express heretofore unacceptable impulses. Any form of therapy, stressed Alexander, under certain circumstances, will encourage the development of such transference and will aim at its resolution in therapy. Accepting these premises of psychoanalytic therapy, Alexander (1965) raised the question of how to deal with the two main aspects of the therapy, the free association and the transference. Here is where his contributions to brief psychotherapy came into play, and around these issues a good deal of controversy took place.

THE CORRECTIVE EMOTIONAL EXPERIENCE

It was the technical application of psychoanalytic principles that caused much discussion in psychoanalytic centers. Some of the echoes of these discussions still reverberate today, although much of what is today practiced as brief psychotherapy is based on his modification of technique. In trying to describe this modification, Alexander outlined the experiences involving the patient in brief psychotherapy—the intellectual awareness of how his behavior is inappropriate and belongs to his past, as well as the emotional recognition that feelings are being experienced in therapy. Here Alexander introduced a now well-known principle of technique, one he felt applied to any form of psychotherapy: namely, the corrective emotional experience. Without that, he felt, there is no psychotherapy to speak of. Very briefly stated, he felt that the difference between the old childhood relationship with the parents and the present relationship between patient and therapist is the central therapeutic element in therapy. The therapist's reaction to the patient's feelings in therapy is completely different from the reactions of the parents during the patient's childhood. He felt that the difference between these attitudes was the cornerstone of the changes that take place in psychotherapy or, for that matter, in psychoanalysis. This difference allows the patient to understand the source of his conflicts. What is more important, the patient becomes aware of the inappropriateness of his emotional experiences. The ego of the patient is afforded a second chance, so to speak; it is helped to adapt to changed situations and to adjust to new and entirely different reality conditions.

Changes taking place in the ego can be ascribed to the psychoanalytic principle of the synthetic function of the ego. However, Alexander did not feel that this corrective experience takes place automatically. It is not enough for the therapist to be objective, nonjudgmental, and empathic for the corrective emotional experience to take place. Rather, the therapist has to work toward implementing such a climate in therapy (Alexander and French 1946, Alexander 1956). He suggested that the therapist ought to generate a climate in therapy that will allow the patient to experience in the transference the difference between the present attitude of the therapist and the past attitude of the parents in similar situations. In therapy, Alexander suggested the positive difference between past and present. If a patient had excessively strict and punitive parents, he advocated a permissive attitude on the part of the therapist. Conversely, if the parents were extremely permissive and catered to all the patient's whims, he recommended an impersonal, reserved approach in the transference.[1]

Alexander strongly defended this modification of the technique against accusations that it was artificial and manipulative. He responded that the therapist's objective, emotionally noninvolved attitude in psychoanalytic therapy was also artificial and does not reflect attitudes between people in real life. If there was one aspect of long therapies that Alexander criticized and tried to resolve, it was the dependency of patients on their therapists. He felt that was a regressive phenomenon occurring in all forms of therapy but encouraged in prolonged therapy. To that purpose he made the suggestion that the emotional experience of the patient be heightened by occasionally decreasing the frequency of sessions in order to make the patient aware of dependent needs and to thus elicit emotions attached to dependency so they can be analyzed.

TERMINATION

Another technical modification had to do with the termination of therapy. Alexander was of the opinion that very long therapies do not necessarily lead to better therapeutic results; he offered as examples the so-called transference cures, in which patients derived lasting benefits after short exposures to therapy.[2] Alexander frequently mentioned in his teaching and writings that the improvement a patient experiences in therapy is often due to the fact that the patient knows he is still in therapy. If his dependency needs are gratified, the patient feels good. If his oral needs are gratified in therapy, the

1. It has often been recounted, and Alexander confirmed the anecdote, of how he first applied this principle. An unusually untidy patient complained for the umpteenth time how few people liked him and how he was avoided by many, even being accused of being untidy. This while the patient was lying on the couch soiling it with his dirty shoes. At this point Alexander remarked that he was not surprised at people's reactions to the patient since at this very moment he was dirtying the analyst's couch. The patient, whose excessively tolerant parents never corrected his attitudes or behavior, was startled to hear his analyst confront him with this different attitude in the transference.

2. One of the research projects he was planning in the last years of his life was to assemble a reasonably large number of "transference cures" and study the length of the therapy, the type of termination of therapy, and the lasting effects of the therapy.

patient can afford in his outside life the luxury of feeling and believing.

To determine the appropriate time for termination, Alexander recommended "experimental temporary interruptions." He hoped that the patient's innate strength and adaptive abilities would be mobilized by these interruptions. He quoted an early statement by Freud that "treatments often reach a point where the patient's will to be cured is outweighed by his wish to be treated." He felt the therapist must apply persistent pressure to make the patient aware that sooner or later he will have to give up his dependency on the therapist and take over the management of his own life. He advocated the view that the therapist ought to tell the patient at the very beginning of therapy that their joint goal is to complete the therapy in as short a period as possible. This is the technique employed today by most workers in brief psychotherapy. He stressed in this respect his views on regression in and out of therapy (Alexander 1956).

REGRESSION

One form of regression, first mentioned by Freud, allows the patient to return to a phase in his life when he was happy. A second form takes the patient back to a painful and traumatic phase in the attempt to master and resolve the consequences of that trauma. These two forms of regression occur in all kinds of therapy. Alexander felt that patients often will regress to early infantile states to avoid dealing in the transference with the painful traumatic situations which genetically took place during a later phase. He felt that very early infancy disturbances in personality development are rare occurrences in patients and that to stress such regression is to keep patients away from later conflictual phases in which most patients find themselves.[3]

Alexander recommended that therapists pay attention to present events and conflicts in the patient's life. He never tired of cautioning that the secret of successful therapy was not to allow regression in the transference to become a good phase, but to carefully control it to

3. This view of Alexander's would be in sharp disagreement with the new views in psychoanalysis on early disturbances of the self and consequent narcissism, as well as much that has been described in recent years by Mahler, Kernberg, and Kohut.

the advantage of the patient. This too is a basic principle accepted today by most workers in this field. A patient with grave ego defects due to early life conflicts will react strongly even to minor conflicts in the present, while the patient with a reasonably healthy early childhood will require a great deal of present life stress to become neurotic. He felt that these latter are the ones that respond best to brief psychotherapy. Today, of course, it is widely accepted that this approach to selection of patients is essential if brief psychotherapy is to succeed. "The understanding of the past should always be subordinated to the problems of the present," stated Alexander (Alexander and French 1946).

COUNTERTRANSFERENCE

He called attention to the problem of countertransference in therapy and was one of the first to question the "blank screen" phenomenon in therapy—the idea that the therapist represents only a mirror onto which the patient can project the images of the important people from his past. Alexander saw countertransference in light of his corrective emotional experience principle; if the therapist's attitudes differ from those of the parents, the patient will be compelled to adapt to new realities. If the therapist's countertransference is similar to the parental behavior toward the patient in his childhood, little if any change will occur in therapy.[4] Alexander's insistence on the importance of the personality of the therapist in the success or failure of the therapy was of particular importance to him. Well aware of his own strong and charismatic personality, he knew that many of his critics attributed his therapeutic results to personal attributes.

What distinguished Alexander's views on theory and technique of psychotherapy was his willingness and enthusiasm in testing generally accepted views on therapy. To that end he undertook, together with a group of experienced psychoanalysts, to test the psychotherapeutic process in all its aspects. This was done under a grant from the Ford Foundation at the Mount Sinai Hospital in Los

4. In this respect Alexander addressed himself to the conscious attitudes of the therapist. He probably assumed that all countertransference attitudes are, or must be, available to the therapist—an ideal goal to reach, but not always attainable. This is of utmost importance in brief psychotherapy, since the therapist does not have too much time to correct his countertransference distortions.

Angeles. A psychoanalysis and a few psychotherapies were observed and studied through a one-way mirror for their duration. Transference, countertransference, insight, corrective emotional experience, and all possible aspects of therapy were examined.[5]

EGO STRENGTH

Alexander cautioned that cases for brief psychotherapy should not be evaluated on the basis of presenting symptoms, but rather on the patient's "integrative capacity or ego strength." Whether a therapy will be long or short will depend on this capacity of the ego. Given this, he felt that "reconstructive change" can take place in brief psychotherapy. (One might question this statement, since Alexander also remarked that the patients most suitable for brief psychotherapy are those who have sufficient ego strength and whose conflicts are not traceable to very early life experiences. One can safely assume that such patients do not need a therapy that implies "reconstructive change.")

GENETIC MATERIAL

He also felt that if short-term psychotherapy is to succeed and to achieve optimal therapeutic results, the therapist must know and understand a good deal not only of the patient's psychodynamics but also of genetic developments and early conflictual areas. One might paraphrase Alexander by saying that to "work fast one has to know a good deal." One cannot stress enough that what distinguishes Alexander from previous proponents of brief therapy, and even from some contemporary practitioners, was his insistence that the therapist be very familiar not only with the patient's present, but with his past as well. This comes through clearly in his writings, as it did in his work with patients. Alexander's insistence on knowing a good deal about the patient stemmed from the fact that the therapist has to appropriately plan the patient's corrective experiences; that can be done only if the therapist is in good command of what it is that has to be corrected.

5. The results of these studies will soon appear as a volume by S. Eisenstein, N. Levy, and J. Marmor.

THE ACTIVE APPROACH

Alexander advocated an active approach in doing brief psychotherapy. Therapy simply cannot be brief if the therapist uses the passive stance observed in long-term psychotherapy and psychoanalysis. This active approach has since been adopted by almost all therapists working with patients in brief psychotherapy. Alexander felt that frequent and planned interruptions of therapy enabled the patient not only to learn about his own resources and how to use them, but also enabled both therapist and patient to learn more about a jointly agreed date for termination of therapy. He stressed consistently that all psychotherapy, whether psychoanalysis or brief psychotherapy, is a *learning experience*. This view is today accepted by most in the field, and many have incorporated it as an important aspect of their technique.

Alexander's insistence that the therapist "know a good deal about the patient" and that the therapist be cognizant at all times of his own countertransference feelings clearly implies that brief does not mean superficial. Brief therapy does not mean improvisation, and it does not include the large variety of therapies that have sprung up in recent years.

In his efforts to modify standard techniques, Alexander recommended using not only the method of free association but also "interviews of a more direct character." He also advised giving patients guidelines for their personal lives, using interruptions of short or long duration as a test for termination, and adapting the transference to meet the special needs of each case. This, of course, is the corrective emotional experience technique. What is significant about these modifications is that the therapist actively plans and consciously makes use of these techniques. Also important is that Alexander advised using these flexible approaches quite early in the therapy. In contrast to classical technique, he did not see the need to slowly and gradually uncover and interpret the resistance before the drive. With Fenichel and other analysts, he did not believe a clear distinction between defense and drive can often be made. When he advised therapists to consciously use these modifications, he added that none of his recommendations were new. In one way or another they had been used before, either accidently or in special cases.

But the significant fact about Alexander's technique was not that he borrowed his methods from previous workers in the field and with them structured a new approach. He did much more. He and his colleagues and students at the Chicago Institute of Psychoanalysis studied and experimented with all these approaches, and only after testing them with patients did he publish his results and recommend new and more flexible techniques. It was his original research in psychosomatic disturbances that led to the experience with all kinds of acute and mild chronic mental conditions. He felt that the short therapy was more effective with the less severely disturbed patient and of greater social value than devoting much time and effort to the treatment of severe and chronic cases.

Alexander saw in our competitive society, and in the conflict between the need to be dependent and the encouragement to become self-sufficient and self-assertive, the source of modern man's emotional dilemma. We are at the same time "friends and rivals." A successful resolution to this dilemma is the exception rather than the rule, and in consequence our culture breeds a great many emotionally disturbed individuals. He viewed the conflict between dependency and competition as the source of most neurotic conditions. Some choose the psychosomatic solution, by developing peptic ulcers or essential hypertension, while others opt for the neurotic solution. He granted that some of these patients may require only moderate reassurance to resume their previous adaptations to life, while others resort to neurotic regressions and escape into fantasy and regressive behavior under life stresses. The faster the patient can learn, through the experience of the transference, to return to the life difficulties from which he retreated the better will be the results of the brief therapy. In this respect he agreed with Rado in opposing the fostering of dependence in the therapy. To avoid that the therapist was asked to systematically encourage the patient to face his life experiences. He found encouragement for this active attitude in Freud's encouragement of phobic patients to face, after a period of therapy, the activities they had avoided in the past. What Alexander actually did was to take what Freud considered a parameter to be invoked in cases of phobia and to make it a cardinal aspect of his new technique.

The neurotic tendency he considered universal; when life stresses become too great for the ego to adapt, acute neurotic decompensation occurs and brief psychotherapy becomes the treatment of choice. Our culture and the stresses of our fast-paced lives foster the acute neurosis. The people who suffer from this condition tend to be very active and to influence the life of the nation to a far greater extent than do severely incapacitated neurotics or borderlines. Parents of young children, leaders at the national and local level, businessmen and workers, teachers, doctors and ministers—these are the people, Alexander claimed, whose emotional problems did not receive the attention they deserved.

The mild chronic cases, the acute neurotic breakdown—these were the ideal cases for his new approach. Classical technique he reserved for the chronic psychoneuroses, for training purposes, and for depression, compulsion neurosis, character neurosis, anxiety neurosis, and all types of hysteria. For acute breakdown under extreme life stress by previously well-functioning individuals, he recommended the brief therapy approach. Interestingly enough, he only grudgingly gave his approval to group psychotherapy. He never practiced it himself, and he would smile mischievously when asked directly why he did not endorse that kind of therapy more openly. Perhaps his roots in classical analysis and his eagerness to fully understand a patient's psychodynamics, both present and genetic, kept him devoted to the dyadic type of therapy.

At the Chicago Institute, Alexander and his collaborators stressed the importance of having a plan of treatment. This plan had to be based on a dynamic and diagnostic evaluation of the patient and the acute problems that brought the patient to therapy. The therapist's task is to decide in each case whether a supportive or an uncovering type of therapy should be used. The choice of method must be determined by the problems the patient presents. Curiously enough, Alexander did not explicitly stress the patient's motivation as a selection criterion for brief psychotherapy, as do such modern workers as Malan, Sifneos, and Davanloo. But those who worked with him are aware that the ability to have insight into one's conflicts, and to recognize the psychological implications of these conflicts, was considered by him a sine qua non.

One should not expect changes in the patient only after the therapy is terminated, he insisted. The patient should be encouraged to perform constructive changes while still in therapy. He ought to be asked to experiment in actual life with what he learns in the relation to the therapist in the transference. According to Alexander, there is no greater therapeutic result than for a patient to be able to engage in life activities he previously avoided and to overcome anxieties he previously was unable to face. This will break the vicious circle established by the neurotic decompensation and will enable the ego to derive great satisfaction from having been able to master obstacles which before therapy seemed insuperable.

Critics accused Alexander of being too active and too manipulative in patient's lives outside the therapy. He replied that "nothing succeeds like success." Let the patient taste new strength, let the ego experience renewed ability at mastery of neurotic symptoms, and that will be the real test of whether these techniques work. In addition, he felt that most therapists, including the classical analysts, have at one time or another, consciously or unconsciously, used all of these techniques. Of course, one should be careful that the patient is not pressed to perform before he is ready. However, when the therapist feels the patient has made enough progress, he should not only encourage the patient but should ask him to try situations he failed in in the past. Alexander placed enormous importance on the therapist's ability and skill to fully understand the patient's conflicts, his weaknesses and ego strength, his genetic background, and his adaptations before the neurotic decompensation. This was why Alexander took so seriously his involvement in the training of young therapists. At the Berlin Institute at the beginning of his carreer, then at the Chicago Institute, and finally at the Cedars-Sinai Hospital in Los Angeles, the teaching and training of therapists was one of his major dedications.

He was insistent with his students on a thorough knowledge of the cases they were treating, and he required a deep knowledge of the literature on the specific case under treatment. When a young resident claimed he was trying to learn from the treatment of a patient and only later check the literature, he retorted with slight irritation, "You have no right to treat a patient by disregarding what others have written on the subject." He could also be encouraging and humorous, as when he told a resident who complained that his patient refused a transference interpretation of a dream, "Doctor, do not feel offended if the patient does not dream every night about you." He encouraged a very flexible approach to the practical arrangements of the therapy. Although he did not advise the use of the couch in brief therapy, he allowed those who could not stare at the therapist to lie down. He discouraged the therapist sitting behind a desk, and if some patients wanted to walk around during the session he allowed them to. He never tired of urging residents to vary their approach according to the type of transference they were planning to develop in the patient.

FOCUSING THE THERAPY AND
SETTING TIME LIMITS

Many have worked and pioneered in the field of brief psychotherapy, but Alexander's influence is the most notable of all. Balint was instrumental in stressing the activity of the therapist in brief psychotherapy and introduced the term *focal therapy* for those forms of therapy that direct attention to a central conflict and a "selective interpretatior". Even here one can detect Alexander's emphasis on strategic planning and limited goals in therapy. Malan emphasizes that concentrating one's therapeutic effort on a focus does not entail a superficial therapeutic goal. On the contrary, he insists that focus and nuclear conflict are often identical.

Most therapists conducting brief psychotherapy today insist on confining their attention and the goals of therapy to control of the focal issue. This is intended to limit the patient's tendency to regress and thus prolong the therapy. Alexander tended to investigate peripheral issues also, but he always returned the work of the therapy to the center. He felt that although the therapist need not work on all issues presented by the patient, it serves the goal of the therapy better if the therapist is familiar with material that is as rich as possible.

Finally, Sifneos (1972) insists that for brief psychotherapy to be successful the patient's focal conflict must be oedipal. In this respect, he approaches Alexander's view, although it is a view not shared by all workers in the field.

There is some latitude in the duration of brief psychotherapy. Sifneos (1972) sees it lasting in some cases for up to a year, and Malan stresses that merely to relieve patients of their symptoms is not enough—the patient must also be willing to accept the necessity of basic changes in his adaptive capacities. Malan (1976) places the upper limit to forty sessions. James Mann (1973), who initiated in 1964 a time-limited psychotherapy program at Boston University School of Medicine and Medical Center, sets a limit of twelve sessions to therapy and insists that the patient must know from the start the date of termination. Davanloo at Montreal General Hospital, in his work in short-term dynamic psychotherapy, favors an upper limit of forty sessions, varying the number of sessions with the severity of the case.

The insistence of some workers on setting a time for termination from the beginning of therapy, advocated in particular by Mann (1973) and Malan (1963), was not considered essential by Alexander. Only in cases of phobia and obsessive-compulsion did he set a time limit, though even here he was flexible and adapted the time limit to the particular case. Although he did not set a time limit to the therapy, he did aim to make it brief. He felt that the type of pathology, as well as the patient's ego strength and capacity for insight, would determine the length of the therapy. He did of course insist on letting the patient know that it would not be a long therapy.

By contrast, Marmor, one of the few who stresses the separation-individuation conflict as being at the center of brief psychotherapy (1979), insists on setting a time limit. Like Alexander, Marmor and Malan also allow patients to return for follow-up sessions after termination. Malan (1976) agrees with Balint's view that extreme chronicity and pervasiveness of illness do not contraindicate brief psychotherapy, provided that motivation for insight is present. Malan will inform the patient at the beginning that the therapy will be brief and that if the patient requires further therapy at a later date he will be transferred for longer therapy to someone else. Malan also informs the patient that he will see him for additional sessions if the patient feels at termination that he needs further help.

THE TRAINING
OF BRIEF THERAPISTS

Generally speaking, then, most authors stress that the time limit of therapy and focusing on a central issue are the two basic requirements of brief psychotherapy. Common also to most brief therapies is that they all follow a psychoanalytically oriented model which implies that the therapist is aware of his own conflicts and assets, as well as of the patient's unconscious conflicts. It takes a good deal of experience to determine in a very few sessions, sometimes even the first session, whether a patient is suitable for brief therapy. Also, to recognize a central or focal conflict and work with it in a few sessions require much ability and insight. It is not uncommon for a focal conflict to appear in the first session only to reveal itself as a "smoke screen," a defense against a "real" central conflict appearing a few sessions later. When this occurs, the therapist must be able to change course in midstream and still limit the duration of the therapy. It is for this reason that Alexander advocated the thorough and expert training of therapists involved in brief psychotherapy.

At the Second International Symposium of Short-Term Dynamic Psychotherapy, held in Montreal in 1976, M. Straker made the useful observation that the efficacy and the time limit of short therapy both have a good deal to do with "who is doing the therapy." We all have different capacities, different preferences, skills, and qualities to function in a variety of settings, and these certainly influence the interaction between the therapist and the patient. Straker comes close here to Alexander's view regarding the role of the therapist in brief therapy, or in any kind of therapy for that matter.

In relation to the training of therapists in short-term therapy, at the same Montreal symposium I made a statement that is probably shared by many who are psychoanalytically trained: "At no time do I think that we aim at short-terming the training of therapists. It is only shortening the therapy of the patients."

In 1962 Davanloo initiated a systematic research program in short-term dynamic psychotherapy at Montreal General Hospital. He stresses that short-term psychotherapy must be based on psycho-analytic principles. He sometimes calls his therapy "broad-spectrum" short-term dynamic psychotherapy. He feels that "such therapy can be the therapy of choice for patients suffering from more severe psychoneurotic disorders of many years' duration." He also thinks that "such therapy can bring about massive charac-terological change in a carefully selected group of patients." This optimism expressed by Davanloo approaches very closely the views Alexander held of the efficacy of brief psychotherapy.

The new brief psychotherapies range from supportive to deep uncovering with unconscious conflict interpretation. In all the types described, however, one can see the influence of Franz Alexander. In his writings and in his practice of brief psychotherapy are to be found all of these interventions. It is due to Alexander's pioneering research and efforts that brief psychotherapy has become such an important therapeutic approach to the treatment of emotional disturbances.

References

Alexander, F. (1956). Two forms of regression and their therapeutic implications. *Psychoanalytic Quarterly* 25:178-4198.

———(1965). Psychoanalytic contributions to short-term psychotherapy. In *Short-Term Psychotherapy*, ed. L. Wolberg. New York: Grune and Stratton.

Alexander, F., and French, T. (1946). *Psychoanalytic Therapy*. New York: Ronald Press.

Davanloo, H. (1978). *Basic Principles and Technique in Short-Term Dynamic Psychotherapy*. New York: Spectrum Publications.

Eisenstein, S. (1966). Otto Rank. In *Psychoanalytic Pioneers*, ed. F. Alexander, S. Eisenstein, and M. Grotjahn. New York: Basic Books.

Ferenczi, S., and Rank, O. (1925). *The Development of Psychoanalysis*. New York: Nervous and Mental Disease Publishing.

Freud, S. (1918). From the history of an infantile neurosis. *Standard Edition* 17:7-122.

Malan, D. (1963). *A Study of Brief Psychotherapy*. New York: Plenum.

———(1976). *The Frontier of Brief Psychotherapy*. New York: Plenum.

Mann, J. (1973). *Time Limited Psychotherapy*.

Marmor, J. (1979). *American Journal of Psychiatry*..

Sifneos, P. (1972). *Short Short-Term Psychotherapy and Cambridge: Harvard University Press*.

4

A *Method of Short-Term Dynamic Psychotherapy*

Habib Davanloo, M.D.

In 1895 Joseph Breuer published observations which are fundamental to understanding and treating neurotic disturbances. The patient, Fraulein Anna O, suffered from severe hysterical symptomatology; and Breuer found that symptoms were relieved when she relived certain traumatic experiences of her past under hypnosis. Her experiences concerned mainly buried feelings about her father, with whom she had had an extremely intimate relationship; and she had nursed him through a terminal illness. During the course of treatment she developed intense sexual feelings for Breuer and had a phantom pregnancy in which it was clear that he was the imaginary father. Eventually she made physical advances toward him, and Breuer was so alarmed that he gave up this work altogether and never returned to it. This case history was based on a series of observations that contained most of the basic principles of dynamic psychotherapy: neurotic symptoms are at least partly the outward manifestation of buried, unacceptable feelings, and these feelings can be recovered.

But a complicating factor is that the patient develops intense feelings for the therapist, which on one hand constitute a threat to the psychotherapeutic process, but on the other hand can be understood in terms of the patient's past.

Breuer's observations triggered Freud's life work, the development of a theoretical system and therapeutic method which he called *psychoanalysis*. The central concepts are *defense* against unacceptable feelings which consequently remain unconscious, and *transference* of feelings onto the therapist which really belong to people in the patient's past. With the aid of these concepts a refined therapeutic technique was developed which contains the following basic elements: the patient's free-associations, interpretation of defense, releasing the buried feelings, accepting and interpreting the fact that some of these feelings involve the therapist, and linking these feelings with the past. In spite of the fact that the documentation of the early cases is not complete, it seems probable that this technique was often therapeutically effective within a short time. In fact, almost all the cases that Freud treated in the very early phase of his work were of relatively short duration, ranging from a few sessions to several months. For example, he treated Bruno Walter, the conductor, in six sessions in 1906; and the composer Gustav Mahler, who suffered from disturbances in potency, was treated successfully by Freud in a single four-hour session in 1908. Perhaps the best documented case is that of the "Rat Man," who suffered from severe obsessive-compulsive neurosis and whom Freud successfully treated in eleven months in 1907. The inference from the early analyses, in the period 1900-1914, is that some factor caused the patients to de-repress their feelings with such intensity and completeness that their neuroses "dissolved." We will never know the answer to this because of the lack of documentation and follow-up, but the "Rat Man" is clearly an example. One might suggest it had something to do with the freshness and the active technique with which Freud and the early analysts came to their fascinating discoveries. At any rate it is clear that in subsequent years something has gone wrong. The art of completing therapy in a few months seems to have been lost. Analysts' reaction to this has been to accept the increase in duration as inevitable and to become increasingly passive in their technique, quite possibly setting up a vicious circle. At the same time there has been an almost total lack of investigation into outcome, so that no one knows what the therapeutic result in the average case is likely to be. The final result is that when they are challenged about the validity of their theory or technique they have no effective answer; and they remain in a state of hidden bewilderment, knowing that they are in possession of fundamental truths about human beings yet unable to convince others, and hiding from themselves the possibility that their methods are not as therapeutically effective as theory suggests they ought to be.

Many early workers from Stekel, to Ferenczi and Rank, to Alexander and French tried to counteract the progressive development of passivity in psychoanalytic technique by activity in various forms, but their attempts foundered on the twin rocks of analytical hostility on one hand and uncertain therapeutic effects on the other.

In the early 1960s I decided to break away from the traditional approach; like the workers before me, but quite independently, I began to reverse the tendency toward passivity, becoming more and more active in my technique, yet adhering strictly to three fundamental psychoanalytic principles: releasing hidden feelings by actively working on and interpreting resistance or defenses; paying strict attention to the transference relationship; and actively making links between the transference and significant people in the patient's current life and in the past. What emerged, to my amazement, was that the hidden conflict became conscious in an unmistakable way; the link with the symptoms became obvious, and the symptoms immediately disappeared, never to return.

This frequently was accomplished in from fifteen to twenty-five sessions; some patients did well in as few as one to ten sessions; and with a few, results were accomplished in up to forty sessions. As I refined my technique further, particularly by working with the transference relationship, interpreting very actively any manifestation of transference resistance and linking the transference with current relationships and with the past, I began to realize that the number of sessions required could be reduced.

In many of these therapies several distinct types of pathology can be dealt with. Based on three systematic researches, we can identify four major groups of patients who can be treated with this technique.

1. Patients suffering from neuroses with a primarily oedipal focus.
2. Patients suffering from neurotic conditions where the focus is loss.

3. Patients suffering from long-standing obsessional and phobic neuroses with more than one focus—e.g., a complicated oedipal focus as well as loss.

4. Patients with more severe psychopathology: those suffering from long-standing psychoneurotic disorders and characterological problems where one cannot delineate a single focus.

In a forthcoming publication based on the treatment of nearly one-hundred fifty patients, I have described in detail seven categories of oedipal psychotherapeutic focus. The major part of this work, consisting of the initial evaluation, therapeutic sessions, and follow-ups, has been recorded audiovisually, and the material is in the process of systematic analysis and publication.

Selection Criteria

The careful selection of patients is essential. The initial evaluation is based on a very special kind of focused interview. One starts not knowing anything about the patient and makes a very careful evaluation of the history and current situation. The interview focuses on the evaluation of those major ego functions which are of primary importance in dynamic psychotherapy. One uses the technique of gentle but relentless questioning and confrontation of the defenses against true feelings. One persistently confronts the patient in the face of vagueness, avoidance, and passivity, and further links him with relation to significant people in his current life, such as his boss, wife, etc. This might mobilize anger in the transference as well as defense against the anger; and this is brought into focus the moment it arises. One persistently confronts the patient, asking what he really feels rather than interpreting it to him. The patient almost invariably experiences relief when he himself is able to say that he was irritated. Very often the anger aroused against the interviewer has links with unexpressed anger in the past, for example, with a controlling mother or an authoritarian father. This in turn may be linked with the patient's maladaptive way of handling anger in his current life situation, and this is brought out as well. I call this a T-C-P interpretation, which is linking the transference (T) with current people (C) and the past people (P), with the patient experiencing the avoided impulse in the transference situation.

This is not a universal technique of the initial interview. If we consider the four major groups we take into treatment, there is a wide variation in technique of the initial interview; and flexibility in the evaluator is essential. The clinician who uses this technique with patients with severe pathology must be very skillful and should be able to detect immediately if the patient is reacting adversely, which requires changing the technique to be more supportive. On the other hand, if a patient reacts positively the technique often brings out fresh material about current and past situations. This technique of initial interview really consists of *trial therapy*, and is the only reliable method of finding out whether a patient is likely to respond. The points to look for by the end of the initial interview, or second interview when necessary, are: Has the psychopathology, the central neurotic structure of the patient's problems, become clear? Has the patient responded positively to the uncovering technique used in the interview? Does the patient respond to interpretation? Has it been possible to make links between the present and the past? Has the patient related in a meaningful way to the interviewer? Were there some meaningful relationships in the patient's past? Does the patient's history justify the inference that the patient can face the uncovering process of therapy without serious adverse effects such as psychotic decompensation, suicide? Has the patient at least potentially the motivation to look at himself and go through the uncovering process with the therapist's help, and the capacity to form a good therapeutic alliance?

Here is an example of an initial interview with a twenty-nine-year-old teacher who presented problems of depression, chronic anxiety, difficulties in her job, and disturbances in interpersonal relationships, especially with men. None of her relationships with men had been satisfactory and they all had ended in disappointment. Her last relationship, where marriage had been planned, broke down a few months prior to the initial interview. During the interview it became clear that at one time she had had a very close relationship with her father which had changed to a disturbed and hostile one. She here with me you are passive, and I am the one who has to question father. During the initial interview the patient was evasive, ruminated a great deal, used a great deal of intellectualization, and focused on trivial issues.

Therapist: How do you feel about talking to me about yourself?

Patient: I feel uncomfortable. I have never done this before, so I don't really, you know . . . I feel I don't really know how to answer some of your questions.

Therapist: Um-hum. But have you noticed that in your relationship here with me you are passive, and I am the one who has to question you repeatedly?

Patient: I know.

The therapist has confronted the patient with her passivity in the transference.

Therapist: Um-hum. What do you think about this? Is this the way it is with other people, or is it only here with me? . . . this passivity, lack of spontaneity.

Patient: Yeah. To some extent. I mean I'm . . . there are a lot of things hidden, you know. Somebody once described me "like a hidden flower" or something. There are a lot of things about me that I don't think I have ever really . . . uh . . . explored that much.

Therapist: Then from what you say you are passive with others. But from what you have told me you indicated that your mother has been a passive person.

Patient: Uh. In terms of the relationship. But she is passive, and she is not. There were situations where she knew what she wanted and wasn't passive.

Therapist: Going back to yourself, do you see yourself as a passive person?

Patient: Yeah.

Therapist: You do . . .

Patient: In certain situations where I don't feel . . . when I get involved with a man . . . I find I tend to take a passive role, and I don't like that.

Therapist: What specifically do you mean by not liking it?

Patient: I feel upset inside.

Therapist: What is it that you experience? You say "upset" . . .

Patient: Perhaps irritated . . . something like that . . .

Therapist: But you say "perhaps." . . . Is it that you experience irritation and anger, or isn't it?

Patient: Ummm. Yeah. Yeah . . . I do.

Therapist: You say you take a passive role in relation to men. Are you doing that here with me?

Patient: I would say so.

Therapist: You "would" say so, but still you are not committing yourself.

Patient: (Long, awkward pause) Well . . . I don't . . . you see, I don't know how to . . . uh . . . I don't know about the situation . . . you know . . . I don't understand this whole situation yet. So I . . . I am here, and I am a passive recipient or a passive participant. I am not passive, really. I am active; I am participating, but I am . . .

Therapist: Are you participating?

Patient: Well, sure.

Therapist: Um-hum. To what extent?.

Patient: (Pause.) I am answering your questions.

Therapist: What comes to my mind is, if I don't question you, what do you think would happen here?

Patient: Well . . . I might . . . I might start to tell . . . I might start something which would indicate . . . would tell you where I am going. It might be very intellectual, though, because I don't really know . . . I don't really understand the source of my depression.

Therapist: Uh-hum. In relationship with me, then, you are passive; and it is the same with all men. (Patient is silent . . . pause.)

The evaluator has made a link between the transference and the people in the patient's current life; and he has already also established that she experiences anger in relation to men, with whom she takes a passive role.

Therapist: How do you feel when I indicate to you that you are passive?

Patient: I don't like it. (The patient is laughing, but it is quite evident that she is irritated.)

Therapist: But you are smiling.

Patient: I know. Well . . . maybe that is my way of expressing my irritation.

Therapist: Then you are irritated?

Patient: A little bit . . . yeah . . .

Therapist: A little bit?

Patient: Actually, quite a bit. (The patient is laughing.)

Therapist: But somehow you smile frequently, don't you?

Patient: It is inappropriate.

Therapist: Hum?

Patient: It is plain inappropriate. It is just nervousness.

Therapist: Let's look at what happened here. I brought to your attention your passivity, your noninvolvement. You got irritated and angry with me, and the way you dealt with your irritation was by smiling.

Patient: That is right. That is . . .

The transference has been clarified. The anger in the transference has been brought out in the open, and a link has been made between the transference and men in the patient's current life.

Therapist: What does this remind you of . . . this situation? Is there any other relationship that may have been like this?

(Pause. The patient is squirming in the chair.)

Now the session focuses on her relationship with her parents. The patient has a great deal of resentment toward her father, and indicates that her mother who appears to be passive is quite a controlling woman, especially in relation to the patient's father. She controls him in a very passive way. Then the session continues; and the therapist brings the parents into focus, linking this with the transference.

Therapist: And this is what you also do here in a passive way. You are controlling me, aren't you . . . intellectualizing, ice-skating around, aren't we?

Patient: (The patient laughs.) I don't know.

Therapist: You are smiling.

Patient: Yeah. And I anticipated that this was going to happen before I walked into this room. I was trying to get my ideas together so that it wouldn't happen this way. But I just didn't know how to do it.

Therapist: Do you think you are a controlling person, or aren't you?

Patient: Hmmm.

Therapist: Let's look at it. You have a problem in life which obviously is seriously interfering, and which is a source of agony for you. Of course you are the one to decide . . . is it, or isn't it?

Patient: Yeah.

Therapist: You constantly repeat a pattern in your relationships with men. And this is a pattern that you very much dislike.

Patient: That is right.

Therapist: And you have come here of your own volition, and no one has forced you to come here.

Patient: That's right.

Therapist: So then you come here to overcome these difficulties . . . so that we can get to the core of your problems; by intellectualizing, censoring yourself, you are defeating the purpose of your coming here. And, obviously, then I would be useless to you as in all your relationships with men.

Patient: Well, yeah . . . I know. I knew that before I walked in, too. . . . I know . . .

Therapist: But is it important that we look at your relationship with me? Don't you think that what is taking place here between you and me in itself is an indication of the core of your problem?

Patient: I know. Right. I know.

Therapist: In other words, you are pulled between two forces. Obviously you have positive forces within you, but there is another part of you that sets you up for defeat, to defeat the purpose of your coming here and to make me useless.

Patient: Defeat . . . that is right. That is very right.

Therapist: Okay.

Thus the evaluator has actively interpreted the transference resistance, which further strengthens the therapeutic alliance. The patient now comes out with a great deal of fresh material. The nuclear conflict unfolds as she begins to talk about the bitter, hostile relationship with her father which developed after the birth of her brother, who became her father's favorite, only son.

Technique

We accept a wide range of patients for Short-Term Dynamic Psychotherapy. The technique used in the initial interview is essentially the technique used in therapy. The patient is gently but relentlessly confronted with his feelings in his current situation, in the transference relationship and in the past, and whenever possible links are made among these three areas.

The technical requirements common to all cases that we have treated within the range of our Short-Term Dynamic Psychotherapy are:

1. Activity of the psychotherapist in using the confrontation technique and maintaining the focus.
2. Very early utilization of the transference; establishing and utilizing a therapeutic alliance; active transference clarification and interpretation.
3. The use of interpretation of all kinds of unconscious phenomena, including fantasies and dreams, but especially transference and resistance.
4. Actively working through the transference resistance.
5. Actively avoiding the development of a symbiotic transference relationship, particularly in patients with a passive-dependent character structure and obsessional character suffering from long-standing psychoneurotic disorders. Avoiding the development of a symbiotic transference is a very important technical issue, and space does not allow me to elaborate on it in detail here. There are a number of factors that are important, such as selection and the use of a technique with frequent confrontation and interpretation of transference resistance. Actively bringing out passivity and dependency with a confronting technique does not allow the development of this kind of transference.
6. Basically, the therapist actively works on two triangles: These are, first, the triangle of conflict: defense/anxiety/impulse-feeling; and second, the triangle of person: transference (T)/significant

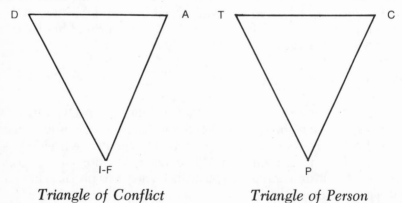

Triangle of Conflict   *Triangle of Person*

people in the patient's current life (C)/significant people in the past (P).

7. A crucial part of the technique consists of making the links in the second triangle, especially pointing out the parallels between the patient's reactions to the transference and current people (the T-C link), and between the transference and the past (the T-P link). The second triangle is completed when all three possible links are made (the T-C-P link).

8. The prognosis is definitely better, and the length of the therapy definitely shorter, the sooner and more often a T-P or T-C-P interpretation can be made in a meaningful way.

Extensive Use of Transference

This method of Short-Term Dynamic Psychotherapy is based entirely on psychoanalytic principles, employing interpretation as its main therapeutic tool and making extensive use of the transference. The emotional experiences of the patient in the transference in both the initial interview and in the subsequent course of therapy are heavily emphasized. In three studies we have come to the conclusion that one of the most striking characteristics of those patients with a successful outcome is a definite rise in the transference in the initial evaluation and a continued high level of transference in the first few psychotherapy sessions. This rise in the transference is associated with an increase in the therapeutic alliance, which obviously brings a rise in the patient's motivation. Any manifestation of resistance should not be interpreted as a decline in the therapeutic alliance. This will be discussed in detail in *The Relentless Healer*. In working with obsessional patients, patients in the third category of our classification, one of the major technical problems is the problem of resistance, which manifests itself in a variety of forms. This can become an obstacle unless one can actively interpret the defenses and work through them.

Using a trial-therapy model of initial interview, which mobilizes resistance and a variety of obsessional defenses, we can make the following general statements:

1. There is a universal appearance of transference resistance by the second interview.

2. There is a significantly higher rise in the transference resistance by the second interview in cases where the therapist, by a process of challenging the patient's neurotic defenses, has been able to expose momentarily the patient's core neurosis;

3. There is a definite rise in the transference and therapeutic alliance and a decrease in resistance when the evaluator has been able to actively interpret the neurotic defenses and has been able to give in a meaningful way T-C or T-P, and more specifically T-C-P, interpretation in the very early phase of the therapy.

In our second study of eighteen patients who suffered from phobic and obsessional disorders, we could make the following two important statements (details will appear in *The Relentless Healer*):

1. In eleven patients with whom we had a successful outcome we noticed a significant rise in the transference and therapeutic alliance in the very early phase of the therapy (i.e., the first to fifth sessions), and there was a concomitant decrease in resistance. These patients came with fresh memories and dreams which threw light on the structure of their neurotic problems. Both the use of transference and the therapeutic alliance remained at a high level throughout the course of therapy, but the patient's resistance was in a state of fluctuation until the middle phase of the therapy.

2. In seven patients outcome was unsuccessful. Here there was no development of a therapeutic alliance, no rise in the transference; and therapy was terminated in the middle phase.

The Man Who Feared Rejection

Since the technique used in the initial interview is essentially the same as in therapy itself, extracts from a further initial interview can be used in illustration.

The patient was in his early thirties and an air-flight controller. His recent divorce precipitated his seeking help. His problems centered around:

1. Disturbances in interpersonal relationships, particularly with people in authority, fear of rejection, bending over backwards in relation to women.

2. After his divorce he experienced anxiety whenever he wanted to approach a woman, as he had before he married, some three years previously. He was intensely involved with his wife prior to marriage; but his feelings for her changed drastically after marriage, when he withdrew from her both emotionally and sexually and became detached.

3. In the initial interview he complained of a lack of self-esteem, a feeling that "he is not as good as others." These feelings of inferiority applied particularly to people in authority.

4. He also suffered from episodes of depression. He had been seen by two other psychiatrists in the front-line services, and finally he was referred to the present evaluator. The interview started with the patient saying that he had already been seen and had given the details of his history.

What follows is the first part of the initial diagnostic evaluation of this patient.

Therapist: Okay, so then you must go through the trouble of repeating yourself, hmm?

Patient: I guess, yeah.

Therapist: Why do you say you "guess"?

Patient: Well, uh, it's . . .

Therapist: How do you feel about it?

Patient: Uh, I think I've been a little angry about it all week. You know, I mean I understand the concept of what you're trying to do here.

Therapist: But still that doesn't help your anger, hmm?

Patient: You're right, right. So I've been kinda going, "Geez, one assessment after another," you know, and this and that; and I gotta go back again and you know, I'd sort of like to get it started.

Therapist: So really you—then you didn't feel that you wanted to come today, hmm?

Patient: No, I wanted to come because you know, it's, well I have to go through the steps you know.

Therapist: But that doesn't still help how you feel?

Patient: No.

Therapist: So let's look at how you feel.

Patient: I was a little angry.

Therapist: You mean you are not anymore?

Patient: (Sigh.)

Therapist: That is the idea that you were and you . . .

Patient: Well, I guess I still am, I don't . . .

Therapist: Again you say you "guess."

Patient: I'm not sure any more. I was angry the day Dr.—phoned me and told me about the session with you.

Therapist: You were angry at whom?

Patient: I didn't tell him. Uh, just the whole bunch in general I think, you know I didn't . . .

Therapist: So it's easier to be angry at the bunch than any individual.

Patient: Well, who could I blame sort of? I couldn't blame Dr.—

Therapist: How did he put it to you?

Patient: Well he asked me you know, if it would be all right and—

Therapist: If it would be all right what?

Patient: For me to, to come and speak to you, you know, it seems that you wanted to speak to me and you know and then . . .

Therapist: So he suggested to you that I want then to see you?

Patient: Yeah, I think so, I believe so.

Therapist: How is your memory?

Patient: Selective.

Therapist: So then let's look at your "selective memory." Because you say . . .

Patient: See what'll happen is, is like—

Therapist: Because he's telling you that I want to see you.

Patient: Right.

Therapist: So then your memory is good, hmmm?

Patient: I believe, I believe that's what it was, you know. I guess what happens is that I—

Therapist: Why do you say you "guess"?

Patient: Well, (sigh) just that I'm never sure of—

Therapist: Is it that you are not sure or because it involves me? Because you see he is telling you that I would like to see you.

Patient: Yeah.

Therapist: So then obviously your anger has a connection with me, isn't that so?

Patient: No, no I don't find that. (Laughing.) I don't . . .

Therapist: You're smiling.

Patient: 'Cause I was just about to say, "I don't think so." Uh, no I don't know you. If I had met you before and you said—

Therapist: I know, but then whom were you angry at?

Patient: Oh everything, everyone, I guess. The whole system.

Therapist: But he told you that I am the one who would like to see you.

Patient: Yeah, but I mean—the only, the only, I don't think I would be mad at you. I would just be mad at the whole system of procedure.

Therapist: Hmmm.

Patient: You know, it's like running into the classical red tape, and you really can't blame the guy who's telling you. You have to go to line C and then go to line B and then go to line D, you know. You can't really blame him. I guess in a way a lot of people would take the anger out on the person who gave him that information. But I was just, I was a little kind of afraid in one sense also you know, 'cause I'd been through two evaluations, right? And the way I understood it is you go through the one evaluation and then, you know, you're almost ready to start the therapy. So I went through two, and then last week you know, when he called me and told me that, you know, you'd like to see me, I kinda started going "uh, I wonder why, you know, why pick on me?"

Therapist: So the idea is that I am picking on you?

Patient: What's so special about me? I mean, you know, I don't think I'm that winged out of it. You know, maybe I'm a classic case of some sort, textbook material and things like that.

Therapist: So one idea was that in a sense there is something specific about your case, something—

Patient: Well that's the assumption that I was starting to make because two sessions—I've been here twice and you know, nothing—from what I can understand the therapy hasn't started. Well, we haven't done anything yet.

Therapist: Hmmm.

Patient: But I couldn't—I don't think I was angry at any particular person, I was just angry at you know, "how dare they treat me like this" sort of thing, I'm coming to them for help and you know . . .

Therapist: How did you feel this morning, coming here?

Patient: Nervous.

Therapist: Hmmm. What is it like when you feel nervous?

Patient: (Sigh.) It's, I don't know, just an uneasiness, you know. You know I find myself doing (sigh) a little more often—I was doing that . . .

Therapist: You were anxious on your way here?

Patient: Yeah, yeah. I am anxious because I was a little afraid.

Therapist: Afraid?

Patient: Of, of why I was being asked to come in for.

Therapist: So there are two things you experienced; one is anger and the other one is nervousness, hmmm?

Patient: Yeah.

Therapist: Do you think there is a connection between the two?

Patient: Oh, I mean I could speculate, but . . .

Therapist: Whatever comes to your mind. Do you think there is a connection?

Patient: Well, maybe, maybe my nervousness is due to my—that doesn't make sense. I was going to say, due to my anger; but maybe my anger is due to my nervousness rather. More the other way around. Uh, I'm a little tense about, you know, I mean I really want to be here and I want to go through the therapy but you know, I'm still tense about it.

Therapist: But do you think that in a sense that there is a link between your nervousness and your anger, that there is some sort of the fear that you might lose control over your anger?

Patient: Not consciously.

Therapist: Hmmm.

Patient: I don't , I don't . . .

Therapist: I'm questioning you . . .

Patient: (Sigh.) Well you know it seems to have brought out that my main problem is my fear of losing control or my inability to, to kind of express those kinds of emotions.

Therapist: What kinds of emotions?

Patient: Anger. I don't do it very often.

Therapist: I know but you have the fear that you might lose control over the—

Patient: Yeah you know the way I've been thinking in the last few years, it seems that I really don't, I don't like to lose control of my emotions in a negative sense. Like I mean it's fine to be laughing my head off on the floor but it's not fine to be angry and mad and demonstrative about it. I somehow feel I'm a civilized man and, and I shouldn't have to let anger get a hold of me like that.

Therapist: Hmmm.

Patient: Not that I am a potentially violent person or—

Therapist: So then this is important because, you see, I raised the question if your anxiety and nervousness this morning, in coming here, was not related to the fear that you might lose control over your anger. Now what you tell me is that you have conflict over anger. Let's look at your relationships with other people, how it is with them.

It is important to see what happens between the evaluator and the patient in terms of the two triangles, the triangle of conflict (defense/anxiety/impulse-feeling), and the triangle of person (transference/current/past people). If we look at the very early part of the interview, the therapist is using one of his standard techniques. He starts by saying, "How do you feel about it? What do you actually feel?" This is the therapist's standard procedure, and this is really the opening move into the patient's unconscious. By this technique he is inviting the patient to do something which he has been trying to avoid all his life—which is to be honest with himself about what he actually feels. This is, in fact, the core of all psychoanalytic psychotherapies; and what inevitably happens every time the therapist does this is that it mobilizes all the patient's resistances.

In this interview, the session immediately focuses on the impulse-feelings, "How do you feel?" The patient admits to a "little bit angry." The patient intellectualizes, and the therapist points out, "It doesn't help your anger." Then he focuses on "How do you experience your anger?" And the patient finally admits to being angry, but says, "Angry with the system." What has come up by now is a set of defenses. The patient repeatedly says, "perhaps," "possibly," and "I guess"; and the therapist also actively deals with this. He maintains his focus at the defense in the triangle of conflict. This defense refers to the transference in the triangle of person. If we analyze the process that has taken place within the first few minutes, the first move, "How do you feel?" mobilizes the different defenses the patient uses and which the therapist interprets, one after another. What follows is the patient saying that he was not only angry on coming to the interview but also anxious. The evaluator is already working very actively on the triangle of conflict in relation to the transference. What comes out is the defense (resistance) in relation to the evaluator (transference). And then he focuses on the impulse-feelings, which sets up more defenses, with the therapist once more interpreting the defense against the impulse in the transference. If we look carefully, the patient has said he is anxious; and he has also spoken of the impulse. What he has not done is link the two, and the therapist asks him, "Is it possible that there is a connection between your anxiety and the fact that you are angry?" The patient eventually admits that one of his life problems is his fear of loss of control. What has emerged is that by dealing with the patient's defenses the evaluator has got to one of the patient's major anxieties: *fear of loss of control,* specifically, fear of loss of control over anger. In this way the evaluator has completed the triangle of conflict in relation to himself, transference.

Having thereby given the patient a certain degree of relief, the therapist has by no means overcome the patient's resistance and defenses; but he has got them out in the open, at least to some extent. What I would like to emphasize is that when one focuses on the patient's feelings one sees at once the resistance; and resistance consists essentially of defenses which are employed in the psychotherapeutic process. And as we know, they are the defenses that the patient has used throughout his life. As we will see later on in this patient, when the evaluator has to some degree penetrated these defenses there is increasing rapport, and the patient in one way or another is more in touch with his real feelings. The tension drops within the therapeutic situation. This is a universal phenomenon. First one sees the defenses rise; and then the defenses are partially penetrated and there is an increase in rapport. One can spot the patient's increased therapeutic alliance. Having done that in the transference (T), the therapist proceeds by saying to the patient, "Let us look at your relationships with other people," which is to focus on the "C" in the triangle of person.

We now take up the interview again.

Patient: Depends on what people?

Therapist: Any, any people. Do you have problems in relationships with people?

Patient: (Sigh.) It's hard to sort of answer that. Uh, I have problems with women.

Therapist: Problems with women, hmm.

Patient: Yeah, for the most part. You know, I do have one or two pretty close female friends who are friends and, you know, very good friends and . . .

Therapist: Hmm.

Patient: But with women I tend to, you know, feel boring, I feel boring about me. You know, like I don't feel like I'm an interesting person, uh, and consequently I tend to start to freeze up, you know.

Therapist: So there is some sort of the inhibition in your relationships?

Patient: Yeah, I feel very inhibited if I'm in a bar and then you know I want to meet a woman that's sitting right next to me and like, I can't, I freeze. With my peer group I'm not so bad, you know, people my own age. I think I tend to be a little bit on the defensive when it comes to, to people like yourself or a policeman, authority figures, you know.

Therapist: What happens?

Patient: I don't feel like I'm on an equal footing with them.

Therapist: Now let's see. With women, when you meet them say in a bar or a social situation, you experience anxiety?

Patient: Yeah.

Therapist: What is it like when you experience anxiety with women?

Patient: I start to, I know, you know, things like my neck muscles, they get tight. I'm not conscious of, you know, I'm really not aware of, of any kind of emotional thing, you know, I'm more conscious of just thoughts whirling around in my mind. You know, very confused, very—you know, you should go and say something to her but no and blah, blah, blah.

Therapist: Okay. You said also with authorities and policemen and people in that category.

Patient: Yeah, yeah.

Therapist: You feel anxious?

Patient: Yeah, I feel inferior. I feel in a pupil-teacher kind of a thing or, or I have to call them sir or something like that.

Therapist: You say you feel inferior to them.

Patient: Yeah.

Therapist: Do you experience this in your relationship in your job, say, for example?

The evaluator explored the situation where he works. With people on his own level he is not afraid he will get angry, but with his superiors, those who control the situation, there is a similar problem.

Patient: I mean I could be out of a job ... sort of, tomorrow type of thing. So uh ...

Therapist: So it's the sort of fear that they would cut you off if you assert yourself?

Patient: Yeah, that's ... that's right, they would exercise the control that they have.

Therapist: In other words they would cut you off, and so forth, huh?

Patient: So like, sure, and then I just become very accepting.

Therapist: Hmmm.

Patient: You know, angry at myself at the same time but you know, kind of ...

Therapist: And what do you do when you get angry with such a person, say, supposedly—

Patient: Nothing.

Therapist: Hmmm?

Patient: Nothing.

Therapist: What happens to your anger? I mean how do you deal with it?

Patient: I don't think I really get—

Therapist: Because you experience anger but there is at the same time fear that they might retaliate with you and they might cut you off.

Patient: Right. So I don't show them that, you know. I don't show them my anger.

The early part of this passage consisted of exploring the patient's *anxiety* (the "A" corner of the first triangle) in two areas, his relations with women and his relations with people in authority, both of which represent the "C" corner of the second triangle. The evaluator asks for specific details in relation to people at work and now receives a crucial clarification of the nature of the anxiety: "I could be out of a job," i.e., that he might be rejected if he didn't behave in an acceptable fashion.

The evaluator at once senses that this almost certainly explains the patient's anxiety at the beginning of the interview, and also, of course, that it has links with the unconscious oedipal feelings. What he now does is to employ another standard technique, which is to use subtly loaded words in order to "speak to the patient's unconscious" and thus try to bring such feelings closer to the surface. This is the reason for the repeated use of the phrase, "fear that they would *cut you off*," the meaning of which to the patient's conscious mind is purely figurative, but to the unconscious may well be literal, in terms of castration.

The passage ends with a clarification of the triangle of conflict in relation to people in authority, namely, that he has to hide his anger for fear of retaliation. The patient states clearly that he understands this.

In the next moment an immensely important phenomenon emerges. Hitherto the dialogue has almost entirely consisted of the patient actively resisting, or reluctantly responding to, the evaluative pressure. An observer would say that there has been hardly any motivation for psychotherapy. Now, however, in response to all this work, for the first time he produces a spontaneous communication which amounts to giving an interpretation of his own defenses: "I think what happens to me is I get depressed." This is the first emergence of the *conscious therapeutic alliance*, which demonstrates with the utmost clarity how the evaluator's relentless confrontation—which might at first sight seem persecutory—is in fact deeply appreciated by the patient and releases his latent motivation. The therapeutic alliance may also have an unconscious component, which is present when the patient starts making communications with hidden meanings of which he is unaware, thus inviting interpretation.

Therapist: So you experience anger . . .
Patient: (Sigh.) I think what happens to me is I get depressed.
Therapist: Hmm.
Patient: Because, because I'm very angry at myself for putting myself in that position where like I have to kind of, you know, back down and constantly scrape and bow and things like that, you know, uh . . .
Therapist: But inside you feel different, hmm?
Patient: I get depressed.
Therapist: Hmm.

Patient: And my trouble is—is separating all the things that I am feeling, you know. I tend to label everything as depression. I don't—

Therapist: Then you experience this anger, and then there is a fear that if you show it then you are going to be cut off, hmm?

Patient: That's right.

Therapist: Hmm?

Patient: That's right.

Therapist: Do you at that moment feel that you want to strike out physically? Not that you do.

Patient: I, there's I—I think I feel a tenseness. I don't feel as loose or relaxed as I was before the conversation with whom I might ever have started. Uh, I do feel—

Therapist: Tense, anxious.

Patient: I feel an anger and I feel a worry, you know, but most of all I think the strongest feelings that I have are—are anger at myself.

Therapist: Is there any specific person in your current life that you experience anger with like this, that you experience anger but you have fear that if it shows they might cut you off and then you experience nervousness? Is there any specific person that you could put your finger on in your current life?

What emerged was that his relationship with his ex-wife was like that, and he said it is the same with his friends and associates.

Therapist: Hmm. So it is a sort of constant fear about—

Patient: People not liking me or people doing . . .

Therapist: That they would reject you; they would turn you down; they would cut you off. So it is the sort of the situation, if I understand it correctly, that you have a need to bend over backwards to please people.

Patient: Yeah.

Therapist: Now would you say this bending over backwards to please is in all your relationships?

Patient: Yeah.

Therapist: Hmm?

Patient: Yeah.

Therapist: Because there is this constant fear that they wouldn't like you, they would turn you down, and so forth, hmm?

Patient: Sure, most of my life is just a facade you know, I . . .

Therapist: So that's quite a problem isn't it?

Patient: Yeah. That's right, and I can't do it any more. I don't want to, you know. 'Cause I'm not happy, and I'm never going to be happy at this rate.

Therapist: Tell me, when you got the telephone call yesterday—

Patient: Last week.

Therapist: Or whatever. You felt angry?

Patient: Right. After I hung up. Well no, even while I was talking.

Therapist: But then today, also, when you came, you felt anxious.

Patient: Yeah.

Therapist: So isn't this exactly like the other situations; namely, was there the idea that if you experience anger and your anger comes out I might retaliate with you?

Patient: I played through a little scenario through my mind, actually, about that.

Therapist: That got in your head?

Patient: Yeah, you would sort of say, "Well if you're not going to cooperate I'm sorry, there's nothing we can do for you. Good-bye."

Therapist: In other words, then I would cut you off. So isn't there a connection between your nervousness and your anger, isn't there? Hmm?

Patient: Yeah I know, I understand. I understand that now.

Therapist: So then it is very clear—to whom you are angry and toward whom also you have fear that he might retaliate with you. That is who? In other words, then, your anger is not toward the red tape or other people; the anger is toward me, but at the same time there is a fear that I "up there" might cut you off.

Patient: Yeah, that's probably true simply because—

Therapist: Why do you say "probably"?

Patient: Because that's my way.

Therapist: No, let's look at it. We are here to look at these things.

Patient: I'm a, I'm a, I'm a in-betweener, I'm a middle man, I sit on the fence.

Therapist: I know, you want to keep things in the state of limbo. That is already clear.

Patient: Yeah, that's right.

Therapist: But let me question you about this; if you are going to keep us in the state of limbo, we are not going to get anywhere. Because here we are to look at these things, okay?

Patient: Well, then I will say you are right, uh, because, like, I was aware also of the fact that you were, I guess, the director—is that it? I'm not sure what your title is—and that you ultimately did have the control over everybody else.

Therapist: So then the anger was directed at that level?

Patient: Yeah, must have been because—but I don't make those correlations you see, that's—

Therapist: But we are here to look to these issues because one of your problems centers around this, that you have to bend over backwards to please others. There is a fear that they might cut you off or they might reject you. Okay? That is a part of your problem. We have discussed that already.

Patient: Yeah.

Therapist: Now you said that you had this in relationship with authorities, policemen, and also with women. Now what happened? You were married?

The early part of this passage consisted of further clarifying the triangle of conflict in relation to people in the patient's current life (C). In particular the *anxiety* has been clarified, namely, the patient's *fear of rejection* if he shows his anger openly. The evaluator knows very well that, before he can pursue "content" and take a history, he must bring this anxiety out into the open in the transference (T). He does this first by establishing what he knows must be true, that this pattern is present in many of the patient's current relationships (C), and then by making the link with the patient's feelings when he received the telephone call giving him the present appointment (the C-T link). There is an immediate response, since the patient now admits that he has imagined the evaluator saying, "If you're not going to cooperate, there's nothing we can do for you. Good-bye."

However, resistance is not over and when the evaluator tries to drive the point home, the patient inevitably starts using once again his defense of vagueness and refusal to commit himself. When the word *probably* is challenged he continues by saying he always "sits on the fence." The evaluator immediately speaks forcefully to the patient's conscious therapeutic alliance, saying that if he is going to do this sort of thing then therapy will get nowhere; and the patient then admits one further important detail of his anxiety, namely, that the evaluator, as the "director," had ultimate control over whether he was accepted for treatment. All this amounts to a very significant corrective emotional experience: the patient has learned that it is possible to express his anger without the disastrous consequences he has always feared.

At last the ground has been prepared for the taking of a proper history. History-taking is, of course, most evident in the initial evaluation, but it is also employed throughout the course of therapy. The evaluator starts with the relations with the patient's ex-wife, in which he has already established that the above pattern was manifest. Later he will go to the past, where almost certainly he will find the pattern once again; and he will be enabled to make a T-C-P interpretation, thus completing the second triangle as well as the first.

It is worthwhile reemphasizing an important point. Whenever this technique is used there will be many times during the interview when challenging defenses makes the patient angry. There is then a standard procedure which is absolutely essential: the therapist must watch for the subtle indications of the emergence of anger, however minor, in the transference. Those who have watched me in action have seen that I often suddenly break into what I am doing and ask the patient, "What do you feel right now?" What emerges is the same old process, "Well... I don't feel anything." And I continue to focus on "What do you feel right now? How do you feel inside?" Then the patient says, "Well... I was a little upset." I say, "Upset?" The patient says, "Well ... I was a little irritated." Finally he admits he was angry. So, again one has penetrated the defenses, which once more increases the therapeutic alliance. Parenthetically I should say that there is a great threat to the therapeutic alliance if one does not use this standard technique.

The evaluator further pursues psychiatric history-taking. My standard procedure is to say to the patient, "You haven't told me anything about your background." From the above patient, for example, there emerged rivalry with his brother, and unresolved oedipal feelings for his mother. Finally, one comes to see that the triangle of transference/current/past is in operation. The therapist is making true progress if he can bring the triangle of conflict in relation to all three of these categories of persons and show the parallels: "Isn't this the way you have been behaving with me?" (T); "Isn't it the way you have been behaving with your wife, or with your boss?"

(C); "And it is the same way you used to behave with your mother, father, brother" (P): In fact, the sooner you can make one of these T-C-P interpretations, and the more often you can make them in a meaningful way, the more effective and shorter the therapy will be.

Process of Therapy

Within the first few sessions fresh memories usually arise which throw light on the whole development of the patient's neurosis. This on one hand brings relief, but as the patient is confronted with his painful feelings he often develops negative feelings toward the therapist. Focusing on the patient's anger as soon as it arises is essential. Once more, showing the patient his defense against anger in the three areas, transference/current/past, has a potentially powerful therapeutic effect. This leads to other kinds of feelings: grief and loss, and forbidden sexual feelings in the patient's childhood. By about the sixth to eighth session therapeutic effects have already begun to occur, and the patient is beginning to show evidence that he is relating to people in his current life in a new way; and there is also a similar change in the transference situation. I do not consider the therapy successful unless the patient is not only free from symptoms but also from all his previous maladaptive behavior, and unless in addition he shows both cognitive and emotional insight into the core neurosis which has caused all these symptoms and difficulties. When this happens termination is considered. This usually comes without difficulty. The process of termination depends on the kind of patient. In patients for whom the focus is primarily oedipal, generally one does not encounter any problem. But for the patients where the focus is loss, the process of working through termination may take anywhere from one to five sessions. Mourning the loss of the relationship with the therapist may become an essential part of termination, but this is by no means a universal phenomenon. Dependence on the therapist is rarely an issue, and the patient usually leaves with the feeling that with the help of the therapist he has done hard work and has achieved many of the results by his own efforts.

What Emerges During Therapy

Obviously every patient is unique, and of course the problems encountered by men and women are different. But what emerges during the course of therapy is extraordinarily similar in many patients and consists of all the buried feelings the patient has been left with by his childhood experiences. In either sex, for example, an early close realtionship with both parents may have been disrupted by the birth of a younger sibling, with heavily guilt-ridden death wishes. In a woman, there may emerge hidden longing for her father and jealousy of her mother, with submission to the latter as a way of defending herself against this conflict—which in turn may be followed by intense hidden grief over the loss of her father through separation or divorce. In a man, childhood sexual fantasies are often revealed, which in therapy can easily be traced to feelings about his mother, coupled with intense buried hostility and fear directed toward an authoritarian father, and a lifelong defense of passivity and submissiveness.

These conflicts are, of course, exactly the same as are those encountered in psychoanalysis itself; but they tend to emerge in a more overt and unmistakable form, rather than having to be gradually inferred and reconstructed, and they are immediately followed by therapeutic effects. They thus constitute a clear validation of Freud's original discoveries.

Evaluation of Outcome

The outcome of the therapy is monitored by a sophisticated technique which involves interviews by both the therapist and an independent evaluator immediately after termination and up to five years later. In addition, we have utilized a specific technique in which the patient himself is the evaluator of the psychotherapeutic process and outcome. The patient observes five randomly selected audiovisually recorded therapy sessions and determines the changes as well as those variables that he considers to be of specific importance in the outcome of his treatment. This is done six months after termination, and the patient does not know about this procedure during the course of his therapy. To put it very briefly, what we consider to be total psychodynamic change is the total resolution of the core neurosis, manifested by substitution of all the maladaptive patterns and defenses by adaptive ones, and freeing of sexual and aggressive drives for constructive use in the patient's life, with a total

change in interpersonal relationships. In other words, basic characterological changes accompany the development of a wholly new
attitude and both cognitive and emotional insight into the core
neurosis responsible for all the patient's difficulties.

Summary and Conclusions

1. In this chapter I have briefly presented a method of Short-Term
Dynamic Psychotherapy based on psychoanalytic principles.
2. This type of therapy is discussed very briefly in terms of
evaluation, selection criteria, technique, process, and outcome.
3. There is a spectrum of cases that do well in Short-Term Dynamic Psychotherapy. At one end of the spectrum are patients with a
briefly circumscribed, clear-cut oedipal focus; and at the other end
are patients with much more severe psychopathology, suffering
from long-standing psychoneurotic disorders, who hitherto have
been considered as some of the most difficult patients to treat, even
in long-term therapy.
4. In terms of technique, I have emphasized the importance of the
therapeutic alliance, which is generated by a dynamic interaction
between the patient and the therapist; the active utilization of the
transference relationship, with active interpretation of transference
resistance and the active avoidance of a transference neurosis. One
works actively on the triangle of defense/anxiety/impulse-feeling
and on the triangle of transference/current/past.
5. In terms of outcome I have pointed out that changes begin to
occur between the fifth and eighth sessions and permeate the patient's entire life by the time of termination; so that at the time of
termination there is definite evidence of the total resolution of the
patient's core neurosis.
6. What I have discovered is that by actively and relentlessly
confronting the patient with his defenses, one forces him to experience his true feelings at any given moment, with the result that the
core neurosis is de-repressed and experienced fully. And it turns out
to be not particularly complicated and overdetermined, but has to
do with simple things concerning all the feelings left over from his
childhood situation—love and hate, disappointment and grief, guilt,
and the oedipal feelings. One does not need endless working through
of yet one more overdetermination; on the contrary, everything is
experienced so intensely that the neurosis is dissolved.

7. Since the changes begin to occur during the first five to eight sessions in patients suffering from long-standing neurotic behavior patterns, and since these changes permeate the patient's life by the time of termination and continue to be present in a follow-up of up to five years, it is hardly possible to say that they were the result of spontaneous remission.

8. What I have presented is based on three systematic studies: one involving the therapy of one-hundred thirty patients, a second of twenty-four patients, and a third of eighteen patients. The majority of this work, consisting of the initial interviews, therapeutic sessions, and outcome evaluation, has been recorded audiovisually; and the material has been in the process of systematic analysis and publication.

Part II

Selection of Patients

5

Response To Interpretation

Habib Davanloo, M.D.

Short-Term Dynamic Psychotherapy refers to a spectrum of brief, dynamic psychotherapies based on psychoanalytic principles and technique and accepts for treatment a wide range of patients suffering from psychoneurotic disorders. Its limits have not yet been fully explored, and the patients we have treated over nearly two decades can be categorized into four major groups: (1) patients with a predominantly oedipal focus; (2) cases where the focus is primarily a loss; (3) patients suffering from phobic and/or obsessional neuroses with one or more foci; (4) patients suffering from long-standing characterological problems with more severe psychopathology, with more than one conflict.

RESPONSE TO INTERPRETATION IS CORRELATED WITH SUCCESSFUL OUTCOME.

We have developed and used a single set of criteria for the selection of patients for the entire spectrum of these short-term dynamic

psychotherapies. As a result of our three studies within a span of
nearly twenty years, including three to seven years' follow-up on
almost 40 percent of these patients, we have come to the conclusion
that response to interpretation has proved to have a highly significant
correlation with successful therapeutic outcome. In the initial diagnostic evaluation we have used a set of criteria which I have described in detail in other publications *(The Relentless Healer)*
Briefly, these criteria are related to the establishment of a psychotherapeutic focus; human relationships, ability to get involved in emotional interaction with the evaluator; the presence of a
give-and-take relationship; the patient's capacity to experience and
tolerate anxiety, guilt, and depression; psychological-mindedness;
motivation; and response to interpretation.

Based on our research data, we have come to consider response to
interpretation one of our major criteria; it has a high value in the
selection of patients and is an important prognostic criterion in
relation to successful psychotherapeutic outcome. We have classified interpretation into different groups. Central to basic psychoanalytic principles and technique are two triangles. One is the
triangle of Impulse-Feelings/Anxiety/Defense, and the second triangle is the triangle of people, which I refer to as T-C-P, the
Transference/Significant People in the Current Life Orbit of the
Patient/People in his Past, parents or parent substitute(s) and others.
In chapter 4 I have indicated that the initial interview is a very special
kind of focused interview. One starts the interview not knowing
anything about the patient and makes a very careful evaluation of the
history and the current situation. The evaluation focuses on the
evaluation of those ego functions of primary importance in dynamic
psychotherapy. The technique is one of gentle but relentless questioning and confrontation of the defenses against true feelings. As
one faces vagueness, avoidance, and passivity, one persistently
confronts the patient with this in the transference and further links it
with the significant people in his current life, such as his wife, boss,
etc. This technique might mobilize anger in the transference and
defense against the anger; and the evaluator brings this into focus the
moment it arises, persistently confronting the patient with how he
really feels. Then the evaluator interprets the patient's defense
against the anger, and invariably the patient experiences relief when
he is able to declare he was irritated and angry. Very often the anger

aroused against the interviewer has links with unexpressed anger in the past, for example with a controlling mother or an authoritarian father. The evaluator then is able to link the patient's maladaptive way of handling his anger in his current life situation (for example with his boss, his wife, etc.), and this link is brought out as well, which I call a T-C-P interpretation. Obviously there is a wide variation in the technique of the initial interview, considering the four major groups of patients we take into treatment; and the flexibility of the evaluator is essential. The technique of the initial interview is discussed further in chapter 7. I consider this trial-therapy model of the initial assessment the only reliable method to determine if the patient is likely to respond to the spectrum of highly interpretative, short-term dynamic psychotherapies.

CATEGORIES OF INTERPRETATIONS

We have classified interpretations into different categories, such as transference confrontation and interpretation, response to T-C interpretation (linking the transference with significant current people), response to T-P interpretation (linking the transference with past significant people), response to T-C-P interpretation (linking the transference with current significant people and past significant people, with the patient experiencing the impulse-feelings in the transference situation), and also response to interpretation of the nuclear conflict. There are interpretations which center around the triangle of Impulse-Feelings/Anxiety/Defense. As I discuss in detail in chapter 7, in the trial-therapy model of the initial assessment the evaluator very actively works on these two triangles. The technique is highly interpretative, interpretation of defense and/or impulse, anxiety, and other interpretations already mentioned. We have scored these responses to interpretation from 1 (excellent) to 5 (poor). The analyses of our three studies indicate that of all these interpretations, response to T-C-P interpretation in the initial assessment correlates most significantly with a successful psychotherapeutic outcome and that there is a definite and significant correlation between the early use of interpretation (and more specifically a T-C-P interpretation) and the length of therapy. Now I will discuss in more detail the response to interpretation by presenting a few segments of the initial evaluative assessment of a number of patients.

The Case of the Masochistic Housewife

The patient is thirty-two years old, married, the mother of two
children. She came to the initial interview depressed, with suicidal
ideation. Her problems centered around disturbances in interpersonal relationships. Her relationships with her husband and her in-laws
were characterized by passivity and compliance. She described a
long-standing conflict with her husband and had obsessional
thoughts that he might die; she called his office frequently to allay
her anxiety. Her intense preoccupation with her husband's health
had been of many years' duration. In the first part of the initial
interview it became evident that her character structure was primarily obsessive, with a strong sense of duty, obligation, dedication,
and a great deal of self-denial and self-punishment. She painted a
self-portrait of a guilt-ridden person with considerable emphasis on
duty, submission, and compliance. The patient has been in conflict
with her husband over her mother-in-law, who is very domineering
and who for the past few weeks had been staying in their home, with
plans to remain there. This was her husband's decision. In relation to
her own mother, she was the same and molded herself according to
her mother's demands. Her relationship with her husband was
similar, and she had a disturbed relationship with her father.

In the first part of the initial interview the patient was very passive
and presented herself as a helpless, weepy person. As the evaluator
repeatedly confronted her with her passivity, she became more
passive. The evaluator continued to confront her, indicating her need
to make him useless. Then he confronted her with her feelings
toward him, and she admitted to her irritation and anger. The
impulse and the defense against the impulse in the transference were
clarified. In the second part of the initial interview the evaluator
brought into focus the patient's hostile feelings toward her husband.

Therapist: How do you feel about the fact that he made the
decision that his mother come to live with you?
Patient: Well . . . I don't want her to stay. (Crying.) I really feel . . .
the house is like a prison . . . her repeatedly telling me what to do. I
have tried to like it, and I have tried to accept it, telling myself she is
an old lady and is lonely; but I feel like I cannot even breathe. It just
depresses me so much, and I don't know why.

Therapist: From what you have told me, your husband also always tells you what to do. And you always comply with his decisions. Now you have your mother-in-law added to the picture, who also wants to run your life. How do you feel about this?

Patient: (Continues to cry.) Everybody tells me I have no choice.

Therapist: But let's see how you feel toward your husband. How do you feel when he decides what is best and you go along with it?

Patient: Well . . . I don't resent that. He is trying to do his best, and I know he loves me . . . you know . . . and I don't feel he is doing anything deliberately.

Therapist: Do you notice that when I questioned you about your feelings toward your husband you immediately said you don't resent him and that you really had to reassure me that you don't have resentment?

Patient: Perhaps I do.

Therapist: Why "perhaps"? Either you do or you don't.

Patient: Well I do, because I don't want to be here. (The patient is sobbing.) I wouldn't have to be here if it weren't for him. Obviously, if I wasn't married to him I wouldn't have to be here. That is right.

Therapist: Now how do you feel when he insists and you find yourself in a situation where you have to constantly comply with his demands?

The evaluator immediately makes a link between her husband and her mother-in-law, bringing into focus the defense-passivity compliance. Then the evaluator looks beneath the defense at the impulse. As he focuses on the impulse, she reassures him that she does not have hostile feelings toward her husband. What finally emerges is an interpretation of the defense against the impulse in relation to her husband (C). And finally she admits to her anger. "I wouldn't have to be here if it weren't for him."

Therapist: But I am talking about your feelings. Do you notice that this is something you repeatedly avoid?

Patient: I don't know. Do you mean do I get angry?

Therapist: What are your thoughts?

Patient: I feel helpless. I feel that I cannot do anything.

Therapist: Do you think your helplessness is a way of dealing with your anger? You have described many situations where you have had to give up your ideas and passively comply with his demands, to the way he thinks is best for you. This is exactly what you described about your mother.

Patient: Uh-hmm.

Therapist: You say you have been pushed around and have molded yourself in the name of "this is what's best for you." You have taken a passive, childlike position in all these relationships, and at the same time you find it difficult to indicate how you feel.

Patient: Uh-hmmm. Yes. I must feel resentful or angry.

Therapist: You see, you are saying "must."

Patient: Hmmm. Yes. I do. I get angry. But then I tell myself what can he do—she dominates him as well.

Then the session focuses on anger and resentment, and the patient brings up what her family physician told her—that her frequent headaches and all her somatic complaints must have to do with something that is bothering her.

Therapist: What do you think about what Dr. ——— tells you?

Patient: I think he is right. I think he is telling me that inside my calm exterior I am a seething mass of anger, which is true.

Therapist: From what we have seen, in relation to your husband and your mother-in-law you take a passive, compliant position. You find yourself helpless, develop headaches and other symptoms; but do you think these are all ways you deal with rage and anger? And from what you have told me, as a young girl at home with your mother you had many of these symptoms—you let her run your life. Would you think that was also your way of dealing with your resentment and anger?

Then the patient recounts two memories. One was when at age thirteen she was going to go fishing with her father. Her mother objected, saying she was a big girl and there would be many men around her father. The patient was very bitter and stayed in her room that weekend, crying and "feeling sick." The other memory was of her constant fear as a child that her mother might die.

The evaluator focuses on the impulse (anger) and the defense against the anger (helplessness), and he makes an interpretation of the defense against the impulse in relation to her mother. She admits to the impulse. Having clarified the defense against the impulse in relation to her husband (C) and her mother-in-law (C), the therapist links this to her mother (P), and a C-P interpretation is made. And finally a T-C-P interpretation is made.

This segment of the interview demonstrates how one sys-tematically works on the two triangles: the triangle of Impulse-Feelings/Anxiety/Defense and the triangle of Transference/Cur-rent People/Past People. First the evaluator brings the transference into focus and makes an interpretation of the defense (passivity, weepiness) against the impulse (anger). After the evaluator has identified the impulse and the defense against the impulse, he then proceeds to give a C-P interpretation, showing the patient her defense against the impulse in relation to her husband and her mother-in-law and linking it with her mother.

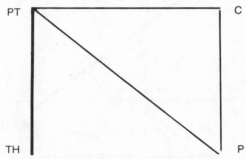

Transference Interpretation

Transference Interpretation is the interpretation of the defense against the impulse in relation to the therapist—the passive, com-pliant, weepy pattern as a way of making the evaluator helpless and useless. The patient finally admitted to her anger toward the evalua-tor for not being comforting and supportive like her husband, and for repeatedly confronting her with her passive, childlike position with her husband and her mother.

C-P Interpretation is the interpretation of the defense against the impulse in relation to her husband and her in-laws, linking it with her mother.

T-C-P Interpretation involves linking the transference with cur-rent people and with past people. Passivity, helplessness, being

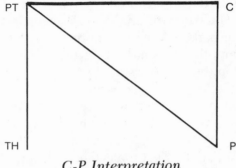

C-P Interpretation

weepy, a defense against anger in relation to the therapist, are linked
with a similar pattern with her husband and her in-laws and further
linked with the same pattern with her father and her mother.

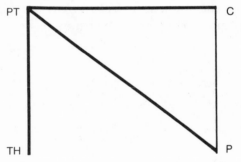

T-C-P Interpretation

The Case of the Passive, Submissive Secretary

When the patient was first seen she was twenty-four years old. At
eighteen she had married a man whom she described as detached,
nondemonstrative, and noninvolved. She had separated from him six
months after marriage. She presented her problems as having been
chronically nervous since adolescense, suffering from episodes of
depression, problems in interpersonal relationships, particularly
with men, and anxiety in social situations. She described herself as
shy and unable to express herself. She became attached to a married
coworker, Stan, who left his wife and moved in with the patient.
Whenever he visits his children on weekends, her anxiety becomes
intense. She is very preoccupied that he might change his mind and
return to his wife.

Her earliest memories indicate a very close relationship with her father. Her relationship with her mother was not a close one. She gave definite evidence of being her father's favorite, which angered her mother. She remembers her mother often saying to her father, "You have other children." When she was eleven she saw the movie *Johnny Belinda* with one of her sisters. Subsequent to this she started having intruding thoughts of her father having sex with her mother, which were disturbing to her. Then her relationship with her father deteriorated, and she became very detached.

During the initial interview the patient was noninvolved, anxious, and passive. By questioning her repeatedly, the evaluator gathered information.

Now we will see a few segments of the initial assessment of this patient, which demonstrate the type of intervention the interviewer made in order to determine if she fulfilled the criteria for Short-Term Dynamic Psychotherapy.

The evaluator has explored her relationship with Stan, which is characterized by passivity, her bending over backward to please him. She admits that inside she feels angry and irritated. She said, "Angry, like in a rage." Then the therapist said, "Then with him you experience anger inside; but you don't want him to know how you feel, and you fear he might drop you?" to which she replies, "Yeah." The evaluator has established that she experiences anger and constant anxiety that he might abandon her and that she takes a passive, compliant role with people in her current life. As she is anxious during the interview, the evaluator focuses on the transference.

Therapist: How do you feel right now here with me?
Patient: Tense. Nervous. I am not relaxed.
Therapist: How do you account for that?
Patient: I don't know.
Therapist: Are you usually nervous with other people, or is this only here with me?
Patient: No. I guess if I am nervous, I, you know, I am with a lot of people. (Pause.) I guess if I am in a group of people I don't really know I feel, yeah, tense. Perhaps it is much more in social situations . . . when you meet people you don't know.
Therapist: I see. Do you find it difficult to talk about yourself here with me?

Patient: Yes. I do.

Therapist: How do you account for that?

Patient: I don't know. I never really thought about it.

Therapist: Well. Let's look at your relationship here with me. Something that comes to my mind is that if I don't say anything what would happen here?

Patient: (Quietly.) We probably wouldn't talk.

Therapist: Hmmm?

Patient: We probably wouldn't talk. (A little louder.)

Therapist: Then what would happen? Let's look at your relationship here with me. I am the one who must question you repeatedly, and in a digging fashion, to go over various events. Is it like this with Stan and with other people, or is it only here with me?

The evaluator has clarified the patient's defense (passivity) in relation to Stan (C) and also her anxiety (the constant fear that he might leave her) and her impulse (hostility and resentment). Then he focuses on the transference and brings into focus her defense (passivity). The defense in the transference is clarified, and finally he makes a T-C interpretation—interpretation of the defense and the impulse in relation to the evaluator and in relation to Stan.

What follows is another segment of the same interview, in which the session focuses on the relationship between the patient and her father, which deteriorated when the patient was ten and her mother gave birth to her youngest sister.

Therapist: You were your father's favorite, and you had a close relationship with your father. Then at around age ten or eleven your relationship with your father started to deteriorate; you started to move away from him. And this was about the time that your mother gave birth to your youngest sister, and also you saw the movie and started having intruding thoughts about your father and mother having sex. Do you think that there is something there—in your feelings toward your father and your father and mother which might play a role in your current problem in relation to men?

Patient: (Smiling, but uncomfortable.) No.

Therapist: I am not saying that you have to agree with what I say, but do you notice that automatically, without thinking about what I said, you rejected the idea; and this is a paradox to the way you described yourself, that you dwell on and think a lot about things. Could we look at this?

Patient: But I don't know why my present problem with Stan has anything to do with my relationship with my father.

Therapist: Let's look at your memories. Didn't you tell me that whenever your father said "my favorite daughter" your mother said, "How dare you say she is your favorite daughter." Wasn't there an indication that you were your father's favorite and that your mother didn't like that?

Patient: Yeah.

Therapist: Isn't there the idea . . .

Patient: I guess.

Therapist: Why do you say "I guess."

Patient: Yeah. I know. But I don't know how she could say that because my youngest sister is her favorite.

Therapist: So if we look at this, there is a triangular situation of you/your father/your mother. And there were your sisters as well. You were the favorite of your father, and there was a close, intimate relationship between you and your father. But suddenly you found your mother was pregnant, you saw the movie you described, the whole thing collapsed, and all your intruding thoughts of your mother having sex with your father began. Was there the idea that your father was not faithful to you any longer, that he preferred your mother to you? You are smiling, hmmm?

Patient: Yeah. Because I never looked at it like that before.

Therapist: Now that you look at it, what do you think about it? What do you see in your current life, particularly in relation to Stan, that might have some connection with some of your feelings about your father and about men in general?

Patient: What I see mostly in relation to Stan is that he is attached to his children and he visits them frequently; I am afraid that he might change his mind and return to his wife.

Therapist: Isn't it now clear? You had your father to yourself. You had managed to become number one among five women, one your mother, the others your sisters; then suddenly your mother is pregnant. Isn't there the idea that suddenly you lost him? And then this was followed by a total detachment; you were angry with your father and punished him. Now let's look at your relationship with Stan. He is married, and there are a few children. And you finally managed to become his favorite; he gave up his wife. Hmmm?

Patient: Yeah.

Therapist: And then to prefer you to his wife.

Patient: Oh yeah. Okay. Yeah. I see.

Therapist: Hmmm? Isn't this another triangle? Stan's wife is angry because he prefers you. Similarly, your mother was angry because your father preferred you.

Patient: Uh-huh. Yeah.

Therapist: Then why did you say there is no connection? Obviously there are many other factors to be explored and understood.

The evaluator then brings into focus the triangular situation of patient/father/mother, with the oedipal implications, indicating that her father had preferred her mother to her. Then the evaluator discusses the birth of her youngest sister. The patient's resistance is intensified immediately. The evaluator continues to confront the patient that she was her father's favorite and that this angered her mother. The patient's vagueness is challenged, and the patient comes up with more fresh material. Again the evaluator focuses on the triangular oedipal situation, and what emerges is the patient saying "I never looked at it like that before." The evaluator links this further with the current situation—that Stan prefers her to his wife. And now that she is Stan's favorite, she fears losing him to his wife. The evaluator also brings into focus that Stan's wife is angry, as her mother was angry. One can say that the evaluator in the last part of the interview is able to interpret the patients' central neurotic structure.

Looking at the data of our three studies, we have come to the conclusion that by the end of the initial assessment we are able to interpret the central nuclear conflict or conflicts of the patient in a great majority of our cases.

What follow are two segments of the initial assessment of another patient that further illustrate on the subject of response to interpretation.

The Case of the Girl in the Golden Cage

When the patient was first seen she was twenty-eight, had a daughter five years old, and had been divorced when her daughter was two.

She complained of depression, anxiety, and problems in relation to men. She had never had a lasting relationship with a man. She described her relationships with men as hostile. She had married at eighteen. Her husband was detached, nonaffectionate, and didn't care. There were sexual difficulties. Eight months before the break-up of her marriage she got involved with a married man with whom she had a good sexual relationship. After she separated from her husband, she gave this man an ultimatum to leave his wife, but she finally dropped him. Then she became very depressed and entered psychoanalytic psychotherapy for almost two years but terminated therapy after she met Jacques, who insisted that she discontinue treatment. She refers to herself in her relationship to Jacques as "a girl in a golden cage." He is wealthy, and she is always afraid she might disappoint him.

What precipitated her seeking help was entertaining the idea of breaking up her three-year relationship with Jacques. Jacques is described as very possessive. He pressured her into giving up her job of eight years as a journalist. He repeatedly telephones to make sure she is at home.

Her mother was always sick and in and out of the hospital, especially during the early years of her life. Her oldest sister, Jacqueline, was like a substitute mother to her. She had two sisters and three brothers. She had a poor relationship with her mother, and at some time in her life she was very worried that her mother would never return home. She had a very close relationship with her father, and most of her early memories are of her father combing her hair every morning, carrying her on his shoulders. She was his favorite, but she was always afraid she would not do her best and would disappoint him. Up to age six she slept with her father in the living room, as her mother was sick and was using the bedroom. Around the age of twelve or thirteen the relationship with her father changed. During the initial interview, after the evaluator had focused on the circumstances that had brought about the change, she remembered two incidents.

One night at a large family gathering her father insisted that she sing in front of the family. She was not as good a singer as Jacqueline. She resisted, but under pressure of her father she finally sang; her grandfather said, "Jacqueline sings much better." She ran to her room crying and did not talk to her father for a while.

Another incident occurred a few months later. She had put on a decolleté dress and preened in front of her father, and he said, "Don't tell me you are Brigitte Bardot?" She ran to her room very upset. Her relationship with her father deteriorated, and some time after that she ran away from home and was brought home by her father.

Her relationship with her father improved somewhat after she married at age eighteen.

The initial interview was characterized by a confronting and interpretative technique. It focused on what happened to her relationship with her father, in reference to the incident of singing.

Therapist: What you say is that that incident destroyed your relationship with him. But do you think that there might have been something else as well?

Patient: There may be, but I don't know.

Therapist: Are you saying that the whole intimate relationship you had with your father and all the pleasant memories you described suddenly changed only because of that incident?

Patient: There may be something else, but I don't know.

Therapist: From what you have told me, all those years you made sure you were number one in your father's eyes. We know about your performance in school, we know about how you kept the house clean and how you cooked for him. In all of this you were number one. It was only that evening of singing when Jacqueline was number one. Are you saying that totally destroyed the intimate, very close relationship you had with your father?

Patient: I never told him anything any more.

Therapist: It is important for us to look at this. There was a lot going on between you and your father. He was very physically demonstrative, affectionate. You played with him. He combed your hair. He carried you on his shoulders. Now this was when you were a little girl. Your relationship started to change around age eleven or twelve. Do you think it might have had to do with the fact that you were no longer a little girl? You were growing up. Do you think it might have had to do with that?

Patient: I don't know.

Therapist: I am not sure if it is that. Do you notice that as soon as I bring up the issue of you and your father you say you don't know? And have you noticed that "I don't know" comes out immediately without your even looking at what I say? Have you noticed that you immediately move away and say you don't know? And at the same time you have given me a picture that you are a person who thinks a lot. But when it comes to your relationship with your father you immediately wipe it out.

Patient: Uh-huh. That is mainly because I don't know.

Therapist: You notice that you didn't give even a minute of thought to what I said, and it is important for both of us here to see what happened to that very close, intimate relationship between you and your father. And it happened around the time, as I said, that your body was growing, your breasts were growing, and you were becoming a woman. And then that relationship dies.

Patient: Well, when you said that my breasts were growing I remember one thing. My mother used to make clothes for other people. I was thirteen, and I remember that there was a beautiful evening gown, and it was very low cut, decolleté. And as you see, I am not very big (pointing to her breasts); and I asked her if I could try on the dress. I was the same height I am now, and I have the same figure. I developed in six months, and that was it. I tried on the evening gown, and I was very proud wearing it. I was looking at myself in the mirror, and my father said, "Who do you think you are, Brigitte Bardot?" I did not answer; I didn't say anything. I was so depressed and sad, and I cried. And so I took off the dress and went to my room.

Therapist: You see? Let's look at this memory. In singing, Jacqueline was better than you.

Patient: She has better breasts than I do, too.

Therapist: So. You are looking in the mirror, and this is the time when you are becoming a woman and you want to see yourself number one in your father's eyes.

Patient: Uh-huh.

Therapist: You have put that special dress on and you want to see your father's interest in you and your body. And what happens is that he compares you with Brigitte Bardot. What thoughts do you have about this?

Patient: That he did not even understand that I could not be Brigitte Bardot because I was not her age.

Therapist: Let's not go into the issue of age. What thoughts come to your mind about what he said?

Patient: Obviously he compared me with the sex symbol of woman.

Therapist: Ummm hmmm. And what does that mean?

The evaluator is not convinced that the singing incident alone could have deteriorated totally her relationship with her father. He confronts the patient with heavy oedipal implications to this effect. This intensifies her resistance immediately. "I don't know." He persists and clarifies the defense, "I don't know," and her avoidance—not looking at and thinking about what the evaluator has said. It is clear that the defenses are mobilized as the evaluator is approaching some anxiety-laden conflict. Then he brings to her attention that somehow the change took place when she was growing up, her body was changing, referring to her breasts. What emerges are fresh memories related to the event when her father said, "Who do you think you are, Brigitte Bardot?" and her anger toward him and the episode of depression. Now the evaluator is able to proceed to make a tentative interpretation of the patient's nuclear conflict.

Patient: That I was not sexually attractive.

Therapist: And that Brigitte Bardot was number one in the eyes of your father. And all those years you had done everything to be number one. Then there was a severe letdown in your relationship with your father at the time you were becoming a . . .

Patient: A woman.

Therapist: Now let's look at your relationship with men. One thing we see like a thread in your relationships with men is a repetition of a pattern. Either you choose men who are married, who prefer you to their wives; and you become number one. That is when you lose interest in them and drop them. Or you enter a relationship in which you put the man on a pedestal, you bend over backward to please him; and, as you referred to yourself, you become "a girl in a golden cage." Now that they are very attached to you, you drop them. Do you think that there is an element of hostility in your relationships with men which has its origin in your relationship with your father? We even see this in your previous psychiatric treatment.

Patient: Uh-huh. It seems like that, but I never looked at it that way.

Therapist: Yet somehow we have to explain what happened to that relationship you had with your father that suddenly turned to the other extreme. You started to give him the silent treatment.

Patient: Yes. It is true. What comes to my mind is Jacques. I am jealous of his work. I am jealous of anything that takes up "my" time. And now I want to terminate the relationship.(The session continues.)

The evaluator finally makes a link between her current problems and the past and gives a tentative interpretation of the nuclear conflict. The patient's response to the interpretation is positive.

In conclusion, we consider response to interpretation one of our major criteria for the selection of patients for Short-Term Dynamic Psychotherapy, and of all interpretations a meaningful response to T-C-P interpretation correlates most significantly with successful psychotherapeutic outcome.

6

Motivation For Change

PETER E. SIFNEOS, M.D.

One of the first discoveries made about patients accepted for Short-Term Dynamic Psychotherapy is that individuals who are eager to understand themselves in an attempt to overcome their difficulties are for the most part successful in their efforts. Investigators from all over the world have reported successfully treated patients who, however idiosyncratic their expression, were all talking about a force within themselves that propelled them to seek help in order to change. It was clear that motivation for change is an important quality shared by a majority of these patients.

At first, of course, the real significance of motivation for treatment outcome was undetermined. It was discovered, however, that many patients successfully treated with Short-Term Dynamic Psychotherapy emphasized in follow-up interviews that their original intent to understand themselves was very possibly the single most important factor in the ultimate success of their treatments. After this, special attention was paid to motivation for change as an important criterion for selection of patients.

ASSESSING MOTIVATION

In the early years, when we were developing Short-Term Dynamic Psychotherapy at the Massachusetts General Hospital in Boston, we decided to devote an entire interview to the assessment of motivation. As a result of this work we were able to arrive at certain general conclusions concerning motivation assessment. This made our task much easier and soon we were able to incorporate these observations into our evaluation interviews. In addition to screening patients' overall interest in understanding themselves, we also developed criteria for selection of appropriate candidates for Short-Term Anxiety-Provoking Psychotherapy (STAPP). As we perfected our selection techniques we were able to drop the special motivation interview.

It is important here to distinguish motivation involving willingness to change from motivation to obtain symptom relief. The former implies activity on the part of the patient whereas the latter is a passive trait involving the expectation that someone else is going to relieve him of his discomfort. Thus an important aspect of the patient's character strength is involved in his being motivated to change.

Following is a list of seven criteria that we use at present to assess motivation for change (Sifneos 1972):

1. *An ability to recognize that the symptoms are psychological in nature.* A patient describes a stomachache every time he has a fight with his supervisor. If he continues to insist, after a medical screening has discovered no lesions to explain his symptom, that he suffers from an ulcer, if he remains reluctant to examine the psychological aspects of his conflict, it can be concluded that he does not meet this criterion. A certain degree of psychological awareness is a prerequisite for doing the psychotherapeutic work necessary for the resolution of such difficulties.

2. *An ability to give an honest and truthful account of one's psychological difficulties.* Honesty about oneself is another indication that the patient has the courage to look at his own defenses objectively, and is willing to speak truthfully about them to the evaluator.

3. *A willingness to participate actively in the therapy.* Here the

emphasis is on activity. The patient wants to stand on his own two feet and take responsiblity for his own treatment, rather than sit back passively and expect to be taken care of.

4. *Curiosity, introspection, and ability to understand oneself.* Self-inquisitiveness entails the ability to raise questions about himself even if they are unpleasant. Instead of boredom and a need to look to the outside world for entertainment, the individual who can discover the wealth of fantasies and thoughts which exist within his own mind will derive an unending sense of pleasure.

5. *A willingness to explore and to experiment.* This fifth criterion is in some sense an extension of the fourth. An individual who is curious and introspective should be able to take action that is explorative in nature even if it cannot guarantee positive results. There is a willingness to experiment to some degree so as to give newly discovered attitudes about himself a chance to develop.

6. *Realistic expectations of the results of psychotherapy.* Expectations of this kind imply modesty, willingness to compromise, and the eschewal of magical or grandiose thinking. This criterion points to strength of character and emphasizes the patient's ability to deal with reality.

7. *A willingness to make a tangible sacrifice.* If the other criteria are met, the patient will demonstrate a willingness to make a sacrifice, to postpone his own pleasure in order to achieve the expected result. Such sacrifices might be financial, or might involve a willingness to make an appointment even if the time is inconvenient.

Patients who meet all seven of these criteria are considered to have an "excellent" motivation for change; six out of seven, "good"; five out of seven, "fair." Patients who score below five are considered to be questionably motivated or unmotivated.

THE CORRELATION OF MOTIVATION
AND IMPROVEMENT

In order to be selected for Short-Term Anxiety-Provoking Psychotherapy (STAPP), patients must score six or seven at the time of their evaluation. They must meet in addition four other criteria for selection. After a systematic history-taking it must be demonstrated that the patient has (1) a circumscribed chief complaint and the ability to choose one area of difficulty to concentrate on; (2) at least one meaningful (give-and-take or altruistic) relationship during early childhood; (3) the ability to work flexibly with two evaluators in terms of expression of feelings; and (4) an above-average psychological sophistication and intelligence. In addition, at the end of the evaluation a specific psychodynamic focus must be chosen by the evaluator and the patient, as this is thought to be the key to an understanding of the patient's neurotic difficulties. Usually for STAPP we choose as a focus unresolved oedipal issues.

In one of our early studies (Sifneos 1968), twenty-two of twenty-five patients who received STAPP and were considered to have improved had "fair" to "excellent" motivation. Motivation for change is also a good guide of the progress of psychotherapy. In a later study (Sifneos 1971) of forty-two patients who received psychotherapy and whose motivation for change was assessed during the first, fourth, and eighth interviews, in thirty-three (78 percent) it increased or remained the same. All thirty-three finished their therapy. Of the nine whose motivation for change decreased, four withdrew after the fourth interview.

Malan (1976) has also emphasized the importance of motivation and has discovered that in conjunction with "parental-transference links"—a key technical requirement of all brief psychotherapies—it constitutes one of the most important factors in successful outcome. Motivation for change, in addition to being an important selection criterion for brief dynamic psychotherapies, also plays an important role in long-term psychotherapeutic modalities. For example, out of a homogeneous group of thirty-six patients who sought long-term psychotherapy and were rated by their therapists as having had "very" or "moderately" successful results, fourteen had "good" to "excellent" motivation during their preevaluation interviews and fifteen had similar ratings at the end of their treatment (Sifneos in press).

DISCUSSION

Every effort should be made to assess motivation during the first interview. In our experience motivation for change is an all-inclusive problem-solving force within the individual. It gives rise to fantasies and thoughts which are then sorted out and synthesized in an effort to find new solutions to old problems, and to avoid such feelings as anxiety, frustration, and boredom.

Assessing motivation for change is not always easy. In reviewing five cases in which STAPP was judged by independent evaluators to have been a failure, we discovered that in the initial assessment we had overestimated the degree of motivation; as treatment progressed motivation decreased rapidly until the patient became totally unmotivated and unwilling to pursue his therapy. In most of these cases it was the patient who interrupted treatment.

Of all the criteria for motivation for change, assessing the patient's willingness to make a tangible sacrifice occasioned the most difficulty. Here is an example.

A twenty-five-year-old mother of two children came to the clinic complaining of marital difficulties. She appeared to have met the selection criteria and was rated as having good motivation for change (score of 6). A question was raised by her evaluator, however, about her willingness to make a tangible sacrifice. When she was offered an appointment in the early part of the week, she refused it, saying that she could not possibly make it because she had difficulties with her baby-sitter. This was considered reasonable and an effort was made to find another therapist, one whose schedule would fit the patient's time requirements. Every time an appointment was offered to her, however, she rejected it as unsuitable. Again the realistic factors relating to a young mother with small children colored the evaluator's judgment, and an attempt was made to find a mutually convenient time. After much effort, a therapist was found who worked part-time on Saturday mornings and had some free time. The patient agreed to see him, mentioning that her husband did not work that day and could stay with the children.

As soon as the therapy started, however, and the therapist tried to help her focus on her unresolved oedipal feelings for her father, which were displaced onto her husband, she became anxious and began to make up excuses for not keeping her appointments. After a stormy session which was thought by her therapist to have been very meaningful, the patient failed to keep her next appointment. When he called her to ask what had happened, she answered that her husband was not capable of dealing with the children and that she had decided to interrupt her treatment. Despite all efforts to find another mutually convenient time, she was unwilling to compromise.

The motivation for change had disappeared, and her therapy ended unsuccessfully.

It should not be concluded, however, that a patient who appears somewhat unmotivated cannot be educated to become motivated. Patients who appear unsophisticated psychologically can be taught by the evaluator what psychotherapy is all about; after a thorough explanation, a seemingly unmotivated patient may understand what is involved and may become more motivated to understand himself. Six of thirty-three patients whose motivation increased during the first eight interviews were considered unmotivated, having received scores for motivation for change of 4, 3, and 2. It is of interest that by the eighth interview the scores of all six had increased and the outcome of their therapy was successful.

Assessment of motivation for change should be an integral part of the evaluation of all who receive psychiatric treatment, whether short-term or long-term. It has proved valuable both in the selection of patients for various treatment modalities and as an aid to prognosis.

References

Davanloo, H. (1978). *Basic Principles and Techniques of Short-Term Dynamic Psychotherapy.* New York: Spectrum Publications.

Malan, D.H. (1976). *The Frontier of Brief Psychotherapy.* New York: Plenum Medical Books.

Sifneos, P.E. (1968). The motivational process: a selection and prognostic criterion for psychotherapy of short duration. *Psychiatric Quarterly* 42:271-280.

——— (1971). Change in patients' motivation for psychotherapy. *American Journal of Psychiatry* 128:718-722.

——— (1972). *Short-Term Psychotherapy and Emotional Crisis.* Cambridge: Harvard University Press.

——— (in press). Motivation for change: a prognostic guide for successful psychotherapy. *Proceedings of the Tenth International Congress of Psychotherapy,* Paris, France. Basil: S. Karger.

7

Trial Therapy

Habib Davanloo, M.D.

The process of initial assessment should enable the evaluator to make a psychiatric, dynamic, and genetic diagnosis, and on this basis to make a psychotherapeutic recommendation. In chapter 5 I outlined a set of criteria to be fulfilled if a patient is to be regarded as suitable for Short-Term Dynamic Psychotherapy. In initial assessment, psychiatric, medical, and social histories are certainly essential, but alone they do not determine the patient's psychotherapeutic potential. In chapter 4 I indicated that one major selection criteria is response to interpretation in the initial interview. This implies that initial assessment is more than a very careful evaluation of the patient's history and current situation and his psychiatric and psychodynamic diagnoses. I have come to the conclusion that no one can really tell anything about the patient's likely response without exposing him to some of the important ingredients of the therapy that he will receive. Therefore a specific kind of psychotherapeutic session—amounting in fact to trial therapy—is an essential part of the initial evaluation process.

In this chapter I will highlight some of the major aspects of the technique of trial therapy. The process is usually accomplished in one interview—sometimes two—of one hour's duration. In the early states the evaluator must of course exclude certain contraindications to Short-Term Dynamic Psychotherapy, such as a history of previous psychotic decompensation, paranoid conditions, poor impulse control, serious suicidal attempts, etc. Once this has been done, the major part of the interview contains exactly the same interventions as are used in the main body of therapy.

The therapist persistently attempts to challenge the patient's neurotic defenses while at the same time constantly paying scrupulous and meticulous attention to the patient's responses. There are many ways in which the patient may respond:

1. This might mobilize resistance, the patient becoming evasive, by using obsessional defenses such as obsessional rumination, intellectualization, etc. This is not necessarily a negative response. The evaluator must gently but relentlessly challenge and work through these resistances. In *The Relentless Healer* I discuss the dynamic interaction between interpretation and motivation for insight. The mobilization of massive resistance should not necessarily be viewed as poor motivation. In this chapter I shall use a clinical example to illustrate techniques that I have found to be effective in working through resistances of this kind.

2. A second type of response is for the patient to become quite consciously resistant, openly refusing to answer certain questions. Again this should not in any way be interpreted as poor underlying motivation. Once more the interviewer has the task of gently and relentlessly challenging the resistance and working it through. In other publications I have described the technical requirements I have developed for working with this group of patients. See "The Case of the Praying Mantis," in *The Relentless Healer* (Davanloo in preparation).

3. The patient may become passive or detached, or may use regressive responses such as crying or being constantly weepy, all of which may be an attempt to put an obstacle in the evaluator's way. Again this is not necessarily a bad sign, and the evaluator must know the technical requirements for challenging the patient's defenses and working them through.

4. At the other end of the spectrum of responses the patient may give evidence of being too fragile to withstand the impact of his own unconscious material, for instance by beginning to show disturbance in his thought processes. The evaluator must immediately change to a more supportive technique. Our systematic work shows that this careful monitoring of moment-to-moment responses prevents the development of subsequent untoward effects. In our work over a span of twenty years with a wide range of psychoneurotic patients this technique has never led to a single serious complication.

5. The patient may respond by producing affect-laden unconscious material, which may throw light on the whole development of his neurosis. This often enables the evaluator to make links between the patient's present predicament and patterns of feeling or behavior in the distant past.

6. A response that is most frequently observed is that under this challenge to his defenses the patient gives evidence of both *anger toward the interviewer* and his *characteristic ways of defending against it*. For instance he may become passive, or anxious and tense, or may make slips of the tongue, or experience moments of thought block. The interviewer handles this not by making interpretations, but by asking the patient what he is feeling at this very moment. In response the patient usually tries at first to evade the issue, but persistent questioning almost invariably brings the anger out into the open. Having reached this, the interviewer is first able to show the patient his patterns of defending himself against his anger and is then able to go further by showing him that these are the same patterns as he has used throughout his life, in relation both to current people (e.g., spouse or boss) and people in the past (especially parents). The ability to make the link between the *transference*, the patient's *current life*, and *significant people in the past*, which I refer to as T-C-P interpretations, has been shown statistically in our three studies to be the most positive prognostic sign of all.

In summary, there is a spectrum of responses to this specific technique. Obviously there also is a wide variation in the details of the technique, which needs to be used with a great deal of flexibility in order to meet the need of each individual patient, with his specific character structure and kind of psychopathology. I hope to demonstrate some of these variables in the patient I present in this chapter.

Here I will present a particular patient together with a detailed
content analysis of the interview, which will provide an illustration of
many of the technical aspects of initial assessment by trial therapy.

The Case of the Little Blond Dutch Girl

The patient was a twenty-two-year-old student complaining of
depression, crying spells, a constant fear of rejection by other
people, a pattern in relation to men characterized by passivity and a
need to bend over backward to please them, and problems with her
parents.

> *Therapist:* I really don't know anything about you except that Dr.
> ——— referred you for a consultation. Would you like to tell me
> what seems to be the problem?
> *Patient:* Yeah. My problem is not knowing how to deal with the
> problem, you know.
> *Therapist:* Uh-huh . . .
> *Patient:* The original reason I came was that I wanted to know
> more about myself, how to deal with myself, the way I act, and how I
> react to other people—which has never been that good. I have an
> escape that I use, and this is crying. But that doesn't do anything
> except put if off for a little while; and then you know, it crops up
> again. It is a vicious circle.

It is worth noting that even though the patient becomes resistant
very quickly, this opening statement of her problem is a hopeful sign.
She does not say, for instance, that her problem is depression and she
wants to be cured of it; she wants to know more about herself, and
moreover she knows that her crying is in some way defensive and
consequently leads nowhere. She is thus already showing genuine
insight and genuine motivation.

> *Therapist:* Would you like to tell me more about these problems
> that you have with people?
> *Patient:* Well with people in general, I don't get along with peers at
> all. I have a very close boyfriend, but other than that I have basically
> no friends. I get along with older people.
> *Therapist:* Uh-huh. Could you be more specific?

The patient is vague, very passive, and has a tendency to ruminate. She gives details, but one cannot get a clear-cut picture of the nature of her interpersonal problems. She says that the reason for her difficulties with her classmates and peers is that many of them smoke, drink, go dancing; and because she doesn't engage in these activities, she feels uncomfortable with them. Questioned about the feeling of discomfort, she says she feels very self-conscious. She further indicates that she feels self-conscious because she is different in terms of her activites. Further exploration reveals that she feels the same way with those peers who don't drink, smoke, etc. Then it becomes clear that this pattern is with everybody. At this point she is unable to give a specific example and ruminates mostly on the smoking and drinking of her peers. The session continues.

Therapist: What do you experience and feel when you feel uncomfortable?
Patient: I blush. (Silence.)
Therapist: You blush . . .
Patient: I chew my lips. When I am nervous I chew my lips.

The patient says what happens to her and what she does, but does not answer the question of what she experiences.

Therapist: (Silence.) So you feel nervous with people? Could you tell me more about it?
Patient: Yeah. I would prefer not being there, yet I would like to be there. I am constantly like this—nervous, shaky.
Therapist: You feel nervous and you shake.
Patient: Yeah. I shake a lot, and I don't notice it, really. I don't consider myself a nervous person.

Thus, having begun to describe something of what she experiences, she then dismisses it. Then the evaluator explores the situations and circumstances in which she feels anxious. It becomes clear that her anxiety is diffuse; she has social anxiety, anxiety in class. It becomes clear that this is a change in her in the past number of years and that she was very "open" when she was younger. In the early years, she says, she was a fighter; later on she became "shy and passive"—somewhere around age thirteen or fourteen she found a change in herself. The patient is not spontaneous, is passive and uninvolved.

Therapist: You said that you have one close friend.
Patient: Yeah. My boyfriend.
Therapist: How is your relationship with him?
Patient: Pretty good.
Therapist: Could we look at it to see what it's like?

The evaluator is gently but persistently trying to get the patient to be more specific and describe what she actually experiences.

Patient: Mostly good, but at times it is rough.
Therapist: Could you tell me what it is like, both the "rough" part and the "good" part.
*Patient:*The rough part? (Laughing.) When it is rough, it is very bad. He is a very good talker, and he used to be able to talk me around his little finger. It is always me who is wrong. It must have been me that was this, me that was that—I take the whole load on myself. I never could come back, and I never could say anything. He could talk me around in a circle.
Therapist: Then you were the passive person?

Something extremely interesting and important happens here. Persistent, gentle questioning has failed to make the patient say very much about what she actually experiences and still less about why she behaves in the way she does. The evaluator therefore used the word *passive*, which is something no one likes to be called and is at the same time an absolutely accurate description of a defense. Stung by this, the patient immediately makes a statment that is far more dynamic, looking beneath the defense to the impulse (fighting back) and the anxiety:

Patient: Yeah. Afraid of fighting back in case something would happen in the relationship.
Therapist: Uh-huh.
Patient: I used to be afraid.
Therapist: Uh-huh. Was it that you were afraid he might lose interest in you? Or that he might drop you? (The therapist makes the anxiety explicit.)

Patient: Uh-huh. That is it.
Therapist: So you were not able to express yourself?

For a moment it seems that her therapeutic alliance is in operation because she now spontaneously mentions another defensive maneuver, namely that when she is afraid of expressing herself she starts contradicting herself. Presumably the meaning of this is that if she avoids standing firm on any particular issue she also avoids the risk of any kind of confrontation with the other person. Moreover, she then lets slip a further important piece of information, namely that this behavior infuriates her boyfriend, which clearly indicates that it can be used as a way of *expressing* aggression as well as avoiding it.

Patient: I was not. Always a fear that if I express myself I generally contradict myself. That is my nature. I contradict myself.
Therapist: Could you be specific about this contradicting yourself?
Patient: Well . . . I will say . . . well . . . like . . . like I was saying to you, "Yes, I like something." And then again I say, "I don't like," right? He used to have fits at the beginning.

Here some evaluators might try to interpret this piece of "content" to the patient in terms of her indirect ways of provoking her boyfriend. Since in fact the patient is still in a state of massive underlying resistance, which is later revealed as having clear transference implications, this would almost certainly have been a mistake and the interpretation would have been wasted. On his guard, the evaluator merely presses her to look more closely at what she does, whereupon the underlying resistance is immediately revealed. She remobilizes her defenses and tries to dismiss the whole issue as unimportant.

Therapist: Could we look at this issue of the contradiction . . . that you say something, and then you say something opposite to what you said?
Patient: I just think it is quite ordinary.

Although it may not be immediately obvious, the clues are now sufficient to make clear that the main issue is in the transference. The

patient has said that she contradicts herself and that this infuriates her
boyfriend. At this very moment she is acting in a contradictory
fashion—on the one hand asking for her difficulties to be looked at,
and on the other resisting attempts to do this—and any therapist
might be forgiven for becoming impatient. The evaluator now
gradually brings these issues to her attention, challenging each
defense as she tries to employ it. Though the tone is always gentle,
the language is extremely confronting, giving the patient no chance
to escape from the impact of what he is saying. At the same time, the
therapist firmly puts the responsibility where it belongs, showing her
that if she defeats her *own* ends it is she that suffers. He thus carefully
prevents the interview from developing into a contest of wills. The
patient herself explicitly acknowledges this, saying that although she
feels scolded, she listens because she knows it has not been said as an
accusation.

Therapist: You said you are a contradictory person. How about
right now here with me?
Patient: Have I contradicted myself?
Therapist: What do you think?
Patient: Well, yeah, I do contradict.
Therapist: You see, right now we are looking into your difficulties.
You said that you have some difficulties and that you want to look at
them.
Patient: Yeah. I suppose . . .

This is a standard situation with a standard response—any vagueness must be challenged. This time the patient does not yield to the
challenge, but defensively continues trying to dismiss her problems
as unimportant.

Therapist: Why do you say "suppose"? Do you, or don't you?
Patient: Well, I have difficulties, sure. I always say, "Well, it could
be worse," you know. And it doesn't seem so bad.

The evaluator makes no attempt to *interpret* this defense, but
brushes it aside and confronts the patient with what she is doing in
the here and now, repeatedly making the link with her behavior in
other relationships.

Therapist: How do you feel about coming here and wanting to discuss your problems with me?

Patient: With you?

Therapist: Uh-huh.

Patient: I feel okay about it.

Therapist: Let's look at your relationship here with me. I have a feeling that on one hand you are here, and on the other hand you are not here. You have not been specific in what you have told me so far. Do you notice that you leave things hanging in the middle of nowhere?

Patient: I am being evasive; I know that.

This word has not been explicitly used before, so the patient is showing very clearly that she understands what the therapist is saying.

Therapist: And that is really the issue. Are you specific, or are you evasive? We are here to see what the problems are, your difficulties. But if you say there is, and at the same time you say there isn't and continue to be vague and evasive, then we won't be able to understand the problem, and we will not have further opportunity to get to the core of your problem.

Patient: I don't try purposely, or I don't do it consciously.

Here the patient is trying to slide out of her responsiblity in the situation and at the same time to elicit sympathy. It would be very easy to respond, "I know you don't." The therapist carefully avoids letting her off the hook in this way, continuing with his examination of the central issue.

Therapist: But let's focus on the issue of your not being specific, your being evasive. You leave every issue in the middle of nowhere, and then I have to go back to the same question. And the most important question for both of us is, "Why are you evasive?" Because from what you have told me you have problems with men.

Patient: Yeah.

Therapist: And you said you contradict yourself with your boyfriend and that he gets angry and has fits. And you have given me the picture that you are very disappointed in him.

Patient: Yeah.
Therapist: Now my question is this: how about your relationship here with me? Obviously you have difficulties in life that are a source of agony for you. And now you have decided to do something about them. And I assume that you came here on your own volition, or didn't you?

This question is both extremely challenging and takes care of the possiblity that she might admit that she had come under pressure from someone else and didn't really want help for herself at all. At the same time, the word *agony* conveys the evaluator's genuine sympathy for her predicament, but not in any way that lets her off the hook.

Patient: Yeah.
Therapist: Now if you continue to be evasive, as you know you do, then I will be useless to you and this session will be of no value to you. If we continue to skate around we cannot get to understand the problem; further, we will not be able to get to the core of your problem, something that we are here to understand. Do you see what I mean?
Patient: Uh-huh. (Silence.)
Therapist: You set up a goal for yourself . . . to come here, as you, yourself, put it, "to understand" yourself, to understand your problems with people. At the same time there is a paradox: namely, by being evasive and vague you are in a sense defeating your goal. My question is, "Why do you do that?" Is this the way you are in every relationship? Is this your way with other people? (Long pause.)
Therapist: What do you think? (Long pause)

The therapist knows that this silence is concerned with feelings aroused by his repeated confrontations, which *must be brought out at once*—particularly as they are likely to include angry feelings.

Therapist: How do you feel right now?
Patient: As though I have been scolded.
Therapist: In a way you didn't like what I said.
Patient: That is how I feel.
Therapist: What do you feel inside?
Patient: Kind of shaky.

Therapist: Do you feel irritated or angry?
Patient: I did for a moment. But I listened to what you said, and you said it not as an accusation. Therefore I didn't really have any right to feel angry.
Therapist: What do you think about what I said?

The evaluator now receives his reward for his hard work on the defenses. The patient becomes much more specific and admits, with feeling, that this self-defeating pattern has run throughout her life for years.

Patient: Well, about setting a goal—and putting up a wall, or whatever, . . . well . . . that . . . uh . . . that has been for like . . . I have done it a lot. (The patient is crying.) This a pattern of my life. I have done it in school because I have tried for an A, but I have always said to myself, "What the heck; I will probably never get an A, and don't be surprised if you don't—so don't get upset." So I don't know if I have ever really tried for an A. This self-defeating system is basically in every aspect of my life. I don't think I could really stand and really try for the highest. (The patient continues to cry.)

This communication bears close examination, since although it contains very important information and is expressed with feeling, it still only scratches the surface and thus can be regarded as a defensive maneuver as well. It would be very easy to respond with a comment like, "So you can't try for the highest because you are afraid of failing." This would be falling into a trap because it would entirely leave out her self-defeating mechanism in relation to people, which—as will clearly be revealed—is concerned with much more anxiety-laden conflict, namely her avoidance of expressing aggression for fear of being rejected. The evaluator intuitively sees this, and in his next intervention he emphasizes both the relation with people in general and the here-and-now, that is, he makes the T-C link. It immediately becomes clear that enough work has been done on the defense for the patient to respond to this, for her next communication contains the following elements: (1) and increase in her *motivation to look at herself*, (2) an emphasis on the relation with people, and (3) crucial insight about the way in which she lets herself be pushed around, which will lead into the whole question of avoidance and expressed aggression. All this amounts to a major increase in the therapeutic alliance.

Therapist: Then, basically, the pattern of your relations with people is similar to the way it is here with me. You find it very difficult to be open about your feelings, what goes on within you.
Patient: Uh-huh. That is why I want to know more about myself. I have a lot of problems in dealing . . . One thing I have to learn to do is . . . and I don't know how to do it . . . is to learn to set, establish my priorities, and not be pushed around, you know, without having something to say (about it). I have a lot of problems with my folks at home, and I've started having a lot more problems in my relations with peers, and problems with establishing my priorities—doing what I really want to do instead of being pushed around and saying, "Well, you know, if you really wanted to, I will do it to you even though I really don't feel like doing it."
Therapist: Would you say that there is a need in you for you to be pushed around because that takes care of the problems—somebody solves it for you whether for your best interest (or not)? And there is a conflict in you, a need for you to stand on your own two feet.
Patient: Yeah. A kind of vacillation between the two—back and forth. But I think I am much more pushed around.

The evaluator now senses that, at last, he can pursue that relation with her boyfriend and will get an accurate picture of the situation between the two of them. What emerges is a catastrophic situation of mutual destructiveness accompanied on her part by self-directed aggression—very different from the vagueness and passivity which she presented at the beginning of the interview.

Therapist: Then you allow yourself to be pushed around more. Could we go back specifically to your relationship with your boyfriend which we left?
Patient: There I let myself be pushed around because there is a constant fear that he might terminate the relationship. But then I let it go for a few days; I get really frustrated and then become very obnoxious. And it gets to the point eventually that he won't bother dealing with me. He just walks away, and that is what gets me more angry.

Then the session focuses specifically on her relationship with her boyfriend. On the one hand she takes a very passive, submissive position, fearful that he might leave her, her fear of rejection. On the other hand, she irritates him and makes him angry and says that when he is angry he is very cynical and very sarcastic with her. She, in return, get very angry. One of the ways she deals with the situation is to cry and go to her room. But there are times when she gets angry and the picture gets worse. During the next passage the therapist employs a standard technique, which is to force the patient to focus on exactly what happens and exactly what she feels in these situations.

Patient: I let my rage take over.
Therapist: What happens when your rage takes over?
Patient: I go nuts. I really start yelling and screaming and crying. Three times I've had fits, if you want to call them fits. I had never had a fit in my life that I can remember until about three weeks ago; I have had three since.
Therapist: What is it like when you have a fit?
Patient: I just get so upset, I start crying, and I get angry . . . well . . . I generally get violent with myself . . . I just hate myself so much, and I just want to hurt myself in some way as a type of punishment. I was with my boyfriend, and we were having problems; I would say something rather obnoxious in front of his friends, and . . . which he said was disrespectful. He was very upset about it.
Therapist: You mean you humiliated him?
Patient: Yeah.

The therapist gets further evidence that the patient manages to humiliate her boyfriend. When he gets angry and upset, the patient becomes passive.

Patient: I keep passive on the outside but enraged inside.
Therapist: Then your passivity is a way of controlling your rage? A way of dealing with your rage?
Patient: Yeah. I just shut up. (Laughing.) It is the only way that I have been able to deal with it because I have let go three times and had just actual fits.
Therapist: Could we look at one of these fits?

Patient: Well, one time I became really upset. I told him off because he told me that if I ever disrespect him in front of people or humiliate him in front of people that that was going to be it for the relationship. That came out, and then I realized what I had done. I was really, really upset. And he just kind of clammed up. And I said, "Well, look . . . I said I wanted to talk to you." And I had told him, previous to that, that I wanted to talk to him. What he did was go into the kitchen and sit, picked up the newspaper, and totally ignored me. I said, "I want to talk to you." He works in a group home, and that is where he lives as well. So this was where (we were). So he said to me, "Well do you want to go to the kitchen or to the living room?" So, anyway, we got up to his room; and he stood there rather quietly, and I just kind of became very, very . . . just raging inside, you know. He kept pushing me away from him, you know. "Leave me alone." Because I tried . . . like I tried to be quite calm. I was crying, and you know . . . like, to say, that I was sorry and (tried) to go up to him, but he would just push me away—and eventually I just said, "I am going." I just started scratching the door; I was upset, and well . . . anyway . . . he did . . . he came over. Then because he realized I was really getting bad, and I started to hyperventilate, he picked me up and threw me on the bed, and told me to "relax, relax"; I just kept getting worse and worse. And I got scared, and I just kept hyperventilating more and more.

Therapist: Was this also the moment that rage was also building up inside (you)?

Patient: Yeah. The time before, I just hit my head against the wall.

Therapist: Then you must have been in a really angry state.

Patient: Yeah. I did that one time. Generally I know what I am doing, rationally, and I know it is wrong. I know I shouldn't be reacting that way, but I have no other outlet.

Therapist: The way you made youself feel better was by scratching the door, hyperventilating, banging your head against the wall, and finally having your boyfriend throw you onto the bed and telling you to calm down. Would you say that this rage was toward him?

Patient: Well. I felt really angry with myself; yet I felt really angry with him.

Then the session focuses on the patient's need to humiliate her boyfriend and their pattern of interaction, particularly the element of rage reaction which is at its peak when he ignores her, a pattern that has been there for the past year, since they have known each other. They have no mutual plans. She has had no other relationships with men except an eight-month-long relationship at age seventeen; this relationship was very disturbed, there were constant fights, and the boyfriend was also cynical and sarcastic. She says about that relationship, "We got together for a good fight."

This completes the first phase of the interview, which has accomplished a very great deal—breaking through the patient's defensive vagueness and getting a true and living picture of her disastrous relations with men. It has also been a therapeutic experiment, in the sense that the patient has demonstrated that she can not merely withstand the therapist's highly confronting technique but can respond positively to it. If at any time she had shown signs of being excessively disturbed by this part of the interview, the therapist would have changed his technique and become more supportive. Once the formal psychiatric history is taken, the other area that has hardly been touched on, the connection between the patient's present disturbances and early relations within her family, will follow quite naturally.

The patient was born in British Columbia; her father, an industrial chemist, is fifty-five years old; her mother is fifty-four; two older sisters are thirty-five and thirty-one; an older brother is thirty-three; and the patient is twenty-two years old. She had a sister three years younger who was killed in an automobile accident when the patient was eleven. Her menstruation started around age twelve; she knew about it from her friends. She had no previous psychiatric treatment. She has had episodes of depression, but no suicidal ideation in the past or present. Regarding her sexual relationships, the patient says that because of her religious upbringing, she had no sexual relationships until her present boyfriend, and that this has been for the past few months. It is satisfactory to her, and she enjoys it. She is a full-time student and lives with her parents. Academically she has done fairly well but not to her potential. Recently there has been a decline. In the early years she always had top marks.

It is clear that the formal psychiatric history confirms the inference from the first phase of the interview, namely that the patient is not seriously disturbed and is a strong candidate for Short-Term Dynamic Psychotherapy. The therapist therefore focuses on an area which he senses may well be crucial, the death of the patient's younger sister.

Patient: My little sister, Becky, was killed in an automobile accident. We were driving along on a Sunday afternoon. I was twelve. My father and older sister were in the front seat; my mother was in the back seat between Becky and me. We were hit, and my little sister lived nine days, until finally she died. And my mother was injured badly. She had severe damage . . . broken bones.
Therapist: Were you injured?
Patient: Yeah. I wore a neck brace for a year and a half.
Therapist: What caused the accident?
Patient: It was the taxi driver's fault. He went through a stop sign and hit us broadside. I never saw Becky again. My mother was in the hospital for months. Nothing happened to my father or to my older sister.

The next question is an abrupt change of subject, and yet the hidden link which the evaluator is seeking is abundantly confirmed. The therapist can use creative free association as well as the patient. Moreover, the earlier work on the patient's defenses now ensures that the information is given in a highly meaningful way, as is shown first by the loaded words *kicked* and *booted,* and then by the clear dynamic sequence from impulse ("I hate her") to overcompensating defense ("I was very protective of her"). Finally, a crucial link which emerges is that *the car,* in which Becky was killed, symbolized one of the ways in which the patient felt rejected after her sister's birth.

Therapist: What is your earliest memory of life?
Patient: I think it was my sister's birth. I remember when we went to pick her up at the hospital, she and my mother. I always had the front seat. We went to the hospital and I was kicked into the back seat and told to stay there. I was about three years old. There were my older sisters and my older brother and me in the car with my father. I was booted into the back seat and told to stay there, and my sister and my father went in for my mother and brought her to the car. And my mother got into the car, and she had a baby in her arms; I remember looking over the seat and just looking at her and said, "I hate her." This is about the first thing I remember. She was one of

those angelic children who never got in trouble—a sweet kid that everybody loved. She looked it too. We were all blond when we were young, but she was a white-haired blond and very blue eyed. She was just good natured and quiet and very pleasant—never really upset. I was very protective of her. No one would dare hit her while I was around. I remember one incident. We were in the basement and my mother went to hit her, and I stood in front. I stood between my sister and my mother, and I wouldn't let my mother hit her. My mother said, "If you don't move I will hit you." So I didn't move, and she hit me. At school I used to try to slip out 'cause we went to the same school for only one year. She was in kindergarten. I was in grade two or three, and I used to try to slip out at recess and make sure that she was okay, make sure nobody was beating her up . . . 'cause I would kill them. I was just very protective of her.

The following passage is best left to tell its own story without interruption, so an advance description of what happens is appropriate. Because of previous work on the defenses and transference resistances, the evaluator senses that it will be meaningful to make interpretations directly about the patient's relation to her sister in the distant past. Although transference interpretations are by no means over and done with, they are entirely absent from this phase of the interview. The patient is very resistant to what the evaluator is trying to convey, and the evaluator—without being nearly as confronting as in the first phase—is relentlessly but gently persistent, using a didactic as well as an interpretative technique ("you have to put the memory of your sister in the proper perspective"). Each time the defenses are challenged, a little more detail emerges, and the full extent of the patient's reasons for hating her sister emerges with increasing clarity. The evaluator relentlessly confronts her with this, while carefully acknowledging that the positive feelings for the sister were genuine as well. At the same time, the fact that she was rejected in comparison with her sister links with her present fear of rejection (the P-C link). Finally, through a description of the funeral, the patient is brought face to face with her guilt about wishing her sister dead, which links with a childhood game that she had played with her sister many years before. The patient first becomes extremely upset and then clearly experiences great relief. The passage begins with an interpretation of the *defense* and the *impulse* in relation to the sister.

Therapist: Do you think that maybe you were overprotective of her because *you also* wanted to beat her up?

Patient: I never had an urge to hurt her.

Therapist: But you see, what you told me here is very interesting, because you were displaced from your front seat, and as you put it, you were "kicked," "booted" out; and the first memory you had at three was that you hated your sister. And then you became over-protective. Isn't that bending over backward to be different? And I don't doubt that you had some very positive feelings, but sometimes one becomes too extreme. By being too understanding and too overprotective and making doubly sure that she was not getting beaten up by somebody, do you think it is possible that some of those old hate feelings were still there?

Patient: I really don't. Well maybe because she is dead. If she were alive, it might be a different story.

Therapist: Let's look at it. The fact that she is dead doesn't in any way detract from the truth. Then what you say is that because she is dead you have to keep the memory good. But if these feelings were there, it is very important for you to see them as they are, to see the truth, because you have to put your sister, even the memory of your sister, in the proper perspective.

Patient: Yeah.

Therapist: What comes to your mind about what I said?

Patient: The problem I have about that is I always felt that my mother wished I had died instead of my sister. I remember that one time after Becky was killed my mother got very upset and said she wished I had died instead of my sister. I didn't like that at all. And I have sensed that my brother always felt the same way. Becky was his favorite; he even named her. I even still feel that I am his kid sister, but he pushes me around a lot. And I get the feeling from him that he prefers . . . he would have preferred it if it weren't I that is still living.

Therapist: So, we have two people. Your mother says that, and that is also the message you get from your brother.

Patient: Yeah. My sister-in-law, my brother's wife—I love her. She is really a great lady, you know. I guess that is because when I was young she told me that—she said, you know—"You have grown up." She said, "You had hell when you were young" because with my little sister—she became the cheese of the family, and I was rejected a lot. I remember, really, a lot of rejection from my sisters.

Therapist: This brings us back again to your feelings. What were your feelings about being rejected?

Patient: I hated it.

Therapist: You have expressed hating to be rejected and that you even bend over backward to let people do things you don't like because you are afraid to be rejected. There it is again.

Patient: Yeah, I know.

Therapist: Now, if we look at this particular situation, you feel rejected by everyone who preferred your sister. My question is, what were your feelings for your sister, the sister who put you out of the front seat? By her coming into the picture, nobody paid any attention to you.

Patient: I admired her, and I wanted to be like her. She was an idol.

Therapist: That is one aspect, but there is more to it.

Patient: I never really thought about it.

Therapist: Here we are, and you can think of it right now.

Patient: I guess it is because there is a block there because I don't want to feel bad things about her.

Therapist: But you did feel bad things about her when you were young.

Patient: Yeah. I know. To be very honest.

Therapist: If you have some negative feelings about your sister, don't you think it is vital for you to get them out in the open? And don't you think it is important that you put things in their proper perspective?

Patient: Okay. Maybe I am trying to forget. But it really wasn't her fault, you know.

Therapist: Obviously it wasn't. She was a good girl. And obviously it wasn't her fault that she came into this world. But the fact is that she did certain things to you, even if she didn't want to.

Patient: Yeah. Consciously.

Therapist: Even if it wasn't her fault. You lost a lot of things. You lost your front seat. Lost the attention. And everybody admired this angelic child. Then let's look at your feelings.

Patient: I remember when she was in kindergarten we used to share a room. I remember on Saturday mornings we always used to play house or play dolls, generally dolls or something like that. One Saturday morning we played dead. I played, then I said, "You are going to be dead." So anyway she lay down. I made her lie down on the bed, and I remember covering her up, right up. She eventually started crying. She didn't like it. She was scared. She fought me then. I remember just looking at her out of curiosity, and then I started crying because I felt very bad.

Therapist: Wasn't it because there was a part of you that wanted her to be dead, and that was what the game was all about? And isn't that what happened in reality?

Patient: I don't know. I guess I thought about what it would be like if she were dead. If she wasn't around. And she died. But, gee, my negative feelings, if there are any, are very deep because I don't really feel them. I have probably hidden them if they are there.

Therapist: You see, you repeatedly say "guess" and "probably"; and you don't want to face your real feelings. And that is the reason you pay such a heavy price, by being insecure, being constantly afraid of being rejected, and not standing on your own two feet and trying to play the role of nice girl in order to be liked by people, giving up your own self, rather than being a free human being—to be you as you really are in your own right.

Patient: After she died I tried really hard to be like her. I remember some friends of my parents at the funeral saying that it was too bad that it was Becky who had died.

Therapist: Then it seems that many people said the same thing.

Patient: I was obnoxious when I was young. (Laughs.)

Therapist: Let's look at this being "obnoxious." What does that mean? Would you think that that was the manifestation of the fact that you were not happy, that you were upset? Now, what were you upset about? Was it that you were pushed off your pedestal?

Patient: Yeah. Before my sister was born I had all the attention for three years. I was also a novelty, a new baby. That whole bit. And I had total attention for three years. And then it was totally robbed from me for a long time, and the only way I knew I could get attention from my parents was to be bad, to do something bad, and then they would notice me. And I knew in school it was the same way. I wanted the attention of the teacher. I couldn't be a nonentity in the class. I wanted to be known. I used to do naughty things. In grade two I beat up the teacher once, and in grade three I ran away from school, and I clawed a teacher, like this—right down her face.

Therapist: A woman?

Patient: Yes. I hated her.

Therapist: Were you particularly angry at your mother?
Patient: I don't know. But I have a lot of problems with women.

Then the patient discusses her difficulties with women, that she has always had a lot of problems with them. Then the session focuses on the day of the funeral. Her mother was in intensive care in the hospital.

Patient: Anyway, when they lowered the casket I felt then, really, a surge of crying; I ran to my neighbor, a woman whom I really don't know very well to this day—but someone I respect, you know. She was at the back. She was nice to me. So I ran to her. I ran right around the casket, right to her.

Therapist: Let's look at the lowering of the casket. What it meant to you.

Patient: That was it. It was just that I knew I would never see her again.

Therapist: Being covered up? And isn't that the game you had played? In the game you covered her up with some sheets. Here it was the same thing.

Patient: Yeah. But this was more final than the other.

Then the therapist questions the patient about what the neighbor had done. The patient says she comforted her, but she didn't stay long in her arms as she felt embarrassed because all her family was there—why hadn't she gone to them? The therapist indicates that she didn't go to them because she felt all of them preferred her sister. The patient said she was afraid of being rejected by the members of her family. And the therapist questioned why they should reject her.

Therapist: What were they going to reject you about? What was so bad about you that people would reject you if they knew it?
Patient: I don"t know. (Crying.)
Therapist: You don't want to look at it. Let's see. What is the worst thing we can think of for which people could reject you if they knew? We know about the "dead" game.
Patient: Maybe they felt that I killed her.
Therapist: And that you were glad about it, too.
Patient: I do remember thinking, "Now I will have my own room."
(Laughing)

Therapist: You were afraid that they may have perceived that, and if they had known that they would have felt you were terrible? And that is why you ran to the lady who didn't know you?

Patient: I guess I wanted to go to someone who didn't really know me.

Therapist: And that was the way to keep your secret. Let's look at your secret.

Patient: That I might have been happy that she was dead.

Therapist: You say "might." Were you happy, or weren't you happy?

Patient: Yes. (The patient is crying and distraught.)

Therapist: But of course this doesn't mean that you didn't also love her. And obviously you had some good things together. But what we have learned today is that your sister had certain advantages that you did not have. You were displaced from the front seat, you lost your pedestal, people preferred her for one reason or another, you had had all the attention for the first three years and lost all that, and then you had to get attention by being bad. So clearly you had a lot of feelings. These feelings have been buried, but they are coming to the surface in this interesting little game you played about her dying.

Patient: It is very strange.

Therapist: When this game became a reality it became intolerable, and what you did with all these feelings was to bury them.

Patient: Yeah.

Therapist: But don't you think it is time that came out, for you to face them for what they are—because they are honest and they are straightforward?

It is clear that though she was at first very upset by this piece of therapeutic work, she is now experiencing relief. The therapist intuitively knows that this is by no means the end of the story, and— encouraged by her response so far—he also senses that she can take further painful revelations. He therefore begins exploring an area which hitherto has been conspicuous by its absence, namely the relation with her father. Because of previous work on her resistances, the information that she gives is highly meaningful and full of feeling; but resistance is by no means over, and it returns as soon as the therapist touches on the possibility of resentment against her father.

Therapist: How would you describe your relationship with your father?

Patient: Then, I remember, I was Daddy's little girl. He used to take me with him, particularly on Saturdays, to his office. I used to go with him then. I used to wrestle with him, and he often used to call me his "little Dutch girl"; then I was very blond.

The session focuses further on her relationship with her father, which indicates that she had a close relationship with her father, and he used to give her a lot of attention. She said he used to put her on his knee or his foot and bounce her up and down, and he used to put her up on his hand and hold her up in the air. He used to take her with him to lunch with a business colleague. Other memories are related to her dressing up like a tomboy and helping her father do things like wash the car. Her relationship with her father changed completely after the accident. She found him unapproachable. He was preoccupied with her mother's hospitalization and the household activities, etc.

Therapist: In a sense, then, you also lost your father after the accident.

Patient: Yeah. I lost my father then. But I did gain a mother. My mother didn't have my sister anymore, and she needed someone. I babysat my mother, if you want to put it that way, for four or five years.

Then the session focuses on the present: the patient said her relationship with her father, specifically, deteriorated. She said that at present it is "horrible," and he has threatened to kick her out of the house. She is very uncomfortable with him and hardly talks with him. She said that it seemed that after the automobile accident, her whole life changed completely—"it was like a dividing point." Further exploration indicates that she was closest to her oldest sister and did not have much of a relationship with her other sister or her brother. The therapist now knows that therapeutically speaking it will be crucial to reach her feelings about the loss of the close relation with her father, if possible through living recollected detail, but he is not yet ready to attempt this. He still wants to fill in detail about relations within the family, and therefore asks first about the relation that her parents had to one another and then about the relation between the patient and her mother.

Patient: It has always been very good. In the whole time, my whole life, I remember only one fight. On one occasion they had an argument. My mother wanted to get away from my father, and there was a lock on the bathroom door, so she closed the door and locked it. And then he tried to get in and she wouldn't let him in. Their relationship is very good. They walk around now still like newlyweds holding hands all the time.
Therapist: You said, "like newlyweds"?
Patient: Yeah.
Therapist: But you are smiling.

The patient clearly has some strong feelings about her parents' relation.

Patient: I just think it is kind of funny. After some thirty-odd years of marriage, it is pretty good I guess.

Then the session moves toward the early part of the patient's life the fact that she was her father's favorite, and her wish that she could have a closer relationship with her mother. She talks resentfully about her father's frequent business trips. And whenever her father was away she used to stay out of the house a lot, riding her bike, which was then her favorite pastime. Now at last it is time to focus on the point at which her relationship with her father deteriorated. What happens now is the crucial passage in the whole interview:

1. The patient allows the evaluator to see one of the reasons why the relation with her father went wrong, but—because her resistance is still very strong—not the most important reason.
2. The evaluator makes an interpretation of the impulse (resentment) towards her father (P).
3. The patient's resistance is immediately intensified ("What do you mean? I don't understand").
4. The evaluator brushes this aside and persists with his interpretation.
5. The patient to some degree admits her resentment.
6. Having got thus far, the evaluator feels it is meaningful to generalize this resentment to other men, i.e., by implication her boyfriend (C)—the C-P link.

7. Perhaps without being fully conscious of it, he is in fact preparing the way for the most important step in the whole interview, namely the understanding of her resistance to the therapist in terms of the relation with her father, i.e., the T-P interpretation of the defense.

8. He has to give the C-P interpretation several times—one of the ways of dealing with resistance is simply to persist relentlessly with the same interpretation.

9. This eventually bears fruit, since the patient now gives a living detail which links her boyfriend with her father, namely the fact that she resents his wanting to travel ("I immediately felt angry, but I didn't realize this before").

10. The evaluator drives this home, even momentarily hinting at death wishes toward him ("Have you ever thought he might never come back?")

11. When the patient even responds to this, the evaluator knows that the time has come for the T-P interpretation, which he drives home with relentless persistence.

12. Since the C-P interpretation has already been given, this completes the triangle of person (T-C-P)

13. Not only this, but the evaluator also completes the other triangle, mentioning the defense (passivity), the anxiety ("There is a constant fear that he might leave you"), and the impulse (hostility and resentment).

14. In other words, the evaluator in effect *interprets almost the whole of the patient's pathology* within a few moments.

15. The response is dramatic: not only does she now reveal the crucial traumatic moment in her childhood, which unconsciously she had been concealing all along, but she reveals it with strong de-repressed feeling, and the interview is essentially complete.

Patient: I think it started because I was in the hospital, I think it was for five days, and he came to see me only once. I had only one other visitor in those five days.

Therapist: Do you think that there might be some element of resentment toward your father?

The patient immediately becomes defensive.

Patient: What do you mean? I don't understand.
Therapist: Exactly what I said. Resenting your father.
Patient: For not being with me?
Therapist: Uh-huh.
Patient: Well, I think he could have got down to the hospital more than once, at eleven o'clock at night. But he didn't.
Therapist: So then you feel resentful.
Patient: Yeah. I was angry about his not being there.
Therapist: Do you think there is some hostility in your relation to men?
Patient: (Pause.) Yeah. There is. And in one way it is the tendency men have to use women. I hate it.

The evaluator bypasses this and continues, making the C-P link explicit.

Therapist: Now the question I have in my mind is that there is also an element of hostility, from what you have told me, in your relationship with your father. And do you think the hostility you have in your relationships with men might be related to the hostility you have had in your relationship with your father?
Patient: Yeah. I think so. Something just popped into my head. My boyfriend wants to go away and travel. And I just realized how strongly, how I feel about that. I immediately felt angry, but I didn't realize that before.
Therapist: Then there is a part of you which resents your father, and there is the hostility you feel in relation to your father. Do you think that this may play a role in your relationship with men, by your displacing your hostility from your father onto other men?
Patient: (Laughing.) Yeah.
Therapist: As you said, when your boyfriend talks about traveling, you have a very intense, negative feeling because immediately it mobilizes your old feelings related to the absences of your father. And the other question that comes to my mind is, has there ever been the thought in your mind that he might never come back?
Patient: Yeah. Very strongly so. And I often think it might be connected to my sister's death—going away and not coming back.
Therapist: From what we have discussed, we can see the elements of resentment and hostility in your relationship with your father.

They have been in your relationships with men in general. How about here with me? Is there any element of resentment and hostility here with me?

(A T-C-P interpretation. The patient is smiling).

Patient: Yeah. I thought that. I just thought about what happened when I said I felt like I was being scolded. (Pause.) I felt hostility for that moment. For a moment I felt you were scolding me like others, like everybody else who scolds me. But then I realized immediately that you were right. I have been making a mess of my life.

Therapist: You said, "for a moment." Does that mean that there is no element of hostility in your relationship with me? Let's look at this interview. At the beginning you were very vague and very passive, and again in the latter part of the interview, when we moved to the issue of your relationship with your father, you became more passive. And we know that in your relations with people, particularly in relationships with men, you take a very passive position.

Patient: When I can't deal with it any longer, yes.

Therapist: From what you have told me, in your relationship with your boyfriend you take a very passive position. There is a constant fear that he might leave you, and at the same time there is a buildup of anger and hostility. From what you have told me you deal with it in one of two ways. Either you start to scratch the door, hyperventilate, and bang your head against the wall. The other is to become extremely passive and take the position of a beaten, passive woman.

The patient now admits both the source of the passivity and the intensity of the anger underneath.

Patient: Yeah. When I can no longer deal with the situation I become very passive. And at the same time I am boiling inside.

Therapist: Then my question is this: Is passivity not a way of dealing with hostility? And is this not in operation with me?

Patient: I don't know you as a person. This is your profession. If I knew you as a person you would probably get the very same treatment.

The evaluator brushes aside this attempt to evade the issue while giving the impression she is considering it.

Therapist: But let's look at this nearly two-hour interview. Don't you think that you have been constantly putting up an iron wall around yourself and hiding behind it? And I have on many occasions had to dig and dig. I am sure that during this interview we have been able to break through some of these barriers, and we have touched on some very important issues; but it has at the same time been only with a great amount of digging. You are always hiding behind something. Is this passive way you take here with me, is this an expression of some hostility in relation to me?

Patient: I know, I know, I know . . . okay. I can tell you. (The patient is crying.) I put up these defenses, like with my boyfriend. And I notice that I put up a barrier and don't let another person get to know me. I do it a lot. Perhaps you are right, that I resent opening up completely.

Therapist: Do you think that at one level it might have its roots in your relationship with your father, with whom you had a very close, intimate relationship? But then he changed completely.

Patient: Uh-huh.

Therapist: At one time you left yourself open and were your father's "little Dutch girl," "little yellow bird." And suddenly he dropped you. Now you don't allow yourself to be open, and we have seen this all through the interview with me.

Patient: All people.

Therapist: Of course. But I am specifically focusing on your relationship here with me and your need to put up an iron wall and not let yourself be open.

Patient: Yeah.

Therapist: Do you think, then, there is a connection between this and your father?

Patient: Yeah. I do.

Therapist: Huh?

Patient: I do. I can tell you exactly when it happened, and what I said to myself. "I am never again going to get close to anybody." It was just after the automobile accident, and Becky was dead by then. My father and my sister used to stay at the hospital until late every night, and I was going to school. And I used to have to go to some friend's place after school. There were a few boys and girls, and I never felt comfortable there; and I worked. I used to do all the dishes and help do the cooking, do everything I could to earn my keep, or whatever it was there. And then I used to come home, and at first, for about two weeks after Becky died, I slept in the same bed with my father, where my mother used to sleep. And one night I was in bed, and my . . . this was actually on a Saturday, I think, I think it was . . . and Dad came upstairs and said, "Go to your own bed now." And I said, "Why?" He said, "Just go to your own bed." So I got up and left the room and went to my own bed, and I remember crying. And it was never the same after that.

Therapist: Let's look at this. Becky is gone forever. Your mother is in the hospital and not home anymore. And then you were faced with the loss of your father. You are no longer his "little yellow bird." You want to take your mother's place in the bed, but you are no longer his favorite. Let's look at your feelings then.

Patient: Well, he thought it was about time I started to stand on my own two feet.

Therapist: Was there something else? You had a very special relationship with your father, and now you wanted to see it in a very exclusive way. But he told you, "Out." What are your ideas about this? Your father didn't want you to take your mother's place in the bed.

Patient: I don't have any idea about this. He didn't want me around anymore.

Therapist: Let's focus at this moment on the issue of not wanting you around anymore, having a very special relationship with your father and suddenly being dropped like that. Then isn't there at one level the element of hostility and resentment? And as you put it so well, "I am never again going to get close to anybody." And as we can see, this has been true in the past two hours with me. And do you think that this might become a problem in therapy? Because obviously for as long as you have to hide behind a wall and take a passive position, we cannot get to the core of your problem, and you will perpetuate your suffering. But I am glad that we were able to break through and touch on some of the very important issues that are the central core of your problem.

CONCLUSION

In this chapter I have outlined a specific technique of initial assessment in the form of trial therapy. I consider this to be the only way of determining accurately whether a patient can withstand the impact of his own unconscious material and is thus a candidate for Short-Term Psychoanalytic Psychotherapy. I emphasized that one of the first tasks of the evaluator is to rule out certain contraindications by careful and skillful questioning. I also emphasized that the patient is likely to mobilize massive resistances and that there are specific techniques by which these must be actively worked through. The patient then gives feedback, which provides direct evidence of whether or not he is able to respond to the technique that will be used in therapy. An important aspect of this feedback consists of fluctuations in motivation. A great majority of patients respond with relief at being understood and having the burden of their neurotic defenses temporarily lifted, and their motivation shows a marked increase. This may take the form of openly appreciating what the interviewer has done or of actively asking for therapy or asking when it will begin. Very frequently the patient shows signs of underlying increased motivation even when on the surface he shows increased resistance, and when this happens it is an extremely good prognostic sign. To sum up, the interviewer is constantly monitoring the patient's response to the very form of therapy that he will receive.

8

Short-Term Anxiety-Provoking Psychotherapy

Peter E. Sifneos, M.D.

Short-Term Anxiety-Provoking Psychotherapy (STAPP) is a technique of short-term psychotherapy based on psychoanalytic principles and technique. The nature of the psychological conflict which underlies the patient's difficulties is oedipal, and it has given rise to circumscribed symptoms related to interpersonal difficulties. The criteria for undergoing STAPP have been developed over a twenty-year period, tested extensively, and their effectiveness in helping pick out appropriate candidates for this kind of psychotherapy has been repeatedly validated. They are the following: (1) a circumscribed chief complaint; (2) meaningful (give-and-take) type of relationship in early childhood; (3) good rapport with the evaluator; (4) psychological sophistication and above average intelligence; (5) motivation to change.

From the proceedings of the Third International Symposium on Short-Term Dynamic Psychotherapy, Los Angeles.

What follows is an initial interview which provides a background for discussion to see if this patient fulfills the criteria for Short-Term Anxiety-Provoking Psychotherapy.

THE CASE OF THE BEATEN BOY

The patient is a twenty-two-year-old part-time student who at the time of the initial interview complained of: (1) anxiety, "a feeling of uneasiness," "nervousness," "sweaty palms," "tight feeling in my stomach." He said that his anxiety intensifies when he gets into conflict with another person, particularly someone in authority, where there is "a little bit of aggression." In such a situation, he says, "I just seem to crumble inside." In social situations he has always felt like an outsider. (2) Disturbances in interpersonal relationships, with particular hostility toward women. He said that in relation to men he cannot stand up for himself.

During the initial interview he talked spontaneously about his violent childhood and mentioned how he was controlled by his mother, whom he described as "rigid and demanding." Some of his memories were of being physically punished by his mother, and of crying. He remembers her telling him, "Stop crying or else I will hit you more." This pattern continued until age fourteen.

He also talked about his hostile feelings toward women, and mentioned his current girlfriend, whom he has been dating for almost two years, whom he knows he is going to end up leaving. When he visited her recently he entered the building without first ringing the bell. The doorman was angry and rude and the patient "started to shake inside."

He described his father as "a very quiet guy," who was completely dominated by the patient's mother.

He talked about being weak and went on as follows:

Patient: I may be dominated by women?

Therapist: Now that is precisely what the picture is, isn't it? Your mother is very strong, very powerful, dominating your father and dominating you as a boy. Now, it would be quite interesting, for you to be in a situation where this would be different. For example, you have a weak girl who even attempts suicide. In that case you are the strong one. Are you doing it possibly because of these early experiences with your mother, because you like to punish women? Is there something inside you that enjoys seeing a woman being weak, threatening to commit suicide or being "a bit screwy," as you say, because of these old angry feelings that you had against women which started with your mother? Do you see what I mean? You displace your aggression at your mother on your weak girlfriend.

Patient: Yes, I see what you mean. Yet, she has a more relaxed attitude. Like, whereas she would attempt suicide and stuff like that if I broke off with her, in other things that would send me for a tumble, she is strong and doesn't tumble.

Therapist: Such as what?

Patient: Mode of life or something that I can't . . . like going to clubs or something . . . I find it very hard to go to a club . . . I find it extremely hard to socialize with people, you know. Whereas she just goes on with no trouble. She meets somebody and talks to them as if she has known them for ten years which I find very disturbing . . . even annoying sometimes.

Therapist: Well, I wasn't trying to put it in an all-or-none way. What I was saying was that it is very possible that under certain circumstances you would be the one who would be anxious, like the episode with the doorman, but that under different circumstances you are the strong one. It is in this sense that when she was suicidal, when she was weak, you had the upper hand. So there seems to be some kind of give-and-take interaction between the two of you, which may explain why you have been staying together for two years despite the fact that she is not the "ideal" girl for you.

Patient: I think what I possess in my strong points, she doesn't; and what she possesses in her strong points, I don't. That is probably it right there.

Therapist: Okay. Do tell me, which are your strong points? What do you think are some of your assets? You told me about your intelligence. What else?

Patient: I think my intelligence is about my strongest asset.

Therapist: What else?

Patient: My logic. I guess that goes under intelligence, taking facts or analyzing them and coming up with a good solution.

Therapist: Anything else?

Patient: No.

Therapist: Okay, now let us go back to your girlfriend. Does she like you?

Patient: I think she is in love with me.

Therapist: She is in love with you! So, obviously you *must* have some assets.

Patient: I know I have a lot of, I could have gone far . . . I could have done a lot of things with my . . . I had ambition. I had intelligence. I had everything, yet I was just crushed inside, you know. I couldn't pursue anything I wanted.

Therapist: When you use the past tense, "I had, I had, I had," are you saying that you don't possess these things anymore?

Patient: No, I still possess intelligence but my ambition has dwindled down. I feel that I am just content to survive.

Therapist: Now, obviously, if this were so, you wouldn't be here. You wouldn't be talking to the other doctor, either.

Patient: I know I am not content in my way of life right now.

Therapist: So, you want to do something about it. Do you think you can?

Patient: Put it this way: I know I can and I know I'd better because it has just been too long.

Therapist: Fine. That is good enough. Now what made you decide to come here? Obviously you have these problems which are long-term. There is something that made you decide to make an appointment. Was there any specific episode or any other situation which made you decide to call?

Patient: You mean the first episode?

Therapist: Yes.

Patient: I had gone to see—well, I hadn't gone myself—but I had gone before to a professional person when I was around sixteen. I had attempted suicide over a big hassle at home. I mean, I was sixteen and I was supposed to be in at ten o'clock or the door was going to be locked from the inside and I was told how to dress, what to wear, how to walk, how to talk, and so on. At sixteen there was rebellion coming out of me. So, if I was to come home at nine-thirty I wouldn't. It was just the fact that I wanted to rebel and I was rebelling.

Therapist: So you did?

Patient: And when we got into fights and everything my parents were extremely physical. Like I said, my mother never thought twice about running and grabbing ahold of my hair or something.

Therapist: And what happened about this episode at sixteen? Why did you attempt suicide?

Patient: Well, things were really getting bad. I felt embarrassed. I would go to school and hear all these people talking in class about bringing home a girl. If I did my parents wouldn't entertain her but would talk about home life instead. And I was utterly frustrated listening to all of this, you know. Why can't I be different? Why can't I sit down with my parents and talk and why can't I bring home a girl as everybody is doing? Why can't I be treated like an adult even at that age, you know, but I just wasn't. I was being treated as a child. I think the turning point came when I was sixteen. It was after the Beatles came in. They still wanted me to go to the barber shop and have a short haircut and you know, no jeans or anything like that. That is probably why I'm wearing hair like this now. Anyway, I went out one day. They kept bugging me for a haircut. "Go and get a haircut." I think they were just trying to be antagonizing. I went out and I got a pretty short haircut and I came back and I was really . . . I was pissed off . . . the way I looked and everything. Like all my friends are sort of different and I can't fit in. I'm having problems to fit in the first place and yet my parents are leading me to even more difficulty. So, I came home and I looked at myself and they said it wasn't short enough. I went back to the barber shop and I told the guy really to trim it short, and he trimmed it as short as he could and was scared to trim it any shorter. I came home, I looked at it in the mirror and I cut off the rest of it. I walked into my room and they wouldn't even go near me. I was just, I never felt like that in my life. I was just completely exhausted mentally. I had just given up and I wanted to die. Put it this way, I don't think at that moment I wanted to die and then . . . well, I slashed my wrist with a razor blade. After I slashed it, immediately I saw my skin open up and I had this big feeling of remorse. I didn't want to die, you know, I know that it sounds contradictory, I yelled for my mother and she saw the whole room full of blood.

Therapist: So you called your mother when you were in distress, the mother who was the cause of your distress?

Patient: It was a . . . I didn't . . . I called, but I didn't call. Well, I wanted to call but I didn't say it in such a voice I was calling. I didn't yell out for her name or nothing.

Therapist: What happened?

Patient: It was just kind of like a sigh. "Ma," you know. Like a slow . . . I wanted her to hear it but I didn't want her to know I was calling

her, you know. Anyway, she came in and first, when she saw me
lying there, she yelled for my father, "Come upstairs and see what
your son did." He came up and I could see that he was screwed up.
He jumped on the phone and called the ambulance. My mother came
into the room and she took off my pants, took off my socks, and
started to wash my feet and said that she didn't want to go through
the embarrassment at the hospital of having the nurses take off my
socks and look at my dirty feet. That was very . . . that really got me
right there. I remember even wondering, "Wow." Here I am lying on
the bed bleeding and she is worried about my dirty feet.

Therapist: Now what does that make you feel? You are bleeding
and your mother is washing your feet?

Patient: Well, right about then, I gave up completely, just completely on them. I said, you know, I was totally disillusioned. There is
no hope for them. After that, I never sat down and spoke my true
feelings or nothing. Right after that incident I said, "That is it, and
they are not even worth it."

Therapist: So, it means that up to the age of sixteen, there must
have been still some positive feelings that you had for your parents
and for your mother in particular—some hopes?

Patient: Well, I think that it is natural even—

Therapist: Yes, but let's not talk about what is natural and what
others think. We are interested right now in *you*. In *your* thoughts.

Patient: Yes, I had feelings. I wanted to have their respect. I
wanted them to respect my opinions, my view. Everything was for
them. They seemed to run the whole show. You do what they want or
else.

Therapist: I see, but let us come back to the present. You saw a
psychiatrist at that time, I presume.

The patient was seen by a neurologist, who thought he should see a
psychiatrist. But he didn't see a psychiatrist. He saw his family
physician, who prescribed Valium. Then he talked about his parents'
twenty-fifth wedding anniversary and the pregnancy and abortion
of his girlfriend.

Patient: Yes, there was an incident right after I came from Myrtle
Beach and it was concerning my girlfriend. This was a very, really
tough thing.

Therapist: What was it?

Patient: Let's see, it was December last year and my parents' twenty-fifth wedding anniversary and I remember arranging everything with my brother to give them a twenty-fifth wedding anniversary because that was something that they had harped on ever since I was young and everything. Everybody did it so I felt obligated to do it. So, I went to a lot of strain. It was just a pain in the neck to go through all of this catering business and hall business and right after that my girlfriend got pregnant and she told me that there was no way of getting pregnant because of some operation. She said that she had plugged up all of her fallopian tubes and I believed her. I was a sucker but I believed her. Anyway, she got pregnant so I said, "What do you want to do? I don't want to marry you." And then her mother found out and she was phoning me for all sorts of things. I know I didn't want to end up married to her. I didn't want a kid. She wouldn't even look after herself let alone handle a kid. So, we decided . . . I say, we together, decided that the best thing to do for her was to have an abortion. So we went around all the hospitals here. She was only seventeen. She only turned eighteen in March, and at the hospital they found out. I thought that they knew that she was seventeen or eighteen so they asked her to leave the next morning. And they phoned her mother up and told her to come and get her daughter. So, we had no choice. I phoned one of these Planned Parenthood associations and we had to go somewhere else for an abortion. Right after we came back she completely changed. She actually had some heated arguments with me and accused me of murdering her baby. And that was my vacation time that had come up that year and I said, "To hell with this. I have got to get out of here." I took my vacation money and I went down there and found out that my mother had raised a big fuss when she went down there a couple of months ago.

Therapist: About the abortion?

Patient: No, no, not about the abortion.

Therapist: Your mother knew about the abortion?

Patient: No.

Therapist: Okay, what happened?

Patient: It was very . . . I never told her nothing. So anyway, I found out that my parents had been down there. My father was impressed with the place. He wanted a job and my uncle got him a job and then when my mother had come down she put up a big fuss. You know, she drank her head off one night and yelled at everybody and insulted everybody. When I went down there, everybody was very apologetic to me. I didn't even know any of the details of the incident. I just know that she made a fuss. I didn't know any details. They were very apologetic. At the same time, they'd also be very sympathetic. Like telling me, "We saw how you were mistreated as a boy." As a kid I used to confide maybe in my grandmother, in my aunt. I wanted to leave when I got older because they were always hitting me. Anyway, I figured well, that is their problem. I said to myself, that it was their problem. Let them worry about it, so I came back to Montreal and I was back to the same crap again, you know. I was smoking a lot. At the age of seventeen and eighteen I used to do almost everything . . . drugs . . .

Therapist: For example . . .

Patient: LSD, you know, meth, speed, you name it. I felt that if I had—

Therapist: Did you take heroin?

Patient: I never took it in its pure form. I think that at one time it was inside a pill that . . . I would say no, but—

Therapist: Now, let's go back a bit. You are how old?

He is twenty-two and has one brother, two years younger than he, and no sisters. His father and mother are both forty-five. One of his earliest memories was of shopping with her. It wasn't fun, it was "hectic." He did not like what she liked, and shopping turned into a battle. Then the session focused on the positive things with his mother.

Patient: Well, I liked her attitude towards nature. If you went for a ride with her in the spring she just seemed so overjoyed with the flowers and it really made you feel good.

Therapist: Do you like nature?

Patient: Oh, I *love* nature.

Therapist: Now, what about your relationship with your father?

Patient: I almost never had a relationship with my father. He was very withdrawn, very quiet.

Therapist: What is his job?

Patient: What does he do? He worked as a butcher.

Therapist: And with your brother?

Patient: Well, with him, it was like cats and dogs until we were sixteen.

Therapist: Who was your parents' favorite?

Patient: My brother was the pet.

Therapist: I see. So what was it that he was doing that would make him the pet? Was he the "good boy"?

Patient: I was smarter. I was getting the high marks in school. I was the guy that if they did have to show off a son that knew something or could do something better, it would be me. Like if I got 95 one month and my mark dropped from 95 to 93 the next month, I would get hell. Whereas, my brother was struggling along with an 85 or 80 and he got no static at all. (Smiling.)

Therapist: Are you saying that your mother preferred your brother to you? I don't get that picture somehow.

Patient: She definitely preferred—*definitely* preferred—because I went into that discussion last week. I was jealous of my brother.

Therapist: I can understand that. But your smile indicated something else. Is it possible in spite of all these fights, in spite of all the difficulties that you had with your mother, somewhere deep inside you felt different. Both of you *loved* nature.

Patient: If this will clarify it. I feel that I have a lot of my mother in me which kind of scares me. I wouldn't want to do to my kids what she has done to me. And I feel as if I would sometimes.

Therapist: "A lot of mother in me!" What does that mean? The two of you are—

Patient: —are kind of alike. I would say alike. There is a definite ... if you had to say to whom am I close to? My mother or my father. I would say my mother. Although, I would prefer my father.

Therapist: You didn't have problems with your father. I understand that completely. But what I am struck by is that the major part of your difficulty is connected with your attachment to your mother. And that, despite all these other terrible things that you have told me about, you are still attached to her and you're caught in between these two feelings.

Patient: No, no, I wouldn't say that. I would say that there is a lot underneath and both are just tearing at each other.

Therapist: I see.

Patient: There is a conflict. It is not like ... I feel like I am holding a rope in each hand and ...

Therapist: Your father was no competition?

Patient: My father was in the background. I think that my mother would have preferred my brother first, me second, and my father last. She even went against him with my brother or me. She played a game. She played one side against the other.

Therapist: What was the attitude about sex in your family?

Patient: Oh *wow*, that was a negative attitude—a real negative attitude. I'm surprised that I haven't come out with some real inhibitions concerning sex. I lead a very vigorous sex life, as a matter of fact. Not too many things shock me.

Therapist: And yet, you said "wow" when I asked you about sex. Obviously, there is something in all this that we have to understand.

Patient: Well, when I was young . . . like I have never seen any physical contact between my parents except maybe once last year for the first time in my life. I went in a room and saw my mother and father with his arm around her in bed. That was the first contact that I had ever seen.

Therapist: But there must have been some.

Patient: Apart from a kiss. There must have been sex, sure, but if there was it was hidden from the kids.

Therapist: Are you saying that your mother was not awfully interested in sex?

Patient: No, no. I sense . . . I never saw them . . . I sense perversion in my mother and I—

Therapist: Perversion meaning?

Patient: It definitely has sexual connotations to it. Like when she used to put the belt to me she always had me take off my pants and my underwear, you know.

Therapist: She was interested in you?

Patient: No, I think she had derived a pleasure of hitting me in the flesh.

Therapist: I see. You said that you were good in school. Good grades. How was it in high school?

Patient: It was very good up until the tenth grade.

Therapist: What happened then?

Patient: That is when I just went downhill all the way after that.

Therapist: Now, as far as your puberty, were there any problems then?

Patient: I had a lot of problems around puberty. First of all, I matured a little bit late. I was about fifteen when I matured, you know, physically. I was very complexed about my height and my size and everything, and to make matters worse, if my mother got mad at me for something, she would have an argument—like this was past the beating age. If she would take the belt to me I would just look at her and she wouldn't . . . like, she knew so she put the belt away and she took to playing with my head. Like, she knew what hurt you and didn't hurt you. She would be a real mother and then ask you to confide in her and tell her what bothered me and I would say, "Well everybody at school is laughing at me because I'm small." But the minute she got into an argument with me, that was the first thing she'd use against me.

Therapist: Did you have any girlfriends in high school?

Patient: I had . . . I could not go for a good relationship. I brought home a girl when I was eighteen years of age and my mother chased her down the street, off the gallery and down the street. I was eighteen when that happened. I was fifteen years of age in high school listening to my friends . . . like telling the teacher that they bring home their girlfriends and the whole family sits down and everything, and I knew I couldn't do that.

Therapist: I see, was it possible that your mother was jealous?

Patient: I think so. I very *much* think so.

Therapist: I see!

Patient: She put up a big fuss at my brother's wedding. My brother just got married last year. She did not accept the wedding and she made a real ridicule at the wedding. Like when the father and mother walk up to the bride and groom, when they get to the doors she walked up, and they are supposed to hand wine and bread or something and the both sets of parents were supposed to shake hands and kiss each other, and my mother handed them the wine and she took off and made a scene in the hall.

Therapist: Now, what did you do after high school?

Patient: After high school I went to college. I went to university.

Therapist: And you majored in what?

Patient: After high school I had taken math and sciences. I had passed with good grades. I think I had the highest mark in geometry. I had a head on my shoulders, a damn good one. I wanted to go into university and I didn't know what I was going to take. They were pushing engineering at me ever since I was born. Everybody's son is an engineer. You have to be an engineer. I just didn't know what I was going to do. I didn't really care for math, you know, until my father asked me what I was going to do when I went into University. I didn't know. I didn't even have a job that first year so I knew that in order for me to go to school I would have to ask my father for some money. So, my parents came up to me and asked me one day what I was going to take and it was getting close to the end of school and I said I wanted to go into fine arts—from mathematics to fine arts. They didn't even discuss it. They just said, "You either take engineering or we are not paying for you and you have to get out!" I was sort of young when I started school. I started at five so I just turned sixteen when I started to go to University and it was a big thing. When your father and mother turn around and say, "If you don't take engineering, you have to get out!" what the hell was I going to do?

Therapist: So you took engineering?

Patient: So I took engineering and I failed every course.

Therapist: Did you graduate?

Patient: I failed every course in engineering and this school sent me a letter saying that I couldn't come back. I worked the next summer after that, at a job at $1.10 an hour. In the second year I got admitted again and I took science. I think I took six credits and passed four of them or something like that. I passed in those subjects that I really was interested in. I failed the ones like math and calculus and stuff like that. Anyway, I passed the first year, more or less by the skin of my teeth and then I quit. I quit and went to night school and I worked during the day.

Therapist: And this is what you have been doing lately?

Patient: No, I worked for awhile and then I had a big beef with my parents. They must have thought their house was a castle or something. "If you don't like it here, leave." And I was just getting fed up with listening to that "if you don't like it here, leave." So—

Therapist: Yet you stayed?

Patient: Ah?

Therapist: You stayed?

Patient: I was only eighteen then.

Therapist: I understand. But there was something, obviously, that influenced you to stay around. There was something that must have been appealing despite the difficulties.

Patient: It was a good . . . aside from all the difficulties, it was a good middle-class home. The food . . . my mother and father weren't alcoholics. The house was clean all the time and my mother had a very deep obsession for cleanliness. It wasn't that she liked the house clean. She was obsessed by it, you know. She would buy a new carpet and put plastic all around it and if you stepped off the plastic, you would get it.

Therapist: So obviously these traits appealed to you above and beyond the difficulties. Okay, now what has happened within the last two years? What are you doing now?

Patient: Well, now I am working as a technician. I work on shifts. I live in. I am just living.

Therapist: And you have been going out with your girlfriend.

Patient: Yes, for roughly two years.

Therapist: Now tell me . . . obviously, we have covered a great deal. As far as you are concerned if we were to put this whole thing in a nutshell, what would you say is the major problem? What would you want to understand about yourself? On what aspect do you want to concentrate? I am struck very much by your strengths and I am also struck by the tendency to give in, such as the suicide attempt or taking drugs or living at home. I understand perfectly well that a kid at a younger age, in particular, can't fight his parents but I don't think that is all. I think that there was something also enticing . . . something that you enjoyed in the relationship. Your mother's cleanliness, the good home, the kinds of talks that you had, nature. There was something in that relationship that was much more than met the eye, despite the difficult times. Now, you have a tendency to emphasize all the negative points, which I can understand, but I wonder, really, whether your attachment to your mother and your "mixed feelings," which is your word, reflect on your difficulties with women. What I mean is that you are still really attached to your mother. That you still have not solved that problem as yet. You smile. What about?

Patient: Well, it just seems that it is a bit like an example of the oedipus complex or something.

Therapist: Let us forget about the oedipus complex and what the books say. The fact is, is this the truth for you or not? That is what counts.

Patient: Yes, it's true. I *know* it is true. I find that the things I look for in a girl are most of the things that my mother possesses.

Therapist: Is your mother attractive?

Patient: She was attractive. I mean, I saw pictures of her when she was young. And I know that I prefer, out of all the girls I prefer blondes with blue eyes and my mother was blonde and blue-eyed. The biggest fights I had with my girlfriend were about her cleaning the house and my mother obsessed with cleanliness. I know this thing but I can't . . . I don't understand it.

Therapist: Okay, I would say this. In my opinion your motivation to try to understand all this is number one. I think we have seen it already here as you just told me. The second thing that I think might be a bigger problem is when you retreat—when you get passive. The "there is nothing I can do" attitude. I am not sure it is genuine. It is put on, and it is neurotic. It is put on and serves the purpose of making you stay close to your mother.

Patient: This is not generally genuine. I know you are right.

Therapist: Okay.

Patient: It was too much. I had to do something, and I became passive.

Therapist: Yes, but you know, this weakness—this passivity is a problem. The fact that you get to the point of cutting your wrists is a serious problem. Now, I think that you know all this. I don't have to tell you all this. Having a chance to go over these things in detail with someone might be a good idea. I have the impression that a great deal can be done. What do you think?

Patient: I think so too. I think inside of me is like a checkerboard where all the checkers are mixed up, and all they have to do is be put in the right places.

Therapist: Okay, with help you will place them where they belong. Good.

Patient: Okay, then. Thank you.

DISCUSSION

Dr. Malan

I was very impressed with this interview. Indeed, I was impressed with this young man, too. He seemed to have a lot in him. My feeling about this is that he fulfills most of the criteria. Quite likely, he fulfills the criteria for Short-Term Anxiety-Provoking Psychotherapy as well as mine. The thing that I am concerned about is the depth of the conflict that he must have about his mother. Sifneos brought out very beautifully the positive feelings that he had about his mother, and the attachment. The actual facts that he told about what his mother did worry me. This boy was making this desperate attempt to get some kind of recognition of his rights by slashing his wrists, and all she was concerned about was whether his feet were clean or not. There was no obvious bitterness, strangely enough, in all the things he said about his mother; but I get the feeling that to work through the degree of ambivalence which he must have about his mother would be a task beyond brief dynamic psychotherapy. I would be willing to have a go, perhaps. I just wouldn't be sure that this was feasible at all. Apart from that, he does fulfill the criteria. There is an obvious focus in the intense ambivalent attachment to his mother. His response to interpretation is . . . I wasn't sure about it until perhaps the very end when Sifneos said something about was his mother attractive, did he look for characteristics of his mother in his girlfriends? And he confirmed this in a most extraordinary way, the blond and blue eyes, and this kind of thing. Before that it didn't seem to me that he brought much in the way of unconscious material, and I'm even not sure that that was unconscious material. I am not entirely happy about a therapist's ability to get in touch with his unconscious, although I think probably it would be possible. His motivation seemed excellent to me. I am still worried about the nature of this problem as to whether it would really be possible to work it through in a short time.

Dr. Dongier

As was pointed out by Dr. Davanloo in his introductory paper, an excellent selection criterion is the patient's response to tentative interpretations. Now, what kind of interpretation? All interpretations have a major projective dimension; and it is quite interesting in this very beautiful interview to wonder about what is going on in the unconscious of the interviewer, which, of course, is the source of the trial interpretations given. I share Dr. Malan's doubts about what can be expected from brief psychotherapy with this patient. I got the feeling that he had deep masochistic tendencies, and I would be worried about that. When he slashes his wrists, even blood fails to work and speak for him! That is the message I am getting from him. And that would have been my own projection in my tentative interpretation: he is telling mother, "See what you have done to me," and the mother reacts in the most unpleasant way, "How clean are your feet?" So he is trying to show his mother what she did to him, and she doesn't understand the message. In the transference situation, whether in long-term intensive psychotherapy or in brief dynamic psychotherapy, we would have to face the same kind of repetition compulsion; and I would be afraid of not being able to deal with that on a short-term basis. In the same way the girlfriend accuses him of having murdered her baby. And that is what he did to his mother. He is showing his mother that *she* murdered her baby by provoking his suicidal attempt. He says, "There is a lot of my mother in me." That was his reply to the interviewer's question about his positive feelings towards his mother; there is a lot of femininity in his overall behavior. This work on his latent homosexual traits. I wonder to what extent it would have to be left aside in a brief dynamic therapy. So that if I had to vote, I would vote against accepting this patient in brief psychotherapy, in spite of his excellent motivation.

Dr. Sifneos

I don't know what Davanloo is going to tell us about this patient. Recapitulating the criteria for selection, I would agree with the two discussants that this patient is not a candidate for Short-Term Anxiety-Provoking Psychotherapy. As far as the second criterion is concerned—which involves the ability to demonstrate that the patient had *one* meaningful relationship with another person—I have been unable to find out any such give-and-take interaction. You heard the discussants clearly bring out the pregenital characterological issues, such as the sadomasochistic traits, the passive withdrawal, and so on. On that basis I would say that indeed he does not fulfill all our criteria for selection. As far as his motivation is concerned, I think it is excellent. There are also some additional elements which are difficult to describe. What I mean by this is the actual experience one has as he is interviewing a patient that even our wonderful videotapes cannot demonstrate completely. As I remember, I had a positive feeling about his interaction with me which I think was more evident during the live interview than you have been able to see on the tape. All in all I would like to see him once more. I want to assess more thoroughly his sadomasochism which was his opening gambit as we see in a chess game. I think that it was exaggerated. It is possible that because we heard so much about it, because he attempted to present to us this "poor me" images that he succeeded in giving us a false impression. It may all be some kind of a smoke-screen. If this is the case, and if he has learned a lesson, for example, that it is not nice to cut one's wrists and to take the passive position, it is possible that he deserves to be given a second chance. If we are not to accept this patient for STAP- because he is not a good candidate, I would like to ask Dr. Davanloo or Dr. Malan whether they would accept this patient for brief dynamic psychotherapy that may go on for about thirty interviews.

Dr. Davanloo

In terms of areas of disturbance, they do not seem to me to be circumscribed. He suffers from anxiety, disturbances in interpersonal relationships, conflict with authorities; and he said that in the face of aggression, "I just seem to crumble inside." He said, further, he is unable to stand up for himself in relation to men. There are also the issues of his sadomasochistic traits and deep-seated characterological issues which need to be understood.

One theme he presented to the evaluator was a stagnated relationship with a young woman whom he found unsatisfactory, going nowhere, and being unable to break off with her. He is stagnated socially, interpersonally.

In terms of a meaningful relationship, he does no fulfill this criterion from the material that emerges from this interview. Here we have a paradox. He interacted very well with the evaluator. He agreed with certain things and he disagreed with others. Is this by itself evidence that he must have had some meaningful relationship somewhere in the past, where he learned his ability to interact with someone in order to be able to repeat it with Dr. Sifneos? In our studies I have frequently been faced with patients who, according to their history, gave no indication of having had a meaningful relationship; yet they somehow or other came across in the interaction with the evaluator in the initial interview with a high score. This paradox needs to be looked into.

Another issue that needs to be clarified is the transference, which was not explored—the way he felt toward the interviewer. The

patient definitely put a heavy emphasis on the masochistic component. He emphasized very strongly the negative aspects of his
relationship with his mother. The transference implication of this,
the way he presented himself to the interviewer, was, "Poor me—I
am so anxious. Look at the terrible things that have happened to me."
But this was not brought into focus. It seems that there is a good
possibility that he had at one time a good relationship with his
mother, and this deteriorated totally after the birth of his younger
brother, who became "Mother's pet." The issue of his brother is very
important and needs full exploration. Was it that he had a very close
relationship with his mother in the very early years and when his
brother came into the picture his relationship with his brother
became a battle over their mother, and he lost her to him? and that
this is what infuriated him, and the relationship with his mother
became negative? Was it that in the early years he did beat up his
brother and then his mother would come into the picture and then he
would get a beating from her, and later on his brother got stronger
and became more powerful and the patient was the beaten one?
Then he had been castrated by both his mother and his brother, and
like his father was helpless and pushed into the corner, furious at both
his mother and his brother. With reference to his father, who was
passive and dependent, and the patient himself is passive and
dependent, what needs to be explored is to what extent did he push
his father out of the picture. Could one say he had castrated his father
as his mother did, that he had pushed him out completely? Something of interest is that his father is a butcher, and the patient
butchered himself. Obviously, from what he described his father
was castrated by his mother. What we don't know are his feelings for
his castrated father. Did he have some relationship with his father,
and then had sided with his mother and his father was then castrated?
Then, having allied with his mother, he suddenly lost her to his
brother—which means that now his father was castrated and out of
the picture, and the patient was the second. Then was his revenge
against his brother, his fury toward him? Then he struggled to
recapture the loss by complying with his mother, becoming passive,
and finally cut his hair short, which was still not good enough for her,
and, finally, in a massive rage toward his mother, he cut off all his hair
and then resorted to suicide by slashing his wrists and yelling for her
to come. This way he castrated himself and called his mother in.

Then came the humiliating situation where he was bleeding and his mother was washing his feet as she didn't want him to go to the hospital with dirty feet.

In terms of psychotherapeutic focus, I agree with Malan that the focus is in the intense ambivalent relationship with his mother; but to me the focus is not as simple as that. The psychotherapeutic focus is much more complicated, and the structure of the patient's neuroses is much more complicated than to say the core problem is related to one focus. In terms of the oedipal conflicts, which definitely play an essential role in the core problem of this patient, they are much more complicated. But a complicated oedipal psychotherapeutic focus is in no way a contraindication for Short-Term Dynamic Psychotherapy.

In summary, what I would want to do would be to evaluate the patient in two or three interviews to get a much clearer picture of this young man, who since age sixteen has been involved in drugs, has made a suicidal attempt, and is still living at home—all of which indicate that this man's biggest problem is his retreat. I would like to have an in-depth knowledge of this patient's problems before I would want to take him into Short-Term Dynamic Psychotherapy, and I would want to clarify some of the very important issues that Dr. Dongier mentioned in his discussion.

9

Evaluation and Selection

JUDD MARMOR, M.D.

THE CASE OF "THE LOSER"

The patient was thirty-three years old and sought psychiatric treatment, complaining of dissatisfaction with himself, lack of ambition, not knowing what he wants to do with his life, and problems in his job and in his marriage. He always managed to be the loser in any competitive situation, a reaction that ran like a thread throughout his life.

I was the interviewer. The interview lasted for fifty minutes, and I went into this interview having no information about this patient.

First we will present the edited transcript of that interview, as a background for the discussions to determine if this patient is a candidate for Short-Term Dynamic Psychotherapy.

From the proceedings of the Third International Symposium and Workshops in Short-Term Dynamic Psychotherapy, Los Angeles, 1977.

Therapist: Could you tell me what seems to be the problem?

Patient: Leading my life, if you will. I feel I have reached the age of thirty-three and have not accomplished as much as I would have liked to. I don't seem to have the aims or ambition and so on that are considered normal. (Pause.)

Therapist: You don't seem to have the aim and ambition, go ahead . . .

Patient: . . . which most people would consider normal ambition, okay? I want to get ahead and so on. But I don't really know myself, what happiness is, what I want out of life, what I expect of myself. I don't know where I have been, really, in the past, speaking objectively. So I came hoping that I would be able to get some kind of guidance or help or whatever in finding what I am and where I am going.

Therapist: How long have you been feeling this way?

Patient: For a fairly long period of time but more markedly so in the past several months, perhaps up to a year, and a dissatisfaction with myself.

Therapist: Did anything specific happen to mobilize these feelings?

Patient: Perhaps to a certain extent something which has probably contributed very greatly to it. I was going into a business venture, going into business for myself, something which I wanted to do for years, which fell through probably right around the time . . . it fell through in May, I believe, of last year. And that sort of, not necessarily demoralized me but I was fairly down because of that. That is probably one of the things which contributed greatly to it, I would say. Although, previously in my negotiations, naturally when things were going well, it looked like it was going to come about. I was pleased and so on, but previous to that again, on a couple of occasions in the past, I felt the same way.

Therapist: Has this kind of thing happened before where you were on the verge of accomplishing something that you wanted and then it fell through?

Patient: It is possibly happening to me again, right this very minute. Again a business venture which I am trying to set and it looks like I am going to have to go into it on a much smaller scale than I originally thought. There still may be some ways of pulling the hand out of the fire, if you will; but it looks somewhat discouraging as far as that goes, this is just a recent development in the last week or so. But on previous occasions, I have had a certain amount of instability in my employment and due basically to a dissatisfaction. I don't know whether I can really say dissatisfaction but disenchantment with what the job became to me, what it consisted of; therefore let it go and went onto something else. And initially only finding which I felt was better.

Therapist: Are these business ventures that you talk of, efforts to get on your own in some way?

Patient: Yes. I don't know why, but for a long time—ever since I can remember, really—I have felt that the best way to succeed in life is to succeed in your own business. These are really the only two concrete efforts that I have really made to go into being independent over the past couple of years or so.

The session now focused on the three attempts he has made to go into business for himself, all of which fell through, and then on his marriage. He has been married for seven years and his wife is pregnant. She was a lab technician but presently is not working. She is French-speaking, and he said they speak French at home. He said his wife was very dedicated to her job. Then the session examined the patient's work history. He had worked in three different companies as assistant sales manager. He left the last company a few weeks prior to the interview with the idea of going into a business venture. The evaluator questioned him. "You quit to go into business before its financing was completed?" The patient said he was dissatisfied with his job—"I may have quit somewhat prematurely." The evaluator then focused on the patient's background.

Therapist: Tell me a little about your background.

Patient: I was born in Edmonton. My father was transferred here to Montreal when I was ten years old. That would make it about twenty-three years ago. He works with the Canadian National.

Therapist: In what capacity?

Patient: I can never quite figure out what it is. It changes every now and then, and I can never catch on to what . . . and right now he has been transferred back to Edmonton.

Therapist: How large a family is it that you come from?

Patient: My brother and myself, that's all. There are two children.

Therapist: Older or younger?

Patient: Older, two and a half years older.

Therapist: And what kind of a person is your father?

Patient: I hesitate, don't I? To a certain extent some of the discussions that I have had with Dr. ———, for example, previous to meeting you, perhaps made me start to think a little bit more about the kind of person my father is. I respect my father very much. I love my father . . . both my parents. My . . . both of them are very outgoing, very sure of themselves, and so on. Very much the conversationalists, if you will. A house full of friends if they wanted it—they don't have people over all the time but very friendly and so on. My father is also very ambitious, very career oriented. He has always been successful in the generally accepted terms, financially and responsibility and so on.

Therapist: What kind of relationship have you had with him?

Patient: I always felt that my relationship with my father was, perhaps to use the term *ideal* is a little idyllical, but always very close. We even on occasion just get together, just the three of us, my brother, my father and myself, and spend a couple of days, just the boys, if you will, together. It hasn't happened in the last couple of years but when, with the family sort of separated, each one going their separate ways, we used to spend time together and so on fairly often. When I was younger my father spent a lot of time with my brother and myself in sports and so on. Stuck up a basketball net over the driveway and the three of us would play basketball and so on. I always felt my relationship with my father was very good.

Therapist: Did he have any favorites between you and your brother?

Patient: Only on one occasion do I remember perhaps feeling that my brother was being favorized, if you will. But perhaps . . . well, not perhaps, I have definitely felt that I am my brother's shadow, just a little in my life. All the way through school I was Frank's little brother, and so on. He was a better scholar, if you will. His marks in school were always better. His accomplishments in school were always, not necessarily better, but numerous. He was well known and well liked in the school and I always felt I had to try and do better than him, which I didn't always succeed at. I gave up golf the day that he came home with a better score. I took up tennis; he took up tennis, became better than me; I gave it up.

Therapist: What about your relationship to your mother?

Patient: My mother, although she has always played a fairly . . . it may seem contradictory, if I say it just the way I was formulating it there. Although she has always played a fairly active role in my life and in the family life, it has always been to a certain extent in the background. In that she was not necessarily subordinate to my father, but took a back seat, if you will. She was always consulted and offered opinions with decisions and so on made around the household, particularly concerning my brother and myself; but didn't play the decisive role, didn't make the final decision . . . not that my father was that aggressive or domineering or whatever, but to a certain extent . . .

Therapist: Now what about her. Did she have any favorites between you and your brother?

Patient: No, I would say that she was more objective, if you will. She didn't seem to have favorites.

Therapist: More objective than your father?

Patient: I suppose that is what I said, yes.

Therapist: So you felt your father did prefer your brother?

Patient: Well, I don't know whether I would go quite that far, but on a couple of occasions, one in particular. Yes, I noticed on a couple of occasions that he did seem to.

Therapist: On a couple of occasions?

Patient: Yes. Getting more and more numerous, eh?

Therapist: He was less objective than your mother, you mean?

Patient: That is a good way of putting it.

Therapist: Did he take pride in your brother's accomplishments versus yours, for example?

Patient: He took pride in both of our accomplishments. There was not really that much of a conflict because of the slight difference in stages of our life, if you will. My brother's accomplishments . . . he accomplished everything before I did because he was a little bit older than I, throughout school and so on. Although my father, none the less, showed pride in my accomplishments also. At least to the best of my memory.

Therapist: You are not sure?

Patient: I can't really remember any great praise that my father ever gave me.

Therapist: What does your brother do now?

Patient: He is working for a textile manufacturer of some kind as a product manager. He . . . one of his accomplishments which I am sure my father was very proud of, recently he had the guts to quit work with a wife and so on and go back to school and get his master's degree. This has allowed him to move up in his job.

Therapist: That is a pretty good job as far as you are concerned.

Patient: From what I understand, yes.

Therapist: He is married?

Patient: That is right.

Therapist: Children?

Patient: He has one son who would be a little more than a year old.

Therapist: What kind of a relationship do you have with him?

Patient: At this stage, perhaps largely due to the distance between us, we very seldom see each other or talk to each other. Always very friendly but . . . when we do see him, but I must admit somewhat distant, perhaps. When we were at home we never really had any great arguments or fights or anything, but we are not as close as we could have been.

Therapist: Are you different in personality?

Patient: I don't really know my brother that well, frankly, to say what his personality is today at any stage. He . . . when we were younger, seemed to be, perhaps, a little bit more aggressive and so on than I. I imagine that has carried through in to today that he is still not overly aggressive but enough so to succeed, if you will, in his career, and of course it takes a lot of aggression sometimes to succeed.

Therapist: What kind of relationship did you have when you were youngsters?

Patient: When we were very young, my mother tells the story of how we were close to the extent that if somebody picked on one of us, the other one would jump on his back, kind of thing. That must have been quite awhile ago because I can never remember that.

Therapist: What do you remember?

Patient: When we were younger, we always played together. I often . . . the basketball net that I mentioned earlier, I used to often play with him and his friends in the driveway with the basketball net. We used to be on a baseball team together when we were younger, organized teams and so on with children. We were fairly active together; I wouldn't say necessarily close, though. A lot closer than we were in later years, but still that was perhaps . . . I don't think we were particularly aware of being particularly close.

Therapist: Were you aware of being competitive with him?

Patient: Not really until high school.

Therapist: What happened then?

Patient: That was really the first occasion where somebody actually said to me, "Ah, yes. You are Frank's brother"—one of the teachers I had the first day. That rankled me. I didn't like being considered the kid brother kind of thing. My brother was very active in many different things in school. And as a consequence, I was even more active. I did just about everything you could possibly do. I was in the orchestra, I was in the band, I was on the football team, the soccer team, the wrestling team, basketball team, name it—I did just about everything you could possibly do. Never really excelled at it, at any one except perhaps at wrestling but . . .

Therapist: You were determined to outdo him?

Patient: Subconsciously, I think so.

Therapist: You weren't aware of it at the time? Go ahead, you were telling me more.

Patient: That is about it.

The evaluator focused on their scholastic achievements. His brother had a much higher average and entered a top-rated university while he ended up at a small university.

Therapist: Was he a particularly good student?

Patient: Not particularly good, I would say, but he worked at it, whereas I didn't.

Therapist: What happened at college?

Patient: I dropped out after three years.

Therapist: Why was that?

Patient: Because I found I was spending more time in the men's lounge playing and so on. I felt that I was wasting my time. First of all, the degree that I was going after, a generalized arts degree, was not really that valid and that I was . . . I may not end up getting it in the long run. And even if I did, it wouldn't do me that much good.

Therapist: Were you unhappy at having to go to a smaller university?

Patient: The only reason I really went to university was because everybody else was. So I wasn't really unhappy with going there.

Therapist: You didn't feel that you had had to settle for second best?

Patient: Not necessarily. I don't remember feeling that way. As I say, one of the reasons I ended up playing rather than studying was because I was somewhat indifferent to going to university in the first place.

Therapist: But of course, being indifferent is a kind of giving up, isn't it?

Patient: Yes.

Therapist: And I am wondering why you gave up. And you gave up golf when your brother hit a lower score and you gave up tennis when he played better. It sounds as though you have been giving up on a lot of things because you couldn't do as well, or thought you couldn't do as well, as he could.

Patient: It does sound that way, doesn't it?

Therapist: What else have you given up on?

Patient: I look back over several things that have happened to me throughout my life and I wonder whether I have not given up on myself. That is one of the reasons that brought me here. To find a goal in life, to be able to . . . not necessarily to make something out of myself because I can only do that myself, the help that I could perhaps get here would be reestablishing myself with myself, reconciling myself with myself, finding out what "myself" is.

Therapist: That sounds like a giving-up attitude—reconciling yourself with yourself.

Patient: Yeah, I like the first one better.

Therapist: I think your coming here is a sign that you are not giving up entirely.

Patient: I hope so.

Therapist: Maybe that is the first step in reversing this pattern of giving up.

Patient: I hope it is not the last step.

Therapist: So, you grew up as a younger brother in the shadow of what appeared to be a successful older brother and you found it difficult to compete with him. You also had a father that you considered rather successful and an outstanding person. You felt your brother was cast in the image of your father much more than you were.

Patient: He even looks more like him than I do.

Therapist: Did you feel that when you were young?

Patient: No, not as far as the looks and so on go. I never really felt competitive to my father; although I did feel competitive to my brother on several occasions when I was younger. Even today, I find that to a large extent I am competing, I think, with my brother in my father's image—in my father's eye, if you want.

Therapist: Do you think your wish to go into business on your own and make a success is part of the need to prove yourself in some way?

Patient: Yes.

Therapist: The last few occasions have been a little disappointing, or at least . . .

Patient: We are still hanging onto this one.

Therapist: When you left college, did you make any effort to pursue your education any further, or did you just—

Patient: Yes, I followed several courses at night and so on. After I left I . . . up until I worked with the . . . last two years I have been working with the ——— company, I have been going back fairly regularly taking night courses and so on.

Therapist: For credit, or . . .

Patient: Yes. Primarily, marketing or economics oriented. A few courses in psychology and sociology and so on, but primarily towards marketing. Perhaps oriented that way because I am in sales, so . . .

Therapist: Now, let's turn to another side of your life. The social and sexual side. Tell me a little more about how that is.

Patient: Okay. Social side of our life as a couple, my wife and myself, is nil. We seldom visit or have people over and so on.

Therapist: You seldom have people over, you say?

Patient: Yes. The last time we had people over to our place, maybe a year ago.

Therapist: Is there any reason for that?

Patient: My wife puts it very bluntly in saying that she doesn't like people. That's very much of an oversimplification. But . . . at least I like to think it is. But she doesn't like . . . she doesn't enjoy sitting around, just sitting around doing nothing and talking to people and so on. The last time that we . . . as a matter of fact, it wasn't too long ago, I had almost forgotten about that . . . we went out with another couple. We simply went bowling and we hadn't been bowling for years. And it was her idea, as a matter of fact. And I enjoyed it thoroughly. That really is the only social contact as such, aside from dinner at the sister-in-law's every now and then, or dropping over to the in-laws which is something that she does more frequently. It is really the only kind of social life that we lead. My social life is a little bit more active than hers in that I am in sales. It requires a certain amount of socializing during the day. I also travel or used to; I therefore would find myself alone in a hotel room at night, which I didn't particularly enjoy, so I would end up downstairs or something in a discotheque or in a bar and socialize. I am more socially active than my wife in that aspect. She will occasionally go with a girlfriend of hers or have lunch and so on.

Therapist: Do you have any close friends?

Patient: I have two friends that I consider close friends, yes. Although, for some reason, I don't know why, I don't see them very often. One of them, I haven't seen for, gee, I don't know how long. The other one is the other couple that I mentioned we went bowling with. Him, I will see maybe once a month or so.

Therapist: Are you disappointed in your wife's reactions to social life?

Patient: To a certain extent, yes. I would just as soon do something every now and then. I would like to have people over every now and then and so on. Go out to other people's places, which we do occasionally, but not as regularly as I would like to say.

Therapist: Do you resent it?

Patient: At first, perhaps. To use a worn out expression, I have learned to live with it. I accept it and since that time I have become, as I say, more active myself socially.

Therapist: Tell me how you met your wife and how your life was before you met her.

Patient: I met her on a blind date where I was working at a summer job.

Then the session focused on his wife, who was academically oriented and the vice president of her class. She was shy. He said he ended up on a blind date with her. He was a student and had flunked out his first year. After they had dated for some time they broke up. He dated many girls for a while and then again met his future wife. They had known each other for six years before they married. He said there had been problems throughout their marriage, sexual problems from the very beginning. His wife does not enjoy sex. At the present time she is pregnant, and the evaluator asked him, "Were you trying to have a baby?" The patient replied, "Yes. It wasn't an accident." He said he has an active sex life outside his marriage, "moreso in the last couple of months." He has a number of girlfriends, "a couple of ladies and girls" he sees every now and then. He said he has no sexual difficulties. Then the evaluator asked if he and his wife had been in treatment, and the patient said yes.

Therapist: What kind of therapy?

Patient: The first year we were married, after about six months we started therapy with a psychologist with a group that lasted for about a year and we didn't feel we got anything from it. The next year, for a period of two years, we were in therapy with the psychiatry department of another hospital here in Montreal. And that helped us a lot in that we now are able to talk to each other much more openly, perhaps understand each other a little bit better, but not necessarily help us as far as the sexual problems that we have had.

Therapist: You haven't sought any help with regard to your sexual problems?

Patient: This was the aim of it. This is what we thought we were getting when we, to a certain extent, when we went to these things. But they didn't . . . it worked out to a certain extent, but with no real great success.

Therapist: The last time being, what? Several years ago?

Patient: It would have . . . when did it finish? It would have been almost two years ago, I suppose, yes.

Therapist: You say, you finished? Were you going alone?

Patient: No. I said, I believe it finished, the course finished or whatever.

Therapist: I see. Do you feel as though you have given up on it now?

Patient: You are getting back to giving up on things, eh? I have almost given up on it, I must admit. In the seven, or almost seven years we have been married, I have . . . my wife has not as yet had a climax. Not once in her adult life has she climaxed, which to me is an important thing for, not only for her, but for myself. It is good for the male ego and she is perhaps somewhat insensitive towards me sexually.

Therapist: You have never sought out actual sex therapy?

Patient: As such, no.

Therapist: Have you read anything about it?

Patient: Very little.

Therapist: With other women, you have no problem?

Patient: No.

Therapist: Before marriage, you had no problem?

Patient: No.

Therapist: How do you feel about your marriage? Are you disappointed?

Patient: Yes. I can't help but feel somewhat adamantly, less passionately about my wife as I did when we were first, we first knew each other. Marriage has lost a lot of its flair. We are friends, almost as though we are boarders in the same house. We talk to each other and so on but . . .

Therapist: How do you feel about her being pregnant under these circumstances?

Patient: A little bit . . . how can I put it . . . mixed feelings. I have never at all been . . . a lot of people, from what I understand, I don't know, I never had any personal experience or discussions with other couples but many people try to save their marriage by having children. This was not our intention. We decided that we would try to have a child.

Therapist: What was your intention?

Patient: That we both felt that we were ready, if you will. We never really felt—we wanted children, but not to the extent—we felt we were ready, that we, at this stage in our lives . . . it would be good for both of us. Perhaps, therefore, good for our marriage, but not necessarily with the marriage in mind when . . .

Therapist: How old is your wife?

Patient: Twenty-nine. She will be thirty this summer.

Therapist: All right, we have run out of time so we will have to stop at this point.

Dr. Eisenstein

We saw an excellent interview, which was to be expected from Judd Marmor. I think he did not leave anything unturned. We also saw a very interesting patient, a very good patient. There are two questions I have. Of course, Dr. Marmor focused on the sibling rivalry, and it was very clear it was there. There were two and a half years between the two brothers. But I wonder how much this intense rivalry with the brother is used as a displacement from competition with his father. When he talked about his father he referred to him as very successful. He is trying to minimize, probably, what is a threatening oedipal competition. I am not dismissing the sibling rivalry; it is there—we all saw it, but he is regressing to a sibling competition as defense against the oedipal competition. The other issue I would like to raise is the suitability of this patient for brief psychotherapy. Here we have to guess. Yes, he suffers, but he is not hurting that much. He is angry that he is not successful, and he is also probably sad underneath it all. But I wonder whether he is not going to do to the therapy what he does with everything else in life. He will try it and then he will give that up too. And then I raise the question: Would a short psychotherapeutic approach hold a man like this? To me this looks like a man who needs to establish, first of all, a working alliance with the therapist—a good strong working alliance in order to keep him in therapy. And of course, this is going to be a very difficult transference. I don't deny he could be treated with a relatively short approach but from what we saw now, it looks to me that it would take a good deal of involvement with the therapist to hold this man in therapy.

Dr. de la Torre

It is difficult to disengage oneself from the pleasure of witnessing such an empathic and sensitive interview, in order to keep in mind the object of our task, which is to try to make some sort of predictive assessment regarding how the patient would respond to short-term psychotherapy. Dr. Marmor conducted the interview with a great deal of gentleness, allowing the patient to follow his own pace and avoiding direct confrontations in order to nurture the therapeutic alliance. Although aware of the nuances of the patient's dynamics, he made his comments gently, as soft suggestions, to which the patient responded quite well.

It was noticeable how at times the patient's reactions were more telling than his verbal communications. For instance, when Dr. Marmor asked him about his father, the patient hesitated, obviously having been touched on an area loaded with anxiety. On a couple of different occasions, when the interviewer mentioned the issue of giving up, there was a change in the patient's reactions. Up to that point, he had been very engaging and appearing comfortable, cool, but on those occasions he became serious and reflective, indicating a capacity and a potential for psychological work that he had not displayed earlier.

Such an interview, it seems to me, ought to be complemented with another one in which some of the issues that were touched upon or only tangentially came up today, could be more specifically followed. One would like to know what was the general effect of this interview on the patient, what amount of curiosity was stirred up by the interaction with the therapist, and how he responded to the interviewer's empathy. Does he remember what went on and the topics of the interview? Was there any particular area that got the patient to think in more psychological depth? Is there any indication about the fate of the dynamic issues that were mentioned in this initial interview that indicates the beginning of a potential "focus" for further work? Was the patient looking forward to a second interview with some indication of increased motivation and greater readiness to do psychological work, or is he going to cover up with denial and repression and go about his merry life as if the session never took place?

Two important issues still remain unclear and will need careful assessment in subsequent interviews. One is how the patient handles his anger and, particularly, how he handles his rivalry. We know that some of his intense competition and rivalry with his older brother was displaced into a great deal of activity with his peers during his school years. The pressure under which he had to compete in all possible athletic activities was very telling. The interview with Dr. Marmor brought that out quite convincingly. The other area of great interest that Dr. Marmor opted not to focus on was the patient's real feeling and concern about his sexual life. We know that he presents himself with a superficial facade of being like a sailor with a girl in every port, but what is really underneath? He wanted to exhibitionistically impress the interviewer with his success, but further exploration in this area and particularly in relation to his present wife will deserve further scrutiny.

Dr. Malan

I am sure we are all extremely impressed with this interview. I was. I think that, as an example of how not to push yourself forward and yet to make just the right comment at the right moment, this interview just couldn't be better. When you have a really beautiful interview like that it seems almost wrong to add questions that you feel weren't answered. There is one minor one and one major one that I would like to raise. The minor one, which doesn't really matter so very much, is: this patient gave a very clear clue that he knew that there was something wrong with his relationship with his father. He kept saying, "I always thought I had a good relation with my father." I would have picked up on that and explored it. I don't think it terribly matters because we know very well that if this patient was taken into therapy, you probably would start with the rivalry with the brother and this would lead to the problems with the father and you can leave that to the future. He seems to have had a basically good relationship with his father, so we don't need to worry.

The second thing which I would have wanted to have asked this patient—I think it is the more crucial one—namely, did he know that his wife was basically frigid before he married her? If he didn't, then, well, all right, you can say this was bad luck, in a way. But I don't believe this was so. This is an actively sexual man. He must have known this before he married her; yet he married her. He set up for himself the profoundest disappointment. The prognosis for someone like that, I think, becomes a bit more doubtful. What on earth is he up to, marrying a frigid woman deliberately? And ending up in the current situation by getting her pregnant deliberately, thus cementing the marriage and storing up an enormous amount of trouble for himself in the future? Well, I suppose the answer is that you could put this into an oedipal focus as well and say that he felt himself unable to have a properly fulfilled relationship with someone he could marry; he could only have relations with casual girlfriends. Maybe this is true. Maybe it isn't. I would want to know about that.

My final comment is that I think that the speakers so far, in trying to apply our criteria to this patient, are ignoring the overall situation. Yes, indeed, I think this is a patient who can work in psychotherapy. I would think that there is every indication that he is that kind of patient; but the setup is not at all a favorable one. Here he is, locked in an unsatisfactory marriage with a baby on the way. You cannot treat that situation by treating the patient, himself, alone. And I am sure Judd, in fact, was working toward that—he asked whether the

couple had ever had sex therapy. It seems to me that it would be
totally inappropriate to put it all upon this man, as a patient in his own
right—what the hell is going to happen at the end of that time? He is
going to maybe overcome his problems about success, but he is
going to be left with as bad a situation as ever. He is maybe going to
be put in touch with his anger about it. I don't think that is going to do
anybody any good. I think his wife needs help. So I am by no means
certain that the treatment of choice for this situation, as opposed to
this patient, is short-term psychotherapy of any kind. I think that
both the wife and the husband need help and the next step is that the
wife must be seen and the depth of her frigidity somehow assessed.
And it sounds to me as though it is very deep. She never had a climax
in her adult life, according to the patient. Of course, is it just a
reaction to this particular man? If it is just a reaction to this particular
man, then there is much more hope of dealing with it. If she is deeply
incapable of responding sexually to a man, then the couple is in
trouble. And this has got to be taken into account. From the dynamics, as Dr. Marmor has demonstrated in this interview, it is very clear
that this man has taken the role of being the loser; and he has played
this role very well throughout his life. He, himself, said he has given
up on himself. The question is, what brought this individual at this
particular point in time to seek help? Dr. Marmor brought into focus
the factor of his job failures, but one wonders if there is not another
factor—the pregnancy, and when the baby is due. His wife is going
to give birth to his "older sibling." And that could present a difficult
problem for him—finding himself even more on the outside.

Dr. Davanloo

There are a number of comments I would like to make. The first has
to do with the technique of the interview. It was very nice to follow
Dr. Marmor's ability to use a combination of open-ended and
forced-choice questions. For example, at one point he said, "Tell me
something about your background." And he said, "Tell me something about your marriage," again open-ended. The other set of
questions were the forced-choice questions, "Do you resent your
wife's attitude about the social issue?" Obviously, each of us does this
kind of thing in our own way. But this technique is of crucial
importance when we are evaluating the patient in technique to utilize

these two types of questions or interpretations to see, in a sense, the patient's responses. And I thought Dr. Marmor demonstrated this beautifully. One thing that came to my mind is that this man has always managed to be the loser, and this was brought into focus by Dr. Marmor—that being the loser goes like a thread throughout his life. But the question is, did he manage to repeat that in the interaction between himself and Dr. Marmor? He was very apologetic, and he was passive, repeatedly useing phrases such as "if you will," "if . . .", and "so to speak." There are many paradoxes he brought into the session, and one wonders what would have happened if Dr. Marmor had confronted him with his pattern of interaction with him—not only linking the current and the past, but also linking the current and the past with his transference responses. In any interview the evaluator has two major tasks. One is to gather as much historical data as he can, and the other is to establish a dynamic psychotherapeutic focus or foci. One of the foci Dr. Marmor established was sibling rivalry, the patient as the defeated younger brother. Obviously there are areas that need to be explored. His relationship with his mother needs to be explored and understood. The area of his relationship with his wife—did he know she was frigid?—as pointed out by Malan. One area Dr. Marmor did not focus on is the patient's anger, both current and past.

In terms of criteria for selection, from what I saw in this interview I would be inclined to say that his problem is more or less circumscribed. It seems he had a meaningful relationship with his father. Of course, we don't know much about his relationship with his mother. He interacted with Dr. Marmor very well. He was in touch with his feelings; there was definitely an emotional interaction between the patient and Dr. Marmor. He is definitely sophisticated. In terms of the psychotherapeutic focus, there was certainly sibling rivalry; there is the issue of failure in competition with men. Regarding the triangular oedipal focus, one needs to explore a number of issues. I would be very interested to know about the issue of competition with his father in relation to his mother. Was he very disappointed with his mother and turned to his father and brother, and then had to retreat in failure because they were so superior to him? We see the same pattern being repeated, in a sense, with his wife.

In terms of Short-Term Dynamic Psychotherapy, nothing succeeds like success. And it seems that a successful short-term dynamic psychotherapy would do more for the patient than going into long-term therapy. Contrary to Dr. Eisenstein's point, a strong psycho-therapeutic alliance is not necessarily a feature of long-term dynamic psychotherapy. In my opinion, a strong psychotherapeutic alliance is one of the major features in Short-Term Dynamic Psychotherapy; a strong psychotherapeutic alliance, both conscious and unconscious, is a major ingredient in all of our successful cases.

In terms of the psychotherapeutic planning, it seems to me that as far as he himself is concerned, he is a candidate for Short-Term Dynamic Psychotherapy. But at the same time I agree with Dr. Malan that the approach to this man's problem must be a multi-dimensional one. Who knows—it might be that his wife is also a candidate for a brief dynamic approach.

Dr. Marmor

I agree with the comments by Dr. Davanloo regarding the patient's relationship with his mother and the need to explore that further. In this case, it seems quite clear that the dominant parent in this family was the father. So that even though there must have been develop-mentally a strong attachment to the mother to begin with, I think as this boy developed and became more aware of the relationships in the family, he had to want the approval of the father more than that of the mother. This became a very important factor in the whole pattern of his life, in his rivalry with his brother, in his effort to achieve more as a man, and in his own pattern of masculine inadequacy.

Dr. Eisenstein raised another very perceptive question and this is, "Is this man going to be unstable in treatment also? Is he going to give up in the treatment also?" I think that is a very real possibility and you may note that one of the things I tried to do in this initial interview also was to give him a corrective emotional experience, a little one, it is true, but nevertheless, a beginning. When he said, "I guess I am giving up. I guess I give up everywhere," after that I jumped in and said, "But isn't the fact that you are coming here a sign that you haven't entirely given up?" I gave him an ego supportive interpreta-tion and I did it deliberately because I felt that in the transference, a father figure, it was terribly important that I become a supportive and approving father figure, not one who is going to repeat the discouraging feelings that he had in his own relationship to his father.

Dr. de la Torre mentioned the ingratiating quality of this patient, that is certainly true. He has a salesman's personality and he demonstrates that in the transference relationship. I am sure that would come up in subsequent interviews in terms of transference interpretation. Dr. de la Torre also raised the question of whether he has a capacity for insight, whether he had a tendency to cover up. I think he does cover up but I had the feeling that he did have a capacity for insight. Dr. de la Torre mentioned a very important thing; and that is his readiness to give up on his marriage just as he gave up tennis and golf and college. I think that is a terribly important issue to be carried further in the therapeutic process. Another example of this pattern of his that Dr. Davanloo and Dr. Malan and others have subsequently mentioned, a point on which we would try to focus therapeutically, is that of doing something about this sexual disappointment rather than giving up on it. I think I have covered the issue of the disappointment with the mother and the turning to the father and the brother raised by Dr. Davanloo. That may well be due to the fact that the mother was not the strong one in the family. This inevitably propelled this man, I think, to turn to the source of strength as children do. They identify with the aggressor and with the source of power. Dr. Malan's point about the relationship with the father should have been explored further, certainly, and would have been had there been more time for a second interview. But I think that at least I identified the issue there and knew that it had to be carried further.

Did he know that his wife was frigid before he married her? A very important point and if we can identify that and clarify it, it might well be another way in which he set himself up for defeat. I don't know whether his wife was totally anorgasmic. Many women who never have an orgasm in intercourse do have orgasms in masturbation and that would be something that would have to be clarified further. My own impulse with this man would be to work with him individually first, and only after he had sufficiently identified his loser syndrome and his tendency to give up would I then feel he was ready and sufficiently understanding to proceed with conjoint therapy or sex therapy and make a more effective relationship out of his marriage. The question of whether the impending birth of a new sibling might not be a factor in bringing him to therapy was a good one. It might very well have been. I think it is a perceptive comment that needs to be looked into further. My initial impression, which may not prove to be correct, was that he saw another disaster looming in the winds. He had gone forward on the new business project. He thought he was going to get rich, surpass his brother, and make a big thing. So he went ahead, prematurely gave up his job, and now he had an imminent sense of profound repetitive defeat coming on him. I think the recognition that there was something seriously wrong with his life pattern was beginning to sink in and it was this, I think, that brought him to treatment with the kind of request that we have often identified as a basis for analytic therapy: that is, "There is something wrong with my life pattern and I think I have to do something about it." But even though this may very well ultimately lead into longer-term therapy, I agree with Dr. Davanloo that there is a great deal that can be done for this kind of patient on a short-term basis.

10

Criteria for Selection

David H. Malan, M.D.

THE CASE OF THE PASSIVE SECRETARY

The patient is a twenty-four-year-old secretary. She came complaining of depression, and disturbances in interpersonal relationships, specifically in relation to men. Her marriage had ended in divorce, and she is currently living with a married man with whom she is very passive. She has an inability to assert herself, fearful she will lose him if she does so. The interview was conducted by myself and lasted for ninety minutes. The edited transcript of that interview is presented here to provide a background for discussion of whether this patient is a candidate for Short-Term Dynamic Psychotherapy.

The evaluator started the session by telling the patient he did not know anything about her and asking what brought her to seek help.

From the proceedings of the Third International Symposium and Workshops in Short-Term Dynamic Psychotherapy, Los Angeles, 1977.

Patient: Why I am coming here? When I started to live with this guy, I can't explain it . . . I have a hard time explaining myself to . . . I just get the feeling sometimes that I am . . . you know . . . like you get frustrated. And I need help, you know. And then, am I doing the right thing? And am I doing what I want? And then I say, "No. No. No." Then I love him, and I want to stay with him.

Therapist: Yes.

Patient: Then you sort of have to say . . . well . . . if I love, and I want to stay with him, I will just have to put up with what happens and what goes on.

At this point the evaluator explored the patient's psychiatric history. She had never undergone psychiatric treatment before. Her main symptom was depression. Further exploration was made to determine the severity of her depression. She said she has suffered from depression for about two years. Further exploration brought out that at its worst she sits and cries for perhaps twenty minutes at a time. Subsequently she feels better. Asked if she knows why she cries, she said she usually does and that it usually follows a fight with Carl, the man she is living with. She said she had made one suicidal gesture. One night, on an impulse, she took some aspirin and had not told Carl and had gone to bed and slept it off. None of this seemed to be in any way alarming. Then the evaluator explored phobic symptomatology. She did not suffer from any serious phobia, but she did talk about a recurrent dream.

Patient: I have dreams of being trapped in an elevator, just an elevator for one person. It is going up and down like a wild ride. Then the door opens, and I am just sort of holding on. And the elevator is going, and there is a tunnel—and I am just hanging on. I have had that (dream) a few times.

Therapist: You are afraid of falling out?

Patient: Yeah.

Therapist: Again, is that a thing . . .

Patient: But this doesn't bother me. It doesn't stop me from getting in an elevator.

Therapist: I think that clears up that area of questioning. That is fine. Let's go back. What you are saying . . . something about coming here because, although you love this guy, Carl, something is going wrong. There is a part of you that feels you want to get out of the relationship. Is this right?

Patient: Not that I want to get out. It is just that I think it could be better. He has two children which he insists—well, he doesn't insist, but he has to see three days a week and then plays hockey once a week and he plays basketball once a week, and I am saying that you have so much going for you, you don't really have time to spend with me. And he will say, "Well, you knew that it was going to be like that until it can change. You just sort of have to live with it." And by change, he means the time when he can bring his children over for the weekend or . . . but he is not ready to do that.

Therapist: Do you foresee there is any likelihood that he ever will be?

Patient: I certainly hope so. He says, yes, there will be. I think so. It is just that his wife won't let him right now and he is not ready to push it, I guess.

Therapist: So he is still living at home with his wife.

Patient: No, he is living with me but he goes over there to see his children. And when he goes, she goes out. He spends the evening with them. And then all day Sunday and he spends the evening with them.

Therapist: So he is still married?

Patient: Yes.

Therapist: So it sounds as if what you are saying is that you are getting frustrated because you don't see enough of him.

Patient: Yes. And then when I do see him I am afraid that he is going to be bored and thinking about the kids and feeling guilty, which he does. I am mixed up. You know, like I want to spend more time with him and I am afraid it is going to bother him not . . . like I was in the hospital. I had an operation, and they did the operation one night and the next night he said he couldn't come to visit me because that was the night he was to see his kids, and I thought he could have come to see me in the hospital and told them, "I'll see you tomorrow."

Therapist: Yes.

Patient: But he said he couldn't come and see me because I understand why he couldn't come but his children wouldn't understand why he couldn't go over.

Therapist: Do they know about you?

Patient: No.

Therapist: They don't. And so what does that make you feel?

Patient: That they don't know about me?

Therapist: No. No, I am going back to that he didn't come and visit you because you would understand and they wouldn't.

Patient: Yeah, but I thought that he could explain to them that he was going to see a friend in the hospital.

Therapist: Yeah. So . . .

Patient: I was quite upset about that.

Therapist: Did you express it to him or not?

Patient: Yes, I did.

Therapist: How?

Patient: I said, "You could have come to see me in the hospital and you could have explained to them that you are going to see a friend."

Therapist: How did he react?

Patient: He gets a little upset, like, you know, "You should understand. They don't."

Therapist: One of the things that is happening is that you are finding it impossible to fight your battles with him, aren't you?

Patient: Yes.

Therapist: It is sounding rather as if you want us to fight your battle for you.

Patient: Well, if I have something to say to him, I'll say it.

Therapist: But it doesn't work, does it? That is what the trouble is.

Patient: How could you fight my battle for me?

Therapist: I don't think we could. It might be that that is what . . . underneath you are really wanting from us. There is certainly a problem there, isn't there? You have got a battle to fight and perhaps it might be true that you have always had difficulty in fighting your battles, have you?

Patient: You mean like sticking up for myself.

Therapist: That is just what I mean. Have you?

Patient: Yeah, I would say so.

Therapist: How has this shown itself in the course of your life?

Patient: I won't bother, you know . . . I will just sort of give up and say, "Okay, fine."

Therapist: And then what?

Patient: I don't really know what you are—

Therapist: What I am really meaning is that it must come out in some other way. You say you give up and you say, "Okay, fine." How did it come out?

Patient: I don't really know. I have never really thought about it like that.

Therapist: You must go . . . It starts by giving up and then you must feel frustrated and resentful inside yourself and this must express itself somehow.

Patient: Usually if I feel that way, I just cry and then I feel fine after.

Therapist: You cry.

Patient: Yeah.

Therapist: By yourself or . . .

Patient: By myself.

Therapist: The trouble with crying like that is you may feel better but it doesn't solve the situation.

Patient: No.

Therapist: Perhaps we had better go back to your marriage. Can you tell me something about this? Can you tell it to me from the beginning? I feel that something similar quite likely may have happened in your marriage and this is how it will happen again.

Patient: I was going out with the guy I married for about . . . since I was about sixteen until we got married; I was about nineteen. We were married for about five years.

Therapist: Yes.

Patient: And then I met Carl. And then I told my husband I wanted a divorce. I didn't want to stay married any longer; I had met someone that I loved and I couldn't see the point in staying with him. Even if I didn't . . . if Carl and I didn't stay together, I wouldn't want to stay married to my husband.

Therapist: That must mean, though, that something had begun to go wrong already, mustn't it? Otherwise you wouldn't have looked elsewhere?

Patient: I think I married him because it was . . . all my friends were getting married. When you figure . . . you are nineteen, I'll never get married and I had never really gone out with other guys before.

Therapist: Yes.

Patient: He was the only guy . . . except, you know . . . no, I had never gone out with other guys before. So he was there and . . .

Therapist: Yes. And the trouble with that is that one doesn't really know . . . one doesn't really have the experience of a lot of different men from whom one can choose. You picked . . . just picked the one that you had known since the age of sixteen. So what happened between you? How did it go? Can you tell me?

Patient: You mean our marriage?

Therapist: Yes.

Patient: It was okay. He worked shift. I was alone a lot. I found it very hard when we first got married. I was from a . . . well, I had three sisters . . . a large family and we lived and they lived quite a distance away and I would come home at night and the house would be empty. I had a hard time to adjust.

Therapist: Yes.

Patient: But I did get used to it. And it wasn't . . . it was okay. Nothing fantastic, really. And then I just met Carl and that was it.

Therapist: I do see something which is repeating itself, because you don't see enough of Carl because he has got all sorts of other activities like his children and . . .

Patient: . . . and sports.

Therapist: . . . and sports, exactly. And the same kind of thing seems to have happened with your husband as well.

Patient: Uh-huh. Yeah. He worked on the weekends too. But before that . . . before we got married, I saw him every night and then he got this job working in downtown and then he started working shift work.

Therapist: Is that after you got married?

Patient: Just before we got married, he got the job.

Therapist: Well, that means that the . . . that at the point at which you got married, in fact, you lost a large part of him. Isn't that true?

Patient: Uh-huh.

Therapist: So one could well imagine you have been very dissatisfied, and let's say disappointed.

Patient: Yes. But I couldn't see myself spending the rest of my life with him; even though I think I had adapted to him working shift, I don't think I loved him. That's it. I couldn't see spending my life with him.

Therapist: When did you discover that?

Patient: That was only after I met Carl that I realized.

Therapist: Yes. What is the difference between the two men? Why do you prefer Carl to your husband?

Patient: That is a very hard question. I know his feelings for me. He is not afraid of expressing them.

Therapist: Can we get your husband a name too?

Patient: Jim.

Therapist: That is different from Carl, was it?

Patient: Uh-huh.

Therapist: Did Jim have difficulty in expressing his feelings?

Patient: I don't know if he had difficulty; he just never did.

Therapist: He never did? Even before you were married?

Patient: No, he just never . . . no. A difference . . .well, sex is a lot better. I mean I don't know if . . . to me that is important in a relationship.

Therapist: Yes, this is important. In what way is it better?

Patient: I just enjoy it more. I am more interested.

Therapist: Why?

Patient: I guess because I find Carl more attractive physically.

Therapist: Yes.

Patient: And he is . . . you know, he likes to satisfy me. And it is not just a little, you know, hop into bed and out and that is it.

Therapist: That is what Jim was like?

Patient: Yes. Well, we very seldom had sex.

Therapist: Did you? How was that?

Patient: You mean why or how often?

Therapist: One of the things that one could say about you is that you are suffering from not really having enough attention paid to you in the current relationship. Is that something that you can see going over your life?

Patient: Going back?

Therapist: Going back, yes. You said you had three sisters, is that right?

Patient: Yes. It could but I . . .

Therapist: And no brothers?

Patient: No.

Therapist: Whereabouts do you come in the family?

Patient: Second oldest.

Therapist: Second oldest?

Patient: I have an older sister.

Therapist: Can you tell me something about your home background, what it was like?

Patient: First of all, my father drinks a lot. That bothers me and I remember when I was young, my mother going out to work and we were left at home and the neighbor next door was minding us and that bothered me too. I was very young. And then when we moved to another house, I know I liked the idea of moving but I had a hard time adjusting to school for some reason. I don't know why I would just sit in class and want to go home and be with my mother.

Therapist: Yes. How old were you then?

Patient: About eight. That was grade three.

Therapist: See there is a pattern. Do you see the pattern?

Patient: No.

Therapist: You don't see it?

Patient: No.

Therapist: Well, have a look at it. I am not talking about the difficulty of adjustment to school—that may be in it—but I am talking about you being left at home.

Patient: That is true.

Therapist: With somebody else . . . in that case with a stranger looking after you instead of your mother. When you have this feeling with the two men in your life, it must have echoes going right back to then, mustn't it?

Patient: Yes. I never thought about it like that.

Therapist: No. All right, let's think about it more.

Patient: I don't know where my father was during those times. He must have been at work too. He must have been at work during the day.

Therapist: If he was at work during the day, that means that he wasn't at work in the evenings; but at the same time, he wasn't there.

Patient: Yeah, he was there, but I know for a while he was in the hospital for his eye. He was gone completely.

Therapist: Going?

Patient: Gone. Like he was in the hospital for a long time.

Therapist: But you said something about he drinks a lot. Did he go out to drink?

Patient: He might have been out. . . . Yeah, he used to go out.

Therapist: Yes.

Patient: But then he used to take us on picnics and to the beach a lot too.

Therapist: He did?

Patient: But my mother wasn't there all the time.
Therapist: No.
Patient: He used to take us.
Therapist: Are you saying that you really feel . . . that you felt neglected by her more than you felt neglected by him? Are you saying that?
Patient: Yeah, probably.
Therapist: I don't necessarily believe "probably." What do you feel?
Patient: I have never really thought about it.
Therapist: You are saying something about that she was out a lot of the time. Other people looked after you, that you remember your father taking you out and that sounds nice. That really sounds close. And yet your mother wasn't there?
Patient: No.
Therapist: And where was she?
Patient: She was at work.
Therapist: She was at work? But when you went out for things like picnics, that would be weekends, wouldn't it? Was she at work over the weekends?
Patient: She worked at night sometimes.
Therapist: So was she doing shift work in a sense, then?
Patient: I don't remember. I don't think she was.
Therapist: But she was working out of ordinary working hours, I mean she wasn't working Monday to Friday nine-to-five sort of thing?
Patient: No, I am sure she wasn't there on the weekends because if we went on picnics, it was on the weekend.
Therapist: And then she wouldn't be there?
Patient: No.
Therapist: What does that make you feel now?
Patient: She should have been there.
Therapist: Yes. At the same time, I suppose you just accepted it. Obviously, one can't . . .
Patient: Well, I didn't like it but you can't . . .
Therapist: There is not much . . .
Patient: There is not much you can do when you are that young.

The evaluator explored further the structure of the patient's family—her relationships with her sisters. She was the second of four girls, and she was very attached to her older sister and was very upset when her older sister left home to get married. What emerged was that her older sister is in the process of divorce and is presently living with a man who sounds like a passive psychopath. Her next younger sister is also divorced. The youngest sister has had a lot of trouble in school with her studies and at present is doing nothing. The patient said with some bitterness that her father seemed to have gone out of his way to defend her youngest sister against various punishments at school, which the patient felt was wrong for him to have done. Further inquiry revealed, however, that there were occasions when he had done the same for the patient. Then the evaluator explored the patient's sexual history, which seemed normal. She said she was orgastic in her relations with Carl.

Therapist: Let's come back. You see, really your problem seems to be about sticking up for yourself. It seems to be about being left alone and feeling lonely, which goes way back. And then what do you do about it, when you are left alone? Is it possible to do anything about it?

Patient: First of all in addition to my job I have joined a volunteer organization where I work once a week. I am very interested in it.

Therapist: I am interested in that too. But it wasn't so much that I meant what you do about it in the sense of finding some substitute. You see I didn't mean that; although that is important too. But what do you do about it when somebody whom you love and need neglects you?

Patient: What did I do? I think of what other things I can do. Like . . .

Therapist: Yes. But that doesn't . . . that compensates your time. It doesn't deal with the basic situation. I think that your problem must be your inability to stick up for yourself and to deal with the basic situation. This is what you are asking our help for.

Patient: I guess so.

Therapist: Well, you say, "I guess so." You are having a problem, in a sense, sticking up for yourself with me, because you know, you are just agreeing with what I say, aren't you? What do you think?

Patient: But I don't see how you can fight my battle. Like, you think that I think that you are going to tell me, "Do this, and do this and do this."

Therapist: I don't know. Do you think that?

Patient: I don't. Because I have heard of people going for help and you are not told what to do; you have to do it on your own. Whatever it is you might want to do.

Therapist: Now what is it you want to do?

Patient: I want to stay with him, but I don't want to keep being pushed aside.

Therapist: Yes, quite. And the question is, "How do you handle that?" Isn't it? What can you do? And I am sure that one of your fears is that if you stick up for yourself, you will lose him altogether. Is that right? Or isn't it right? You see you are agreeing with me again.

Patient: That is right.

Therapist: Then you see, what happens is that you can't stick up for yourself because you are afraid you will lose him and then you have to hold your angry feelings inside yourself. Then you get depressed and then it comes out as crying and you feel better for a bit but it doesn't solve the basic situation. It just happens over again. I am sure that is what the problem is.

Patient: So I guess I could solve my own problem by just sticking up for myself, really. This is what really you are trying to say to me.

Therapist: I am sort of saying that, but I am also saying that your pattern of reacting this way goes back a long way and it may not be quite so easy to solve as all that. I could say to you, "Well, if you go out and fight your battle in some way—." I don't know. You mightn't find it so easy. What do you think?

Patient: I might?

Therapist: Mightn't.

Patient: Well, I don't think I will find it easy.

Therapist: But you are quite right. You see, we can't do it for you.

Patient: I know that.

Therapist: All we can do is acquaint you with what the problem is and try to support you in a way, while you try and deal with it yourself. How do you imagine us helping you?

Patient: Well, just coming for sessions and talking, I imagine it would make me feel better. You know, having someone to talk to and ... I guess I do want someone to say, "Well, you are doing the right thing, or you are not doing the right thing."

Therapist: If they were to offer you treatment here, would you come?

Patient: I would come.

Therapist: Yes. You say, "I would come."

Patient: Like, I came here in the first place because I thought I needed help, so obviously, if they called me and said, you know . . .

Therapist: Are you able to get time off from work in order to come during the day?

Patient: Well, I probably could, but I don't really like to tell them why I want the time off.

Therapist: No. So you would want it to be out of working hours if possible. That may not be possible. Supposing it is not possible?

Patient: Then I would take time off work.

Therapist: All right. I think that is probably all I want to ask you.

Patient: It is just that I don't, like you figure people at work, you tell them why you are going home. . . . Well, first, when I came for the first session and then after a while and then when I hadn't had a phone call, I figured, oh good, I don't need treatment. With people watching me, I figured, well, maybe I do. I am asking you if you think I need it or just, you know . . .

Therapist: Well, I think that I should really put that question back to you, you see. Maybe you can fight this battle yourself. Maybe you don't need our help, I don't know. You see, I am not God. I can't answer that question. You might be able to fight it yourself, mightn't you?

Patient: You are just turning it around.

Therapist: Well, I am just turning it around. You know you have got an opinion too, you know. This is . . .

Patient: That is why I came because I thought I did.

Therapist: You thought you did need treatment?

Patient: Yes.

Therapist: All right, now we have talked about it and a few things have perhaps become clearer. You see, you are trying to rely on us rather than on yourself.

Patient: Yeah.

Therapist: So what is your opinion?

Patient: Yeah, I do.

Therapist: Need treatment?

Patient: I think so.

Therapist: Yes. All right. You feel . . . I am sure if you want help that they would be willing to offer it. (The patient begins to become visibly upset.) Now what's going on?

Patient: Now I am just thinking when I sit here and talk I get very . . . I can't explain it. Like, I just want to cry.

Therapist: Do you? Tell me about that then.

Patient: I can't. I don't know why.

Therapist: Let's explore it. You know something has happened today, has made you feel you want to cry.

Patient: Maybe it is because I have been so keyed up about just thinking about coming.

Therapist: All right. How are you going to go away? Are you going to go away relieved, or sorry, disappointed, or . . .

Patient: I think, relieved. Not sorry that I came or disappointed, no.

Therapist: You could be disappointed. I mean, you can be disappointed with what has happened, couldn't you?

Patient: I think so, yes.

Therapist: All right, then we will talk about that.

Patient: I could come here and just leave and say you know, well, I haven't been helped at all.

Therapist: Ah. Now when you say you haven't been helped at all, what do you mean?

Patient: Being able to sit and talk to someone and not, you know, they have their opinion of me. You have done this and you have done that.

Therapist: I don't quite understand you. Look, can we try to be more specific? You can . . . obviously, you are saying you came with certain hopes here and I think you are also saying that I haven't fulfilled them.

Patient: No, I haven't said that.

Therapist: Haven't you?

Patient: No.

Therapist: I think you did.

Patient: No. When I say that, I am thinking about my sister.

Therapist: Your sister? Now, why?

Patient: Okay, I think she was very upset when my husband and I broke up and I guess I expected her to say to me, "Well, you should do what makes you happy." She never did. She sort of went on, "You know, you have hurt Jim." And stuff like that. They see him all the time. I guess I sort of feel she has sort of condemned me.

Therapist: So, surely what you are saying is that you came to us for reassurance that you shouldn't be condemned.

Patient: I don't think I should, no.

Therapist: But you came hoping that we would say that what you have done is all right.

Patient: No.

Therapist: No? Go on then.

Patient: Well, I don't think you are going to tell me, "Yes, you did the right thing," or "No, you didn't." But . . .

Therapist: No, but . . .

Patient: You sort of want me to decide for myself if I have done the right thing.

Therapist: But that is not good enough, is it?

Patient: I guess not.

Therapist: What you are saying here is that almost certainly you felt guilty in relation to Jim about what you have done. And your sister, instead of reassuring you, said . . . reinforced your guilt and said that you had done wrong.

Patient: Yes.

Therapist: Perhaps you were hoping that we would give a different opinion.

Patient: No, I don't think I expected to come here and have you say, "Yes, you have," or "No, you haven't."

Therapist: Well, I don't think you expected it quite as literally as that but perhaps you expected to come here and go away with some of your guilt relieved.

Patient: Yeah.

Therapist: And I haven't done it, have I?

Patient: No. No.

Therapist: So you are going away disappointed?

Patient: No, I am not. No, I don't think I am.

Therapist: Yet you are wanting to cry.

Patient: Well, I can't explain that.

Therapist: You are making it very difficult for me because first of all you say so and so and then I put it back to you more or less in the same way, and then you say, "I didn't say that at all."

Patient: You are saying that I am going away disappointed.

Therapist: Yes.

Patient: But I don't think I am. I don't really know what to expect when I come here.

Therapist: No, of course you don't.

Patient: But I don't think I am going away disappointed or . . .

Therapist: But, aren't you showing the same pattern with me as you show outside? In a sense, that first of all you have tried to hide what your real feelings about the interview were and to go away making me think all is well. Then fortunately, I managed to somehow bring out that actually when you are going away, you want to cry. Then it seems that you are sort of half saying that there is something about reassurance that you wanted from us that I haven't given.

Patient: No.

Therapist: See, you are agreeing with that, aren't you?

Patient: I am agreeing that you haven't given me reassurance about anything, but, I didn't expect to get it, you know.

Therapist: I feel that what you are doing all the time is trying to pretend you didn't want things that you haven't got from me. This is obviously what I meant to say—I don't know what I did say. And then if I am not careful I am going to go away not knowing that there were things that you wanted. You are going to go away and feel that there was something missing. That you haven't communicated your need to me for what you want. And even if I try to put it into words for you, you deny that it is there. And don't you see that you must be showing the same pattern with me that you show in your relation to Carl? And, of course, this leads into a terrible vicious circle because he doesn't know how much you need different things so he goes on with the same old behavior, ignoring you. You get ignored, you get more and more upset, you can't say what it is you really want. Then you get depressed and you cry, but you don't know why you are crying. He doesn't know why you are crying. So you are not communicating to him what you really need, and that somehow this is what goes on and on in your relationships. It surely must be.

Patient: In the last year . . . you just put into words what I can't do.

Therapist: Yes, and what you want help for. This is right. Now I agree with you, you can't. Now I am trying to say that you should. I am just trying to bring out how much this pattern runs through your life and somehow not putting your own needs forward. And then getting things going wrong because you haven't put your needs forward because you don't know how. It is something right there you need to know, learn as well.

Patient: I agree with you.

Therapist: You see, ten minutes ago, I said, "Shall we stop?" But a lot has happened in that ten minutes, hasn't it?

Patient: Yes.

Therapist: What do you feel now?

Patient: I don't know. I just feel like crying.

Therapist: Well, there is nothing to stop you.

Patient: I just feel like, what you have just said, you are right. You know . . . what you have just said is true.

Therapist: What you are crying about is all the amount you have lost because of this, isn't it?

Patient: All I have lost?

Therapist: Yes. You have lost lots of things that you might have had if only you had known how to ask for them. This is what I am trying to say.

Patient: Yes.

Therapist: What are you going back to now? Are you going back to work or have you got the afternoon off?

Patient: No, I took today off. I have four weeks' holiday. So I take a few days off now and then when I decide I would like to have a day off.

Therapist: Yes. And so you will be going home to do what?

Patient: To do what? Oh, I don't know. To watch TV or go to a movie.

Therapist: All by yourself.

Patient: Yes. Is it so terrible to go to a movie by yourself? Like, I have always been afraid to do things by myself.

Therapist: Afraid to do things by yourself?

Patient: Like go to a movie or go out to lunch by myself.

Therapist: Why are you afraid?

Patient: I don't know. Some people would say, "Oh, look at her at the movie all by herself."

Therapist: What would that mean?

Patient: She has no one. But now I don't know. It is different. It doesn't bother me as much any more.

Therapist: When is Carl due to come back?

Patient: He has to go visit his children tonight.

Therapist: Does he? So is it all right if we stop?

Patient: Yeah.

Therapist: I hope it is all right.

Patient: Sure.

Dr. Sifneos

I was very impressed with the interview and Dr. Malan's ability to elicit from the patient's psychodynamics the motivation for therapy. The strenuous effort made by the evaluator in a situation like this with a patient who is so passive and so anxious is very hard. I like the way he introduced the transference. I also would have liked to ask her, "Do you have any feelings that I will not reach you?" Since the psychodynamics of this patient have to do with being neglected by so many men in her life she may have similar feelings for the evaluator. There is no doubt that she is depressed, so I wonder whether a brief approach to her problem is suitable. Since we are focusing on the issue of criteria for selection, I have some doubts whether this patient is suitable for a very brief period of therapy. How can one deal with a loss that goes back to early life, which Dr. Malan so well connected it with her current life? How can this be dealt with in fifteen or twenty sessions? I was also impressed with his gentleness in handling her. In terms of psychotherapeutic focus, I am not entirely clear whether the focus is really the loss of her mother and, therefore, is essentially a pregenital problem which would give rise to a depression and require a long-term psychotherapy, or whether the loss is associated with her father and therefore possibly it could be approached in a somewhat different way. I would have tried to find out why is this woman the way she is? Is it possible that there is an oedipal focus? If so, is this in terms of the loss of her father? Is she then repeating this pattern over and over with everyone else? If this were the case, then possibly psychotherapy of shorter duration may be the treatment of choice. At this point I don't know.

Dr. Malan

To the question of what those fights were like, it is quite clear that in this interview I didn't really ask her about that, although I got the impression that the fights mostly consisted of her not really being able to protest, getting depressed, going away and crying by herself. Obviously, I should have explored if she ever lost control and tried to hit, screamed, threw things. I think one would be much more encouraged about this patient if she had done so. This is a piece of information that I did not acquire.

With regard to the interpretation, I, in my own mind, interpreted the dream about being trapped in the elevator and being afraid of falling out as being a fear of loss of control, in fact. But you know there are many ways you can interpret it. Anyhow, I did not go into that dream.

Regarding her crying, she cried at the point at which I started to draw the interview to a close. And I think it is by no means clear that I found out why she was crying. In fact, I had a fixed idea in my mind. I am not certain that it was right by any means.

In terms of the psychotherapeutic focus and the question related to oedipal and preoedipal, this distinction, this black-and-white split between oedipal and preoedipal, is something that I don't like. People need other people at all stages of their life, and women need mothers even when they are five, which is after the so-called oedipal stage. And the fact that this patient suffered losses of both women and men is no evidence whatsoever that the problem is preoedipal. The evidence that you are going to get for that is about the quality of dependence in the patient, the type of passivity which might have the quality of the need to be looked after like a little child. But I certainly did not feel this, and I did not in fact feel that it was a preoedipal problem.

Regarding the question of suicidal risk, I very carefully explored the issue; and obviously one of the things that one needs to do when a patient talks about a suicidal attempt is to assess the fantasied risk to life and actual risk to life and the circumstances in which the suicidal attempt was made and what happened subsequently.

If in one's evaluation one gets a story that the patient took a hundred barbiturate tablets and went to a place where no one would find him, then you have to take that pretty seriously. But in this specific case it was nothing more than a gesture between her and herself. It wasn't even a cry for help, and she did not actually tell Carl she had done it, so he never knew. On that basis one would consider her in no way suicidal.

The next question is why is she seeking teatment at this very point in her life. As far as I can understand she sought treatment after a particularly difficult period with her boyfriend, which presumably convinced her that things couldn't go on like this forever and she had better try and do something about it.

Follow-up Comments and Discussion By Dr. Malan

These comments were written after a gap of several years, during which my interviewing technique has been considerably influenced by that of Davanloo.

The aims of an initial interview are exceedingly complex. They often cannot be fulfilled in sequence and need to be approached by the interviewer concurrently. In roughly logical order they can be listed as follows:

1. To take a full psychiatric history in order to check on features that may constitute dangers to interpretative psychotherapy—particulary short-term therapy—such as potential psychosis, poor impulse control, or serious suicidal tendencies. This should result in the possibility of making a psychiatric diagnosis.
2. To make a comprehensive formulation of the psychodynamics.
3. To decide whether the patient is suitable for an attempt at trial therapy in the interview itself.
4. If so, to test the patient's response to trial therapy.
5. In the light of this response, to decide whether the patient is suitable for interpretative psychotherapy, and if so, whether this can be short-term.
6. If the patient is thought to be suitable for short-term therapy, then to formulate a therapeutic plan or focus.
7. To test out, and if necessary to attempt to increase, the patient's motivation.
8. To take care of the consequences of the interview for the patient, and especially to avoid leaving him or her with a mass of unresolved feelings.

The present interview needs to be judged in the light of these aims.

1. With respect to the early part of the interview, severe pathology was effectively excluded. The patient is probably suffering from mild reactive depression in the setting of a character problem. Suicidal tendencies do not seem to be serious.

2. The psychodynamics can be inferred with reasonable certainty. A pattern of feeling neglected by the people close to her runs through her whole story, starting with both her parents, continuing with her husband, and now occurring with her boyfriend. Her reaction to this has been extreme passivity, almost certainly a defense against a great deal of resentment. Moreover, since she married her husband in the full knowledge that he was unsatisfactory (unable to express his feelings), the element of "compulsion to repeat" a relation in which she feels neglected is very clear. This process seems to have continued into her present relation.

3. Therefore, there seemed little doubt that she was suitable for trial therapy in the interview.

4. Her response to trial therapy was equivocal. The pattern of passivity was manifested in the interview with the utmost clarity. The interviewer repeatedly pointed out this pattern without really being able to penetrate it.

5. However, she was able to interact with the interviewer in a meaningful way, which shows that she is almost certainly suitable for interpretative therapy. Whether this can be short-term will be discussed below.

6. There seems little doubt of the therapeutic aim or focus, which must be to break through her defensive passivity and reach the anger about the way she has been neglected at all phases of her life.

7. Because this breakthrough was not successfully achieved in the interview, the patient's motivation remained equivocal to the end.

8. The interviewer made a determined attempt to bring out the patient's feelings about the interview before she left. It is by no means certain that he succeeded, and the reason for the patient's tears at the end never quite emerged. She remained essentially evasive about what she was really feeling, which was probably a consequence of the interviewer's not having penetrated the passivity earlier. She may well have been left with a number of unresolved feelings, which may have made it more difficult for her to accept treatment when it was offered to her.

In spite of the above shortcomings, however, the interview was probably adequate—with reservations—for the purpose of deciding whether the patient was suitable for short-term therapy. Here it is essential to emphasize something that was never quite clear to the discussants at the time, namely, that three different kinds of short-term therapy are being considered—represented by Sifneos (Boston), Malan (London), and Davanloo (Montreal), respectively—for which the selection criteria are different.

First, as Dr. Sifneos says explicitly in his discussion, the question of whether the patient is suitable for the Boston type of short-term therapy hinges on the balance between the patient's disappointing relation with her father, on the one hand, and with her mother, on the other. The more the element of maternal deprivation is present the less suitable the patient. This question is not adequately answered by the interview, and it therefore remains uncertain whether the patient is suitable.

As far as the London school is concerned, the following can be said: (1) Without question there is a focus: the patient's defense of passivity against her anger about neglect. For this type of therapy the problem of the balance between paternal and maternal neglect is of far less importance. (2) The patient has responded to some extent—though not as much as one would like—to interpretations on this focus. (3) There are no obvious dangers to taking the patient into interpretative psychotherapy. (4) The patient's motivation is equivocal and needs to be increased by vigorous interpretation.

On balance, my opinion is that she is suitable, but the success of therapy will depend entirely on the therapist's ability to break through the passivity.

Finally, as far as the Montreal type of brief therapy is concerned, the patient is almost certainly entirely suitable. She represents a type of patient with whom Davanloo has extensive experience, and with whom he has regularly achieved successful results. His confronting technique is admirably suited to breaking through the kind of passivity that this patient shows. Once this has occurred, the patient's motivation is likely to show a marked increase, and I would predict an excellent result with her.

Part III

The Family

11

Dynamic Family Therapy

SAUL L. BROWN, M.D.

How does a chapter on dynamic family therapy fit into a volume devoted to brief dynamic psychotherapy? Are we mixing apples with oranges? The answer to this question will come in the telling. My personal participation in this volume is justified by the fact that my clinical experience has been as a part-time psychoanalyst, part-time general psychotherapist, part-time child therapist, and part-time family therapist. I am not offering this as an advertisement for myself. It is a serious statement about the mixed clinical experiences that lead to my particular views about the usefulness of family therapy and to the first-cousin relationship it has with brief dynamic psychotherapy. It is that mixture of clinical experience that allows me some confidence in asserting that given the appropriate clinical circumstances, relatively brief dynamic family therapy may facilitate the kinds of objectives that we seek to accomplish in individual dynamic psychotherapy. The objectives I am referring to for the latter are:

1. Individuation of a realistic sense of self with coincidental improvement of self-esteem
2. A reduction of self-punitive and ego-restrictive superego functions
3. An increased capacity for gratifying interpersonal relating
4. A reduced rigidity and greater fluidity of ego defenses
5. A greater ease with emotionality and emotional expression

In stating the above, I must draw attention to the word *facilitate*. I use it advisedly and in preference to words that imply cure or total resolution of a syndrome of pathology. My belief is that the direction of therapist action in all psychotherapy is toward a release and vitalization of developmental levels of the patient's psyche that may have become rigidified or suppressed, or simply left dormant, as a consequence of confusing or frightening or experientially deficient family experience.

Just as rigid and self-defeating ego functions and defenses may become structurally embedded in an individual psyche, so devitalizing and growth-inhibiting interpersonal subsystems may become structurally embedded in a family system. Loosening of these structures, whether interpersonal or intrapsychic, usually requires some kind of intense emotional experience in which a person discovers alternative emotions and behaviors. Successful continuation of the new behaviors and emotional states requires continuous practice through the medium of ongoing interpersonal relationships. The transference situation in individual psychotherapy provides one avenue for such discovery and practice to occur. Group therapy provides a different kind of therapeutic context in which individuals can try out and practice alternative interpersonal behaviors and become acquainted with unfamiliar or new feeling states. Family therapy presents a most potent context in which all of this can occur. However, just as with individual psychodynamic psychotherapy, a patient must fit the modality. It does not work for everyone. So with family therapy, when properly motivated and sufficiently endowed with certain kinds of integrative capacities, members of a family can benefit significantly from a fairly brief family therapy, achieving some of the objectives that I noted earlier. Of course not all family members benefit equally. While benefit from family therapy must ultimately be reflected in the feelings and behavior of individuals if it is to have meaning, the therapeutic process and goals for the family as an entity are best described according to an interpersonal systems frame of reference. Using the language and concepts of that frame of reference the following list of objectives and criteria for therapeutic change is pertinent:

1. Improvement of communication between members. (This includes the ability to explicitly state ideas, feelings, and reactions; and to listen to each other with deeper attention. It also includes greater alertness to nonverbal communications and their meanings.)

2. Clearer definition of roles, role expectations, role functions, and a better understanding of the intergenerational structure in the family, including the nature and limitations of the parental-marital dyad.

3. Increased sensitivity to the individual needs of each other person in the family, and greater ease with open and empathic encouragement of individuation and associated autonomy.

4. Acceptance of each one's limitations, accompanied by the ability to correct exaggerated projections and projective identifications that have been operating between the members of the family.

5. A reduced anxiety in each person relative to expressed or veiled anger, and a lessened fear in each person of separation loss resulting from anticipated rejection, withdrawal, or ejection.

6. Improved mechanisms for acknowledging and resolving interpersonal conflicts about tasks and actions that occur in the daily life of the family.

As a very general statement of what one hopes to achieve for the family system, I would emphasize the notion of an enlarged repertoire of constructive interpersonal behavioral alternatives for each person in the family, with a resulting facilitation of the kind of change outlined earlier that we hope to achieve in individual psychotherapy.

Lets turn to the common ground shared by both individual dynamic psychotherapy and dynamically based family therapy. Hopefully the reader will come to understand why I characterize them as "first cousins."

BREVITY IN FAMILY THERAPY

Justifications for brevity in family therapy can be more economically and empirically presented than for brief psychodynamic
psychotherapy. The latter being viewed as an impure derivative of
classical psychoanalysis appears to require more elaborate validation at a theoretical level. Based upon his work in a child guidance
clinic in Israel, Mordecai Kauffman published a paper in 1963 titled
"Short-Term Family Therapy." In it he offered a model for brief
family therapy process, which he was careful to point out worked
well for selected cases. Earlier, perhaps the first clinical description
of a family therapy was published by John Elderkin Bell (1961).
Based upon a ten-session therapy with a family, he delineated the
following sequence of phases.

1. First conference
2. Child-centered phase
3. Parent-child interaction
4. Father-mother interaction
5. Sibling interaction
6. Termination phase

While most family therapy does not fall into quite such a precise
sequence, Bell's outline does give some insight into how the process
may unfold over several interviews, especially if the named patients
are young children.

Gerald Zuk, a longtime contributor to the literature in family
therapy, recently commented (1967) that his experience as well as
those of a large number of family therapists with whose work he is
familiar tend toward relatively few contacts with any single family,
usually less than six sessions. Zuk's view is that only a relatively small
number of families are motivated for a longer series of family
sessions. On the other hand, the published cases by Salvadore
Minuchin (1978), especially related to treatment of anorexia nervosa,
indicate a much longer series of treatment sessions with individual
families. However, Minuchin's clinical approach includes many
variations on the central theme of meeting with an entire family in a
group. Relatively intensive work with individual patients may occur
in addition to the family meetings.

Nathan Ackerman, one of the most influential figures in the history of family therapy, repeatedly emphasized his view that clinician flexibilty was a keystone of the modality (1958). He believed it was clinically unrealistic to pursue a "pure" model of family therapy. Ackerman viewed family therapy sessions as a clinical base from which a variety of therapeutic efforts could proceed. He worked alternately with the entire family, with various subunits, and ultimately with the marital dyad. He arranged for individual sessions, and he also involved individual family members in group therapy separate from the family sessions when it appeared to him to be of value.

Because of my commitment to the principle of flexibility in psychotherapeutic work, I have become inclined to think of family therapy as a series of family interviews. It may turn out that such a series is an unbroken one of weekly meetings with the whole family. However meetings with individuals or with subunits of the family may occur intermittently or even regularly. Also one or several family members may be in a concurrent individual therapy with other therapists. Thus rather than becoming locked into a set procedure, I feel free to vary the clinical interventions according to what issues have arisen and to what I have learned about the family's therapeutic responsiveness. I find it most helpful to view family therapy as providing a matrix for clinical management. A series of family interviews may become the dominant modality, but variations are not unusual. The length of time during which the family is involved in one form or another varies from a few weeks to two or three years. Six months to a year is not unusual.

THE NEED FOR THEORY

Relying upon flexibility as a guide for choice of clinical modality does not mean that one can proceed without an organizing set of theoretical concepts. Just as with brief dynamic psychotherapy of individual patients, comprehension of transference and of psychodynamics is essential for well-focused clinical work. But in addition to these, effective clinical work with families requires a feeling for and a keen comprehension of systems theory as it relates to intimate interpersonal relationships. Without such comprehension, the therapy of a family tends to drift toward a series of parallel individual psychotherapies with the various family members. While one-to-one therapeutic exchanges between the therapist and the individual family members inevitably occur during each session, the therapeutic payoff in family therapy lies not so much in interpretive dyadic exchanges as in the shifts and changes in role functions, and in the character of the transactional subsystems that result from the total process occurring in the family sessions. Knowledge of family systems as well as of transference (and countertransference) and of individual psychodynamics keeps the family therapist on the road, but his or her spontaneous participation in the action of the family system is what provides the therapeutic fuel, remembering that facilitation of developmental change is the ultimate goal.

TRANSFERENCE AND SYSTEMS THEORY IN AN INTERVIEW

Individual transferences to the therapist from each family member certainly occur. They can include most of the elements of transference occurring in individual psychotherapy, namely idealization, depreciation, regressive expectation, wishes to incorporate and impulses to eject, competition, envy, projection, etc. However, direct exploration of any of these transference reactions occurring during a family therapy is usually very brief. Most often they are sidestepped. Whenever possible I redirect the overt or covert transference reactions to me back into the interaction between the family members themselves. Instead of inviting associations to a dream or to thoughts and feelings about the therapist, the family therapist is more likely to respond to transference material as an opportunity for drawing out feelings that a particular family member has not yet formulated toward others in the family or has been fearful of verbalizing.

In a particular session (approximately the fourth or fifth), my response to a severely agoraphobic young woman who said she feared I would grow tired of her and her family and discontinue the family therapy, was to say that I thought she was fearful there would be a repetition of her earlier adolescent experience with her mother. I knew from preceding family meetings that her mother had become coldly critical of her when she reached puberty. Both parents were present in the meeting, and as one might expect, mother responded defensively to my comment. She did not see herself quite in the negative light that my interpretation to her daughter cast upon her and was not inclined to recognize that her behavior toward her daughter several years earlier could have played a part in her daughter's fear of expressing any kind of independent or rebellious or angry comments to those upon whom she depended. Nevertheless I felt free to say what I did because during the course of several family sessions preceding this one, the mother had developed a relatively positive transference to me. This was based upon various supportive statements I had made about her when she and her husband argued, and I could now trade on that bit of our mutual history as I redirected the daughter's transference anxiety away from me and back to the original object, her mother. As I've noted, the father was also present in this session and a consequence of my commentary to the daughter was an activation of his already idealized transference to me. My comment reenforced his view of me as a supportive champion of his daughter, with whom he felt allied. He viewed her as helpless in the face of any battle she might have with her mother. He felt me to be a protective paternal ally who he could feel aided him in managing a difficult woman (his wife). He did not disguise his delight with my comment. Understandably this did not warm his wife's feelings toward him at that moment. However, rather than interpreting his idealized transference reaction to me, as one might do in individual psychotherapy, I showed him that he was now forming an alliance with his daughter against his wife. (I had said similar things to him in previous sessions and did so many times in subsequent sessions.) When the mother showed her distress over my earlier comment, I used the moment to remind her of how she tended to be demanding of herself and that behind her critical reaction to her daughter's early sexuality had been a genuine fear that she as mother might not be protecting her daughter enough. (This was certainly what might be called an "inexact interpretation" since it left out the reality of mother's hostility toward her daughter's sexuality. However I believe interpretations of motivations must often be incomplete when one works with parents.)

Where, one may ask, is the therapeutic payoff in what I have described? My answer, which follows, will involve a mixture of family system and individual dynamic statements.

1. By interpreting and thereby redirecting the daughter's trans-

ference anxiety, she and mother were forced to reengage in the never-resolved adolescent level of individuation-separation process that should have occurred in their relationship many years earlier. While my comment to the daughter about her fear of evoking her mother's hostile withdrawal evoked discomfort in both of them, the safety of the therapeutic setting preserved them from a defensive regression into wild and nonconstructive and nonresolvable adolescent-versus-mother battling. The fact that I only commented, but avoided any encouragement of battle with each other, left them with breathing space. There would be time later for more constructive confrontations in which the daughter might practice individuating from her mother in age-appropriate ways. (This occurred slowly over several months of the family meetings.)

2. My comment to the father disrupted the affective flow of his alliance with daughter against mother. She was freed, momentarily, from the growth-inhibiting tie to him and experienced a brief glimpse of freedom from both parents. Disrupting this alliance pushed her to stand on her own. It moved her one more step toward the realization that her existence did not depend upon a continuous clinging to the parents. Also it helped her recognize that her father could survive separate from her, and that her mother could withstand separation from her.

3. My pointing out to both parents somewhat later in the same interview that they were in a stalemate with each other was only a reiteration of what I had said to them in previous sessions. Several times we had weathered hateful exchanges between them. Since in this session I felt both parents were left somewhat in limbo as I worked toward detaching their daughter from them, I felt the need to address them as follows: Speaking to the parents, with daughter listening, I reminded them of how each offends the other—he by trying to pressure and control her, she by withdrawing into cool disdain or by snapping at him. It was clear that I judged neither of them, but facts are facts. Externalization of interpersonal reality by a nonjudgmental family therapist relieves the anxiety of alienation that each person feels in a troubled marriage. Loosely stated, both are "sinners," and at least in that sense they each find a companion in the other. Meanwhile, the therapeutic process occurring in this way attenuates the danger of self-punitive superego reactions. When guilt rises in individual psychotherapy, it often becomes transformed into

a paranoid transference projection in which the analyst-therapist is felt to be judging or even tormenting the patient. Marital relationships often include transference distortions and projective identification between spouses. This marriage was no exception! But a direct confrontation of that theme would have been relatively futile at this time. My goal is to reduce the guilt each marital partner feels and with it, the need to project hostile intentions onto the other.

4. Even in this session, but particularly in earlier ones, mother experienced a sense of validation and support when she heard me restrain her husband's compulsive controlling behavior of her and of the daughter. This helped to reduce her feeling of helpless rage in dealing with his criticisms of her and left her with more available warmth for her daughter. I would not suggest however that it changed her basic character defenses nor her underlying ambivalence about the independent assertion in her daughter.

5. My interaction with the father was one in which I could ally with his superego in a limited sense. His more integrated self did not wish to stifle his daughter's individuation through an alliance with her, nor did he wish to badger and try to control his wife to the degree that he repeatedly fell into. My alliance with the constructive aspect of his superego helped him restrain his impulses, and he expressed relief about this. However in order to manage other levels of anxiety that he experienced, he sought periodic consultations from another psychiatrist, concurrent with the family therapy. I encouraged this. Meanwhile, the daughter, in observing my confrontations of her very energetic and intrusive father and seeing that he did not become undone by the process, found herself relieved of conflict about disengaging from him and also became more free to carry out her own confrontations of him when he became too controlling.

Much more than what I have described in the preceding paragraphs occurred in the complex therapy with this family during the course of weekly meetings for about one year. (An older sister of the agoraphobic patient was also a participant, and many of the sessions involved her in significant ways.) Also the agoraphobia, which had all but immobilized the young woman for close to ten years, and during which she had been in an analytic psychotherapy two and three times per week for about five years, and also during which she had been hospitalized briefly, gave way. At the end of the first year of family meetings, a resident who functioned as my associate therapist began weekly desensitization meetings with the patient and later, a dynamic group therapy. He became her primary therapist. Before the middle of the second year (the family meetings were now discontinued), she became able to seek and find employment, date men, and learn to drive—all at the age of thirty. This was a dramatic change from the previous ten years of her life.

THE INNER PROCESS OF THE FAMILY THERAPIST

This presentation allows for only a brief commentary. My own inner process includes constant attentiveness to my own reactions—realistic and countertransference—to the family members. While I am concerned with the family system and responding to the subsystem transactions, I never lose track of my reactions to each person in the family, and I feel I must find something to like about each if I am to be able to work with them. Each person in the family I have described sensed my positive feeling. While I could hardly feel enthusiastic affection for the mother when I perceived her capacity to be cold and aloof toward her husband or her daughters when they offended her, I did genuinely respect some aspects of the way in which she had managed a very difficult life, and I appreciated her sense of humor. Also, I genuinely identified with her distressed feelings when her husband mounted his compulsive pressuring campaigns against her. On the other hand, he too had met extreme difficulties in his life in a way that aroused my admiration. It was he who had faced the failure of her previous therapy and sought out a new approach. His profound devotions to the cause of helping his daughter was constantly impressive to me. The daughter, who was essentially the designated patient, was easy to like even though her recurrent stubborn retreat into clinging to the family stirred my impatience at times. Stiff reminders to her of the need for her to commit herself to struggling with her phobia were frequently necessary. I and my associate therapist had to be gentle but firm taskmasters at these times. The sister, who was older than the patient, was a wallflower who needed to be drawn out. She responded fairly well to this. Rarely had anyone shown her such focal attention, it seemed.

In attempting to build a bridge between the objectives for individual psychotherapy and the use of dynamic family therapy the following generalization become pertinent:

Individuation of the self. The degree to which psychotherapy contributes to this is a function of a far more elaborate set of factors than the psychotherapy per se. Preexisting character defenses of the patient, reality circumstances, individual motivation for change, therapist skills and orientation are all significant. The questions of frequency and depth of therapy are alway present. Withal, the process of individuation is never an inner maturational process only. It occurs through interpersonal experience. The intensified interpersonal experience occurring in even a very few family interviews, as illustrated by my case example drawn from the fifth family session, facilitates the process enormously.

Diminution of punitive and ego-restrictive superego tensions. Much of the process of individual therapy, especially when it occurs within the context of a positive transference, relates to reduction of the patient's sense of shame and the fear of being judged and criticized. The archaic superego reveals itself in the transference, and the patient is helped by the therapist to reduce its pervasiveness and intensity. In the family sessions the emotional safety of the situation provides the family members with freedom to try out what each has always felt to be forbidden. Precisely because the family members are present, these are not just intellectual exercises in guilt reduction; they are often intensely felt interchanges which reach deeply into each person's past. Discovering what happens if one tells forbidden feelings or ideas to others in the family facilitates the long and difficult process of reducing superego restrictions much as they occur during the course of individual psychotherapy. In the case example, at least the daughter discovered a new freedom. Her sister, whom I have barely referred to, also discovered this in some degree. The mother was helped to reduce guilt, but at a more superficial level of psychic organization. The same might be said for the father. For both parents, the relief of participating in a constructive effort for their daughter was a guilt-relieving experience—and I believe, a life-saving one.

Loosening of rigid ego defenses. Defenses, rooted as they are in very early life experience, do not loosen magically in any kind of therapy, especially if the patient has major rigidities. The relatively "normal" person does experience a freeing up of old and nonproductive defenses through many kinds of experiences, many of which are not considered psychotherapy. Moving to California is enough to do it for many! "EST" does it for others. And so on. Individual dynamic analytic therapy is one way to reach for the golden ring. We reach it less often than we might wish, although certainly we do reach it for many patients, given appropriate and facilitating factors. Family therapy does no better than other therapies except in those cases where facilitation itself is perceived as the golden ring. From that viewpoint, the intense exchanges of the family meetings become opportunities to try new behaviors and give up old and self-defeating defensive ones. This in turn affects inner defensive structures and releases developmental process.

The daughter began, slowly, to confront her father's compulsive controlling of her. She felt great anxiety as she did this in the sessions (and at home), but she also felt the support from the family sessions—and the transference to the therapist. The father, too, experienced anxiety when both daughter and therapist limited his compulsive behavior and also when his attacks on his wife (displacements from old fears and angers toward his mother?) were disrupted. Furthermore, his identification with his daughter, which was disrupted by the family therapy, also evoked anxiety in him since his identification with her fulfilled deeper defensive needs in his psychic structure. But anxiety is not the sole issue here. The partnership between myself and each family member provided a kind of parental support which made each feel safe to "let go," at least for awhile, of rooted defensive behaviors. Letting go in this way allowed each an opportunity to view relationships in a somewhat new light. The designated patient was the one who could benefit most through viewing the microcosm of her world in alternative ways.

Increasing the freedom for gratifying relationships. The practice that occurs in family therapy of stating feelings and ideas in an increasingly open fashion, and the modeling provided by the family therapist of empathic and supportive listening, facilitates growth of these capacities in the various family members. For many families this is a totally new experience, namely the one of expressing not only negative but also positive and supportive feelings to each other in an open fashion. In the family I have described, there was already a great amount of positive support between them, in spite of the sharp hostility that regularly occurred between the parents. And even the mother made positive comments about her daughter from time to time.

Improvement of emotionality and emotional expression. The process in family therapy must be emotional if something useful is to occur. This may not always happen. But when it does, the sheer experience of letting feelings flow facilitates a new way of being for many in family therapy. On the other hand, for those who live in families where excessive emotionality abounds, learning to contain and to appropriately direct raw emotion can be equally facilitative of personal growth, again the "golden ring."

THE FACILITATION OF DEVELOPMENT

Beginning with a brief commentary about my views of what we hope to accomplish in dynamic psychotherapy, I attempted to show some of the potential for overlap between those objectives and the objectives one seeks in family therapy. In order to discuss the latter, a systems frame of reference is necessary, and I touched all too briefly upon that frame of reference. I have defined the "golden" link between the two modalities as the one of facilitation of developmental progress or growth in each individual. Using facilitation of development as the integrative concept allows one to bypass issues of ultimate "cure" and to address the operational aspects of what either modality attempts to accomplish. Flexibility of modality and in therapist remains my keynote.

In the case that I have offered for illustration, it was evident after two or three months of weekly interviews with the family that the relationship between the parents was not likely to change very much. However, the dread each seemed to have of losing the other, in spite of their pain in living together, made it clear that having everyone together in family meetings reassured each that even as the patient changed and moved out into the world, their emotionally painful but essentially secure interpersonal world would not collapse. The patient herself needed to see her parents maintain some kind of "steady state" while she learned to express what had always felt to be forbidden. Drawing upon the fact that five years of analytic psychotherapy with her had accomplished little, I concluded her ability to "let go" and individuate was more promising if she could keep an eye on her parents as she became emancipated from them, reassured that they were alive, even if in distress. I believe this is an oft-misunderstood issue by therapists who become committed to emancipation and individuation of adolescents and young adults. What those therapists lose track of is the existential reality of the adolescent or young adult, which includes the need for sustaining family ties, even as the individuation process occurs. The capacity of a family to encourage and allow individuation is something more than just shoving each member out into a sea of individually autonomous beings. It is a capacity that occurs only out of respect for the intricacies involved in separation of one person from another even as each seeks relative autonomy. This is just one more way to emphasize my basic message about facilitation and how it links individual dynamic therapy with family therapy.

References

Ackerman, N.W. (1958). *The Psychodynamics of Family Life*. New York: Basic Books.

Bell, J.E. (1961). *Family Group Therapy*. Public Health Monograph, U.S. Department of Health, Education and Welfare, No. 64. Washington, D.C.: Government Printing Office.

Bowen, M. (1976). Theory in the practice of psychotherapy. In *Family Therapy: Theory and Practice*, ed. P. Guerin. New York: Halsted Press.

Brown, S.L. (1969). Diagnosis, clinical management and family interviewing. In *Science and Psychoanalysis*, vol. 14, ed. J. Masserman. New York: Grune and Stratton.

———— (1972). Family group therapy. In *Manual of Child Psychopathology*, ed. B. Wolman. New York: McGraw-Hill.

Kauffman, M. (1963). Short-term family therapy. *Family Process* 2:216-234.

Minuchin, S., et al. (1978). *Psychosomatic Families, Anorexia Nervosa in Context*. Cambridge: Harvard University Press.

Sager, C.J., et al. (1968). Selections and engagement of patients in family therapy. *American Journal of Orthopsychiatry* 38:715-723.

Zuk, G. (1967). The go-between process in family therapy. *Family Process* 5:162-178

12

The Family in Crisis

SAUL L. BROWN, M.D.

COMMON SENSE ABOUT FAMILIES AND CRISIS

Assuming that there is some kind of functional family unit, it seems a common-sense realization that if a major problem affects one member in a family, reverberations will occur throughout the family system. Conversely, an event or a series of circumstances that seriously disrupts the ongoing life of the whole family will inevitably affect each person in the family. Framed in psychological terms, an acute decompensation of psychological function in one or more family members cannot fail to evoke major psychological and emotional reactions in at least some of the others. That is not to say that all such reactions are of clinical significance. Indeed disruptive events may result in a spontaneous consolidation of family functions leading to a vitalization of interpersonal relating in a family and to improvement in each person's psychological function. Clinical intervention in those situations might be superfluous. On the other hand, certain families that previously have had successful experiences with family therapy interviews become oriented to calling upon a family therapist when disruptive events occur. In this way they are able to avoid unnecessarily fragmenting and painful consequences. One family comes to mind in which a widow had received a sudden diagnosis of a fulminating abdominal cancer. When it was clear that she would not survive, her two sons, a niece who was close to her, and one daughter-in-law requested a family interview to discuss how they might manage their reactions and be most helpful to each other as well as to the patient. In this case the patient herself was not included in the meetings. The family was an emotionally volatile one, but two interviews with the group served to avert what would have become mutually destructive behaviors and to assure the family integration at a time of potential disruption.

Acknowledging that common sense alone is not a sufficiently convincing criterion for involving family members in the clinical treatment of a crisis situation, the need for a more systematic presentation of indications for such clinical action becomes evident. A full presentation and discussion would need to include much more than this single chapter allows for. I will therefore review only a few guiding principles that I believe may provide some orientation for mental health professionals who must respond to crisis situations.

DIFFERENTIATION OF FAMILY INTERVIEWS FROM FAMILY THERAPY

A first principle is that family interviewing is not necessarily synonymous with family therapy. Once differentiating the two processes from each other, therapists may feel freer to use one or more family interviews in the clinical management of a crisis, without feeling locked into a full-scale family therapy. I emphasize this as a first principle because my experience has been that many clinicians fail to consider family interviews when it appears obvious, to those of us who are familiar with the process, that even one such interview might be of profound significance for all family members. I have concluded that one reason for this failure to do the obvious is that in the minds of many therapists even a single family interview is equated to beginning family therapy in the full sense. Since they do not feel qualified to carry this out, the result is a reluctance to use a valuable clinical intervention. It is exactly because family interviewing lends itself to limited goals that it is well suited for resolving a crisis situation. The decision about whether to carry out a more extensive family therapy can be deferred or reached according to what happens in the preliminary family interviews. The following illustrates how an initial response to a crisis situation using family interviews was of profound importance and long-term value for several members of a family.

A woman called for an appointment in the hope that I might help her. On the telephone she sounded reasonable but at the same time extremely pressured and desperate. She said her twenty-year-old son had needed to leave college because of a "breakdown," had been hospitalized for a few weeks, and was now living at home. He was seeing a therapist three times a week, but the therapist would not communicate directly with her and her husband because it might undermine her son's therapeutic relationship with him. The mother felt at wit's end. She said she was unable to sleep, felt overwrought, and was at a total loss about how to deal with her son's extremely variable moods, his silences, his long retreats to his room, and his refusal to eat dinners with the family. Also he had broken off contact with all of his former friends and tended to give long lectures to his two younger sisters on philosophical issues which they did not want to hear. They felt so embarrassed about him that they had become ashamed to bring their friends to the house. One of them had begun to awaken nightly with nightmares. In addition to all this her husband, always a busy executive, had taken to drinking three or four cocktails each evening and slipping off to bed early, leaving her to feel very alone and increasingly panicky about the family situation. She confessed that complicating this whole situation was a rising mistrust in both her and her husband about their son's therapist and the value of the treatment he was receiving. From the telephone conversation, my impression was that here was a woman approaching a state of crisis, and a family on the edge of crisis as well.

I suggested that all members of the family come in for a family consultation. This was to include the son if he would come and if his therapist felt it was alright.

Following are several of the objectives that I anticipated would be accomplished through a single or perhaps a series of family interviews.

1. In a meeting with all family members I could assess whether the crisis that I sensed in the mother on the telephone was essentially her own, or whether others in the family and the family as an entity were also in a state of imminent crisis.

2. With all family members present, productive ventilation of what I sensed were rapidly intensifying feelings of anger, frustration, and even despair in the siblings as well as in the mother and probably the father might occur.

3. With the son participating, it might be possible to clarify the nature of his problem and help each person in the family to evolve a cognitive frame of reference for managing the difficult feelings they were experiencing about him.

4. Through meeting with the family as a group, an evaluation could be made of the capacity of the marital dyad to maintain integration and leadership of the family system at a time of threatened fragmentation. Such an evaluation is essential if clinical management is to occur in a sensible and realistic fashion and if therapeutic measures are to have long-lasting value.

5. By participating in one or a few family meetings, the disturbed son might be helped to perceive how his behavior was affecting members of the family. I have found that if I can be both sensitive and cautious in such a circumstance, I can help reduce the disturbed person's guilt by suggesting more appropriate avenues for his behavior in the day-by-day family interactions. Very specific suggestions about how to communicate his feelings or his impulses to the others and what to do when he feels overwhelmed or confused can be helpful.

In this case, I met with the whole family twice in the first two weeks, met with the parents weekly for the next two, met with the two sisters together on one occasion, and the whole family group once every two weeks for about four months. The disturbed son continued with his independent psychotherapy. Early in the series of interviews the father became able to acknowledge that he was avoiding emotional involvement in the family stress by drinking just enough when he was home to create emotional distance from his wife and children. One of the sisters became able to talk about her former idealization of her brother and her disappointment as well as her anger over his failure to live up to her childhood view of him.

Also her guilt over these feelings was actively discussed by everyone in the family. The other sister shared her feelings about needing to close off from the family distress by becoming absorbed in intensive socializing and school activities. Once having talked about this openly, her parents became less blaming of her for seeming to be unsympathetic and detached. The son's behavior in the sessions varied. On some occasions he tended to be a lecturer to everyone. On other occasions his obsessional defenses gave way to asserting delusional ideas about religion. A few times he was able to comment critically about his father's arbitrary personality, but often he listened closely to the others. My own comments to him were always supportive and careful. A few times I took note of his ambivalence toward his parents and his great difficulty expressing angry feelings, but I did not encourage an active expression of these and I repeatedly supported his continuing individual therapy. My basic stance with both parents but especially the mother was to try to reduce guilt by emphasizing the constructive side of their efforts.

In summary, what I have described in this case example is the use of a series of family interviews for meeting a crisis occurring both in the family as a whole and in the various individuals as well. The effect of the sessions was to neutralize rapidly intensifying disintegrative forces at work in the family equilibrium, even while the major stress upon the family of the son's disturbance continued and would doubtlessly be present for some time. Returning to the first principle I addressed in this section, namely the differentiation of family interviewing from family therapy, a full-scale family therapy effort would have included more complex objectives and a different kind of commitment from the family members than what I described. Since it is not possible in this writing to enter into detail about what make up the elements of a full-scale family therapy, I will only briefly summarize that it would usually include at least the following: (1) active attention to the conflict-resolving subsystem of the family, (2) clarification of the problem-solving subsystem with a related examination of how authority and power are managed, (3) a sustained study-in-action of the subtleties of the communication subsystem, with efforts to help the family members improve it, and (4) an intensive review of the marital relationship and the intergenerational boundaries. Other subsystems would inevitably be dealt with in the process. While I realize that the methodology for family therapy is a subject in itself, my point here is that while in working with a crisis situation the therapist interviewing a family may have those subsystems in mind, he does not attempt a systematic approach to them. Instead, with the family I have described, the objective was limited to that which is the usual one in crisis therapy, namely to help the family members return to a previous level of equilibrium or homeostasis. In this situation the objective was related to the family system as a whole, as well as to the several members individually and the mother specifically.

CLINICIAN CONVICTION ABOUT THE VALUE OF FAMILY INTERVIEWING

A second principle related to the use of family interviews for crisis situations is that the clinician must have a positive personal conviction about its value. This kind of conviction can occur only as a result of having had successful and gratifying experiences in the use of family interviews in the clinical management of crises. Prerequisites to this are interviewing skills that are not necessarily present in all clinicians. Included are a facility for following as well as leading group process, an ease with role theory, an ability to talk easily with people of several age categories, from the very young to the very old, a capacity to avoid taking sides even while being fairly active in directing the communication process, and a willingness to "tolerate the heat" that often occurs in the intense and often poignant, but also openly angry interactions between family members. Because a family interviewer must be fairly active in formulating and clarifying what is going on from one phase of an interview to the next, he or she needs to feel an inner certainty about the ultimate importance of the process for each person in the family as well as for the one who is in crisis. Without such a feeling, a clinician is not likely to take on the difficulties that may arise in attempting to involve several family members in the clinical effort. These difficulties are often very real and practical ones. Logistics and scheduling of interviews may not be the least of these. A spouse of the person in crisis may need to be at work; siblings of children must attend school, may be studying for exams, may be on an athletic team or whatever; transportation may not be available for all members. Also physical illness or old age may be deterrents to participation; long-standing grudges against the person in crisis may cause some family members to reject invitations to participate; in addition to all this, the therapist's time and the cost of family interviews may be a problem since a family interview should always be at least a full hour and often somewhat longer.

FAMILY SYSTEMS THEORY AND CRISIS

A final guiding principle rests upon the ability of the clinician to perceive what I believe to be an intimate linkage between what we have learned about family systems on the one hand and about crisis on the other.

In most instances, a crisis state occurs in association with a recent or an imminent or even a threatened loss. If the loss is of a person, that person may be a lover, a parent, a spouse, a child, a grandchild, an employer, a teacher, a physician, or even someone who is not in fact a part of the real life of the individual. Such a person would be of symbolic importance such as a Franklin Roosevelt or John Kennedy or perhaps a religious or an intellectual leader or a sports hero or a film celebrity. Rather than the loss of a person, what may be lost in association with a crisis state is a familiar or long-established belief system, a faith, or loyalty to a cause or a belief in one's fate or role or destiny. The loss may be one of social status or of professional or vocational role. Perhaps a most common precipitant of crisis is the loss of physical vitality or of a full state of health. Other losses are a function of the normal transitions of life: children growing away from home, parents aging, old friends dying. A loss, threatened or anticipated or real, that is among the most powerful of all in its impact upon an individual is the loss of economic security, since it has implications for almost every level and area of an individual's existence. Formulated in psychological terms, loss is an event which results in or is a precipitant of psychic disruption. What is disrupted in association with loss are familiar and stable inner feeling states and predictable interpersonal patterns and relationships that provide a sense of continuity in daily existence. Clearly every person is at risk for experiencing disruption of inner equilibrium arising from loss. When events in an individual's life bring about an acute disruption of inner experiences of the kind associated with loss, he immediately needs supportive response from those who make up his human environment. When that environment is a vitally functional one for the individual, the inner disruption is likely to be transitory. A kind of self-healing occurs. However when the intimate interpersonal environment (usually the family) of the person experiencing loss of inner equilibrium is unresponsive or essentially nonfunctional in its capacity to provide emotional support, that person becomes unable to sustain integrated relatedness to other people. The consequence of this is a rapid compounding of the feelings of loss and an extending and deepening disruption of inner equilibrium. The weaker a person's ties to his or her interpersonal world, the more vulnerable he is to this kind of disintegrative process once it begins. Conversely, the less vitally functional the intimate interpersonal world of the individual, the less able it is to offer the reassuring, anxiety-reducing, emotionally supportive, and personally validating experience that might halt the progression of disruptive emotions in the troubled individual. A spiral of mutual distancing occurs as the patient and those who should be close to him "lose each other." Those close feel increasingly helpless and become defensively hostile over their impotence to reverse the deteriorating situation.

It is here, in referring to the vitality of the patient's intimate interpersonal environment, that an understanding of family-systems theory becomes of value. I am equating "intimate interpersonal environment" with family. These days one is inclined to define *family* as any close grouping of people that elects to consider itself a family. So it includes certain communal groups or people living closely together who have accepted a certain dependency upon one another. What makes for vitality of family function is the effectiveness of the subsystems that we have come to recognize in family life or in intimate group life.

Those subsystems most commonly designated by family theorists are: the *communications subsystem* through which feelings and thoughts are externalized through complex reciprocal and circular processes of verbal and nonverbal exchange, the *emotional expressive subsystem* through which essential interpersonal relatedness occurs the *conflict resolving subsystem* through which differences of interpersonal need or impulse or viewpoint are negotiated between individuals to a constructive end point, the *empathic subsystem* through which mutual identifications with one another's inner experience occur, the *problem-solving subsystem* through which mutuality of constructive effort is carried out, the *mutual validation subsystem* through which each person supports the other's autonomy and self-esteem, and the *authority-power subsystems* through which executive and administrative functions of the family occur. There are others that have been well described in the family literature. But my purpose in this brief and incomplete listing is only to provide depth to my contention that a comprehension of family-system theory leads clinicians to the realization that the mobilization of a family system at times of crisis in one or several members may be the most powerful resource available. A clinician interviewing a family in response to a crisis may not address any of the subsystems in a directly analytic or interpretive fashion. In fact his style of approach to the family in an interview or series of interviews may be entirely spontaneous while at the same time limited to specific objectives such as facilitating a ventilation of undercurrent emotions, encouraging verbalization of supportive comments, and reducing the level of hostility. But the indirect result of these seemingly surface clinical actions is to free up the various subsystems so that empathic emotional exchanges and clear communications can occur while hostile distancing from one another lessens. The sense of loss and disruption occurring within the various individuals in the family and especially in the one who is in crisis reduces as vital family function and a feeling of group integration take hold.

SUMMARY

In my work as a clinician in crisis situations I view my responsibility as one of providing response to the desperate need that persons in crisis have to sustain their psychic integration. Since I believe that there can be no genuine or substantial state of individual psychic integration in the absence of an integrative interpersonal environment of some kind, my clinical responsibility includes an effort to mobilize the intimate interpersonal environment of the person who is in crisis to become supportive and constructive. Also because I believe that a crisis in one person in an intimate group has ramifications for everyone who is related to the group, the clinical response should be to each member of the group as well as the group as a whole. The goal is to strengthen the integrative processes in the group. Through family interviews, the opportunity is present to move in all directions at once, although not to a full end point in any of them. Clinical reality sets limits for what can be accomplished. Clinical reality includes not only what family members can afford to pay for service but also the full range of factors that all clinicians know about: namely, the clinician's skills, the characterology of the family members, the psychopathology of the family members, the existential circumstances of both the family and the clinician, and ultimately, the nature and quality of the functional subsystems in the family or in the close interpersonal environment of those experiencing crisis.

I hope that in this chapter I have succeeded in clarifying why the inclusion of a family or intimate interpersonal group in the management of an individual's crisis rests upon more than a common-sense point of view. Through presenting guidelines for the clinician I have sought to provoke a deeper-than-usual appraisal of pros and cons about the choice of a particular modality and have tried to explore some of the dynamic factors that underly my choice of clinical modality. In a sense, the use of family interviews turns the traditional process of clinical management on its head. Conventional or traditional approach, within the medical model, is based upon a history taken from and an examination of an individual patient who presents with some kind of discomfort. Family members in conventional practice may or may not be called upon for additional history or to provide aid if major environmental action is needed. But the approach to crisis that I have discussed tends to avoid total focus upon one individual even while his or her problem is seriously addressed. Instead, the surrounding interpersonal system is invited to reorganize or revitalize itself. This is not simply because the family members should be good samaritans, but because they too have an absolute need to maintain their individual and group integration. Their individual and collective need is just as desperate in the long run of their family existence as the need of the person in crisis. Just as the actor needs an audience, so the audience needs an actor if the play is to reach a gratifying end.

References

Ackerman, N.W. (1966). *Treating the Troubled Family*. New York: Basic Books.
Barten, H.H. (1971). The expanding spectrum of the brief therapies. In *Brief Therapy*, ed. H.H. Barten. New York: Behavioral Publications.

Brown, S.L. (1969). Diagnosis, clinical management and family interviewing. In *Science and Psychoanalysis*, vol. 14, ed. J. Masserman. New York: Grune and Stratton.

—·—— (1971). Family group therapy. In *Manual of Child Psychopathology*, ed. B.B. Wolman. New York: McGraw-Hill.

——— (1973). Family experience and change. In *Family Roots of School Learning and Behavior Disorders*, ed. R. Friedman. Springfield: Charles C. Thomas.

Caplan, G. (1964). *Principles of Preventive Psychiatry*. New York: Basic Books.

Lindemann, E. (1944). Symptomatology and management of acute grief. In *Crisis Intervention: Selected Readings*, ed. H.J. Parad. New York: Family Services Association of America, 1965.

Minuchin, S. (1965). Conflict resolution in family therapy. *Psychiatry* 28: 278-286.

Norman, W.C., Fensterheim, H., and Schregel, S. (1971). A systematic approach to brief therapy for patients from a low socioeconomic community. In *Brief Therapies*, ed. H. Barten. New York: Behavioral Publications.

Parad, H.J., and Caplan, G. (1960). A framework for studying families in crisis. In *Crisis Intervention: Selected Readings*, ed. H.J. Parad. New York: Family Services Association of America, 1965.

Pittman, F.S., De Young, C., Flomenhaft, K., et al. (1966). Crisis family therapy. In *Current Psychiatric Therapies*, ed. J. Masserman. New York: Grune and Stratton.

Rappaport, L. (1971). The state of crisis: some theoretical considerations. In *Brief Therapy*, ed. H. Barten. New York: Behavioral Publications.

Zuk, G.H. (1975). *Process and Practice in Family Therapy*. Haverford, Pa.: Psychiatry and Behavior Science Books.

Part IV

Crisis Intervention

13

An Overview

MANUEL STRAKER, M.D.

Crisis has always been part of the human condition and comes in various shapes and sizes. While crisis is attended by emergency reactions in those affected, the responsive intervention depends upon the urgency of presenting symptoms and the extent of failure in adaptive coping. The San Mateo County General Hospital Emergency Clinic reported that only 3 percent of their applicants were true emergencies (Thier and Levy 1969). These data suggest that crises include a wide assortment of clinical disturbances.

HISTORY

In order to better understand current behaviors in operational psychological terms, it is important not only to know the nature of the precipitating stress but also to identify the psychodynamic components which reflect the shaping influences of past developmental experiences and which determine the adaptive defenses. In fact, the systematic study of human behavior under crisis conditions has its roots in Freud's hypothesis of causality and psychic determinism. Applications of psychoanalytic theory have stimulated the development of varied models of short-term psychotherapy, among which crisis intervention is one.

Contributions from many investigators and theoreticians have led us to present-day concepts. Rado (1942) identified the importance of motivation in adaptive success or failure. He stated that brief treatment methods rely upon the same basic psychodynamic understandings needed in longer treatment, but the techniques are employed in different combinations and toward different ends. He also recommended that it is necessary to practice new solutions for current reality problems. This clearly places learning within the scope of psychotherapy.

The recognition of crisis as a normal developmental experience has been brought to us by Erickson's work (1959), which describes the sequential periods of maturational identity crises during human growth, and by Mahler's insightful observations (1961) of the infantile crises which revolve around object loss and separation-individuation.

Alexander (1946) experimented persistently with brief forms of treatment. It was his opinion that the major task is initially to reduce anxiety, gratify dependency needs, and facilitate abreaction. As soon as it can be tolerated, the stressful situation is to be reviewed with the aid of an active therapist who can manipulate the situation as needed in order to foster restabilization. If the abreaction occurs in a supportive setting, new coping skills and new judgments can develop. Under optimal conditions, this becomes the "corrective emotional experience." He also emphasized the importance of early intervention and early treatment termination "to permit further independence and ego growth to continue unaided." These writings represent an obvious departure from the established psychoanalytic practices of his time and clearly have significance to the management of crisis episodes.

Attention to external situational crises surfaced in the psychiatric literature with increasing frequency. The World War II military literature described brief treatment for the combat neuroses and for the transient disorganizations due to exhaustion or injury (Office of Surgeon General 1973). However, the emergence of definitive crisis intervention is most clearly related to the work of Lindemann (1944) and Caplan (1964).

Lindemann studied onset, process, and grief work in catastrophic bereavement. Stressful mourning is attended by somatic symptoms, depression, guilt, hostility, a sense of unreality, and loss of the usual behavioral patterns. If the grief work is successfully concluded, there is reconstitution of the ego and further growth can then occur. If not, a chronic regressive maladaptive reaction develops and persists. The therapeutic task is to carry out a careful review, redefine and reformulate the stressful crisis, and help to mobilize the patient's repertoire of problem-solving skills so as to achieve resolution.

Caplan studied the successive adaptive reactions in crisis. The first rise of tension activates the usual range of coping mechanisms. Should these prove inadequate to meet the stress demands, emergency coping responses appear. An initial reaction of dazed shock may be followed by primitive fight-flight reactions. Thus a coping failure leads to disorganization and/or apathetic resignation. Renewed coping attempts are now initiated at a more regressed level. On the other hand, successful coping is accompanied by a reformulation of the crisis event. There is symptom reduction and resolution.

Social psychiatry has further focused attention upon social precipitants and external events and studied their impact on illness. Holmes and Rahe (1967) designed a quantitative social readjustment rating scale to value weight a variety of stressful life events which precede crisis. When their scale total exceeds 300, there is a high risk that a major depression or other illness will develop within the year. Other studies have identified the special stresses associated with pregnancy (Bibring 1961), parenthood (Benedek 1959), migration (Koranyi et al 1963), family disruption (Langly and Kaplan 1968), retirement (Straker 1963), catastrophic illness (Visotsky and Hamburg 1961), rape (Burgess and Holmstrom 1976), and the impact of unusual environments such as prisons (Cormier and Williams 1966) and concentration camps (Straker 1971). This by no means exhausts the list of noxious stresses.

During the period since WW II, psychiatry has moved rapidly into new directions of service delivery. The inclusion of such services within the general hospital placed the psychiatrist in outpatient clinics, into the emergency room, and out to various hospital wards as liaison-consultant. The development of mental health centers, crisis clinics, walk-in clinics, etc., and the expansion of private psychiatric practices have placed the professionals into new roles and into contact with a variety of emotionally disturbed patients who present problems different than those seen in an institutional setting and which require different strategies and therapeutic techniques. The hospital emergency room has become a crisis center in addition to its more traditional roles. "The psychiatric emergency usually involves some acute condition with people who are frightened, desperate, hopeless, driven by self-destructive impulses or paralyzed by conflict or anxiety" (Farnsworth 1970). "The emergency may be a state in which there are personal overwhelming feelings of catastrophe, irrespective of any particular diagnostic category of mental illness" (Wayne 1966). The presenting syndrome may be a panic attack, assaultive or suicidal behaviors, a drug intoxication or a psychotic process, among others. This also includes patients whose commitment is initiated in the crisis setting. "The kinds of patients for whom involuntary confinement may be deemed appropriate are typically panicked and terrified. They are wary and distrustful or agitated and difficult to reach. Their families and friends are often exhausted and desperate after having been caught up in the patient's pathology and their own responses to it. The complicated human dynamic of crisis is what the psychiatrist must confront" (Stone 1977). This brief scanning of the range of crises makes it clear that the appropriate therapeutic response may be psychological, biologic, pharmacotherapeutic, environmental manipulation, or control by brief hospitalization or various combinations of these strategies.

Recent contributions to the psychologic theory and treatment of crises have come from Jacobson (1965) and from the work of Horowitz (1973, 1974, 1976). Jacobson distinguished generic and individual approaches. The generic approach rests upon the tendency for specific life crises to evoke similar responses in different persons, e.g., in facing bereavement, retirement, or other common life stresses. The therapist may use this knowledge regarding the universality of these stresses to provide support, reassurance, and help to the distressed patient in facing the crisis by sharing and benefiting from the experiences of others. The attention is thus focused upon the specific crisis and how it may be resolved. On the other hand, the assessment may demonstrate that intrapsychic factors are of special importance in shaping the crisis response, so an individualized therapeutic approach may be more appropriate. He therefore emphasizes that it is essential to assess not only the problem but also the person with the problem.

Horowitz (1974) has pointed out that major stress evokes a general stress response, which is marked by individual variations according to personality predisposition. The characteristics of the stress response syndrome include: (1) onset of symptoms after a latent period, (2) compulsive tendency to symbolic repetition of some aspect of the traumatic experience, (3) phasic alternation between denial (numbness) and intrusive repetition, (4) at some point an acute stress response syndrome, (5) profound protracted stress that leads to permanent chronic effects no matter what the structure of the prestress personality. This formulation incorporates the clinical findings from studies of concentration camp (Krystal and Niederland 1968) and Hiroshima survivors (Lifton 1968).

Horowitz interprets the denial "numbed" phase as symptomatic of overcontrol, while the intrusive thoughts and feelings signify undercontrol. In both information and emotional processing, the therapeutic efforts are to be directed toward specific goals and fulfilled by the use of technical maneuvers which are phase determined. He has emphasized that there is individual variation for time in phase, oscillation of phases, and also in presenting signs and symptoms. In more recent work, he has stated that treatment should not only be phase specific but also reflect recognition of the individual variations which will take into account the habitual individual defenses.

CRISIS DEFINITION AND GOALS OF INTERVENTION

Crisis has been described as an upset in the steady state accompanied by failure of coping and problem-solving behaviors (Hankoff 1969). This occurs as a signal of strain in an individual going through a major transition period, when the threats and adaptive demands are beyond the coping resources (Rapoport 1965). It represents a situation "where the adaptive tasks demand the mobilization of new resources in psychological competence and social skills" (Adams and Lindemann 1974). The acute state of dysequilibrium reflects a sudden shift of internal homeostatic defenses and at times may be precipitated by the overuse of drugs or alcohol or be signaled by a suicidal attempt (Spitz 1976). The crisis disruption is marked by a temporary state of increased fluidity which causes a rise in the patient's susceptibility to therapeutic intervention (Stierlin 1968). This means that the temporary state of heightened susceptibility presents an unparalleled opportunity for internal boundary realignments. It is an opportunity for better—or for worse.

The goals of crisis intervention are both therapeutic and preventive. A time-limited, problem-focused intervention aims to identify, confront, and resolve the crisis, repair the disrupted equilibrium, and support the development or return of appropriate adaptive responses. The reduction of symptoms and the restoration of equilibrium indicate that a maladaptive regressive disorganization has been prevented. In uncomplicated situations, a number of therapeutic objectives may be telescoped and condensed into as few as one or two contacts. The mastery of a stressful life crisis may enhance the range of coping skills, leading to an unanticipated maturation (Wolberg 1954).

Preventive intervention for high-risk populations and for those in high-risk life situations remains an area relatively unexplored, although some studies have been published. Preventive psychological support, exploration, and education may indeed be appropriate prior to surgery, retirement, to assist the dying, and for others facing major life stresses. It is already established that timely crisis intervention may prevent or reduce hospitalization to a brief period and reduce the total burden of morbidity (Spaulding et al. 1976, Rhine and Mayerson 1971, Straker et al. 1971).

PSYCHOPATHOLOGY OF CRISIS DEVELOPMENT

A crisis develops when the customary adaptive coping mechanisms are inadequate for the perceived threat, whether actual or impending. In such a situation, the anxiety level rises and mobilizes idiosyncratic ego defenses. Horowitz (1974) has described the particular operational defenses in hysterical and obsessional personalities, also indicating how this should decide the selection of therapeutic strategies. If a coping failure ensues, there is a loosening of ego boundaries, with an initial regressive confusion. There is a release of primitive emergency affective responses, and a sense of unreality develops. Under such conditions, cognitive processing is also impaired.

If new resources for reestablished psychological competence adequate to meet the stress become mobilized, there is a reduction in the emergency state. This can be aided by external support and by a reformulation of the crisis situation into less-threatening terms. Anxiety-laden assumptions are modified, options are examined, choices are made and tested in real-life action, and then evaluated. As coping mastery returns, appropriate actions replace the previous panic, and homeostatic equilibrium is reestablished. During the recovery period, tentative or proposed solutions are reviewed, reassessed, reinforced, and thoroughly integrated. This is essentially a process which involves new learning (Beebe 1975). If resolution fails to take place within a period of four to six weeks, a chronic maladaptive state ensues. While phases can vary in time, the usual crisis is normally self-limiting, and by six weeks the crisis is over or the patient has settled into a chronic symptomatic disorder.

In a recent paper on battlefield psychiatry, Koranyi (1977) reviewed stress concepts, crisis, and the theory of emotions. He makes an effort to correlate recent neurophysiological, biochemical, and endocrinologic data as they may apply to acute stressors and the range of adaptive responses which follow. The gaps in our current knowledge still continue to pose an insurmountable barrier. "The exact mechanism whereby a homeostatic storm produces perceptual distortion and cognitive misreporting ranging at times to dramatic mental phenomena, is still an unresolved question."

MODELS FOR CRISIS INTERVENTION

The locale of treatment may be the patient's home, the physician's office, the hospital bedside, the emergency room, or the walk-in clinic. A number of variables will determine whether a protective environment or brief hospitalization is necessary (Spaulding et al. 1976, Rhine and Mayerson 1971, Straker et al. 1971). These are determined by the nature and severity of the crisis, the extent of personality disorganization, the capacity for adaptive reintegration, and the availability of external supports, and may be the best provided in a hospital setting. This may be the case if a psychotic process or serious suicidal risk is identified. The treatment most appropriate may be a supportive psychotherapeutic approach, mobilizing the assistance of helpful others, the temporary use of medication, or providing a brief period of protective security. It is clearly necessary to assess crisis, the patient's response and resources, and the total setting in which the dramatic events are set.

To assist in such clinical decisions, the examination process will define the following issues:

1. The disruptive current life event is known to patient and therapist. This is not always the case at first, and persistent efforts may be necessary to establish which recent happening is the significant precipitant.

2. The patient is capable of establishing a therapeutic alliance. When chaotic disorganization is part of the presenting clinical syndrome, the initial need may be for calm, supportive reassurance, taking over decision making until ego functions can be restored, and providing suitable medication to shield the patient from overwhelming affective flooding.

3. The patient has the motivation to engage in the necessary task. This will be influenced by the crisis perception of the therapist's intervention.

4. The capacity for reality testing and affective response is evaluated.

5. By history from the patient or others, data are collected about the adaptive resources and responses to past life crises, whether similar or otherwise.

6. Suicidal risk and lethality potential are evaluated.

The application of these criteria will sort crisis patients for immediate management purposes, regardless of the clinical diagnosis. It will identify those who are suicidal, psychotic, extremely dependent, grossly immature and/or especially impulsive. For these patients, the appropriate intervention may combine a number of therapeutic approaches.

The developments of emergency room psychiatry have tested and established clinically useful management techniques (Straker 1975). The major neuroleptics given I/V or I/M and carefully titrated can be extremely helpful for an assaultive, explosive or excited patient and can rapidly reverse a psychotic decompensation. The minor tranquilizers are extremely helpful to diminish unbearable anxiety or as adjunct in convulsive disorders. Drug or alcohol intoxications can be rapidly assisted by psychotherapeutic support, rest, and I/V haloperidol, librium 50-100 mgm I/V or Valium 10-20 mgm I/V. This is not the place to review medication use in detail, but there is substantial agreement that when the goal is a resumption of normal behavior, psychotropics, when carefully titrated in relationship to the clinical condition, are very useful to ameliorate target symptoms. Under such conditions, drugs are not given as an alternative to psychotherapy, but rather to enhance the conditions for psychotherapy (Rosenthal 1968, Ostow 1968).

On the other hand, the patient who is immediately accessible, highly motivated, verbal, and can actively participate in a problem-solving approach will quickly be identified. Assessment of the adaptive resources will also indicate whether the patient is likely to stick to the task until a satisfactory resolution is achieved or whether special risks exist that should be taken into account in the therapeutic encounter.

Crisis intervention can be described under three major models:

1. The oldest is the intervention which depends upon providing reassurance, support, help of a practical kind, and reducing anxiety by "taking over" while there is a temporary impairment of capacity to think clearly and act appropriately. This is essentially an empathic, caring, human response to one who is temporarily overwhelmed or terribly frightened. "A variety of people can do crisis intervention. The intervention has to be practical—it is not the best time for fancy psychological interpretations. It is the time for action and for practical things" (Shneidman 1973). What is most important is the immediate availability of help from an active and supportive therapist. The value of this method is well indicated by results achieved from even one or two contacts (ultra-brief therapy) in some cases. Another suggestive finding is the pattern of "patient dropout," as the crisis condition abates and the patient's need to return for further help no longer is evident.

2. The second model arises from psychoanalytic applications. As above, the reaching out with immediate support and encouragement is important, but the assessment includes a psychodynamic formulation, and a deliberate effort is made to mobilize and maintain a positive transference to sustain and motivate the patient. The transference is helpful in keeping the patient focused upon the presenting

crisis problem. While the patient is receiving support, confrontation and abreaction are important segments of the working-through process toward resolution. While interpretations are made as these relate to the connections between events, behavioral patterns, and relationship sequences, the patient-therapist transference is not, as a rule, specifically interpreted. The detached, distant, and uninvolved therapist does not do well with this approach. However, the therapist who is energetic, interested, capable of risk taking, and hopeful is an important asset and ally for the anxious patient (Frank 1968).

3. The third model approaches crisis intervention as a focal dynamic psychotherapy in which interpretation of ego defenses, the transference, and a flexible use of interpretative skills are essential strategies (Horowitz 1973, 1974, 1976). In many respects, this development in the field of crisis intervention parallels the recent work of Sifneos (1967), Malan (1976) and others in Short-Term Dynamic Psychotherapy.

STEPS IN CRISIS-INTERVENTION THERAPY

1. A supportive, anxiety-reducing rapport is established. The psychiatrist is trained to listen empathically and help the patient gain perspective on both internal and external environments and to work collaboratively for potential solutions (Sullivan 1954).

2. As the working alliance develops, data are collected to identify the crisis, precipitants, and sequence of events. Special attention is directed to elicit the crisis life incident and to focus efforts toward reformulation and resolution. The background history establishes the adaptive ego resources, external supports, and the nature of the transference.

3. While supportively monitoring the anxiety levels, the therapist clarifies, connects events, sums up, and offers simple, focused hypotheses or explanations. As the patient's understanding expands, a cathartic reexperience of the crisis situation becomes possible.

4. Encouraged and guided, the patient modifies irrational assumptions, considers the options, and selects the most practical ego-syntonic solutions. Working through and new learning are taking place.

5. The patient's own solution is accepted, supported, tested, and reinforced. When the problem subsides, the contact ends (Beebe 1975).

6. Within the first therapeutic encounter, a "contract" is developed which defines the intervention objectives and limits the time and number of sessions to no more than six weeks.

The approach is essentially a problem-solving one. The crisis situation is assessed, its evolution and component elements are analyzed, possible outcomes are considered, and a treatment plan is developed. The latter must recognize the individual's coping resources and limitations. The intervention includes support, active reassurance, summing up, clarification, educative reinforcement, counseling and guidance, facilitating catharsis, "reopening the social world," and reinforcing the resolution methods which are chosen.

The process of exploration covers precipitants, the specific crisis event in detail, the patient's own perceptions of the problem, the solutions already tried, the habitual life style and coping patterns, the external supports, and what special risks are present. The inquiry is supportive and extends to include past similar experiences. The aim is to develop an explanation of the query "Why now?" Possible casual explanations are offered tentatively while evaluating the range of patient reaction and agreement. The "right" explanation is usually greeted by relief and vigorous assent from the patient. The focus is kept upon the crisis problem, with confrontation of resistances and defenses as tolerated. When the crisis is over, the therapeutic intervention stops. The average number of sessions does not exceed six interviews.

Different intervention styles call for a variety of skills. Many crises can be managed equally well by a wide range of mental health professionals. Aynet (1965) reported a large series of patients treated with brief psychotherapy, in which outcome was similar with treatment by social worker, psychologist, or psychiatrist. However, Bellak and Small (1965) emphasized the importance of diagnosis and the need to understand the problem in a psychodynamic context. The therapist is active in the sense of intervening frequently to develop the crisis situation and to provide support. A great asset is the capacity to know when short cuts are in order (Menninger 1963), to take risks, and to be able to conceptualize and pursue short-term goals rather than long-term objectives. Indeed McGuire (1965) recommends a selective inattention to data which relate to characterologic or long-range issues. The therapist must be skilled in interviewing, in developing and maintaining transference, in being an advocate for focused attention, and above all, in demonstrating clinical judgment in choosing the timing and style of intervention and interpretation. Even simple educative reformulations or clarifications can produce remarkable results at times. When the crisis is associated with some medical problem, as is often the case in consultation-liaison work, a medical background is an invaluable asset.

TERMINATION AND OUTCOME

The acute crisis usually does not last beyond four to six weeks, either resolving by that time or settling into a chronic symptomatic state. The average number of interviews does not exceed six as a general rule. By agreement, the treatment contact is terminated when the crisis is over. This leaves the patient with a continuing positive transference. This helps the patient to think of return in the future if a new life crisis occurs, and this is aided when termination is left open ended, with the shared understanding that the contact can be resumed, if necessary. The time-limited approach encourages maximal responsibility for self-direction, supports self-esteem, and minimizes the risk that strong dependency needs will surface. Maximal flexibility can be exercised in varying both the frequency of contact and the interval between visits. This is decided by an agreement which reflects both patient wishes and clinical judgment. The shared goal is the disappearance of crisis symptoms and the return to the pre-illness state.

The expected outcome is not invariably attained. A common exception occurs when the patient drops out of treatment prior to the agreed termination point. In many such instances, the therapist has failed to perceive the actual progress of resolution or has unwittingly set longer-term goals without the patient's concurrence. Some psychotherapists suffer a nagging disbelief that much can be accomplished so quickly. The other frequent variation is that dependency needs complicate the initial aims and objectives, and as termination approaches, symptoms reexacerbate. Under such conditions, it becomes clear that some patients should continue with more prolonged treatment as these issues relate to characterologic problems.

Good results are reported in about 80 percent of the patients treated. While controlled studies are few, Malan's work (1975) is a careful documentation which demonstrates beyond doubt that powerful therapeutic effects can follow a single psychodynamic interview. In that study, it was demonstrated that 25 percent of such patients manifested significant psychodynamic change and further growth.

The clinical conviction is that timely crisis intervention is extremely helpful for most patients. It is also inexpensive, is associated with rapid recovery, and can be offered by medical and nonmedical, trained providers. Some risks do exist to temper an unqualified enthusiasm for this technique. Legislators in search of cost-effective procedures sometimes make overinclusive decisions. It would be disastrous if the brief therapy model were offered as a panacea or suitable replacement for all other forms of psychotherapy. Clinical judgment reaffirms the importance of individualizing each treatment plan to fit the patient's needs. Crisis intervention can be the treatment of choice in a crisis situation and for selected patients, but the method is hardly the unchallenged successor to all other forms of psychotherapy. Much work remains to be done in testing the limits of application in a wide variety of clinical and life situations.

References

Adams, J. E., and Lindemann, E. (1974). Coping with long-term disability. In *Coping and Adaptation*, ed. G.V. Coelho, D. Hamburg, and J. E. Adams, pp. 127-138, New York: Basic Books.

Alexander, F., and French, T. (1946). *Psychoanalytic Therapy*. New York: Ronald Press.

Aynet, H. (1965). How effective is short-term psychotherapy? In *Short-Term Psychotherapy*, ed. L. Wolberg. New York: Grune and Stratton.

Beebe, J. (1975). Principles of crisis intervention in psychiatric treatment. In *Psychiatric Treatment: Crisis/Clinic/Consultation*, ed. C. P. Rosenbaum and J. Beebe. New York: McGraw-Hill.

Bellak, L., and Small, L. (1965). *Emergency Psychotherapy and Brief Psychotherapy*. New York: Grune and Stratton.

Benedek, T. (1959). Parenthood as a developmental phase. *Journal of the American Psychoanalytic Association* 7:389-417.

Bibring, G.L., Dwyer, T.F., and Huntington, D.S. (1961). Study of the psychological process in pregnancy and of the earliest mother-child relationship. *Psychoanalytic Study of the Child* 16:9-44.

234 MANUEL STRAKER

Burgess, A.W., and Holmstrom, L.L. (1976). Coping behavior of the rape victim. *American Journal of Psychiatry* 133:(4)413-418.

Caplan, G. (1964). *Principles of Preventive Psychiatry.* New York: Basic Books.

Cormier, B., and Williams, P. (1966). La Privation Excessive de la Liberté. *Canadian Psychiatric Association Journal* 11:47-484.

Erikson, E. (1959). *Identity and the Life Cycle.* Psychological issues, Monograph No. 1. New York: International Universities Press.

Farnsworth, D. (1970). Psychiatric emergencies. *International Psychiatric Clinics* 7:227-235.

Frank, J.D. (1968). The role of hope in psychotherapy. *International Journal of Psychiatry* 5:383-395.

Hankoff, L.D. (1969). *Emergency Psychiatric Treatment.* Springfield, Ill.: Charles C Thomas.

Holmes, T.H., and Rahe, R. (1967). The social readjustment rating scale. *Journal of Psychosomatics* 11:213-218.

Horowitz, M.J. (1973). Phase oriented treatment of stress response syndrome. *American Journal of Psychotherapy* 27:(4)506-515.

———— (1974). Stress response syndromes. *Archives of General Psychiatry* 31:768-781.

———— (1976). Diagnosis and treatment of stress response syndrome. In *Emergency and Disaster Management,* ed. H.J. Parad, H.L. Resnick, and L.G. Parad, pp. 259-269. Bowie, Maryland: Charles Press.

Jacobson, G. (1965). Crisis theory and treatment strategy. *Journal of Nervous and Mental Disease* 141:209-218.

Koranyi, E. (1977). Psychobiological correlates of battlefield psychiatry. *Psychiatric Journal, University of Ottawa* 2(1):1-19.

Koranyi, E., Kerenyi, A., and Sarwer-Foner, G. (1963). Adaptive difficulties of some Hungarian immigrants. *Comprehensive Psychiatry* 4:(1)47-57.

Krystal, H., and Niederland, W.G. (1968). Clinical observation on the survivor syndrome. In *Massive Psychic Trauma,* ed. H. Krystal, pp. 327-348. New York: International Universities Press.

Langley, D., and Kaplan, D. (1968). *Treatment of Families in Crisis.* New York: Grune and Stratton.

Lifton, R.E. (1968). Observations on Hiroshima survivors. In *Massive Psychic Trauma,* ed. H. Krystal, pp. 168-189. New York: International Universities Press.

Lindemann, E. (1944). Symptomatology and management of acute grief. *American Journal of Psychiatry* 101:141-148.

Mahler, M. (1961). On sadness and grief in infancy and childhood. *Psychoanalytic Study of the Child* 6:332-351.

Malan, D. (1976). *The Frontier of Brief Psychotherapy.* New York: Plenum.

Malan, D., Heath, E.S., Bacal, H.A., and Balfour, F.H.G. (1975). Psycho-dynamic changes in untreated neurotic patients. *Archives of General Psychiatry* 32:110-126.

McGuire, M.T. (1965). The process of short-term insight psychotherapy. II: Content, expectations and structure. *Journal of Nervous and Mental Disease* 141:219-230.

Menninger, K. (1963). *The Vital Balance.* New York: Viking.

Office of the Surgeon General (1973). *Neuropsychiatry of World War II*, Vols. I and II. Washington, D.C.: Department of the Army.

Ostow, M. (1968). The consequences of ambivalence. *Psychosomatics* 9:5.

Rado, S. (1942). In *Proceedings of the Brief Psychotherapy Council*, p. 44. Chicago: The Institute for Psychoanalysis.

Rapaport, L. (1965). The state of crisis: some theoretical considerations. In *Crisis Intervention*, ed. H.J. Parad. New York: Family Service Association of America.

Rhine, M.W., and Mayerson, P. (1971). Crisis hospitalization within a psychiatric emergency service. *American Journal of Psychiatry* 127:1387-1391.

Rosenthal, H.M. (1968). Drug therapy in breaks and breakdowns. *Treatment Monographs on Analytic Psychotherapy* 2.

Shneidman, E. S. (1973). Crisis intervention: some thoughts and perspectives in crisis intervention. In *Crisis Intervention* (Continuing Series in Community-Clinical Psychology, Vol. II), Chapter 1, ed. G. A. Specter and W. L. Claiborn. New York: Behavioral Publications.

Sifneos, P. (1967). Two different kinds of psychotherapy of short duration. *American Journal of Psychiatry* 123:1069-1074.

Spaulding, R. C., Edwards, D., and Fichnian, S. (1976). The effect of psychiatric hospitalization in crisis. *Comprehensive Psychiatry* 17(3): 457-460.

Spitz, L. (1976). The evolution of a psychiatric emergency crisis. *Comprehensive Psychiatry* 17(1):99-113.

Stierlin, H. (1968). Short-term vs. long-term psychotherapy in the light of a general theory of human relationships. *British Journal of Medical Psychology* 41:357.

Stone, A. A. (1977). Recent mental health litigation: a critical perspective. *American Journal of Psychiatry* 134:273-279.

Straker, M. (1963). Prognosis for psychiatric illness in the aged. *American Journal of Psychiatry* 119:1069-1075.

——— (1972). Survivor syndrome. *Laval Medical* 42:37-41.

——— (1975). The psychiatric emergency. In *Consultation-Liaison Psychiatry*, Chapter 13, ed. R. Pasnau. New York: Grune and Stratton.

Straker, M., Yung, C., and Weiss, L. (1971). A comprehensive emergency psychiatric service in a general hospital. *Canadian Psychiatric Association Journal* 16:137-139.

Sullivan, H. S. (1954). *The Psychiatric Interview*. New York: Norton.

Thier, T., and Levy, R. (1969). Emergent, urgent and elective admissions. *Archives of General Psychiatry* 21:423-430.

Visotsky, H., and Hamburg, D. (1961). Coping behavior under extreme stress: observation of patients with severe poliomyelitis. *Archives of General Psychiatry* 5:423-448.

Wayne, G. (1966). The psychiatric emergency: an overview. In *Emergency Psychiatry and Brief Therapy*, ed. G. Wayne and R. Koegler. *International Psychiatric Clinics* 3:3-8.

Wolberg, L. (1954). Brief of short-term psychotherapy. In *Techniques of Psychotherapy*. New York: Grune and Stratton.

14

Crisis Intervention and Short-Term Dynamic Psychotherapy

Judd Marmor, M.D.

The spectrum of short-term psychotherapeutic approaches extends from emergency treatment at one pole to Short-Term Dynamic Psychotherapy at the other, with crisis intervention in between. Although broad distinctions can be made between these three approaches, they are by no means sharply delimited from one another. It is not unusual for emergency treatment to merge into crisis intervention or for crisis intervention to merge into Short-Term Dynamic Psychotherapy. Nevertheless, there is a difference of focus in these three approaches which merits discussion.

Emergency treatment implies the provision of immediate relief or help to persons who have decompensated psychologically and who are unable to cope with the stress situation in which they find themselves. In other words, in emergency treatment one is dealing with individuals whose adaptive mechanisms have broken down, who are unable to cope, and who require immediate help and relief from their disabling symptoms.

Crisis intervention implies the provision of relief, or the attempt to provide relief, to persons who are in danger of decompensating from a specific stress situation, either internal or external, and are coping poorly. The approach of the crisis interventionist may be simply to try to remove the stress situation or ameliorate it, or to provide emotional support to the person in crisis. Some crisis theorists, however, make a distinction between crisis support and crisis intervention. They designate as crisis support those approaches that aim merely at providing support or modifying the stress and reserve the term *crisis intervention* for approaches that go beyond support to helping the individual cope more effectively with the immediate stress situation as well as similar future ones. When crisis intervention techniques move into the area of attempting to modify the coping behavior of the individual, they are edging into the borderline area between crisis intervention and Short-Term Dynamic Psychotherapy.

In Short-Term Dynamic Psychotherapy one is dealing with individuals who may or may not be caught in a specific stress situation as exists in crisis intervention. In short-term psychotherapy the patient may or may not present with a crisis, but there is always an underlying conflict situation, and the emphasis in Short-Term Dynamic Psychotherapy is on the resolution of the conflict and the modifying of the coping techniques of the individual toward the goal of more adaptive functioning.

SIMILARITIES BETWEEN CRISIS INTERVENTION AND SHORT-TERM DYNAMIC PSYCHOTHERAPY

There are a number of similarities between the techniques of crisis intervention and Short-Term Dynamic Psychotherapy. (1) In both approaches the patient is seen in a face-to-face situation. The analytic couch is not a part of either technique as a rule. (2) In both approaches a time limit is set for the total duration of the therapy. The number of hours may be clearly specified, or occasionally in Short-Term Dynamic Psychotherapy there may be simply a time limit that is set in terms of weeks or months. In crisis intervention the time limitation is generally a briefer one. As a rule, crisis intervention encompasses not more than six visits, although occasionally as many as ten may be employed. In contrast, the length of Short-Term

Dynamic Psychotherapy ranges in the neighborhood of twelve to twenty visits, as a rule, although the number may go as high as forty. (3) Both crisis intervention and Short-Term Dynamic Psychotherapy are focused approaches, but there are some differences in the focus, which will be clarified below.

DIFFERENCES BETWEEN CRISIS INTERVENTION AND SHORT-TERM DYNAMIC PSYCHOTHERAPY

Focus. In crisis intervention the focus is primarily on the stress situation: What is the problem? Why is the patient upset? What is the immediate factor that is causing him/her to be in danger of decompensating? How can the stress situation best be dealt with? (Parenthetically, in emergency treatment the primary focus is neither on the stress situation nor the core conflict but on removing the presenting and disabling symptom as rapidly as possible. Secondarily, efforts may be made to deal with the stress situation, if time and circumstances permit.)

In Short-Term Dynamic Psychotherapy, on the other hand, the primary focus is on the core conflict and on enabling the patient to develop more effective techniques in coping with the core conflict. In contrast, crisis intervention deals only secondarily with improving the coping capacity of the individual. I am not implying that crisis intervention is not concerned with the patient's coping capacity, but that its primary goal is the restoration of homeostasis. It is only fair to point out that there are crisis theorists who disagree with me and who would say, "That isn't enough of a goal. The good crisis therapist goes beyond the restoration of homeostasis and hopes and tries to improve the coping ability of the patient so that in future similar stress situations the patient will be able to cope more effectively." I do not deny this, but I would insist nevertheless that the primary focus, the primary effort in crisis therapy, is on restoration of homeostasis. Obviously, if one can, if one has the time, if the case load permits, if the patient's psychodynamic potential permits, then one can move over into some kind of limited short-term psychotherapeutic approach. On the other hand, the primary goal of Short-Term Dynamic Psychotherapy is basically to improve the patient's ego-adaptive capacity. So, its focus is from the beginning basically a different one from that of crisis intervention.

Termination. How do the two approaches compare as regards the question of when treatment is terminated? Again, there are indistinct borders, but at least in terms of immediate goals, the termination point of crisis intervention is reached when the crisis is resolved. Once the crisis is resolved, one has arrived at the end of the crisis intervention unless both therapist and patient agree that they want to go beyond that. In contrast, in Short-Term Dynamic Psychotherapy, termination takes place at the end of the contract, which is usually a specified number of visits. However, if the number of visists is not specifically indicated, the termination point of Short-Term Dynamic Psychotherapy is when the patient shows evidence of being able to cope more effectively with the core conflict situation which brought him or her into treatment.

Degree of emotional support. A third important difference is that crisis intervention is generally a more supportive approach than is Short-Term Dynamic Psychotherapy. Inasmuch as the immediate goal of crisis intervention is to deal with the stress situation and to restore homeostasis, the crisis therapist generally tends to be more supportive than confronting. In contrast, in Short-Term Dynamic Psychotherapy, the emphasis is much more on confrontation and interpretation than on emotional support. Again, this is not to imply that the crisis therapist may not utilize confrontation and interpretation or that the short-term therapist may not be supportive, but only that the primary emphasis in each approach tends to be different. When I say that the short-term therapist is confronting, I am not implying that he or she is directive. There is a distinction between being active and being directive. In crisis intervention there tends to be a greater degree of directiveness, though not necessarily. Since the goal of such therapy is not so much to improve the coping techniques of the individual as to resolve the emotional crisis, the crisis interventionist may be directive, e.g., tell the patient what to do or what kind of environmental manipulation ought to be involved in removing the stress situation. For example, a young housewife in crisis because of an overextended visit from her mother-in-law might be advised to ask her husband to get his mother out of the home. Thus there might be a direct intervention technique which would result in the mother-in-law leaving the home and the crisis being resolved. In Short-Term Dynamic Psychotherapy, however, such a directive technique would not be characteristic. The main goal of the therapy is to improve the adaptive capacities of the patient. Although the therapist may be active, just as the crisis interventionist is active, the technique in Short-Term Dynamic Therapy is less directive, more interpretive, and confronting.

Time focus. Still another difference is that crisis intervention generally deals only with the here and the now. It is concerned with the presenting problem and with enabling the individual to resolve the presenting problem. By contrast, inasmuch as Short-Term Dynamic Psychotherapy is an interpretive and uncovering technique, its goal is—as much as possible—to link the past with the present in the context of the transference interaction between the patient and the therapist. Thus one has what Karl Menninger has called the "triangular" goal of interpretation, linking together the past, the present, and the transference relationship to the therapist whenever the opportunity to do so exists.

Therapeutic context. Still another difference is that, in general, Short-Term Dynamic Psychotherapy is a one-to-one technique. That is not to say that it cannot at times be utilized in a group context, but thus far in the history of Short-Term Dynamic Psychotherapy, it has been utilized primarily as a one-to-one technique. In crisis intervention, however, there is a more flexible approach to the context of the therapeutic process. In the interest of resolving the crisis, the crisis interventionist may call in the spouse and work in conjoint marital therapy, or may decide to convene the entire family and try to resolve the disturbances in family dynamics that are behind or underlying the crisis situation, or may decide that in the interests of resolving the crisis, the individual might be dealt with best in a group context. Thus, in crisis intervention there is a broader spectrum of approaches and techniques. Even though crisis theory grew out of analytical theory and was developed primarily by analytically oriented people, the modern crisis interventionist is nevertheless not limited technically just to psychodynamic techniques, but may find it useful at times to employ behavioral techniques or any other kind of immediate intervention that might help to modify the crisis situation.

Duration of symptoms. In general, in crisis intervention one is dealing with an acute situation. By definition, a crisis implies a stress situation of relatively short duration. On the other hand, in Short-Term Dynamic Psychotherapy the duration of the symptoms is not of primary importance. In Short-Term Dynamic Psychotherapy one may be dealing with a problem that has been in existence for a long time. The duration is not a primary determinant.

Severity of symptomatology. The difference here are not sharp. It is true that, in general, crisis interventionists feel that they work best (as indeed who doesn't!) with individuals who are not too severely disturbed. Nevertheless, assuming that one is not dealing with a patient who requires hospitalization, a crisis interventionist can work with an individual who is severely disturbed because the emphasis is not really on the severity of the disturbance of the individual as much as it is on the severity of the stress situation. An individual may be extremely disturbed due to a very severe stress situation, and modifying that stress situation may relieve the severity of the symptomatology. Thus the focus in crisis intervention is not on the severity of symptomatology so much as it is on the question of whether the removal of a stress situation will help. In World War II, individuals were sometimes seen who had very severe symptomatology, bordering or paranoid-schizophrenic reactions. The symptoms had appeared under inordinate stress situations, say at Guadalcanal, where soldiers were being subjected, day and night, twenty-four hours a day, to intense bombardments and shelling. Removing the stress situation relieved those very severe symptoms rather rapidly. This was a form of crisis intervention that did not involve any interpretive techniques—they were really not even indicated.

Diagnosis. When we talk about severity of symptoms, we also come into the area of diagnosis. What kinds of diagnoses are suitable for crisis intervention versus short-term stress situations? In both situations we find that we don't particularly focus on diagnostic classification as such, but rather on what the balance is between the ego-adaptive capacities of the individual and the life situation with which they have to deal. The difference here is that in crisis intervention there is not as much focus, nor as much need to focus as strongly, on the ego-adaptive capacities of the individual as there is in Short-Term Dynamic Psychotherapy. Since in crisis intervention the primary focus is on the removal of stress, one can deal with a patient in crisis even though the ego-adaptive capacities of that individual may not be all that one would like them to be. One may move on from there into a psychotherapeutic relationship, but the primary focus is on the stress. On the other hand, since the primary focus in Short-

Term Dynamic Psychotherapy is on improving the ego-adaptive capacities of the individual, one has to be concerned that the patient is capable of working within the context of a short-term dynamic framework, and therefore the selective criteria with regard to Short-Term Dynamic Psychotherapy make a greater demand on the coping patterns of the individual, as indicated in his/her past history and interpersonal relationships, than they need do in crisis intervention.

Socioeconomic status of patients. Do socioeconomic factors have any bearing on whether one employs crisis intervention or Short-Term Dynamic Psychotherapy? They do and they don't. As a rule, blue-collar people and working-class people are not as attuned to psychological thinking and uncovering techniques as are middle-class, upper-middle, and upper-class people. That is to say, the cultural background of the patient sometimes has a bearing indirectly on his or her readiness to work with one technique or another. However, this is not an absolute thing. Some upper-class people may be quite insensitive psychologically; on the other hand, one can run into an individual of lower socioeconomic status who is psychologically sensitive, aware of unconscious factors, and emotionally resonant to his or her feelings. Such an individual may well be a candidate for an uncovering therapeutic approach. But, in general, clinical experience shows that individuals who are less advantaged culturally are more apt to seek immediate relief by the modification of the stress situation wherever that is possible, than they are to involve themselves in psychodynamic uncovering techniques.

15

The Technique of Crisis Evaluation and Intervention

HABIB DAVANLOO, M.D.

THE CONCEPT OF CRISIS

As formulated by Eric Lindemann, crisis refers to the state of a reacting individual who finds himself in a hazardous situation. It seems that the words *crisis* and *stress* are often used interchangeably, but the term *hazardous situation* is preferable and is the phrase Eric Lindemann used in his conceptualization and formulation of crisis theory and therapy. Historically, the development of a crisis theory and its practical application to the technique of crisis intervention date back to 1942.

On a Saturday in November after the big Boston College-Holy Cross football game, eight-hundred people were celebrating in one of Boston's oldest night clubs, the Coconut Grove, when the club suddenly caught fire. This tragic event is referred to as the Coconut Grove Fire; nearly five-hundred persons died, and another two-hundred were hospitalized, leaving hundreds of families in a state of bereavement. It was Lindemann, at the Massachusetts General Hospital, who studied the survivors and published his classic paper, "Symptomatology and Management of Acute Grief," which appeared in the American Journal of Psychiatry in 1944. These observations were the prime stimulus for the development of the concept of emotional crisis, which has been further expanded on by Caplan, Sifneos, and many others.

Sifneos defines emotional crisis as "an intensification of a painful state which has the potential of becoming a turning point for better or for worse."

The state of emotional crisis as a rule follows a hazardous life event, which in some persons who have been emotionally healthy sets the stage for emotional crisis. But not all individuals faced with the same hazardous event will be in a state of crisis. There are, however, certain common hazardous events, such as loss by death and its sequelae of grief and bereavement, which will induce a state of crisis in nearly all individuals. In view of the universality of this phenomenon, in this chapter I will focus primarily on crisis evaluation and intervention as it relates to the individual who is facing a loss by death. Due to the fact that cognitive and emotional responses in relation to death at various phases in life are not identical, here I will confine my attention to adults and will begin by reviewing some of the fundamental contributions of Lindemann in the area of the clinical picture of grief and mourning, pathological grief reaction, and those complicated factors that contribute to the development of a pathological mourning. Finally I will focus on the technique of crisis evaluation and intervention through a detailed analysis of my first and second interviews of a patient who lost her son.

GRIEF AND MOURNING

> When it is a beloved and intimate human being that is dying, besides the horror at the extinction of life there is a severence, a spiritual wound, which, like a physical wound, is sometimes fatal and sometimes heals.—Tolstoy, *War and Peace*

Freud defined mourning as a reaction to several forms of loss. In his paper "Mourning and Melancholia" (1917) he gave the following as the clinical features of mourning:

1. A profoundly painful dejection
2. Loss of capacity to adopt a new love object.
3. Turning away from any activity not connected with thoughts of the lost person
4. Loss of interest in the outside world

Nothing was added to Freud's views until Lindemann's work in the early 1940s.

Lindemann described acute grief reaction as a definite syndrome with psychological and somatic symptomatology and indicated that the syndrome appears immediately after a crisis. He further indicated that the syndrome might be typical or atypical. In some persons it may be exaggerated, and in others it may be delayed or it might be apparently absent. He referred to the atypical picture as a distorted one and indicated that by appropriate technique the distorted picture can be changed to a normal grief, with its resolution. He further noted that the individual's reaction to either the death or the severe injuries of a loved one may take one of several forms, which can be summarized as follows:

1. Normal grief reaction
2. Pathological grief reaction; prolongation of the state of emotional crisis which was not resolved as a result of a maladaptive pattern of behavior
3. Regressive reaction, such as the development of a severe depression or a pathological pattern of responsiveness such as suicide

CHARACTERISTICS OF A NORMAL MOURNING PROCESS

What are the characteristics of a normal mourning process? A normal mourning process is characterized by a set of phenomena which was well described by Lindemann in his early work:

The presence of guilt. Preoccupation with feelings of guilt. The bereaved searches the time before the death for evidence of failure. Our clinical experience shows that the intensity of the guilt feeling is usually in proportion to the hostility that the mourner had in relation to the deceased and that there existed a strong ambivalence in relation to the deceased. When there had been the presence of hostile impulses in relation to the deceased, the mourner may view the death as the fulfillment of a wish, which gives rise to strong guilt feelings. At the start of mourning guilt feelings might be overwhelming, and the mourners attack themselves: Why didn't they go to such and such a place that the deceased asked them to? Why didn't they seek different medical care earlier?

Among the most important sources of guilt are the presence of a hostile and ambivalent relationship with the deceased, as I mentioned; reproaches that the deceased is causing him the painful state of mourning; and the mourner's relief that someone else is dead, not he, himself.

Angry, hostile reaction. Anger and hostile reaction might be present toward the deceased for dying. The origin of anger might be related to a number of factors. Death brings the pain of mourning; the mourner may react with anger toward the deceased. Death might bring further deprivation; the bereaved is left helpless. In some cases we see a displacement of anger; here hostility toward the deceased is displaced onto another person. This anger might be directed toward anyone and anything at the slightest provocation. The bereaved might be angry with the world. The anger might be directed at the physician or the surgeon. Obviously, anger mobilizes more guilt feelings.

Emancipation. This phenomenon is seen particularly in cases where the mourner feels that he has gained his freedom. We have seen this in a number of cases of adolescents who had a disturbed relationship with their father and subsequent to his death felt free and ended up showing acting-out behavior. Obviously in these cases the process of grief work is interfered with. One does not see the normal psychological work of the ego in relation to the loss, and the acting out is a regressive defense against experiencing the painful emotional state typical in the process of normal mourning.

Relief. This phenomenon is most often seen when a prolonged, painful illness has terminated in death. What we have are two interrelated ideas. One idea is that the deceased is now free from pain and no longer suffering. The second is that now the mourner is freed of the burden of taking care of the deceased.

Anxiety. This is another symptom we often see in a mourner. Freud in "Inhibitions, Symptoms, and Anxiety" (1926) outlined some of the sources of anxiety subsequent to a loss, namely; fear of being left helpless and an anxiety over a closer incestuous relationship with the other parent.

Reactivation of old unresolved conflicts. The reactivation of an old unresolved conflict over the loss by death or separation is often seen.

Helplessness. This phenomenon may be related to the total inability of the mourner to go through the pain of loss, the painful state. Another source of helplessness is that he must continue in life without the support of the deceased.

Denial. Denial might be the initial reaction to death. It usually lasts for a short period and is followed by the process of mourning. The process of denial, that the person is not dead, and the reality that he is dead may fluctuate for a while; and sometimes it may continue long after the loss. Denial may pass the boundaries of normal mourning and be classified as pathological mourning.

Absence of emotions. Such an absence may be a mechanism attempting to postpone the painful work of mourning. In normal mourning this usually lasts for a short period.

There are a number of other symptoms which are a part of the clinical picture of a normal mourning process. Sensations of somatic distress occur in waves lasting from twenty minutes to an hour at a time. Typical sensations are: feeling of tightness in the throat, choking with shortness of breath, marked tendency to sighing respiration, empty feeling in the abdomen, intense subjective distress described as tension or mental pain, restlessness, and an inability to sit still. The individual may move around in an aimless fashion.

These waves of somatic discomfort are precipitated by visits, by mentioning the deceased, or by receiving sympathy. Respiratory experience is most conspicuous when the patient is going to discuss his grief. Many patients complain of a lack of strength and exhaustion.

Lindemann emphasized five major points as pathognomonic for grief:

1. Somatic distress
2. Preoccupation with an image of the deceased
3. Guilt
4. Hostile reaction
5. Loss of pattern of conduct

He described a sixth characteristic: the appearance of traits of the deceased in behavior, especially symptoms shown during the last phases or the behavior which may have been shown at the time of the tragedy. Lindemann indicated that the six characteristics are shown by individuals who border on pathological grief reaction.

PATHOLOGICAL GRIEF REACTION

Prolongation of mourning. This is one of the major characteristics of pathological mourning. It is a maladaptive defense of avoiding the difficult task of experiencing the painful emotions involved in the process of mourning. The mourner holds onto the idea that the dead person lives. Freud in "Mourning and Melancholia" (1915) comments on this, indicating that there are hypercathexes of memories. As we know, the process of introjection and identification normally is the ego's attempt to give up the lost object through a process of piece-meal cathexis. But in the prolongation of mourning the process of mourning is broken down: there is internalization of the lost object; the ego holds onto the object, denying its loss; and the ego avoids confrontation with reality.

Delay and rejection of grief. Lindemann in his paper in 1944 indicates that delay and rejection of grief may occasionally involve many years. He further indicates that some patients in acute bereavement following a recent death may be preoccupied with grief about a person who died many years ago. In our own series of seventy-two patients seen in a state of grief, almost 25 percent of these patients seen subsequent to a recent death were preoccupied with grief over the tragic death of a close relative many years ago.

Grief reaction of abnormal intensity; distortion (Lindemann 1944). The normal reaction of the mourning process such as guilt, anger, anxiety, etc., might be present in various combinations with a very high intensity. The process of mourning is disturbed, and our clinical data indicate the presence of a chronic conflict with the deceased. Lindemann describes six categories of distortion: guilt with an obvious need for punishment; somatic symptoms, usually belonging to the last illness of the dead person; insomnia; denial of feelings and an appearance of woodenness; altered relationships with friends; and increased hostility and irritability.

PSYCHIATRIC AND PSYCHOSOMATIC
CONDITIONS AS A REACTION TO THE DEATH

A group of investigators and clinicians, among them Lindemann, Cobb, Anderson, and Lidz, have described a number of clinical entities precipitated by bereavement: obsessional reaction, anxiety neurosis, depression, ulcerative colitis, rheumatoid arthritis, asthma, and hyperthyroidism.

Bereavement very often precipitates clinically recognizable psychiatric illness. In our series we saw three adolescents with delinquent and severe acting-out behavior subsequent to the death of a parent. They had no previous history of acting-out behavior, which in our view was a clear manifestation of a maladaptive response to the mourning process.

NORMAL MOURNING REACTION AND
PATHOLOGICAL MOURNING REACTION

The question is how to differentiate between a normal mourning reaction and a pathological one. The differentiation is to a great extent based on the degree and intensity of those features that are characteristic of a normal mourning reaction. As was described, anger, guilt, preoccupation with the image of the deceased, waves of somatic discomfort, and other features in combination or all may be present in the process of normal mourning. These reactions in certain individuals may present themselves in an exaggerated way. In certain individuals we see a delayed reaction. If the symptomatology of a normal grief is excessively intense, or if the process of mourning is unduly prolonged, (for example, a persistence of denial, persistent absence of emotion), we may be faced with a pathological mourning reaction. In my experience the dividing line is at times very difficult to determine. There is a spectrum of mourning reactions. At one end of the spectrum are those individuals who present a clear-cut picture of normal mourning, and at the other end of the spectrum are those who demonstrate a clear-cut picture of pathological grief; in the middle we see a wide range of cases who present a mixed picture.

The process of grief work. As described by Freud in 1917, the process and the work of mourning consists of a gradual dissolution of every tie the individual has with the lost person. The loved object does not exist any longer, and the individual is very conscious of the loss. There is a libidinal withdrawal from the lost object, which is very painful; it is a very painful emotional state. The pain can be so intense that the individual might turn away from reality and refuse to believe that the lost person is no longer there. When the process and the work of mourning have been completed, then we notice that the ego becomes free.

Thus the work of mourning is a slow and painful process, and often in the initial phase there is shock and disbelief. There are those individuals who experience numbness, which has a defensive function against the very painful emotional state. After the very initial phase we see the phase when the full impact of the loss is felt. The work of mourning is painful, repetitive work. Lindemann referred to the work of mourning as a piecemeal review of the patient's life with the deceased.

The process is both an emotional and a cognitive process—going over all past experiences, looking at everything that has taken place, until finally the bereaved is able to break the bondage to the deceased. How successfully the process is carried out, as Lindemann has pointed out, depends on the grief work, the mourning process, which involves three elements: (1) freeing the mourner from bondage to the one who died, (2) a readjustment to a new life situation without the deceased, and (3) the building of a new relationship. It is obvious that the success of this grief work is dependent also on how well the mourner overcomes the tendency to avoid the pain and distress of grief.

FACTORS CONTRIBUTING TO
PATHOLOGICAL MOURNING

As described originally by Freud, the process of mourning is a painful one. He raised the question, How can we explain the painful process? He was perplexed with respect to the pain involved during the process of withdrawing the libido from the lost object. In "Inhibitions, Symptoms, and Anxiety" (1926) he attempted to explain the painful process. "Similarly in the case of the object loss, the pain of separation is due to a mounting and unsatisfiable cathexis of longing for the object during the reproduction of the situation in which the mourner must undo the ties that bind him to the object."

Freud in his further writings indicated that some ambivalence exists even toward those we love.

Lindemann in his contribution indicated that there are certain factors that disturb the normal mourning process and produce a pathological mourning, factors such as low tolerance for pain and manner of death. His work was a stimulus to our own work at McGill. We have asked what factors are involved when certain individuals avoid the intense emotional pain associated with grief by employing maladaptive defenses. And we have been very interested in developing techniques by actively working with these cases of pathological grief reaction. In our series we have come to see that certain variables in varying combinations might bring about pathological mourning:

1. Highly ambivalent and hostile relationship to the deceased. Our case material indicates the presence of a highly ambivalent and hostile relationship with the deceased, of overidealization of the dead person; the ego's attempt to cover up the unpleasant features of the relationship, a complete denial that there was a hostile relationship between the patient and the deceased.

2. Unexpected, sudden death, particularly if during the period prior to the death there was some exchange of hostility with the deceased.

3. The manner of the death, and if the patient was in some way responsible for the death.

4. If the deceased died in a tragic accident, and the bereaved was a witness and escaped death.

5. Ego-adaptive capacity; inability of the patient to experience and tolerate anxiety and depression and painful affects.

6. Ego state. The ego might be in a state of exhaustion due to the painful circumstances preceeding the loss. We have seen this in cases where there previously existed active conflicts or painful situations, and in cases where the bereaved had been nursing and taking care of the deceased, who was suffering from a long chronic illness, and at the same time was working to support the family and had active death wishes for the deceased.

In our work we have been very interested in developing techniques and timely interventions to alter the process of a pathological mourning to a normal one. In our series there are cases where the normal mourning process has been disturbed, with subsequent crystallization of neurotic disturbances: phobic neuroses, obsessional neuroses, and other psychoneurotic conditions. We have developed techniques for treating these patients with Short-Term Dynamic Psychotherapy. I have given the details of the technical requirements of the treatment of these patients in another publication (in press). Here I will focus primarily on the techniques of crisis evaluation and crisis intervention of a woman whose infant son was found strangled in his crib.

CRISIS EVALUATION

The Case of the Mother Whose Son Strangled in His Crib

The patient is married and has a full-time job as a sales representative for a company. One afternoon while at work, two weeks prior to her first visit, she was called home urgently; when she arrived at home she found her son had been strangled on the string of his pacifier while he was in his crib. The patient had left her family in Denmark at the age of eighteen and met her husband, who comes from Italy. They married and have been living in this city for the past ten years. The son was their only child.

In terms of the technique of crisis evaluation, it is obvious that one cannot conduct the interview purely along the lines of evaluation in this type of case. But at the same time it is essential that the therapist make a rapid appraisal of the patient's character structure, her ego-adaptive capacity, and the presence of any character defects, to determine to what extent the patient's coping mechanisms are maladaptive, to what extent the adaptive mechanisms are prominent, and to what extent the character structure has been free of neuroses—the patient's adjustment to work, family, marriage. Such an evaluation is essential in order to decide if the patient is a candidate for crisis intervention or if the patient is a candidate for crisis support.

Crisis intervention, or dynamic crisis intervention, is a specific psychotherapeutic technique for helping this patient, who is in a state of emotional crisis, with the aim of replacing her maladaptive psychological reaction with an adaptive one and preventing it from becoming crystallized into a neurotic disturbance.

During the first interview this patient indicated that her husband

and her in-laws don't leave her alone and that they tell her she should not let the death of her son affect her. Both she and her husband had been avoiding thinking about their son's death and looking at anything that belonged to him. She had gone back to work to forget him. It was clear from the beginning of the initial interview that the patient's maladaptive responses were predominant, compared with the adaptive ones, and that she and her husband were in collusion in reenforcing those maladaptive responses. The important question in the evaluation of this patient is if this patient fulfills the specific criteria for selection of patients for crisis intervention. But, as I mentioned before, one should immediately recognize that the initial interview aimed at evaluation is always mixed with intervention, and this patient is a typical example that demonstrates that the line of demarcation between evaluation and therapy is not well delineated. The criteria for selection of patients for crisis intervention are more or less similar to those for Short-Term Dynamic Psychotherapy; psychological mindedness, motivation to overcome the psychological crisis to demonstrate clear evidence that she is making an active effort to deal with the crisis, and flexibility in the ego's defensive structure, etc. We will see as we go through the initial interview that this patient fulfills these criteria, which I have described as briefly as possible.

In terms of the technical requirements, the therapist makes an active attempt to establish a therapeutic alliance and the psychotherapeutic work becomes a joint venture with systematic exploration and clarification into those stages that have brought about the state of emotional crisis. In this specific patient the immediate focus is active exploration of the circumstances that caused her son's death and the patient's reactions, with repeated confrontation with her maladaptive psychological reaction in dealing with her painful state of emotional crisis. We will see some of these technical requirements in more detail as we proceed with the first and the second interviews of this patient.

Initial Interview

The patient entered the interview room detached and silent.

Therapist: When did this happen?

Patient: It happened two weeks ago yesterday.
Therapist: How old was . . .
Patient: Fifteen months.
Therapist: Boy or girl?
Patient: A boy. Our first.

The patient maintains a detached attitude, is silent and noninvolved. The evaluator attempts to establish a rapport with her and explore the event surrounding the death of her son.

Therapist: What happened?
Patient: (Somewhat irritated.) To tell you quite frankly, I received the death certificate yesterday, but I haven't looked at it carefully. He died of strangulation.
Therapist: Strangulation?
Patient: In his bed. Yes.
Therapist: How did it happen?
Patient: (Irritated.) I don't know. Maybe he had a pacifier with a little string attached. (The patient is silent, and the evaluator prefers to continue the dialogue without reflecting to the patient that she is irritated and that she prefers not to participate.)
Therapist: Pacifier with a string attached . . .
Patient: Which we used sometimes if he was in his little carriage and he was taking his nap, I assume. I don't know . . . I think my husband knows more about it than I do. And I think he played with it.
Therapist: Played with the pacifier . . .
Patient: By not having it in his mouth maybe he played while he was awake, while having his nap. And I assume that then it happened. I don't know.
Therapist: What sort of idea do you have?
Patient: That is just my idea . . .
Therapist: That it had to do with the pacifier?
Patient: Uh-huh.
Therapist: And the string of the pacifier . . .
Patient: That is right. I think so.
Therapist: When did it happen?
Patient: In the afternoon during his nap. He always takes his nap from one to three, so it must have happened during that time.

As we notice, the patient is detached and takes a noninvolved position. She is irritated and does not want to explore with the evaluator the circumstances surrounding the death. The evaluator pursues gently, with the aim of establishing a therapeutic rapport and to maintain the focus surrounding the death.

Therapist: You were at home?
Patient: No. I was at work.
Therapist: And who was at home?
Patient: A babysitter.
Therapist: So she was at home.
Patient: Uh-huh.
Therapist: And then how did you find out about it?
Patient: The police called me up . . . said that I had to come home urgently, and they didn't tell me what for. So I rushed home.
Therapist: You were in your office?
Patient: Yeah.
Therapist: Then you didn't know then . . . in your office . . . what was the . . .
Patient: No.
Therapist: What did you think had happened, that they wanted you home urgently?

The patient maintains a noninvolved attitude. She is rather perplexed, and the therapist continues to explore the events. She says she had thought it had something to do with her husband because his car insurance had expired. Then she thought maybe he had been in an automobile accident. She said it was because the police had told her there had been an accident. Then the evaluator focuses on the time that she arrived at home.

Therapist: And when you got home, do you remember how things went at that moment?
Patient: Do I have to repeat it?
Therapist: How do you feel about it?
Patient: At this moment, very bad.

There is a turning point here in the interview. At first the patient was detached and noninvolved, but now she is showing signs of being in a state of emotional pain. She wants to use avoidance, and the evaluator's technique is to get her to review in detail those few hours from the time she entered the house to the time when she finally saw the dead body of her son.

Therapist: All of this must be very hard on you.

Patient: It is. This was our first child after ten years.

Therapist: After ten years . . .

Patient: Go ahead. I hope the purpose of these sessions is actually to try to overcome the present situation we are in.

Therapist: Do you remember the situation when you arrived home . . . when you went in and found out exactly what it was?

Patient: I don't know except that it happened when I saw my husband. He was very upset, of course, crying and just blaming the pacifier. So I imagined how it had happened. And that is all I saw. Shortly after, we went to the hospital because I did not believe it. I did not know at that time that he was dead. I only thought that he was in the hospital.

Therapist: He was taken to a hospital?

Patient: The kid was taken to the hospital, and we were taken to the hospital. At that time I did not believe that he was dead already. I didn't know it, either. At the hospital they showed us he was dead.

Therapist: You saw him dead?

Patient: Yes.

Therapist: It must have been very traumatic and painful for you . . . that moment.

Patient: It was . . . seeing his little body as white as paper.

The patient is trying not to experience the total impact of this tragic event. She talks about these events, but at the same time is detached. The therapist's attempt is to bring about a shift from avoidance and detachment to see that she is in touch with the total impact of the death of her son. The attempt is to rechannel her maladaptive response to a more adaptive one.

Therapist: What was your reaction at that moment? It was so sudden.

Patient: I think I had no reaction. I couldn't believe it. I couldn't cope with it. It seemed untrue, unreal.

Here we see the initial phase, disbelief—as she puts it, "unreal," "untrue."

Therapist: At that moment you couldn't believe that he was dead.
Patient: No. It took me more than a day to realize that he wasn't . . . that he was dead. That is the only reaction that I had.
Therapist: Then your initial reaction was disbelief: it couldn't be true. But how about feelings-wise?
Patient: How do you expect one to be feeling? I don't think that one changes, but I think . . . I don't know. I just took it. I don't want to say that I accepted it. I just realized it. And there was so much commotion around that you just followed the chain—like an animal. Whatever there is, what had to be done, and you just follow whatever was being done with you, or whatever it is.
Therapist: Where was your mind that evening? You see, this was a sudden and unexpected tragic event that happened to you.
Patient: My mind? It was where it is today. I was mad—blaming myself for not being there.
Therapist: You have been blaming yourself.
Patient: For not having been there. Maybe it wouldn't have happened. I don't know.

What we see here is the patient's attempt to avoid, and the therapist is actively and persistently focusing on the circumstances. The patient indicates that she is gradually accepting the reality. We notice the presence of guilt, and there is an angry, hostile reaction toward herself, that if she had been at home this might not have happened.

Therapist: So, it is this thought that comes into your head . . . that if you had been at home then . . .
Patient: It will always be in the back of my mind. The more you think about it, the more you think about it . . . maybe your act was selfish. I don't know. Everything was running okay, beautifully—no complaints whatsoever.
Therapist: So your mind obviously wanders around your relationship with your son, Michael.

The patient is still preoccupied with guilt feelings and sees herself responsible for the death of her son. What she is really saying is if it had not been for her professional ambitions then Michael might not be dead. And then there is her angry, hostile reaction toward herself; she continues to blame herself.

Patient: Maybe I wasn't there often enough. I don't know. It is difficult to say whether it is because of the child now, or because of my husband now, or because of the guilt factor. There are so many factors coming into it, and I don't know. I am the one . . . maybe I just try to ignore everything and just think of nothing . . . just try to be empty . . . which is not the correct way.

Therapist: But there are many ideations that come into your mind, and in a sense you are trying to analyze yourself to see what is what. So could we look at them?

Patient: Sure.

Therapist: You were saying you have thoughts about your husband and you have thoughts about yourself . . . if you were there, if your husband had been there, and the idea that if you had been home then this might not have happened.

Patient: Yeah. My thoughts are on all of these issues. Maybe I should have spent more time with him, not thinking just about work. These are the thoughts that go through my head.

The evaluator explores into the nature of her job. She is the sales representative for a company and works full-time, is very efficient, and very much enjoys her work. She has been working there since she came to this country.

Patient: Maybe I should have been there when it happened—that means always being with him, not thinking, maybe, of my work, of my ambition, of our ambitions.

Therapist: The idea is then that you needed to work.

Patient: No. I don't think I have a need to work.

Therapist: In terms of ambition?

Patient: I don't know. I have been working all my life, for many years in this job, a field which is very interesting.

Therapist: Did you previously have thoughts of not working, or is this idea that you should not have continued to work the kind of idea that has come into your head since Michael died?

Patient: Yes. Since that time. Prior to that I never had such a thought. In a way everything came too lucky. I wouldn't know . . . in "lucky." If you want to say so, in a way. I wanted to keep my position, as I said. Selfishness, maybe. I don't know. On the other hand, I was needed. Then we brought over a young student. She is fifteen years old. So . . . the circumstances she was living in, they are different from here. So we thought of combining, trying to give her as much education over here, giving her a home, giving her schooling, and at the same time she might look after Michael whenever I was not around. That is what happened.

What we see at this point in the interview is that the patient is in a state of tension with tightened facial musculature. She has accepted the fact that Michael is not there any more, but there are expressions of guilt feelings, that if she had been there this might not have happened. Then she goes on to her husband. Then she goes back to blaming herself for putting all her thoughts on her work, expressing anger and hostility toward herself for being a career woman. And finally she brings up the baby-sitter, and obviously there is implied the idea that she is a young student—was she qualified?

Therapist: So she had been taking care of Michael for the past fifteen months?
Patient: That is right, yes.
Therapist: And you were satisfied with the way she took care of Michael?
Patient: Very. Very much. No complaints whatsoever.
Therapist: What are the thoughts that come to your mind about Michael?

At this point the patient indicates that in the past two weeks there have been a lot of visitors, and the family of her husband is there. Everybody tells them that "one has to survive," "one has to continue." The evaluator's attempt to bring to focus her memories and her feelings is not successful. She indicates that they have a very good marriage. They enjoy life very much. Her husband wanted a child two or three years after marriage, but her view was to wait for a few years—to enjoy life and build up economically. Her pregnancy was a planned one, and she was fully occupied with her job. When Michael was born he brought a nice change in their lives, and she looked forward to the end of the day, to go home and take care of him. Life was no longer monotonous. She said that, "With the birth of Michael our happiness was complete." Then the evaluator again makes an attempt to focus on her memories and feelings about Michael with the hope that the maladaptive responses of denial, "life has to continue," might be replaced by more adaptive responses and facilitate the work of mourning.

Therapist: You give me a picture of trying constantly to fight the inner turmoil, the memories and feelings you have about Michael.

Patient: It is very painful, and sometimes you try to ignore it.

Therapist: As you say, they are painful, and your way of dealing with it is ignoring it.

Patient: It is very difficult to explain the way it comes in waves. Sometimes I try to ignore everything, to ignore everybody. You hate everybody, even . . . we still have my mother-in-law around. Other family is around. You hate everybody around you, and then you detest yourself while you think that way. So, as I said, it is coming and going. On the other hand, I have to realize that everything has to go on, and I will have to cope with it.

Therapist: You see, you describe these waves of discomfort during the day, and you also talk of feeling irritable. But at the same time repeatedly you say that life has to go on, or others tell you that, which has to do with the idea to wipe out the whole thing. Do you find yourself not wanting to be bothered by people? To be left on your own? Do you often feel that way?

Patient: Yeah.

Therapist: Then you have these waves of distress that come over you, which must be associated with thoughts about Michael; and this is the moment you don't want people around, you want to be left on your own—you and your thoughts and feelings about Michael.

Patient: That is right. But you see, there is a commotion around the house. Everybody wants to socialize; they want to talk with me.

Therapist: And then you feel irritated.

Patient: You are right. These waves of distress come over me frequently, you know; they come and go. But the people talk a lot. They tell me it is not the end of the world. In the first days I just tried to close myself completely. I am that type. If I have problems, I am not the type to want to discuss them, to talk. On the other hand, my husband always tried to convince me to talk. He wants the family around. And as I said before, we only visualize in front of our eyes, to only remember the joy and the happy days we had. So that is what we are doing.

Therapist: To avoid the inner turmoil, and to visualize the joy and the happy days. . .

Patient: My husband and I are trying to keep the memories of the good days with him. And I have a big house. What can you do? I couldn't stand it at home anymore. Neither could I stand going around looking at people . . . going shopping, whatever was suggested. So I went back to work.

Therapist: So you are working now. How do you find yourself there?

Patient: I am just sitting in my office trying to occupy myself, and in a sense—I don't know whether that is correct or not—trying to forget.

What we notice at this point is the process of the work of mourning. She describes waves of physical distress, the painful emotional state. She expresses a need to cut off all relationships, which is the expression of an exclusive devotion to mourning. She wants to be left alone. She is preoccupied with an image of her son. But this process is totally disrupted by the presence of the members of the family. There is irritability and anger toward these people, but at the same time she expresses guilt for feeling that way.

Therapist: Let's look at this. You have these waves of distress which come and go. There is this painful inner turmoil, and the thoughts and memories of Michael. I wonder why it is that you have been trying to fight them.

Patient: I don't know.

Therapist: And also you said that you don't want to be bothered with people; you don't want them to visit you; and you get irritated when they are around, which is in a way related to your thoughts and memories of Michael.

Patient: Right.

Therapist: So then why should you tell yourself that you have to switch your mind away from something that is there, because it was quite a tragic event that happened to you? And why should you switch it to other directions? What sort of memories come to your mind about Michael?

Technically speaking, the patient presents a defensive pattern of avoidance of grief work, and the therapist very gently confronts the patient with her maladaptive way of handling the situation, repeatedly insisting that she should not avoid going through the painful emotional state. The therapist's technique is to focus on the memories associated with her life with Michael and specifically the period immediately prior to his death, in an attempt to bring to focus the painful emotions associated with her memories. The patient finally focuses on the event of going to the hospital and seeing Michael's dead body. What emerges is the intensification of the painful emotional state.

Patient: At this moment I will tell you quite frankly the picture of when I saw him at the hospital.
Therapist: Could you describe the picture you have in your mind of him?
Patient: His lips were blue. His face was a little angel, like usual. When I looked at his body it was blue and red bruises all over the place. That comes constantly back to me, which is very painful; I try to see only his little picture. I prefer to see his little picture. I prefer to see his little picture, always running around the house, up and down the stairs, all over the place. But I can't. The other picture of his dead body is more powerful . . . coming into my mind.
Therapist: One is the picture of his dead body, blue and red bruises; and the other one is the picture of him when he was alive.
Patient: His activities. (There is a sudden intensification of a painful emotional state. She is near to having tears in her eyes but is fighting it.)
Therapist: What were his activities like?
Patient: He was a very active child.

Now we notice that the maladaptive responses have been broken down and the painful process of mourning has begun. A piecemeal review of the patient's life with Michael is the focus, but most importantly the therapist focuses precisely on the dead body of

Michael and brings the patient to describe in detail his dead body. She does this and indicates that it is very painful, and that she prefers the pleasant memories.

Therapist: What do you remember about Michael? What were your activities with him when you were at home?

Patient: He was just starting to walk . . . two or three months ago. He was . . . when you came home he was taking your hand. He wanted to run through the house, or go with you through the house, opening all the drawers; showing you the house. He could do that repeatedly and repeatedly. Look into each room . . . switch off the light . . . little things he developed at his age. He started to talk the last two or three months. He crawled into the bed, or into the crib. Hugging . . . But you know, since he was seven or . . . or six (months) he started to crawl.

Therapist: He was a very active boy. . .

Patient: In January of this year we went to Bermuda. So in the plane he became a . . . "the little boy."

Therapist: Could we look at the memories of that trip?

Patient: This was our first trip with him. During the summer we went camping with him. This child . . . he hardly cried . . . he never cried. He was always happy. He always laughed. He had a beautiful laughter. . . since he was small. I was very proud of him.

There is a gradual buildup of a painful emotional state. The patient is becoming increasingly sad, has tears in her eyes. Her attempt at control is breaking down, and she is in touch with her inner feelings. The technique of a piecemeal review of her life with Michael is effective. The evaluator reviews further with her the trip to Bermuda.

Exploration indicates that she met her husband in Europe. From the beginning, he wanted to have children, but she didn't. Her idea was to enjoy life before starting a family. They traveled and enjoyed themselves as much as they could. Then they moved to Canada, and the idea of having children went into the background. She has a sister who lives in Denmark, and the patient does not feel close to her. She describes her mother as "domineering and demanding." Her father is described as a "passive" person. Her earliest memories of family life are that she spent a lot of time with her parents but never felt very close to them. She left her family at the age of eighteen. Then the evaluator proceeds.

Therapist: Is there any time that you get so depressed that you feel fed up with life, or you feel like doing away with yourself?

Patient: Yeah. Sometimes I ask myself . . . it is hard to describe it. As I said, we have been married for ten years; suddenly there was this little boy who changed our life completely. Now it is back again as it was before that time. It is not the same, but I mean the situation. I am alone with my husband. I don't know . . . suddenly you realize, what was it all about before? What did you care about so much in your life, for yourself? When I say to myself, "What is the value of continuing living?"

Therapist: So it is a very difficult and painful situation. Suddenly he is not there.

Patient: Sometimes you think, there was this little creature—at least you had a job, to take care of him, a job to try to educate him, to give him as much love as we can, whatever has to be done. At least there was a function for you, which before you were married . . . I should have a function for my husband. But maybe it was only a function for the enjoyment of yourself. What is the whole use of continuing?

The patient has become increasingly depressed, tearful.

Therapist: Is there any problem with your sleeping?

Patient: Well, we have not been sleeping very well. And we are both light sleepers. One way or another. But now I find it more difficult to fall asleep. I wake up frequently.

Therapist: What wakes you up?

Patient: The silence of the house.

Therapist: Silence . . .

Then the evaluator proceeds to complete his evaluation. She dreams a lot but cannot remember her dreams, and there has not been any increase in her dreams in the past two or three weeks. There is a definite indication that her husband's way of dealing with the death of their son is maladaptive with denial and constantly also reinforces his wife in that direction. Both of them avoid going to

Michael's room, and he, by bringing his family around and socializing, makes a constant attempt to deny and avoid. It was on that basis that the evaluator, after clarifying this with the patient, suggested it was important that he see her husband. As he was in the waiting room, he was seen immediately after the interview with his wife. The interview with him took the form of an intervention. The therapist was able to break through his maladaptive defenses, and the process of mourning and grief was greatly facilitated. The decision was to see the wife for a second interview.

Very often there is no clear-cut boundary between crisis evaluation and crisis intervention. This case is a typical example of a blend of evaluation and intervention. At the same time that the evaluator is making an intervention, he is attempting to evaluate those major ego functions essential for a dynamic type of intervention. What we finally saw was that she is a person with a healthy character structure who is facing the tragic loss of her son and is using a mixture of adaptive and maladaptive responses, with the maladaptive responses more predominant than the adaptive ones. Finally we have evidence that she fulfills all the criteria for a dynamic type of crisis intervention.

Crisis Intervention

Now we will see some segments of the second interview with this patient to demonstrate some of the technical aspects of crisis intervention.

The patient starts the session by saying that she has become more depressed that her thoughts are most often on the death of her, son, and that she was looking forward to this session.

Patient: I thought maybe it is because on these occasions when I come here I take the opportunity to talk about the subject. More or less, whatever I do every day is drifting away or . . . not drifting . . . but the negative side . . . is like living in a dream, if you want to say so. During the day I feel as if I am performing everything manually or automatically as I have done in the past—maybe with another face. When I come here I don't feel that I want to hide. I was taught to hide, I think.

Therapist: So outside of here you have more of a tendency to hide. Could we look into that?

Patient: It isn't that I like to hide it, but I am getting ready every morning, going to work. At work actually I try not to think about my personal problems, just try to concentrate on my job. And I have to— I mean I have responsibilities. Otherwise I shouldn't have decided to myself. So I have to concentrate on my job. That is what my decision was, and that is why I went back. But the pain starts when I get home.

Therapist: So during the day are you saying that these thoughts about your son don't come?

Patient: Oh, no. They come to my mind. I just try to push them away.

Therapist: Then you have a struggle. What are these thoughts?

Then the patient says that shortly before Michael died, her friend, a co-worker, took a few pictures of Michael one afternoon. The patient had taken Michael to her office. This friend had had these photographs developed, and the patient had at first left them on her desk. Recently she has been carrying them in her purse but has been afraid to open the envelope and look at them.

The patient is reluctant to take the photographs out of her purse, and the therapist persistently focuses on the patient's attempt to avoid looking at the photographs, just as she avoids entering Michael's room, indicating to the patient that looking at the photographs might bring about waves of painful emotions. This technique of getting the patient to look at the photographs is important, as the photographs bring to life the notion of object relations and object loss. The photograph is an object that brings back to life the gifted, precocious, bubbling, perfect being that is Michael.

Therapist: What is he doing in those pictures?

Patient: You can see the pictures. I have them here. He is just looking.

Therapist: What is he looking at?

Patient: At me.

Therapist: He is looking at you, and who took the picture?

Patient: It was just before it happened—one week before, in my office.

(The patient is emotionally charged, her face very sad, crying.)

Therapist: Before? Before he died? So this is the last picture that you have of Michael.

Patient: Yes. It is just . . . It is a mass of big eyes. That is all. (The patient is crying, and her voice is shaking with sighing respiration.) Actually I have a picture on my desk. Again, there are the innocent, big eyes. And I have been covering it up with papers. I can't look at his face.

Therapist: You avoid looking at his picture?

Patient: (Heightened emotional distress.) No, I can't . . . especially at the office because I would get emotionally upset at the office.

Therapist: How about outside the office? Do you look at it?

Patient: No. Neither can I look at the pictures outside the office. No . . . I'm not over that point yet. Since my visit with you, a number of times before going to bed I decided to look at the pictures, but then I decided not to.

Therapist: Do you remember the day that these pictures were taken?

Patient: Yes.

Therapist: Where were you?

Patient: I was in my office with him. I had taken him to the office. I took half a day off, so I took the baby-sitter and the boy downtown. He is like . . . in my company it is like a family. So he grew up. Everybody liked him. From time to time I take him to the company, and this time I sent them out shopping for an hour or two, and I picked them up again; we all had lunch together in the company. And afterward we went home. It just so happened that one of my colleagues took some pictures.

Therapist: So one of your colleagues that day took these pictures?

Patient: Yeah. That's right. And she also framed one of them for my desk in an enlarged form. And ever since he died I have covered it up.

Therapist: How many days did you have the picture on your desk before he died?

Patient: I have had it only since Monday.

Therapist: And you find it very difficult to look at them, particularly the eyes.

Patient: It is only a picture of big eyes anyhow.

Therapist: But you like to look at it, but somehow you hold back.

Patient: I would love to . . . yeah. I would love to. But I cannot yet without getting emotionally involved.

Therapist: Obviously it is a painful emotional state . . . this whole tragic event. But you are repeatedly saying that you don't want to get emotionally involved, and you constantly want to avoid.

Patient: I think I cannot afford it while I am in the office. I can't let myself go.

Therapist: But we are talking right now here at this moment.

Patient: Sometimes I ask myself why I am here.

Therapist: Now let's look at this. I have been saying that you are avoiding going through the motions of your feelings and your thoughts. And you now say, "Why am I here?" And a while ago I had a feeling that you wanted to open your purse and look at the pictures, but somehow you avoided it. And now you are smiling.

Patient: It is not that. Sometimes I think, "Why am I here?" But at the same time I realize that it is in order that I can overcome this emotional situation that I am in right now.

Therapist: But obviously you cannot overcome this state that you are in by avoiding and making an attempt to bury them in the back of your mind.

Patient: I realize that. And I realize that I am trying to postpone it, to put it aside. I think now I can. Talking with you . . . yes, I can. (The patient is indecisive.)

Therapist: A moment ago you said that you wanted to look at those pictures, but then you postponed it. Why? If you wish to look at them right now, why do you postpone it?

Patient: I don't know why I postpone it. Maybe because I feel embarrassed about getting emotionally involved. Maybe I'm embarrassed, letting my feelings come out. I feel embarrassed, maybe, in front of you.

Therapist: The idea is that I might have some reaction, some negative reaction, if you go through your feelings, and if you share with me your ideas and memories with you son.

Patient: I don't know. I just feel embarrassed because I don't like to show my feelings in front of others. And as I said before, I never had experienced having treatment like we have now. So I mean, maybe it is just because it's public. I'm afraid of letting myself go. It must be that. The last time, when we talked about it, you said, "Why are you always trying to hide behind something?" I gave it some thought at that time, and it might originate, I think, from my job, from my work.

Therapist: Let's look at it. Isn't it that you have difficulty to be honest with yourself? I use "honest" in this sense, that if you basically are choked up with a lot of feelings and then you smile. I don't know why you don't want to be emotionally honest with yourself.

Patient: Okay. I agree.

Therapist: Let's look at the situation here. There is denial and avoidance in going through your thoughts, ideas, and feelings that you have about your son; you are constantly rationalizing in order to avoid them, bringing in the issue of your job, embarrassment, people, to avoid it. And your repeated smile here is a cover-up. And you know that these painful waves have been coming over you for the past, say, half hour; and you have constantly been making an attempt to avoid them . . . to cover them up . . . while at this very moment we both know that you are heavily choked up with a lot of feelings. And right now, also, again you are postponing what you wanted to do.

Patient: I wanted to show you the pictures.

Therapist: To show me the pictures, or we look at the pictures?

Patient: I have them with me.

The patient is using all types of defenses to avoid looking at the pictures, and the therapist persistently confronts the patient. This persistent, confronting technique is essential in crisis intervention of this kind, while one cannot do this with patients who have some character defect, who can benefit only from crisis support—which will be discussed in detail in chapter 16.

At this point the patient takes out of her purse those photographs that were taken of Michael shortly before his death.

Patient: This is . . . if you want to see it . . . this is my son's first birthday. And this is the picture that I have . . . actually it is in a round little thing . . . the last picture taken of him. (The patient is showing the photographs of her son to the therapist.)

Therapist: And this is the other one?

Patient: It is the same as this.

Therapist: This was taken how long before he died?

Patient: Which one?

Therapist: This one.

Patient: This one. It is from his birthday.

Therapist: This is in your office?

Patient: That is right.

There is intensification of the painful, emotional state. Her lips are trembling, and she is very tearful.

Therapist: And this is in January? What idea does this bring to your mind when you look at it?
Patient: That I am looking into two big innocent eyes. (The patient is crying.)
Therapist: Innocent.
Patient: Especially that last picture where he is sitting in the office. The other one gives me more joy looking at it because he is facing his birthday cake.
Therapist: What other idea comes to your mind related to that office and that afternoon?

We see the psychotherapeutic effect. There is a lot of change in the patient's facial expression, and the therapist continues the piecemeal review, facilitating the process of mourning, bringing out the painful emotions of associative memories. There are two processes going on concomitantly—cognitive memories and associations connected with her dead son and the affective ties between herself and her son. We notice also some preoccupation with Michael's eyes—the way he looks at her—which strongly suggests the presence of guilt feelings.

Patient: I guess a lot of ideas.
Therapist: Could you talk about these ideas?
Patient: I could think about all sorts of things. One. Both. All three of us. Or him, alone, who is missing right now.
Therapist: Could you talk about it?
Patient: (Very tearful.) Say, when I drive home . . . say if I see a kid . . . I get emotionally affected by it. I am always sorry, and it is very painful . . . the points which I am missing now. That he is missing. We can't enjoy them together anymore . . . especially this last picture.
Therapist: The office picture?
Patient: Yes. As I said, it is the most painful. It is a whole picture of eyes looking at me innocently, and asking, "Why? Why has everything happened? Why has everything discontinued?" (The patient is quite upset and crying, but is very well able to verbalize her ideas.)

Therapist: You were opposite him in that picture?

Patient: Yes. I think so. It was . . .

Therapist: Why do you say, "I think so"? You mean you don't remember?

Patient: I don't remember. No. To tell you quite frankly, I don't remember. But I think I was standing beside the girl who took the picture. Yes. I was.

Therapist: You were opposite him?

Patient: Yeah. He was looking at me while the girl took the picture, trying to make him smile.

Therapist: Do you remember what you did after she took the picture?

Patient: I played a little bit with him in the office. He got toys and . . .

Therapist: And what does the other picture bring to your mind?

Patient: I just think how grown up my little son was. How serious he can be concentrating on the candle. It was a birthday—his first birthday.

Therapist: Do you remember the day of his first birthday?

Patient: Oh, sure. I remember the birthday. If you just look at this picture it brings back a lot of nice memories. When he is sitting in his chair. It was actually taken in the kitchen. (The patient is quite upset, crying.) I remember him eating, feeding himself, which was part of the birthday party at home.

Therapist: What else does it bring to your mind?

Patient: That one? As I said, sometimes before, even if I look at these pictures, or even at the other pictures, it sometimes seems that you are looking at the picture and you don't even realize that it is your son. It is like a dream. As if I am not related to it. But sometimes I think that is the feeling. Then I look at all the pictures and say, "Yes. It is your son. That is your son." But, again, it looks like a dream, that it was never real. That I had a son that . . . I have it now in pictures that I could never touch. As I said, it is so confusing sometimes. On the other hand, sometimes I do have the desire to just remember . . . trying to hug him, to kiss him . . . whatever there is . . . feeding him. So sometimes it seems so real. Sometimes it does not seem real. (The patient continues to be upset and tearful.)

Therapist: It must be very difficult for you, this painful emotional state which you have to go through.

Patient: It happens mostly at night when I go home, or on weekends when we are at home. Again it is the same . . . like in walking. I feel that I can be two different persons—one just entertaining or doing business, the other one like last Sunday, which was a very bad night. I couldn't sleep at all. As you say, I was letting myself go, in touch with the pain that he is not going to be there anymore.

Therapist: You mean that last Sunday you had a lot of these waves of discomfort?

Patient: Yes. It was as if I was with him. My thoughts were going over some memories of what I used to do before this happened. And I cried a lot. I was crying, and I thought of all the things coming to my mind. I got so involved in it that I just started stopping it. Then I tried not to think of anything, just tried to relax. That is how I calmed down and finally fell asleep. Then, of course, routine work started as of Monday, and I am back in the office. I am like a machine. Since the last session my husband and I have talked about Michael, and I get depressed when I talk about it. And when I come here is the best chance I have to talk about it.

Therapist: How about the things that belonged to him, because as you pass around . . .

Patient: I haven't entered his room yet. Maybe, as you say, I am trying to avoid.

Therapist: Have you felt that you wanted to go into his room?

Patient: Perhaps it is like the pictures. Sometimes I want to do that. But then I end up to avoid it.

Therapist: But at one time not long ago you were looking forward to going into his room.

Patient: I have the desire to look at his clothes, to go to his cupboard, touch his clothes; but somehow I end up to avoid it. I end up crying in my bed.

Therapist: But you see, you would like to go to his room, his cupboard, to touch his clothes, to be totally in touch with your memories, thoughts, and feelings; but somehow, one way or another, you end up avoiding it. You see, these waves of painful emotional states which are associated with a lot of memories of your life are going to come and go. But the striking thing is that you don't allow yourself to be honest about what goes on within you. These are memories related to a person that you felt very close to, but I have to again repeat to you this need in you to avoid. And, indeed, in it is the element of self-denial. Why should you make two persons of yourself? And why should you deny to yourself the way you feel? Last time you said you went to Bermuda with him, and you were very proud of the way he behaved on the plane. Could we look at your memories of that trip?

Here we notice the therapist adheres to the fundamental principle of maintaining the focus, facilitating the process of grief work, breaking through, over and over, the maladaptive responses, and confronting the patient over and over with her avoidance and denial.

Dr. Katherina Marmor

This is a poignant and moving interview; it presents so many aspects that it is difficult to narrow one's discussion. The patient comes in with a classic bereavement situation to which she has been unable to adjust. In the first interview she appears to be a person immobilized by emotional crisis. In the second interview, although she is crying, she is beginning to pull herself together with a strong defensive pattern. She is an externally oriented person who depends on the outside world for validation. She takes pride in her work and places great value on her relationships with her co-workers. When she speaks, she shows more investment in her work and co-workers than she does in her family life. She presents a picture of an emotionally isolated person, a person who feels she can depend only on herself for survival.

Dr. Davanloo handles the interviews very impressively. He combines information gathering with evaluating the patient's ego strength and makes his therapeutic decisions at the same time that he is engaging the patient in a therapeutic alliance. This is done most skillfully, and it is impressive to watch the way the interviews progress. The focus he selects is to facilitate the process of mourning by confronting her persistently with her true feelings, and in a gently persistent way he breaks through her maladaptive defense pattern. He succeeds in this process when she finally looks at the pictures of her lost son, something she had resisted doing up to this time. The point at which she bursts into tears and is able to experience her repressed painful emotions is a dramatic and moving moment. The question may also be raised as to whether there may have

been some unconscious guilt in this patient in relation to the loss of
her child. She is a working mother who is very involved in her office
work, much more than her nuclear family; the tragic incident took
place while she was working. Her preoccupation with the child's
eyes—the way he "looked at" her—strongly suggests such guilt
feelings. It is also possible that this patient was ambivalent about
mothering since we know that she did not want to have a child for
many years.

Normal mourning is distinguished from pathologic mourning by
the ability of the patient to experience the real affects that are
attached to the person being mourned. In pathologic grief the
maladaptive defenses stand in the way. In this patient the major
defense was an obsessional character structure that did not permit
her to experience her real feelings. To lose control is very threatening
to persons like her.

But what is important is the therapist's ability to break through this
maladaptive defense pattern, her maladaptive way of dealing with
her emotions. This was Dr. Davanloo's primary focus, and it was
striking that he was able to overcome the defense in so short a time
and enable the patient to experience her repressed affect. He chose
the technique of encouraging her to look at her son's pictures and
persuading her to talk about her memories and feelings. The result
was an impressive therapeutic effect.

Dr. Peter Sifneos

I would like to discuss this patient along the following lines: the crisis
intervention, the concept of psychological crisis, and the nature of
the interaction between the evaluator and the patient. In this particular case the evaluator is also the therapist.

It is clear that this patient is facing an intensification of strong
feelings as a result of the death of her only son. She is handling these
feelings in two ways. On the one hand she uses some flexible
defenses, which are on the whole adaptive ones; for example, she
tries to remember past memories, to look at the pictures of her son, to
recall the pleasant experiences which took place between the two of
them. On the other hand she often uses maladaptive defenses, for
example, she attempts to deny, to cover up, and to hide her feelings.

The intensification which I mentioned already, and which she describes so clearly, is typical of a psychological crisis, the feelings one experiences in waves, particularly at times when she is alone. It is then that she allows herself to experience her feelings. On the contrary we observe a diminution or almost an absence of feelings during work. It is then that she is using maladaptive defenses and is avoiding the awareness of her affect.

In terms of the technique, the evaluator is clearly attempting to encourage her. At first he proceeds cautiously. He inquires about her feelings and wonders why she is fighting to hide them. He wonders why she is avoiding old memories and why she refuses to look at the picture. As a result of the repeated confrontations the patient starts to move. The emphasis therefore on the part of the evaluator-therapist is to undercut the maladaptive defenses of denial and avoidance and to facilitate the expression of sadness and grief. Finally the patient is able to do her own grief work, which results in her ability to free herself; finally she is able to overcome her cruel predicament. What is striking here is the gentle but persistent confrontation on the part of the therapist to get the patient to become aware of and to express her feelings. This is exemplified beautifully in the way he encourages her to look at the pictures of her son. He also urges her to continue looking at the pictures, not only when she is alone at home, but all the time, even while she is at work. The patient puts up obsessive defenses by rationalizing; she emphasizes how society expects people to hide their feelings, how life must go on, how the job requirements must take precedence. Despite all this she fails. She fails because the therapist let's her, because he is persistent. She fails to pursue this maladaptive denial and avoidance, and finally, slowly, and steadily, she cooperated with the therapist and is able to look at the pictures. This is the most dramatic moment in the session. It is very moving to see her looking at the picture of her son and bursting into tears.

Crisis intervention as a therapy is, of course, for all intents and purposes, most often dealing with issues of loss. Crisis theory and crisis intervention are the brain children of Eric Lindemann. He was the originator of the necessity to understand psychological crises. The therapeutic intervention was essentially what has already been described: the attempt to undercut maladaptive defenses, the effort to help the patient to do the grief work and to become aware of feelings which are appropriate for the loss until finally the loss can be put into proper perspective and the crisis can be overcome. In these two sessions we can see how clearly and systematically the therapist follows the above pattern.

One last word should be said about flexibility. Flexibility, which implies an access to a variety of defense mechanisms during the crisis, even if these defense mechanisms are temporarily pathological, is a healthy sign. I have specified that this patient is indeed using some maladaptive defense mechanisms, yet it should not be forgotten that she is in pain, and when on is in pain one wants to overcome it by any available means. The flexible way in which she deals with the problems, the ups and downs, the waves of feeling and so on, help her finally to overcome her crisis.

I am convinced that the outcome in terms of her future behavior will be uneventful; I predict that she is going to experience progressively a lessening in the intensity of her feelings and an ability to express them appropriately. In this sense this dramatic and painful experience in retrospect could be viewed as helpful because it has taught her how to deal with critical life events.

SUMMARY

In this chapter I have outlined the concept of crisis theory, crisis evaluation, and intervention along the lines of the classic work of Eric Lindemann. I reviewed the clinical picture of normal mourning and pathological grief reaction, the process of grief work, and outlined some of the factors which can disturb the normal process of mourning and contribute to the development of pathological mourning.

Due to the fact that an individual in crisis is in a state of flux, a dynamic therapeutic approach based on psychoanalytic principles is necessary. In order to identify patients who can benefit from such an approach, one must determine if the individual fulfills the criteria, as outlined, for crisis intervention, which is a specific psychotherapeutic technique for helping an individual in a state of crisis, with the aim to uncut his maladaptive psychological reaction, replace it with an adaptive one, and avoid the crisis becoming crystallized into a psychoneurotic disorder.

As I indicated, the criteria for selection of patients are more or less similar to those we use for Short-Term Dynamic Psychotherapy in spite of the fact that the focus and aim are different. The process of crisis evaluation and intervention was discussed in the context of the first and the second interviews of the mother who lost her son and who was using predominantly maladaptive psychological reactions.

In terms of the primary focus, the aim was to undercut her maladaptive psychological reaction—her denial, avoidance, obsessional defenses—and to facilitate the process of mourning, to work through her rage and guilt, to recapture her self-confidence, her self-acceptance, and to go ahead and have another child.

The course of the intervention is very brief, but the course of normal mourning will continue and may last for many months to a year.

The psychotherapeutic intervention with such a patient should take into consideration many factors—cultural, religious, family. For example, the attitude of the family of this specific patient, as she indicated, was very strict. They told her she should not let herself be upset. In some very religious families we might see the attitude that one should not be very upset—"The innocent child is now in heaven."

The most important task of any crisis interventionist is to have the clinical skill to spot who has the potential to deal with his crisis maladaptively, and within the spectrum from crisis support to dynamic crisis intervention to choose an intervention which he hopes will bring a resolution to the crisis and bring about a stable equilibrium and prevent the crystallization of a neurotic disturbance or in a very vulnerable patient prevent further ego regression, depression, and suicide.

References

Adams, J.E., and Lindemann, E. (1974). Coping with long-term disability. In *Coping and Adaptation*, ed. G.V. Coelho, D. Hamburg, and J.E. Adams, pp. 127-138. New York: Basic Books.

Anderson, C. (1949). Aspects of pathological grief and mourning. *International Journal of Psycho-Analysis* 30:48-55.

Barry, H. Jr., and Lindemann, E. (1960). Critical incidence for maternal bereavement in psychoneurosis. *Psychosomatic Medicine* 22:166-181.

Barry, H. III., and Lindemann, E. (1965). Dependency in adult patients following early maternal bereavement. *Journal of Nervous and Mental Disease* 140:196-206.

Beck, A., Sethi, B., and Tuthil, R. (1963). Childhood bereavement and adult depression. *Archives of General Psychiatry* 9:295-302.

Beebe, J. (1975). Principles of crisis intervention in psychiatric treatment. In *Psychiatric Treatment: Crisis/Clinic/Consultation*, ed. C.P. Rosenbaum and J. Beebe. New York: McGraw-Hill.

Bibring, G.L., Dwyer, T.F., Huntington, D.S., and Valenstein, A.F. (1961). A study of the psychological processes in pregnancy and of the earliest mother-child relationship. *Psychoanalytic Study of the Child* 16:9-72.

Caplan, G. (1964). *Principles of Preventive Psychiatry*. New York: Basic Books.

Davanloo, H. (1978). *Basic Principles and Technique of Short-Term Dynamic Psychotherapy*. New York: Spectrum Publications.

—— (in press). *The Relentless Healer*. New York: Jason Aronson.

Deutsch, H. (1937). Absence of grief. *Psychoanalytic Quarterly* 6:12-22.

Freud, S. (1915). Mourning and melancholia. *Standard Edition* 14:237-258.

—— (1926). Inhibitions, symptoms and anxiety. *Standard Edition* 20:87-172.

Lindemann, E. (1944). Symptomatology and management of acute grief. *American Journal of Psychiatry* 101:141-148.

Lipson, C.T. (1963). Denial and mourning. *International Journal of Psycho-Analysis* 44:104-107.

Loewald, H.W. (1962). Internalization, separation, mourning and the superego. *Psychoanalytic Quarterly* 31:483-504.

Mahler, M. (1961). On sadness and grief in infancy and childhood. In *Psychoanalytic Study of the Child* 6:332-351.

Rado, S. (1928). The problem of melancholia. *International Journal of Psycho-Analysis* 9:420-438.

Rapoport, L. (1965). The state of crisis: some theoretical considerations. In *Crisis Intervention*, ed. by H.J. Parad. New York: Family Service Association of America.

Schulberg, H.C., and A. Shelton (1968). The probability of crisis and strategies for preventive intervention. *Archives of General Psychiatry* 18:553-559.

Shoor, M., and Speed, M. (1963). Delinquency as a manifestation of the mourning process. *Psychiatric Quarterly* 37:540-558.

Sifneos, P.E. (1972). *Short-Term Psychotherapy and Emotional Crisis*. Cambridge: Harvard University Press.

Spitz, L. (1976). The evolution of a psychiatric emergency crisis. *Comprehensive Psychiatry* 17(1):99-113.

Spitz, R.A. (1946). Anaclitic depression: an inquiry into the genesis of psychiatric conditions in early childhood II. *Psychoanalytic Study of the Child* 2:313-342.

Stern, K., Williams, G.M., and Prados, M. (1951). Grief reactions in later life. *American Journal of Psychiatry* 108:289-294.

Stern, M.M. (1968). Fear of death and trauma. *International Journal of Psycho-Analysis* 49(2-3):457-461.

Winnicott, D.W. (1954). The depressive position in normal emotional development. In *Collected Papers*, pp. 262-277. London: Tavistock, 1958.

——— (1965). A child psychiatry case illustrating delayed reaction of loss. In *Drives, Affects and Behaviour*, Vol. 2, ed. M. Shur, pp. 212-242. New York: International Universities Press.

Zetzel, E.R. (1960). Symposium on depressive illness: introduction. *International Journal of Psycho-Analysis* 41:476-480.

16

The Technique of Crisis Support

HABIB DAVANLOO, M.D.
PETER E. SIFNEOS, M.D.

CRISIS EVALUATION

Is there a clear-cut difference between evaluation and therapy? It seems that it is not possible to separate them entirely, and a patient in a state of crisis is in a painful psychological state. From the moment the therapist and the patient meet, the clinician's responsibility centers around working on the patient's problem. In spite of the fact that the line of demarcation between evaluation and therapy is not well defined, it is helpful to try as far as possible to distinguish between evaluation, the attempt to understand what the crisis is all about, and the beginning of intervention, which is therapeutic in nature. Sometimes the beginning of the therapeutic process does really occur during the first evaluation interview. It must take place, however, after the evaluator feels confident that he clearly understands the problem. He sometimes intervenes as a way of assessing how the patient reacts.

Under ideal circumstances the evaluation should be complete before the therapeutic intervention takes place. This is of crucial importance. There are other practical considerations, however, that should also be kept in mind. For example, in a patient in crisis one's primary aim is to deal with the immediate problem. And it is the clinician's responsibility to arrive as quickly as possible at a therapeutic decision, as time is of the essence in crisis evaluation. The evaluator must observe what type of adaptive and maladaptive responses the patient is using to determine if the patient is overwhelmed with maladaptive responses and to judge the characteristics of the patient's maladaptive coping mechanisms, such as excessive fantasy, somatization, regressive patterns of behavior, magical thinking, hypochondriacal preoccupation, withdrawal from reality, acting-out behavior, etc. On the other hand the patient might be using predominantly adaptive coping mechanisms such as task-oriented activities or goal-oriented behavior. For example, the patient is aware of his feelings, he is conscious of the problem, has the ability to verbalize appropriately, and to discharge tension. At one end of the spectrum we might see patients who use primarily adaptive psychological reactions, and at the other end there are those who use predominantly maladaptive psychological responses. Between these two extremes are those individuals who use a mixture of both.

In situations where the crisis is not an acute one the clinician might want to try to see those positive components of the patient's adaptive responses in handling his crisis. This evaluation is important as the therapist would want to reenforce these adaptive patterns of behavior as much as possible. An effort is made to actively assist the patient to deal with the crisis. If the evaluation indicates that the patient is able to use adequate adaptive coping mechanisms, then the therapeutic intervention is rapid and the patient is expected to return rapidly to a state of emotional equilibrium. Thus, as already mentioned, the correct evaluation of the individual's coping mechanism is crucial in determining the nature of the crisis therapy. For example, with a patient who takes a somewhat masochistic, self-destructive pattern, with the feeling that he was responsible for his son's death, one observes that predominantly maladaptive responses are used in coping with his crisis. On the other hand, one may detect certain positive and adaptive aspects of the patient's character structure, such as his being a successful businessman, his involvement in community activities, and his active interest in the welfare of his family.

Within this spectrum we also see patients with character defects, and long-standing poor interpersonal relationships, who when faced with a hazardous situation might decompensate rapidly. The rapid evaluation of the character structure to determine the patient's ego-adaptive capabilities is the key to determining the kind of crisis therapy which will be offered to meet the patient's idiosyncratic needs.

Crisis therapies can be classified into two major categories of psychotherapeutic intervention: crisis intervention and crisis support.

Crisis intervention was described in detail in chapter 15, and here we will focus primarily on crisis support.

CRISIS SUPPORT

Crisis support is a specific therapeutic intervention designed for those patients who have a history of long-standing psychological problems and who decompensate easily in the face of stressful situations. They usually give a history of poor interpersonal relationships. The aim of crisis support is to modify or remove the stress, provide emotional support, restore the patient's equilibrium, and as far as possible to improve the maladaptive coping mechanisms with adaptive ones.

Criteria for Selection

The criteria for selection of patients for crisis support include the ability to maintain a job, to recognize that the difficulties are psychological in nature, to appeal for help by realizing that they face a hazardous, stressful life situation which has given rise to a great deal of anxiety, and to know that they are decompensating. In a way, the criteria for the selection of patients for crisis support are similar to those for short-term supportive therapy, except that these patients are facing an acutely hazardous life situation and are in the midst of a state of crisis.

TECHNICAL REQUIREMENTS

An essential ingredient of the technique is the immediate development of a therapeutic rapport. The patient is seen once or twice a week lasting up to six or eight weeks, but one may have to see the patient more often. In terms of focus, the therapy concentrates on the events that have brought about the disequilibrium. The therapist makes a careful assessment of the steps that have led to the crisis, and he assesses the degree and intensity of the painful feelings which are experienced. He also helps to mobilize the forces necessary to support the shaky disequilibrium in which the patient finds himself. The clinician's duty is to mobilize every concurrable resource that will help prevent further deterioration.

In crisis support, medication may be indicated, especially since the level of anxiety is so high that the patient is no longer able to make decisions for himself. Since the aim is an intervention within a short period of time, a sizable number of these patients are usually placed on medication as soon as possible.

In a sense, the therapist lends to the patient some of his own executive ego functions, exploring various possibilities and making decisions appropriate for him.

The technique aims basically at concrete assistance and environmental manipulation.

When the crisis has been resolved and the previous equilibrium has been established, it is time to terminate.

In crisis support, in contrast to crisis intervention, it is the therapist who does most of the work or even all the work.

The following interview, which was conducted by Dr. Sifneos, demonstrates the technique of crisis support of a woman who slashed her wrists subsequent to an argument and disappointment with her boyfriend. She was admitted to the surgical ward and was interviewed while in the hospital. The case demonstrates a blend of crisis evaluation and crisis support.

The therapist starts the session by asking details about what happened, indicating to her that he has no previous information. The patient says she has been going out with a man for five years and that they had been living together for the past two years. She said that her boyfriend likes to make little jokes like, "When are you going to move out of the house?" Then he laughs. This has been upsetting to her. He has had affairs with other women, and the patient has told him repeatedly that if he wants to get rid of her to let her know. Her relationship with him is characterized by his spending most weekends away while she sits and worries. One night he was drunk and he told her about his other women; they had a bitter argument which led to a physical fight. She was in a rage and attempted suicide by going to the kitchen and slashing her wrists with his straight razor. She said in the interview, "I just lost my head for a moment; I didn't even realize I had done it until I looked up and said, 'What the hell have I done?'" She is worried because she cut two tendons, around her wrist.

Patient: I am going to have an operation on Monday, and it is the first operation I have ever had, eh ... and it is kind of, well, it is the first operation. You are bound to worry, eh, because I am concerned about my fingers; and I don't know what the operation is going to be like. I was talking with my doctor last night, and he told me that I have tendons split. I don't know anything about medicine. This is just a ... you know, a thought I have got. I am not a doctor. And I said, "I have got great visions of you having to make a slice up here to catch them there and put them back." And then he says, "No, we might just have to cut down here." God!

Therapist: Now tell me, when did all this happen?

Patient: February 15.

Therapist: February 15.

Patient: 11:00 P.M.

Therapist: One thing I don't understand is why did you take it against yourself?

Patient: I don't know. I didn't plan to use it on myself. I was trying to scare him into the truth.

Therapist: Yes.

Patient: And I had lost my mind for one moment, and then I looked and I came back to reality. I said, "What the hell have I done?"

Therapist: But you were angry at him.

Patient: Yeah.

Therapist: ... for mentioning something that you felt was the most horrible thing.

Patient: If I had my mind really ... (crying) ... I would have just said, "The hell with you. I will leave." I know that is what I should have done.

Therapist: Why did you hurt yourself?

Patient: I don't know. I just lost my mind. I didn't even realize that until after I looked at myself and I said, "My God, what the hell have I done?" And I went into hysterics after.

Therapist: Uh-huh. Now, let me ask you another question which I am not clear about. Why is it that you felt that his going with other women was so devastating a thing for you? Why was it so upsetting?

Patient: Because I loved him.

Therapist: Okay, but why does it have to be such a terrible thing?

Patient: Because I was true to him, why should he go behind my back?

Therapist: I understand that you may prefer it that way, but when it gets to the point where you injure yourself, when you may die from loss of blood, when it means that you don't want to live anymore if he carried on like that, how can you say as you did awhile ago that the most important thing would have been for you to say, "The hell with it"?

Patient: Yeah, I know. This is what I am thinking now because I am going through all that trouble with the worries in my fingers and everything.

Therapist: Exactly.

Patient: I never thought at the moment that the damage would have been . . . I never gave it a thought to start with.

Therapist: So it was just an impulse. It came . . .

Patient: It was an impulse to scare him into the truth.

Therapist: Yes.

Patient: To get him to stop joking all the time because he is always joking. During the week he is most cooperative, but then on the weekend he will go and drink, and then he started his hunting. It was the third weekend he had gone hunting, and I was on my nerves' edge worrying about him and everything.

Therapist: But what is it about him that you like so much? You told me the negative things. He left you alone for three weekends to go hunting. You told me that he joked all the time, and didn't like that. You told me that maybe he went out with other women. What is it about him that you like?

Patient: Well, I loved him. I loved him. He was intelligent. He is well, first of all, I have been with other guys before I went with him and I had sexual relations, and it never really meant anything to me, but with him I found something different as if it was real.

Therapist: Uh-huh.

Patient: . . . real love.

Therapist: Now, this was for five years you have been going together. Well, let's just leave this just for a minute. Now, tell me something about yourself. How old are you?

The patient is twenty-five years old. Her parents are living here. She has one brother, five years older. The session continues.

Therapist: What were your early life experiences at home? Were you happy?

Patient: Oh, yeah. Mommy and Daddy were strict though. They were . . . Daddy was telling me last week, "Maybe we were too strict with you."

Therapist: What is the earliest thing that you remember . . . way back?

Patient: I fell off my tricycle and split the back of my head open. I can still remember that.

Therapist: That is painful, isn't it?

Patient: Well, at three years old, I guess you don't have as much pain.

Therapist: But it is something that happens to you, and it is traumatic and it has something to do with . . .

Patient: Yeah, stitches, pain.

Therapist: Yeah, so you started with pain very early in life?

Patient: Yeah, my mom had told me not to play on the tricycle, and at three years old you want to play on the tricycle, and I fell off and split the back of my head open.

Therapist: Uh-huh.

Patient: I keep kidding her today that I lost my brain then.

Therapist: So the problem had to do with your mother?

Patient: No, I would say it has more to do with my father.

Therapist: In what way?

Patient: Well, my father is protective. Mommy is very sympathetic with everything, and my dad is soft underneath but he shows a hard core, eh? He would give you the shirt off his back, like I am in trouble now. I am twenty-five. He doesn't have to take me back into the house but he wants to, to help me, to get me back on my feet. This is why he suggested a psychiatrist.

Therapist: It was your father who suggested a psychiatrist?
Patient: Well, he is going to a psychiatrist.
Therapist: I see.
Patient: Because of his job and pressures and everything.
Therapist: But you never thought of it yourself? That you might need some help?
Patient: No.
Therapist: Now, what was it like when you were a little girl, when you were five, six years old? What was your relationship with your father like?
Patient: Well, I remember when we were living in . . . I used to get up in the morning, and he would give me some of his poached egg on toast. I remember that.
Therapist: Did you feel good about it?
Patient: Yeah. It was good.
Therapist: Were you his favorite?
Patient: Yeah, I was his little girl. I guess I am still his little girl.
Therapist: I see.

The evaluator explored the area of sibling rivalry, and the patient said that the children were treated equally. Her brother is a machinist. She says she had a good relationship with her mother.

Patient: I found that Daddy, when he started becoming nervous, I didn't want to bother him.
Therapist: When did he become nervous and upset?
Patient: When he quit smoking about seven years ago.
Therapist: But that is more recent. Let's stay back to that early time. Your relationship with your brother . . . Now let me see, he was five years older than you are. How did you get along when you were children?
Patient: Well, we always used to play Davey Crockett. I would be the Indian and he would beat me up all the time, and I would go squealing.
Therapist: He would beat you up?
Patient: Well, just in play. (Laughing.) He never really hurt me. He used to be Davey Crockett all the time, and I would always be the redskin.
Therapist: But, you know, there is a pattern here, things are

happening to you. You fall from the tricycle and you split your head, you are the Indian and you are being attacked and . . .

Patient: Always the low man on the ladder.

Therapist: And look at you now. Is this a pattern in your life that you somehow or other are injuring yourself, somehow or other finding yourself in situations like that?

Patient: Don't ask me. I don't know.

Therapist: I am asking you because you are the only one who knows.

Patient: I guess it is fate.

Therapist: Is it fate or is it something within you?

Patient: Well, a kid falling off a tricycle, three years old. I don't think that that is a planned accident or something.

Therapist: Well, planned obviously it is not, but to accept the position of being the Indian and always been beaten, even if it is not serious, is something that you choose to do and we should take into account.

Patient: Well, I was thinking, well, he is my brother. He is older. He has got the right to choose first.

Therapist: Not necessarily.

Patient: He liked to be Davey Crockett better than I did.

Therapist: I am not saying that is what it is. I am asking. Now, how were things in school? Did you have any close friends?

Patient: Oh, yeah.

Regarding her menstruation, she said that her mother had prepared her, and in talking about the incident of her first period she said that nevertheless she was not at all pleased. The session continues.

Therapist: So you didn't want to grow up.

Patient: Well, at the age of twelve you are still playing around with the kids and on the bicycle and everything. You don't want the responsibility of having a period.

Therapist: Hmmm.

Patient: Because you are still young, eh?

Therapist: So you were not very happy.

Patient: Well, with the period—Have you ever had a period?

Therapist: No, I have never had a period. That is one thing that I don't know anything about.

Patient: The trouble with it and everything about . . .

Therapist: But you see, some girls have different reactions.

Patient: Uh-huh.

Therapist: They feel very proud. They feel they have grown up. They feel all kinds of things, but in your case it was a nuisance.

Patient: Well, Daddy was always kidding Mommy. "Oh, don't talk to the old lady. She is bitchy. She has got her curse."

Therapist: So, you mean to say, your father disapproved also?

Patient: Well, he must have been happy because I remember one time when we were living in . . . he said don't bother your mother. She is late on her period and she is very worried and she was kind of older, eh, so I was what, seventeen, eighteen, and it was kind of unexpected to have another kid come along.

Therapist: What was the attitude about sex in the family?

Patient: Well, my father always told me, "What you have got . . . what you are sitting on is a treasure, and don't put it up for grabs for every guy." But I didn't have every guy. I was with one guy. I was with one guy. I wasn't with . . .

Therapist: What did you . . . what was his meaning? How did you feel? What was your father trying to tell you?

Patient: Well, he was trying to put an old head on young shoulders.

Therapist: Uh-huh. And?

Patient: And you have to learn by your own mistakes.

Therapist: But obviously he had concern about you and love for you.

Patient: Yeah, yeah.

Therapist: What was your feeling about him? At that time.

Patient: At that time, I was young. I was thinking the old man . . . what is wrong with him and all of this? Well, every teenager goes through that, eh?

Therapist: Uh-huh.

Patient: How come he is telling me that? Gees, if you love a guy, aren't you supposed to do something with him?

Therapist: I see.

Patient: And every time I went with a guy it was when I love him, but if I didn't love a guy, I wouldn't . . .

Therapist: How old were you when you had your first boyfriend?

She started dating at age fourteen and had her first sexual experience at age seventeen. She described that it was painful, and she feared she might get pregnant. She was afraid her parents might find out and be disappointed as they had often warned her about having sexual relations. She described herself as an average student, finished grade eleven. Then she talked about her father, who is on antidepressants and who is not at all stable. The evaluator explored her work performance. After high school she worked as a secretary and did well and liked it but was laid off. Then she worked in a bank, didn't like it, and quit. She moved to the country where her parents had a farm. There she met the man she lived with.

Patient: We were both drunk and we went . . . I was living on the farm. My parent were living in . . . still. And we had come back from a bar, and we were both drunk, and we decided to make love, and I still didn't know anything, really, about it, eh? And I was nineteen at the time, and I was afraid that I might get pregnant, and then he said, "Well, if you are pregnant, I'll marry you." And then as time went on, we didn't make love that much anyway. Maybe about ten times a month. That is not really a lot.

Therapist: Hmmm.

Patient: And then I went on the pill, and then we went to Florida and he didn't trust the pill at all. I was on the pill for about three months before he would go through with everything, eh? Using safes in the meanwhile. He didn't trust the pill, eh? Although I didn't either. I was kind of leery of it, eh? I would try . . . I was afraid that I would end up pregnant. I was on the pill. And then I was on and off it. Going on it for six months, off it for six months. You know, try and give my body a rest and everything, and at the same time just to see if he'd be going out with me just because I was on the pill.

Therapist: Uh-huh.

Patient: But he stayed with me. We bought . . . we got other stuff to use because a man he was working with said that a foam his wife had been using for quite a while was good and she never got pregnant. Well, she had one child that they had planned. So we used that while I was off the pill.

Therapist: But you lived together?

Patient: Yeah, we went out for two years, two and a half years, almost two and a half years before we lived together.

Therapist: Were you working at the time?

Patient: Yeah.

Therapist: What were you doing?

Patient: I was working in an electronics shop.

Therapist: I see.

Patient: His brother was living upstairs with a girl and his other brother now is living with another girl. His parents were there. First of all, his real father died, eh? And the mother left the three of them. Well, my boyfriend's name is Jack. He was three years old when his father died, and his mother must have gone through hell because she had had the youngest by her first husband around the time that he got killed in the mine and she was at her mother's, living at her mother's, eh? And in one room there was the coffin of her husband and the other was her newborn baby, so I guess she must have gone through some hell, eh?

Therapist: Yes. But did you want to get married to him?

Patient: Yeah, and then he kept telling me, play the other way. Say you don't want to get married. When we got engaged, I told him, I said, "Look, you want to get engaged?" Because he had been saying that we would get engaged one day, or that we will get engaged another day. We will get married here, get married there. You know, on and off, and I was getting kind of fed up. I said, "Make your mind up." And I told him, I said, "Look, you want to get engaged, let me know. If you don't, don't bother me. I don't want to hear about . . . You want to get married? Let me know. If you don't, don't talk about it." His brother who was living upstairs with his girl, they had been going out for about two months or a month and a half or something and decided to get engaged at Christmas, 1972, 1973. So I told Jack, "You know, we have been going out for two years and you, you can't get off your ass and make some decisions. Look at your brother. What is wrong with him or what is wrong with you?" And I was kind of mad.

Therapist: I see.

Then she said that two weeks later her boyfriend bought her an engagement ring, which made her happy. On Christmas Eve they were going to get engaged, and his brother was going to get engaged the same night. This was at the home of his parents. But Jack was too drunk and the patient was in a rage, as she found him in a disturbed state. He had drunk a bottle of gin in the barn, had fallen into horse manure, and was so sick that he had to be put in bed. The patient, in a very angry state, wanted to return the ring but changed her mind. The session continues.

Therapist: Well now, how do you feel about him after all this trouble?

Patient: Well, I am still going through heartbreak. Well, after five years.

Therapist: But is it. . . .

Patient: I am concerned about my arm.

Therapist: Okay.

Patient: And I am nervous about the operation because I have never had an operation before.

Therapist: Yes. But now, tell me one thing. Are you . . . do you feel your relationship has ended?

Patient: Well, I am going to try and forget it. That is for sure.

Therapist: And what is your plan? What is it that you would like us to help you with?

Patient: For you to help me?

Therapist: I mean, this clinic, you said you wanted to see a psychiatrist? What is it that you wanted?

Patient: Well, it was my father's idea to see a psychiatrist.

Therapist: But do you think it is a good idea or not?

Patient: Well, I don't know. For me, I think that I am just going through heartbreak.

Therapist: But you don't think that it is . . .

Patient: But Mommy . . . Mommy was down on Saturday to get my clothes, and she said that she had told Jack that I had a cast on one side, eh? He said, "How come she had got a cast?" "It is because she has very bad cuts and she can't move her fingers, and the doctor wants her to stay set." And he said, "Oh, she cut the tendons, eh?" And he is concerned. He knows he has pushed me a little bit too far.

Therapist: Has he come to see you?

Patient: He is too afraid because Mom told him Saturday when she was down, "You know you should be lucky she is not here because she would probably go bang right on your head with the cast."

Therapist: You mean to say that since that time you haven't seen him?

Patient: I saw him when he brought my parents into the hospital.

Therapist: Uh-huh.

Patient: And I told him not to worry them.

Therapist: Okay, now tell me, what are your fears about your hand?

Patient: Well, I'd like it to get going.

Therapist: Of course.

Patient: Because this city is not my kind of life anymore. I am used to a quiet town.

Therapist: What is it that you would like to do?

Patient: Well, I would like to be able to move my fingers.

Therapist: This I understand but what is it? I mean, you said that this city is not your . . . What are your plans?

Patient: My future plans?

Therapist: Yeah.

Patient: Well, he lives in the outskirts. He is buying a house there, and he is working there. As far as I am concerned he can stay there and work. He said that he is going to pay my first rent on an apartment because I have got a job there too. I am working for an electronics company, and I enjoy it. It is interesting.

Therapist: But if he wants to get married, would you marry him?

Patient: This I don't know. I think I would give him one big run around and make him . . .

Therapist: So you are still mad at him?

Patient: . . . out to drink every night and worry about me like I used to worry about him and see him go on nerve pills to try and quiet things down.

Therapist: So you want to punish him. You are still mad at him.

Patient: Well, shouldn't I be?

Therapist: Well, I don't see any reason why you shouldn't be. Instead of taking it all against yourself. What did your poor arm do to you to deserve what you did to it?

Patient: I don't know. But I lost my mind for a second, and I think it is Jack that pushed me to this.

Therapist: Uh-huh.

Patient: . . . because of his joking and joking and then after having the nerve to say that it was a joke.

Therapist: Well, I don't know the nature of your lesion, but I am sure that with surgery everything is going to be all right, but not right away. It takes time. First of all, the tendons do not go all the way up there, but they start from the elbow, and it seems likely that you have cut them. They are going to repair them.

Patient: Well, I am getting . . . I was on penicillin pills, and I am getting little spurts as if it is going to awaken.

Therapist: Yes, but you feel all right then?

Patient: It is still numb a bit but . . .

Therapist: . . . a little bit.

Patient: But I feel inside it is going up.

Therapist: Well, you probably didn't cut a nerve, so chances are that this will take a little time but you would get full use of your fingers and . . .

Patient: Because I enjoy my job a lot.

Therapist: Of course, on the other hand, I hope that this is the best lesson for you—that this is not the time to turn things against yourself.

Patient: Don't worry.

Therapist: . . . if you are angry at somebody else.

Patient: Hit him. Bang.

Therapist: I am not suggesting that but . . .

Patient: Maybe I should have hit him on the head with the bloody beer bottle.

Therapist: Hmmm.

Patient: Knock him out.

Therapist: Then it would be his blood and his head, and you would be feeling just as bad. I don't think that these things have to be expressed in this way, but I certainly think that you could express it in a verbal way. If there are certain things that you don't like . . .

Patient: Oh, I have expressed it in verbal ways, but he can't take an argument. He will go and drink first.

Therapist: Well, maybe then that is not such a good plan.

Patient: Once in a while I will have a beer with . . . like when we were working up north there, I was alone in the house, and I was going to see my girlfriends during the day, and everything, and I don't know, they seemed to turn against me or something. I don't know because I guess they were jealous because I was living with the guy I loved and everything and him buying a house and I helped him. Well, it was me who did all the painting in the house and putting shag carpets in and keeping a clean house and working and I was going out on the weekend just to get out of the house and go to the bar and talk with some people and everything, you know. Socialize, not to go on a drunk or anything. I went on a drunk a few times. The morning after you don't feel better. You still have your problem, and you have a bigger problem. You have a hangover, or you are sick. I remember one time I had twelve ounces of vodka under the table, drinking it in a bar with a can of orange juice, and Jesus, I was sick. Oh, God. But that doesn't solve anything.

Therapist: No, it doesn't solve anything.

Patient: It solves it for the night. You feel good. You are all happy, but the next morning you have got a heck of a hangover.

Therapist: Yeah. But the question is, do you really think that Jack is the man for you or not, after all that happened?

Patient: Not now because I sort of blame him for pushing me, eh?

Therapist: Yeah.

Patient: In the future I don't know.

Therapist: Are you going to forgive him? How do you feel?

Patient: I don't know. If I ever forgive him he is going to have a real runaround.

Therapist: Uh-huh.

Patient: I'll know how to treat a guy next time because Mommy was always telling me to treat a guy like dirt and I was starting to treat him like dirt and telling him, "Well, you want to go and drink tonight, no supper." You know: "Take your choice between your beer or your good supper." Because I used to make him really good suppers and keep his house really clean while working forty-five hours a week on a really tough job, and I didn't mind. I like to keep active. This is another thing that was practically driving me up the wall and around doing nothing and I am used to, you know.

Therapist: So maybe after all, after all this tragedy, maybe you learned a lesson.

Patient: I learned a lesson.

Therapist: And if you learned a lesson this may be the best thing that could happen.

Patient: I learned a lesson. Don't trust a nice guy, and my father was always telling me, "Never put all your eggs in one basket."

Therapist: Okay, so maybe he was right.

Patient: Yeah, and he had a kind of procedure, throwing everything back in my face, the silent way too, and this hurts me more because I know that I am a disappointment to him.

Therapist: Uh-huh.

Patient: But Mom, she is understanding. She realizes what I am going through, and she is mad as hell at Jack too.

Therapist: Well, thank you for coming and talking to me.

Patient: Okay.

Dr. Peter Sifneos

It seems to me that the important question for the evaluator is the degree of intervention without a history. It is true that it might be perfectly appropriate to take less history and emphasize the here and now. But by doing this, one is faced with another problem, namely: How can one understand the here and now without having a picture of her character structure, of what she is like? In this specific case it was through careful history taking that it became apparent that she is passive and impulsive, the characteristics of her suicidal attempt have become clear.

A crisis occurred within a split second; her maladaptive defense was to deal with it by cutting her wrists, which was done very quickly. With patients such as this the evaluator must judiciously decide how much he must focus on assessing and how much on supporting.

I very much agree with the point that one should leave it up to the patient to decide if she wants help. I would say, "It is up to you to decide, really." In other words, one has to start to break through her passive process from the onset.

In terms of psychotherapeutic planning, one possible focus would be to tell her, "Let's look at the situation you are in. You have been living with Bob for five years. You may break up with him, or you might get back together and want to get on with it in a way that is meaningful to you. In a way, you have some unfinished business with Bob." If she accepts this, then I might add, "Do you think it might be helpful to discuss with me your relationship with Bob so that you might be able to work through this unfinished business, however it ends up?" There is a possibility that she would be quite eager to engage in therapy with such a focus because it would make a lot of sense for her.

Would it make a difference if this patient had a female therapist instead of a male therapist? Certainly for patients who are candidates for Short-Term Dynamic Psychotherapy it doesn't make any difference. But regarding this patient, who is not a candidate for STAPP, I don't think it makes much difference. I explored very carefully to see if she had any special feelings for her father or for her mother. She presented both her parents in a bland way. They were both supportive. She needs a supportive therapist, male or female— it makes no difference.

Dr. Habib Davanloo

I think Dr. Sifneos made a very thorough evaluation with this difficult patient. It was a blend of crisis evaluation and crisis support. The interview demonstrates the process of evaluation of a young woman who had recently made a suicidal attempt. She starts the session by expressing worries about if her little finger is going to function. She presents herself in a very passive way, and what emerges immediately is a repetition of a recurrent pattern, which Dr. Sifneos explored very well and brought to her attention; but I did not get the feeling that she paid much attention. In terms of technique, Dr. Sifneos's attempt was to undercut the malignant type of defense mechanism she uses, in terms of suicidal attempt, the maladaptive process of being passive. In terms of the therapeutic alliance and the therapeutic focus and contract, she represents the type of patient with whom the development of a therapeutic alliance is very difficult. Her passivity and indecisiveness were the highlights of her relationship with the therapist. "What should I do, Doctor? What do you recommend?" And whenever Dr. Sifneos confronted her, she responded by saying, "I don't want to think about it now. "I will think about it tomorrow." This again was another prominent feature of her interaction. There was the process of being passive, somehow or other almost dissociative, that these things happen to her from outside, that she has no say in what happens. In terms of the question of therapeutic foci, it seems that there were two possible contents to engage her about, and Dr. Sifneos very sensitively picked them up. One of them was her relationship with this man, and she talked about her "heartbreak." The other was the pending operation. Around these two possible foci, Dr. Sifneos repeatedly questioned her about what she expected the outcome to be. And as we noticed, her answer was, "The outcome will be what it will be . . . fate." She indicated what her boyfriend wants and what her mother decides.

In terms of her psychopathology, there is definite indication of poor impulse control. I see her as a volatile person, and she gives a clear picture of being capable of having rage reactions. She does not have much capacity to experience and tolerate anxiety and depression. Regarding the circumstances of her suicidal attempt, she said that she did not know what had happened for a moment. There is anger underlying the suicidal attempt and the fear of impulse control. She is terribly frightened that she has no control over her impulse. There are patients like this who come to the first interview with such a passive tendency and say, "I have no control over myself; I don't know what is going to happen to me. Am I going to go crazy?" The question in my mind was what to do about the affect that is behind this young woman's defenses, this woman's passivity against aggressive impulses which have become self-directed. What this patient presents is an entire life history of a long-standing characterological pattern of being passive and wanting to be taken care of. About her suicidal attempt she said, "It is not my fault that I have injured myself." The way she put it was something like, "A razor was in my hand, and a lot of blood came out. I don't remember it. Now I am injured, I am hurting; it is no fault of mine. I need you to rescue me and to take care of me."

This woman presents herself as a patient who has not really separated from her parents. She has never completed the psychological work of separation and has not undergone the maturational process of separating from her parents. She has not developed an independent identity.

Her relationship with her boyfriend is part and parcel of this problem. Dr. Sifneos's evaluation clearly indicated that they have a very ambivalent relationship, and they don't know what they want to do. They don't know if they want to get married or if they want to break up. Their relationship has been a hostile one, and it has been like this since the onset of their relationship five years ago.

It seems to me that if her relationship with her boyfriend breaks up, she will be desperate to reattach herself to someone. This, in my experience with this kind of patient, is an important point of departure. What I have in mind is that if at the point of the breakdown she could attach herself to a reliable mental health professional, he/she might help her toward individuation and might provide a period of maturational development. But the other side of the picture would be that she would deal with the breakdown of the relationship by attaching herself to another relationship.

In terms of technique of crisis support, there are two possible areas one could work with. One is to help her, to get her to go through the surgery she needs, preventing ego regression and a further suicidal attempt. The other is, as I indicated before, if her relationship with her boyfriend breaks down she would be in a desperate state to reattach herself; this would be the point at which a skillful mental health worker could enter the picture and help her in the work of individuation, an engagement of self-exploration and self-development to gain some degree of independence and to enter into a healthier relationship. But if the question to me is, "Is she a candidate for Short-Term Dynamic Psycotherapy?", to work with her in terms of her mental health potential, I don't believe she is a candidate.

But one of the most important technical considerations in taking this woman into treatment is that one would like to leave it up to her to decide and have her come back not because the surgeon suggests it or her father wants it. One has to break through this passive process by getting her to decide for herself from the very early phase of the therapeutic work. In terms of her dependency, there are those therapists who say that you must permit dependency and that you must allow it to occur in the beginning. But on the other hand there are clinicians who say you must not permit this to occur. Obviously one must not get trapped, in the therapeutic approach, into supporting her maladaptive system.

17

The Persistently Suicidal Risk

KATHERINA MARMOR, PH.D.

HISTORY

The scientific and objective study of suicide as a complex socio-psychological phenomenon can be said to have begun with the publication of Emile Durkheim's famous book *La Suicide* in 1897. His was one of the first examples of an organized use of statistical methods in social investigation. Durkheim's book, written at about the same time that Sigmund Freud was beginning his investigations into the nature of unconscious factors in human behavior, is remarkably perceptive and is justly regarded as a classic. His basic theme was that suicide could be explained etiologically via the social structure and its ramifications. He categorized three basic types of suicide: (1) egoistic, (2) altruistic, and (3) anomic, although various mixtures of the three can and do exist.

The first type, egoistic suicide, occurs when the individual is a relatively isolated person with insufficient or inadequate ties to a family or community. The second, altruistic suicide, is one that is expected or required by society, and is in effect dictated by society, with the individual having little or no choice. To live, under dishonorable circumstances, is ignominious; to die is honorable. Hara-kiri (Japan) and Suttee (India) are examples of altruistic suicide. The third type, anomic suicide, the one with which Durkheim's name is uniquely associated, refers to the self-inflicted death that occurs when the accustomed relationship between an individual and his societal environment is precipitously disrupted. Thus a sudden loss of one's fortune, of a job, of a significant other, or of any other central factor in one's support system can precipitate what Durkheim called an anomic suicide.

Fundamentally, Durkheim's approach and emphasis was a sociological and statistical one, although he was not unaware of the existence of individual psychological factors. Numerous English and American sociological studies of suicide have followed the Durkheim pattern, all demonstrating the differential suicidal rates in relation to various sociological and demographic factors, such as age, religion, sex, race, economic class, rural-urban differentials, and ethnic identity.

Historically the development of the psychological or psychodynamic approach to suicide was parallel in time with that of the sociological approach and began with Sigmund Freud's major insights into the role of unconscious motivation in human behavior. It was Freud who first called attention to the role in suicide of unconscious hostility turned inward, with the suicide "murdering" the introjected object. In psychoanalytical terms all the psychological elements manifested in suicide are explicable by the life history of the individual and the way in which basic psychological configurations have been channeled through the dynamics of family relationships.

Investigators of suicidal behavior emphasize that it is a multifactorial problem and that both sociological and psychological factors must be taken into consideration in studying the problem. As far back as 1930 Maurice Halbwachs, a student and friend of Durkheim, emphasized that there was no necessary antithesis between the social and psychological approaches to suicide and that they were actually complimentary. In more recent times Farberow alone (1973), with Shneidman (1955), and Litman (1970), and others

(Levi 1972, Stengl 1969, Kiev 1977) have all emphasized that a comprehensive approach to the etiology of suicide must include both the general socioeconomic aspects of the human condition in Western civilization as well as how people's inner needs and conflicts mesh with the demands of their life situations.

SOME GENERAL ASPECTS OF SUICIDE

Suicidal attempts tend to occur when an individual's habitual coping techniques fail badly, leaving him or her with feelings of hopelessness and helplessness. Hopelessness has been shown to correlate more highly with suicidal behavior than does the actual severity of depression. Feelings of hopelessness and helplessness due to the inability to meet either internal or external expectations tend to create the conviction that suicide is the only feasible way to resolve the impasse and obtain relief from the intolerable inner tension. Yet the ambivalent nature of most suicidal reactions is revealed by the fact that the majority of suicidal patients, after initiating an attempt, make an effort to reverse the process by seeking or calling for help. This is further indicated by the finding that surviving a serious attempt often seems to symbolically destroy the past and can lead to a rebirth of hope, although the hope is short lived if the underlying problems are not dealt with.

In persons with poorly organized ego structures, once the psychological defenses against suicidal behavior have been breached and an attempt has occurred, the possibility for future suicidal acting out under conditions of extreme emotional tension tends to be facilitated. It is possible that a prior attempt enhances the secret omnipotent fantasy that one really won't die and thus lessens the inner barriers against the suicidal action.

Suicidal attempts rarely occur without some background of depressive symptoms. Feelings of self-depreciation, emptiness, isolation, persecution, rejection, and frustration are frequently encountered subjective reactions in this population group. These symptoms most often occur in the context of interpersonal conflict, but the conflict can also be strongly intrapsychic. Actually, both types of conflict are almost always present although one or the other tends to predominate.

Different groups of suicidal patients tend to experience and react to different varieties of stresses. Thus older patients, more than younger ones, tend to suffer from the effects of physical illness, retirement, changing life-style, social isolation, separation, loss of identity, and widowhood. In younger married people, marital conflicts, role adjustment problems, and threats of separation are commonly encountered suicidal stresses. In younger single individuals one tends to see stresses growing out of sexual or drug problems, identity problems, parental pressures, social isolation, dependence-independence conflicts, transitional life-adjustment problems, or sociopathic activities that have brought them into conflict with the law. It should be recognized that these presenting stresses are sometimes offered as rationalizations for crisis symptoms that are really due to deeper underlying psychopathology in the individual.

Some lethal attempts appear to be sudden and impulsive but are, in fact, culminations of weeks or months of withdrawal and rumination that have totally absorbed the individual. On the other hand, severe interpersonal conflict may precipitate a succession of impulsive, dramatic, and desperate suicidal attempts. Some individuals lack the self-restraint to stop themselves once they move to the brink of dangerous action.

THE PERSISTENTLY SUICIDAL RISK

In the early history of the suicide prevention movement, suicide was regarded primarily as a response to an acute situational crisis, and suicide prevention centers were designed mainly to evaluate the seriousness ("lethality") of suicidal callers and to make appropriate recommendations and referrals for crisis intervention. In recent years, however, a subgroup within the suicidal population has been gaining increasing attention because a short-term crisis approach has been insufficient for them. This group, variously estimated at 30 to 50 percent of those seeking assistance at suicide prevention centers, present life patterns of long-standing maladaptation to stress and have come to be designated as chronically suicidal because of recurrent attempts and persistent suicidal ideation. Patients in this group are distinguished from those in the situational crisis group in that their angers, psychological losses, and somatic complaints are long-standing and persistent, even though they may present themselves recurrently in states of acute crisis. Many of these patients reveal histories of repetitive adaptive failures due to ineffectual problem-solving techniques and poor interpersonal relationships.

Others, however, seem to function externally at good levels most of the time, but their inner conflicts and needs are such that they react repetitively with self-destructive behavior.

In persons who become chronically or persistently suicidal, the sources of stress are more likely to be due to internal characterological problems than to external objective life difficulties, even though the latter may reinforce the former. In such patients, ordinary life problems tend to become greatly magnified due to their impoverished inner resources, their inadequate interpersonal relationships, their suspiciousness and distrust of others, their poor impulse control, and their impaired self-concepts. Their distorted perceptions most often lead them to react aggressively to imagined wrongs, and the consequent retaliation by others then serves to confirm their suspicions.

Another characteristic of this group of patients is the strong tendency toward patterns of behavior that Karl Menninger (1938) has described as "partial suicide." Some of these frequently encountered patterns are abuse of alcohol or potent narcotics, purposive accidents, multiple surgery, gambling, sexual deviance or promiscuity, or various forms of counterphobic behavior in which these individuals risk their health or safety in an effort to deny inner feelings of weakness or inadequacy.

Such behavioral tendencies in chronically suicidal individuals render a purely statistical approach to suicide difficult. Although the number of completed suicides in the United States ranges from twenty thousand to forty thousand annually, individuals who die as an indirect consequence of self-destructive patterns—e.g., accidents, reckless driving,[1] surgery, alcohol or narcotic abuse, or even

1. Not all such deaths are necessarily suicidal. A recent study that questions the traditional assumption that a large proportion of accidents necessarily share the same intention toward self-destruction as does suicide is Tabachnick's *Accident or Suicide* (1973). Tabachnick found that only 4 percent of his auto accident series had marked suicidal features and only 25 percent showed elements of depression "which made them closer to the suicide group." He contends that the "accident" person often is utilizing a propensity toward risk taking for various psychodynamic reasons. The action of the alcoholic intake that is commonly seen in both suicides and accidents illustrates the difference. Alcohol resolves the ambivalent conflict in the suicidal person over whether to live or die by dulling the realistic and critical life-evaluation and self-preservative functions. In the "accident" person, it heightens the lethality of a realistically dangerous activity, i.e., driving, by seriously impairing the quick and sharp use of his faculties.

injuries sustained at the hands of others but provoked by their own courting of danger—are usually not recorded as suicides.

One group of chronically suicidal patients who are often overlooked or inadequately treated are the talented, successful, bright, "special" people, who carry the burden of an external image that they can neither sustain nor relinquish. Included among these are respected public servants like policemen; professionals like physicians, teachers, scientists, and engineers; and famous public figures like artists, writers, and politicians. Individuals in these groups often find it difficult to ask for help, and their friends, families, or colleagues tend to minimize or ignore the telltale signals of decompensation that they would recognize more easily in others.

Patients in this category share the same inner fears, feelings of loneliness, and lack of self-confidence that are experienced by less gifted or economically or educationally less advantaged people, but their suicidal propensities can be missed if the clinician fails to look behind their bright facades into the chaotic inner person. If, due to early traumatic life experiences, these individuals have sustained damage to their egos or impairment in their ability to form a meaningful relationship with a significant other, the very special quality of their personalities tends to increase their sense of emotional isolation.

Although these people are often able to use their trained skills for long periods of time to compensate for their inner emotional poverty or tensions, their psychological rigidity makes it difficult for them to cope adaptively with unexpected losses or life changes. The culturally admired roles of these individuals tend to reinforce their psychological defenses of denial. For them to seek help is a loss of ego status, and thus they often try to help themselves by reinforcing their external role activities at the expense of obtaining more rational sources of psychological support. When life circumstances block or interfere with their ability to function effectively or to derive satisfaction from their work, they have no inner resources to fall back on. Their initial response to such a situation is to try to restore their ego-support systems and respected self-images by compensatory overinvolvement in their work activites or by attempting to shift to a totally different lifestyle or locale. When these extraordinary efforts fail to resolve their inner turmoil, then their feelings of despair tend to increase, accompanied by a sense of worthlessness, self-blame, withdrawal from others, resort to narcotics, immobilization, and suicidal ideation.

The personality characteristics most often encountered in chronically suicidal individuals can be summarized in seven major categories,[2] as follows: (1) defect in affectional relationships; (2) impaired sense of identity, with vacillations between intense self-depreciation and grandiose self-inflation; (3) depressive mood disturbances; (4) pervasive feelings of anger, feelings of victimization and self-hatred for unmet self-expectations; (5) rigidities of thought and perception, as manifested by constricted thinking and difficulty in finding new or alternative solutions for their emotional difficulties; (6) rigidity of behavior, including tendencies to repeat self-defeating patterns and an obsessive need to be in control in interpersonal situations; (7) impulsivity of behavior as manifested in various patterns of antisocial behavior, deviant or promiscuous sexuality, dependency on drugs or alcohol, outbursts of irrational rage, dramatic somatic symptoms of unexplained origin, or attempted suicide.

In terms of actual lethality, the most important indicator is the impairment of affectional relationships with others and the sense of emotional isolation, loneliness, and alienation that ensues therefrom. This corresponds with the findings of a number of other recent investigators—Breed (1972), Maris and Lazerwitz (1973), Weisman and Worden (1975). As Breed points out, it is not only the social isolation (and absence of a support structure) that is so destructive, but also the repressed anger due to frustrated dependency needs. It is interesting to note that Weisman and Worden found that when these characteristics were present in terminally ill people with cancer, such patients tended to die much sooner than did similarly ill patients who were not socially isolated.

The affectional alienation that is experienced by these individuals has wide ramifications in the way they relate to other people. As an example, when they do have paired relationships they tend to substitute control for affection; they enter into neurotic marriages in which they attempt to hold onto their partners by keeping them in a kind of dependent bondage which conceals their own profound

2. Not all these categories are necessarily present in all such persons, nor do they fall into any single diagnostic classification. Statistically the highest incidence occurs among the schizophrenias, affective psychoses, paranoid psychoses, and borderline personality syndromes.

dependent needs and emotional isolation. As might be expected, the spouses of such individuals, after a while, initiate separation or react with a variety of behavioral and symptomatic patterns: somatic complaints, depressive symptoms, alcoholism, overmedication, sexual acting out with others, or emotional withdrawal. These patterns in turn cause depressive crises or acute panic reactions (due to the threatened loss of control) in the hitherto dominant partner. These are often misinterpreted as being the primary problem by helping agents, who do not recognize the deeper and more chronic psychopathology behind these acute depressive reactions or attacks of panic. Often these individuals, who present particularly rigid defenses, seek help not for themselves but for the symptomatology of their spouses. They present themselves as concerned rescuers of a problematic or inadequate partner, although what they are really looking for is help in reestablishing control over the relationship.

TREATMENT

The treatment of the persistently or chronically suicidal patient requires a different approach than does the approach of acute suicidal crises in persons with previously intact egos who are reacting to a situational trauma or loss. With the chronically suicidal person, coping with the immediate crisis situation alone is not enough; treatment *must* include preventive efforts to modify the underlying interpersonal difficulties and intrapsychic conflicts. If the helping agent, influenced by the enormous perturbation and panic that such patients usually present, becomes overly anxious about their persistent suicidal ideation or their potential suicidal acting out, his therapeutic stance and judgment will become impaired. Maneuvers to prevent imminent self-destruction are the first order of importance and must be actively attended to, but if the therapist continues to function primarily as a "rescuer" beyond the acute suicidal phase and fails to confront the chronically suicidal patient with the underlying psychodynamics that have led to the acute crisis, he impairs his therapeutic usefulness to the patient.

After an initial suicide attempt, follow-up treatment becomes a critical factor in preventing subsequent suicide episodes. Suicide attempts, like other crisis situations, involve both a threat and an opportunity. The threat, of course, is to life; the opportunity is that the attempt can serve to alert both the patient and/or others to the existence of important and soluble problems that may hitherto have been concealed and thus lead to the seeking of professional help. Often a suicidal crisis leads to the discovery that the individual has been suffering from chronic depression, masked behind somatic symptomatology or chronic feelings of fatigue, apathy, or boredom.

Adequate therapeutic intervention in such cases requires a careful exploration of historical background as well as of existing psychological, economic, biological, and social factors, and of internal as well as external stresses.

As in all forms of psychotherapy, the patient's motivation and capacity to accept the existence of an underlying problem are crucial to the success of therapy and to the eventual prognosis. Patients who manifest unconscious resistance by utilizing excessive denial or rationalizing all their difficulties as being due to external circumstances or past events that can neither be modified nor altered are the most difficult to treat and have the most doubtful prognosis. These are the patients who will often call for help, but then find all sorts of excuses for not keeping their appointments, or else engage in futile pseudotherapy.

A serious problem that one often encounters in public clinics and suicide prevention centers is that of getting adequate information about previous therapeutic interventions. Patients come in with histories of escalating life difficulties that have brought them into prior contact with a variety of agencies and health workers, but one seldom encounters any coordination of information between such groups or any efforts at follow-up treatment or even follow-up investigation of the postsuicidal patient's subsequent course. Thus many of these patients "hop" from clinic to clinic and from therapist to therapist, sometimes even attending more than one clinic or therapist at the same time. Different prescriptions and treatment approaches may be received from each clinic or therapist, or the same prescription may be duplicated without the knowledge or coordination of the therapists involved. Indeed, sometimes the treatment approaches negate each other to the serious detriment of the patient. Although similar failures to communicate can occur in other areas of health-care delivery, the mental health field is particularly prone to it because of the understandable concerns that exist in that area about breaching the patient's confidentiality. This creates an especially difficult obstacle in the treatment of chronically suicidal patients, not only because there is an actual information deficit that presents an obstacle to good therapeutic management, but also because superficial treatment contacts tend to reinforce the patient's distorted conviction, based on early life experience, that people don't really care and cannot really be depended upon.

A clinical feature characteristic of these patients that contributes strongly to this problem is their lack of basic trust, and the depressive constriction that impairs their communicative processes. This leads them to seek multiple sources of assistance, in none of which they have confidence. Seeking absolute or magical answers for their conflicts and insecurities but having no confidence in their problem-solving abilities or that of the helping agent, they are incapable of pursuing any consistent course of action, thus defeating the therapy as well as presenting a manipulative pattern to the helping agents.

Family physicians are often the first ones to see the suicidal patient. Litman (1970) states that 75 percent of completed suicides consulted a physician within the six months preceding their action. He also estimates that the average family physician encounters about half a dozen potentially suicidal patients in his practive every year, and will have ten to twelve actual suicides among his patients over his lifetime.

Unfortunately patients do not always reveal their suicidal ideation. Instead they may present themselves to their family physicians with unexplained somatic symptoms that mask their underlying depressive diathesis, and they may even deny any existing emotional distress.

This denial of emotional difficulties often makes suicide attempters inaccessible to conventional therapies and increases the need for management, follow-up, and outreach through other avenues. A number of innovative programs that attempt to deal with this problem have been devised by various suicideologists. Thus Motto (1974), at the Langley Porter Clinic in San Francisco, set up a program to maintain long-term contacts with high-risk posthospitalization patients by periodic telephone calls or brief letters expressing an interest in their welfare and inviting their responses. Litman and Wold (1976) devised a similar program for high-lethality outpatients at the Los Angeles Suicide Prevention Center, assigning a specific worker to make regular, periodic telephone calls to each patient. The results in both programs were considered beneficial for the life-styles of these patients, but the long-term effect on their rate of suicide still remains to be seen.

Farberow, working at the Los Angeles Suicide Prevention Center, has emphasized the value of varied group therapy programs for this same patient population, with the sharing of responsibility by cotherapists. The theoretical basis for choosing a group therapy format rested on two major elements among others: (1) a group situation lends itself well to dealing with the feelings of loneliness and emotional isolation in these patients and their strong needs for acceptance and support; and (2) peer support, peer feedback, and peer-role modeling in a group context become valuable therapeutic adjuncts.

Based on these considerations, under the direction of Farberow, there was organized at the Los Angeles Suicide Prevention Center a comprehensive program embracing socialization groups and drop-in groups as ongoing support systems for postsuicidal-attempt patients, and short-term and long-term psychodynamically oriented group therapy programs for those who showed a potential for insight (Farberow 1974, Marmor and Farberow 1974, Marmor and Farberow 1976).

A basic element in the treatment of chronically suicidal patients is establishing a trusting patient-therapist relationship with them. Although these patients can be helped in their recurrent crises by either long-term dynamic therapy or short-term therapeutic techniques, it is of major importance to them to know in the latter instance that the same therapist will be available to them in a crisis if they feel they need to return. Sometimes this transference relationship can be established to the clinic or institution as well as to the therapist so that the sense of continuity can be maintained even if the therapists change.

CONCLUSION

In summary, we have attempted in this chapter to describe the personality characteristics of a large subgroup of suicidal patients who because of multiple suicidal attempts or persistent suicidal ideation often present themselves in states of recurrent crises at clinics, suicide prevention centers, or therapists' offices. The recognition of these personality characteristics is critical in a preventive sense because if they can be identified at an initial suicide attempt, or prior to it, it may be possible to prevent the development of the chronic suicidal syndrome or to reduce its severity. This issue is important because the first direct or indirect cry for help from such persons is apt to be to family members, school counselors, and/or family practitioners who more often than not fail to recognize or heed its significance.

References

Breed, W. (1972). Five components of a basic suicide syndrome. *Life Threatening Behavior* 2:3-18.

Durkheim, E. (1897). *Le Suicide: Étude de Sociologie*. Paris: Alcan.

Farberow, N.L. (1973). Research in suicide. In *Suicide Prevention in the Seventies*, pp. 45-80, eds. H.L.P. Resnick and B.C. Hawthorne. Washington, D.C.: U.S. Government Printing Office, 1970.

——— (1974). Group psychotherapy in the Los Angeles Suicide Prevention Center. In *Proceedings of the Seventh International Congress on Suicide Prevention*, pp. 456-463. Amsterdam: Swetz and Zeitlinger.

Farberow, N.L., and Shneidman, E.S. (1955). Attempted, threatened, and completed suicide. *Journal of Abnormal Psychology* 50:230.

Halbwachs, M. (1930). *Les Causes du Suicide*. Paris: Alcan.

Kiev, A. (1977). *The Suicidal Patient*. Chicago; Nelson-Hall.

Levi, L. (1972). Stress and distress in response to psychosocial stimuli. *Acta Medica Scandinavica* 191 (Supplement 528).

Litman, R.E. (1970). Management of suicidal patients in medical practice. In *The Psychology of Suicide*, pp. 449-459, eds. E.S. Shneidman, N.L. Farberow, and R.E. Litman. New York: Jason Aronson.

Litman, R.E., and Wold, C.I. (1976). Beyond crisis intervention. In *Suicidology: Contemporary Developments*, pp. 528-546, ed. E.S. Shneidman. New York: Grune and Stratton.

Maris, R., and Lazerwitz, B. (1973). Toward a general theory of self-destructive behavior. Unpublished manuscript.

Marmor, K., and Farberow, N.L. (1974). Post-crisis-oriented time-limited group therapy of suicidal patients. In *Proceedings of the Seventh International Congress on Suicide Prevention*, pp. 464-470. Amsterdam: Swetz and Zeitlinger.

——— (1976). Process and termination in group work with post-suicidal borderline patients. Paper presented at American Association of Suicidology, 9th Annual Meeting, Los Angeles, CA, April 30, 1976

Menninger, K.A. (1938). *Man Against Himself*. New York: Harcourt, Brace.

Motto, J.A. (1974). Suicide prevention by long-term contact. In *Proceedings of the Seventh International Congress on Suicide Prevention*, pp. 426-434. Amsterdam: Swetz and Zeitlinger.

Shneidman, E.S., Farberow, N.L., and Litman, R.E. (1970). *The Psychology of Suicide*. New York: Jason Aronson.

Stengl, E. (1969) Recent progress in suicide research and prevention. *Israel Annals of Psychiatry and Related Disciplines* 7:127-137.

Tabachnick, N., ed. (1973). *Accident or Suicide*. Springfield, Ill.: Charles C Thomas.

Weisman, A.D., and Worden, J.W. (1975). Psychosocial analysis of cancer deaths. *Omega* 6:61-75.

Whitebook, D., and Farberow, N.L. (1974). Drop-in groups as crisis and post-crisis therapy in suicide prevention centers. In *Proceedings of the Seventh International Congress on Suicide Prevention*, pp. 471-477. Amsterdam: Swetz and Zeitlinger.

Part V

Evaluation of Outcome

18

The Nature of Science and the Validity of Psychotherapy

DAVID H. MALAN, M.D.

Since there will be no lack of evidence in the later pages of this essay, I shall start by asking a number of questions and answering them—most unscientifically—without evidence.

The first question is, What is the truth about the effectiveness of dynamic psychotherapy?

More than twenty years of systematic follow-up work have convinced me of the following four-part answer:

1. On the whole, dynamic psychotherapy as usually practiced is ineffective.
2. On the other hand, in certain patients dynamic psychotherapy is extremely effective.
3. This effect occurs through the operation of specific factors, which can be identified and have been understood for decades.
4. But such patients represent a very small proportion of the general psychotherapeutic population.

The second question is, What is the truth about "spontaneous remission"?

My answer to this is that true improvements do occur without therapy and that the mechanisms mostly involve normal maturation interacting with life experience.

These statements together account at once for the fact that so many controlled studies of psychotherapy have given results that are positive but *not* statistically significant: the genuine good results of psychotherapy are too few to outweigh significantly the cases of spontaneous remission.

Now a third question: If these statements represent the truth, why have they not been demonstrated unequivocally by thirty years of research?

The answer is complex, but I believe a large part of it to be as follows:

The majority of psychotherapy researchers have been trained in a tradition that overvalues scientific method and basically does not understand the true nature of science. The result has been the blind and compulsive application of methods that are inappropriate because they are too exact, and the neglect of indirect and less exact methods that are the only ones likely to give the true answers. This is one of the tragedies of our field and is the theme of the present essay.

The rest of the essay falls into two main parts. First I examine aspects of the history of four sciences, contrasting the situation in bacteriology, on the one hand, with that in biology, chemistry, and cosmology on the other. As I hope to show, at certain vital stages in the development of the latter three sciences, direct methods were impossible. The indirect methods that had to be used lay very far from the crucial experiments so often demanded in the field of psychotherapy and involved forms of argument that lay very far from the rigorous logic that so many people consider essential in any subject deserving the name of science.

I then turn to a detailed examination of two studies of brief psychotherapy (Malan 1963, 1976), frequently drawing parallels with the logic of these other sciences. I show how the cumulative circumstantial evidence leads inescapably to the conclusion that in these carefully selected cases major therapeutic effects follow from the operation of specific factors.

THE TRUE NATURE OF SCIENCE

Bacteriology

Here we may take as an example the problem of the cause of anthrax. Much condensed, the sequence of events was as follows: (1) the discovery by a French physician named Davaine of the *invariable presence* of certain rod-shaped bodies in the blood of animals that had died of anthrax; (2) the demonstration by Koch that these rods could be grown in culture outside the animal's body; and (3) Koch's further demonstration that these cultures, when injected into healthy animals, reproduced the disease.

These three observations in combination (which have come to be generalized as "Koch's postulates") virtually proved that the rod-shaped bodies were the causal agents of anthrax.

The point of this summary of events is that it represents not an idealized situation in scientific inquiry, but an *ideal* situation, because it really happened. But the trouble is that many people are led to believe that this is the only type of situation to occur, which they illustrate by carefully selected examples of crucial experiments which confirm or disprove a given hypothesis, such as the observation in 1919 of the bending of light by a gravitational field, which seemed to confirm the general theory of relativity. But this ideal situation does not always occur—crucial experiments are not always possible—and then it is necessary to fall back on methods that are very different. In the excitement and fascination of describing the ideal logic of science, these other situations—which may indeed be the rule rather than the exception—tend to be forgotten. To emphasize this again and again and provide additional examples, we will look at aspects of the development of three other sciences.

Biology: The Origin of Species

The traditional view of the origin of species, which Darwin himself originally shared, was that each species was immutable and independently created by God, perfectly adapted to its environment. However, the more observations he made, the more evidence he began to see which suggested an alternative hypothesis, namely, that species had changed and evolved over the course of time, in response to natural selection or the "survival of the fittest."

Here then were two alternative hypotheses. How was it possible to choose between them? The natural answer that springs to mind is that he must perform crucial experiments. But any attempt to use this type of scientific method met difficulties that were totally insuperable. The difference between the problem facing Koch and that facing Darwin is purely in the time scale: anthrax takes a matter of days to infect its victims, while the time scale of major steps in evolution is often measured in millions of years. Thus the sequence: hypothesis, prediction, crucial experiment, though not impossible *in principle*, is impossible *in fact*. The result was that Darwin was forced to act on the principle that "something might perhaps be made out on this question by patiently accumulating and reflecting on all sorts of facts which could possibly have a bearing on it"—in other words, on the principle of *cumulative, indirect, and circumstantial* evidence. The result was a vast accumulation of independent lines of evidence which favored one theory over another—so much so that today the theory of evolution is regarded as a scientific fact.

A few examples will give a feeling of the arguments used in this hard-hitting yet extraordinarily nonpolemical report of scientific work.

The arguments cover a series of observations, each of which can readily be explained on the theory of natural selection, but seem arbitrary or irrational on the theory of special creation:

1. The presence of special adaptations that are *irrelevant* to the environment in which a given species is living, e.g., webbed feet in upland geese which rarely go near the water. Presumably these geese, originally living near water, have succeeded in colonizing a new environment, to which they are well adapted in other ways.

2. The fact that the species found in very similar oceanic islands, e.g., the Galapagos Islands off South America and the Cape Verde Islands off Africa, resemble not each other but those living on the nearest mainland. This can easily be explained by the hypothesis that colonists came to these islands from the mainland and subsequently underwent modification.

3. The fact that corresponding or "homologous" parts in different animals, e.g., the bones of the foreleg in mammals, seem to have been produced by extensive modification of a basic ground plan rather than by a special design suited to each function.

After describing each of these observations, he writes a passage rather like the following:

> On the ordinary view of the independent creation of each being, we can only say that so it is;—that it has pleased the Creator to construct all the animals and plants in each class on a uniform plan; but this is not a scientific explanation.
> The explanation is to a large extent simple on the theory of successive slight modifications. . . . [Darwin 1859, p. 435]

The argument really involves two principles, one being the universally recognized principle of *economy of hypothesis;* while the other consists essentially of what we may call *intuitive probability*, based on speculation about the mind of the Creator.

But one thing that this argument does not do, of course, is to disprove the hand of God in the creation and distribution of species. God may be postulated at any point in the process; if any of the observations that Darwin describes seem arbitrary, well "God moves in a mysterious way," and perhaps he had his reasons. It is, after all, a pretty unproductive exercise to speculate about the mind of the Creator—an argument that can be used to dismiss every one of the points that Darwin puts forward and is quite unanswerable.

The final result is that the *Origin of Species* (1859) reads as much like a speech in a court of law as an exposition of scientific argument, with Darwin presenting his case like an advocate—not quite like a judge giving a summing up, because the jury is being very strongly directed. But it differs from an advocate's speech in that there is a total absence of special pleading or polemics or any attempt to gloss over the difficulties. He is an advocate who has become convinced that the difficulties and improbabilities will one day be overcome. It is up to us, the jury, to make up our own minds, but in the end the verdict will be based, like any verdict in law, on what it seems reasonable to believe and on nothing else. This is the major difference from the crucial experiments of Davaine and Koch described in the previous section.

Chemistry: Atomic Weights and the Search for Meaningful Regularities in Nature

The story of atomic weights is touched on in every elementary textbook of chemistry. It is a subject which many students find infinitely boring, and yet it has a profound bearing on the nature of science as it really is and not as philosophers of science would like it to be. The theme once more is the problem of reaching a conclusion when crucial experiments are impossible.

Toward the end of the eighteenth century the atomic hypothesis was put forward, according to which each chemical element consists of indivisible particles which combine with one another in simple numerical proportions. An intrinsic property of each element was then the weight of one of its atoms relative to that of the lightest of all elements, hydrogen, a quantity called the atomic weight.

Now the problem of determining the atomic weight of a given element was one of the most intractable in the history of science. In the words of Aaron Ihde in *The Development of Modern Chemistry* (1964), this problem "was so formidable that it taxed the ingenuity of the best chemists of Europe for half a century." The reason is as follows: it was easy enough to determine the combining weight, i.e., the weight of the element that combines with unit quantity, say one gram, of hydrogen. For oxygen this is about 8 grams, and the result is water. If we assume that one atom of hydrogen combines with one atom of oxygen, i.e., that the chemical formula of water is HO, then the combining weight and the atomic weight are equal; but of course this is not necessarily so. If the chemical formula of water is H_2O, then the atomic weight of oxygen is twice times 8, or 16; if it is HO_2 the atomic weight is 8 divided by 2, or 4; and so on. All that can be obtained, therefore, is a series of possible values; there is no way of knowing which of these to choose, and no further progress can be made. In Ihde's words: "The dilemma is evident—formulas are needed to calculate atomic weights, and atomic weights are needed to determine formulas." Once more, crucial experiments are impossible.

The only hope is to make a start somewhere, which has to be done either by a guess, or else by using what evidence there is and making an *assumption* about how this is to be interpreted. The leader in the field, the Swedish chemist Berzelius, made use of an observation of Gay-Lussac's, namely that gaseous elements seem to combine in simple proportions by volume, for instance *two* volumes of hydrogen combine with *one* volume of oxygen to form water. If we *assume* that equal volumes of gaseous elements contain equal numbers of atoms (which of course on purely common-sense grounds seems improbable since one could be forgiven for supposing that heavier atoms would occupy larger volumes) then this suggests that the formula of water is H_2O, giving an atomic weight for oxygen of 16.

By arguments such as this, Berzelius succeeded in drawing up a list of atomic weights which possessed self-consistency if nothing else.

Each time a new element was discovered, however, chemists were faced with the same problem. The combining weight could be measured, but since the chemical formulae of its compounds were unknown, the atomic weight was undiscoverable.

The only way of getting round this problem was to *argue by similarity*. When a new element was discovered, its properties were compared with those of known elements, and if sufficient similarity was found with any particular element, then the inference was made that the chemical formulae were similar. Since the formulae of the compounds of known elements were themselves based on insecure assumptions, this was an example of inference piled on inference, assumption on assumption. Moreover, similarity is a highly subjective concept. Which are the *fundamental* properties and which the incidental ones? There was nothing to indicate the answer except intuitive insight based on a wide experience of chemistry. This was thus an example of subjective methods playing a major part in the determination of absolute and immutable quantities in physical science. Yet with the aid of this method and with the good fortune that the assumed formula of water was correct, Berzelius's list of atomic weights bears an astonishing resemblance to that used today.

Another method which helped to choose the correct values for atomic weights resulted from the discovery of an *empirical law*, or in other words an unexplained regularity. It was discovered that if one took a given solid element and multiplied its supposed atomic weight by its specific heat, giving a quantity that was named the "atomic heat," then in a high proportion of cases one obtained approximately the same number. With modern atomic weights this number usually lies between 6.0 and 6.5. This is the Law of Dulong and Petit.

At this point the following kinds of inference can be made: First, since one has found an unexpected regularity, one is "on to something"; the regularity reflects something important in nature which one day will be explained. The argument here is based on a fundamental *assumption: that in nature regularities do not happen by chance.* Yet of course exactly the same argument could be used against this as was used by the opponents of Darwin's theory of evolution, namely that "it has pleased the Creator" to make this regularity and that the explanation is thus essentially unfathomable.

Well, if it pleased the Creator to make this regularity, there were times when it didn't please Him, since the Law of Dulong and Petit possesses notable exceptions. The atomic heat of carbon in the form of diamond, for instance, is about 1.2. What about this?

Here one is immediately faced with a dilemma. There are three possibilities: (1) The Law of Dulong and Petit is wrong; (2) the value used for the atomic weight of carbon is wrong and should be altered to bring the atomic heat in line with that of other elements; or (3) carbon is simply an exception to the law, and one day this too will be explained. It was in fact the third of these possibilities that was accepted.

Since these accounts of problems in other sciences are all given for their bearing on the validity of psychotherapy, I find it useful to pause and consider what a hostile counsel would make of the evidence. One can hear him asking: "What is the use of an empirical law to which you arbitrarily admit exceptions? Either it is a law or it isn't."

To this the defending counsel can only answer: "But the evidence in favor of the law for a large number of elements is overwhelming. I cannot even explain the law, let alone the exceptions, but I believe that one day both the law and the exceptions will be explained."

This reply may seem pretty lame and will be dismissed by the opposing counsel with contempt, but in fact, of course, it is correct. In the twentieth century both explanations were found.

However, precisely because crucial experiments were impossible, there was room for complete disagreement, and the result was that by the middle of the nineteenth century the whole question of atomic weights was in a state of confusion.

Finally in 1858, Cannizzaro published a method of determining atomic weights with far greater certainty—though still with the aid of assumptions and therefore not a crucial experiment—and at last the interlocking measurements contained such a degree of internal consistency that it was almost impossible to doubt their validity. Now the way was paved for the discovery by Mendeleyev of the most fundamental concept in the whole of chemistry, the Periodic Table of the elements.

This happened through a method of investigation that is common enough in science but very far from a crucial experiment; namely the *retrospective arrangement of data into patterns,* with the additional methods of changing the pattern wherever necessary to suit the data, and of *cheating* whenever the data seemed to contain exceptions and anomalies. The result was a pattern which was extremely striking on the one hand and extremely complex on the other. Its existence seemed to indicate both that the list of atomic weights was essentially correct and that atomic weights reflected some quite fundamental property of the chemical elements.

It is obvious that this kind of arbitrary, retrospective juggling with data is to say the least a hazardous occupation. The point is, however, that—as with the Law of Dulong and Petit—*the regularities were so striking as to outweigh the discrepancies.* This was hardly apparent to many of Mendeleyev's colleagues, who remained sceptical and acted as the hostile counsels postulated in the present essay.

However, even in his lifetime Mendeleyev was completely vindicated. This arose from his courage in making *predictions* from his pattern about elements which remained to be discovered. When these predictions were fulfilled, the hostile counsels were silenced forever. Yet, if these elements had already been discovered, predictions would have been impossible, and the retrospective arrangement of data would have been the only method he could have used.

In all this story there is a fundamental point. As I have implied many times, "truth" in science often arises not from any crucial experiment but from an *overall assessment of the evidence.* This has nothing to do with rigorous logic, but much more to do with a concept that might be supposed to be more characteristic of law than of science, namely *a conclusion based on what it seems reasonable to believe.* Because this has nothing to do with logic, circular arguments are perfectly permissible.

The following is one of the circular arguments implied in the story of atomic weights:

1. We have determined atomic weights by means of various uncertain hypotheses and empirical rules, which themselves seem to represent some underlying regularities in nature.

2. The atomic weights so determined fit into a complex but extraordinarily beautiful pattern.

3. This pattern in turn is only a hypothesis, but it also seems to represent some underlying regularity in nature.

4. We do not believe that this pattern can have arisen by chance.

5. Therefore *both the original hypotheses* on the one hand, *and the pattern* on the other hand, are essentially valid and reflect the truth.

Nowadays, of course, crucial—or nearly crucial— experiments on all these questions have been performed.

But during the nineteenth century none of this was possible, and all that could be done was to make observations, search for patterns, and pile one hypothesis on another. On the one hand the story illustrates the utter confusion resulting from this situation; but on the other hand it illustrates that *the correct answer can arise from the confusion without the use of crucial experiments.* This is the relevance to the problem of the validity of psychotherapy.

Cosmology: The Dimensions of the Universe

The distances of the nearest celestial objects can be measured by triangulation—measuring the angles subtended by the object at the two ends of a baseline of known length, ultimately the diameter of the earth's orbit round the sun. But for the vast majority of celestial objects the differences in angle are too small to measure. Once more, the crucial experiment is impossible.

This deadlock was broken by a complex set of circumstances. At the beginning of the twentieth century Henrietta Leavitt of the Harvard College Observatory began studying the Clouds of Magellan, two dense clusters of stars then thought to be part of our own galaxy. She found that the clouds contained a type of star whose brightness varied over the course of time in a regular manner, usually with a period somewhat more than a day. She then made the crucial discovery of an empirical law, namely that there seemed to be a constant relation between the length of the period on the one hand, and the brightness of the star on the other.

Now since each of the Clouds of Magellan appears to be a cluster of stars, the individual stars in each cloud may be assumed to be all at roughly the same distance from us. If they are all at the same distance, then the empirical relation between the period and the apparent brightness becomes a relation between the period and the true brightness, and if we can find the true brightness, we can find the distance by the inverse square law.

The problem, then, is to calibrate the equation, which—if the empirical law is reasonably exact and always holds—means finding the true brightness of at least one example of this kind of variable star. This, of course, can be done only if we know its distance; and the trouble is that though similar stars occur elsewhere in our galaxy, even the nearest of them is too far away. So we come full circle, facing exactly the same kind of problem as was faced over the question of atomic weights.

When this kind of situation arises in any branch of science, it has to be circumvented by any means available, however precarious and uncertain these may be. Then, once more, the universally used circular argument is brought into play: if the results seem to make intuitive sense or give rise to new regularities, then it is tentatively concluded that both the results and the methods used to reach them are essentially correct.

The method used depended on the following principles:

1. Variable stars that seem to have the same properties as those in the Clouds of Magellan are found scattered throughout our galaxy.

2. Stars that are not too far away—though still too far for their distance to be measured by triangulation—change their positions in the sky over the course of years because of their motion at right angles to the line of sight. In other words, their angular velocity can be determined.

3. Might there be a way of determining their true velocity? This, together with their angular velocity, would enable their distance to be calculated.

4. A step toward this can be made by the fact that the component of their velocity in the line of sight can be measured by means of the Döppler shift in the lines of their spectra (red shift if they are moving away from us, blue shift if they are moving toward us).

5. It is then necessary to make the *assumption* that the directions of their motion are completely random, so that on the average the component of velocity in the line of sight and the component at right angles to it are equal. If this can be carried out for a sufficient number of stars, then it provides a measure of their average velocity at right angles to the line of sight.

6. With this assumption the average actual distance moved can be calculated, and hence, by simple trigonometry, the average distance from us.

7. From the average distance and the average apparent brightness, the average true brightness can be calculated, and the equation is calibrated.

8. The true brightness of the variable stars in the Clouds of Magellan can now be calculated from their periods, and hence finally their distance.

The Clouds of Magellan were then found to be far enough away to be lying outside our own galaxy.

The essential point concerns the number of plausible yet questionable assumptions on which the whole chain of reasoning is based:

1. The assumption that the Clouds of Magellan are not appreciably extended in the line of sight. This was by no means certain—after all, the Milky Way *appears* to be a flat band of stars stretching across the sky, whereas we now know that it is a disc seen edge on with a diameter of about a hundred thousand light years.

2. The use of an *empirical relationship without known explanation* in order to measure unknown quantities. The trouble with this is that there is no way of telling how far the empirical relation is applicable or when there may be exceptions to it—compare the law of Dulong and Petit discussed in the previous section.

3. The assumption that the motions of stars are random, when we know very well that these motions contain all sorts of regularites.

4. The assumption that an empirical relation which holds for stars in the Clouds of Magellan holds for other stars in the galaxy.

Once more, anyone who wished to approach the evidence as a hostile counsel could destroy it to his own satisfaction in a moment.

This method could be used to measure the distance of the nearer galaxies, and other methods, also involving reasonable yet questionable assumptions, were developed for those futher away. Then came another pair of observations for which by now wonder has been dissipated by familiarity. First, when astronomers began to examine the spectra of these distant celestial objects, it became clear that the lines in the spectra of galaxies are all shifted toward the red. The natural explanation for this is that the galaxies are all receding from us at enormous speeds. And second, the speed of recession was found to be roughly proportional to their estimated distance from us—once more this was the discovery of an empirical law, an unexpected and unexplained regularity in nature.

Now it became possible to turn the equation around the other way, for the most distant objects to use the empirical relation between velocity and distance to measure distance. The essentially circular nature of this argument should be clear.

But we can go much further than that. The implied circular argument is similar to that used in connection with atomic weights and the Periodic Table, and runs as follows:

1. By a number of "reasonable" assumptions, we have developed a means of measuring the distance of galaxies.
2. This method leads to the discovery of a regularity.
3. Therefore the assumptions, and the method of measuring distance, were valid.

This is a type of argument that is universally used in science.

Again we can go further. There is now a new circular argument:

1. The regularity admits of an extraordinarily simple explanation.
2. Therefore the regularity itself, the explanation for it, and the methods used to discover it, are all valid.

The regularity, as already described, is the relation between velocity of recession and distance. This can easily be explained if the current state of the universe is the result of a single colossal explosion which occurred several thousands of millions of years ago. Provided there is no large force to change the velocity of the resulting fragments to different degrees, it follows inescapably that after a reasonable lapse of time, the fastest-moving fragments will become the furthest away and that the distance will be proportional to the velocity. Moreover, by simple arithmetic—since *time* equals *distance* divided by *speed*—it now becomes possible to calculate the number of years ago that the explosion must have occurred, which at that time came out to be a few thousand million years.

But did this figure fit in with other evidence? The answer was no.

Much cumulative evidence suggested that the age of the solar
system—which, after all, is part of the universe—is about 4.5 thousand million years; since this exceeded the above value for the age of
the universe as a whole, there must be something wrong somewhere.

The answer to this paradox illustrates the uncertainties of relying
on empirical relations that no one understands. It eventually became
clear that the fault lay in the fourth of the assumptions listed above.
There were in fact two kinds of variable stars, and the equation had
been calibrated with one kind while the distances of galaxies had
been measured with the other kind. The discrepancy was such that
all these distances, and hence the age of the universe, had to be
doubled. The evidence now became self-consistent.

Again we can imagine what a hostile counsel would make of a
method of measuring distances that is so uncertain that it apparently
gives half the correct value. On the other hand, it could also be
argued that we have just illustrated one of the strengths of scientific
method, namely that in spite of the circularity of the arguments,
there are independent checks that in the end enable us to discover
errors and correct them.

THE VALIDITY OF PSYCHOTHERAPY

Of course it is true that the only way of proving or disproving the
validity of psychotherapy beyond reasonable doubt is by means of a
true controlled study. In such a study the sample of patients is
divided into two, the first of which is given treatment while the
second remains untreated, and the changes in the two are then
compared.

The difficulty with this design is that many changes—representing
both improvement and deterioration—are known to occur during
the period after termination. This means that an essential part of any
valid study is a follow-up of many years; therefore the controls must
be left untreated for a period equal to the length of therapy plus
follow-up. This is virtually impossible for both ethical and practical
reasons. The ethical problem is obvious; the practical problem
concerns the difficulty of preventing patients from finding treatment
elsewhere during so long a period. Additional problems arise from
the natural wastage of patients, the funding of such a prolonged
research project, and the need to keep the research team together.

The relevance now appears of the examples from other branches of science given in previous sections. The length of follow-up required can be said to be analogous to the evolutionary time scale or to cosmic distances—in both cases sheer magnitude makes direct observation or measurement impossible. Is it true, therefore, that evidence about the validity of psychotherapy is impossible to obtain?

A reading of the material in the foregoing sections will immediately indicate my answer to this question: No, it is not impossible. Indirect methods not only can, but must be used. This means, as Darwin wrote, that "something might perhaps be made out on this question by patiently accumulating and reflecting on all sorts of facts which would possibly have a bearing on it."

In other words it means the use of all the types of evidence and argument used in other sciences, whether the less exact biological sciences or the extremely exact science of chemistry—methods such as the examination of cumulative circumstantial evidence, measurement of questionable validity, empirical relationships with exceptions for which one seeks explanations, circular arguments, and finally the examination of the overall picture, with a verdict that can never be anything but subjective and based on "reasonable probability." The whole subject has of course not been deficient in hostile counsels, and these will never be convinced; but for those who have an interest in finding out the truth, the evidence may possibly be worth considering. It is this basic, universally recognized scientific principle—universally recognized, that is, except in the least exact of the sciences, the psychological, to which it is most applicable—that has occupied my research life for the past many years.

EVIDENCE FROM TWO STUDIES OF BRIEF PSYCHOTHERAPY

The Material

This consists of two series of patients treated by a team of experienced therapists under the leadership of Michael Balint. The original aim of the project was purely clinical, namely to investigate psychoanalytically oriented brief psychotherapy from first principles. The design was elementary in the extreme: to take on patients thought to be suitable, treat them, and see what happened. I then carried out a single-handed study of the first eighteen patients (the first series), which was published in *A Study of Brief Psychotherapy* (1963, 1975); this was followed by a far more rigorous study of the second series (thirty patients), published in *Toward the Validation of Dynamic Psychotherapy* (1976). Follow-up was extremely long—between four and nine years after termination, with very few exceptions.

In the present essay I do not intend to get involved in the "fine print" of the evidence, for which the reader is referred to the above two publications. What I shall present is the broad sweep of the two studies, with special reference to the nature of scientific evidence as illustrated by the examples from other sciences given above. I shall hope to show that the cumulative evidence is very strong, not merely that therapy was responsible for the improvements in these patients, but that the therapeutic factors were specific rather than nonspecific, that there are clear indications of what these specific factors are, and that these in turn are the same as those that psychoanalysts have always believed to be operating in psychoanalysis itself.

Evidence from the Duration of Disturbances

Let us suppose that a disturbance that has lasted twelve years is reported in the fourth therapeutic session as having shown a sudden improvement, ten weeks after the patient was first seen, and that when the patient is followed up seven years after termination the improvement has been maintained (in quoting these figures I have an actual case in mind).

In this particular case the ratio of twelve years (the duration of the disturbance) to ten weeks (the duration of therapy before the disturbance improved), which we may call the *duration ratio*, is about 55. It is surely straining credibility to suggest that the improvement "just happened" to occur at this point; if we could show that our series contained a number of cases of this kind, credibility would be strained even further.

In fact, careful examination of the thirty cases in our second series reveals that there were eleven in which the duration ratio, very conservatively estimated, was greater than ten. This suggests very strongly that some factor or factors concerned with therapy were associated with—indeed, probably *caused*—at least some of the improvements. For simplicity I shall refer to this as a single factor in subsequent discussion.

Evidence from the Relation between Outcome and Number of Sessions.

The distribution of these two variables in the two series taken together is shown in Fig. 1.

FIGURE 1.
DISTRIBUTION OF 46 BRIEF PSYCHOTHERAPY PATIENTS
ACCORDING TO LENGTH OF THERAPY AND OUTCOME

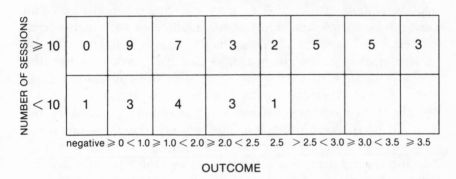

NUMBER OF SESSIONS	negative	≥ 0 < 1.0	≥ 1.0 < 2.0	≥ 2.0 < 2.5	2.5	> 2.5 < 3.0	≥ 3.0 < 3.5	≥ 3.5
≥ 10	0	9	7	3	2	5	5	3
< 10	1	3	4	3	1			

OUTCOME

As will be seen, there is an "overhang" on the right-hand side of the diagram, there being fifteen out of thirty-four longer-stay patients, and only one out of twelve shorter-stay patients, who scored more than 2.4 for outcome; and thirteen longer-stay patients, and *no* shorter-stay patients, who scored more than 2.5.

Now because of the large number of longer-stay patients who gave poor results (the top left-hand corner of the diagram), the hypothesis suggested by this distribution is not that, statistically speaking, the more sessions the patient has the better the outcome, but that *a certain minimum number of sessions is a necessary condition to a satisfactory outcome.*

This evidence marks the beginning of a long progression which steadily narrows down the factors that we are seeking. The evidence from "duration ratio" suggests only that there is some factor concerned with therapy that is associated with favorable outcome. The evidence just presented suggests that really favorable outcome occurs only in association with a certain minimum quantity of this factor, whatever it may be. In other words, the factor is probably something that is given in therapy, whether specific or nonspecific, and not simply the fact of being taken on for treatment.

The Study of Motivation

In the first series I studied eight different selection criteria and found that the only one that gave a significant correlation with outcome was motivation.

This result needed to be examined very carefully. First, we have to ask, motivation for what? The answer to this was that motivation must not be merely for help but for the kind of help that is being offered, which is essentially concerned with insight and nothing else. Moreover, most patients do not know that this is the kind of help that they will be offered until some point after therapy has got under way, which will therefore be the point at which motivation may best be judged. In accordance with this, it was found that when fluctuations in motivation during the first few sessions were taken into account, the relation to outcome was strongest.

In the second study I had the help of an independent judge, Dr. Peter Dreyfus, who could score motivation entirely uncontaminated by knowledge of outcome. Shorn of excessive detail the results were as follows:

1. Of ten criteria studied at initial assessment, motivation gave the highest correlation, but this could clearly have arisen by chance ($p < 0.1$ but > 0.05).

2. When fluctuations in motivation were considered, none of the correlations with outcome was significant during the first four contacts with the Clinic, but there was a strong tendency for them to become significant during contacts five to eight.

The Study of Focality

One of Balint's original hypotheses about this kind of therapy was that it should be "focal," i.e., the therapist should plan in advance the main area of pathology which he wanted to work through, and by selective attention and selective neglect should concentrate his interpretations upon this planned theme.

In order to test this hypothesis, Dreyfus worked out a method of judging the degree to which the therapist had succeeded in keeping his interpretations on a single theme. This variable, called *focality*, was scored by both of us independently on each of the first eight contacts in the second series.

It is important to note that whereas motivation is defined as motivation for insight, in the patient focality is complementary to this, being concerned with the giving of insight by the therapist.

The following observation now emerged: Exactly as with motivation, the scores for focality were at first unrelated to outcome, but tended to become significantly correlated with outcome during contacts five to eight.

Meaning of the Studies of Motivation and Focality

As has already been discussed, the relation between outcome and number of sessions suggested that a minimum quantity of some factor was necessary for a really satisfactory outcome, but this observation offered no evidence about what this factor is, or whether it is specific to psychoanalytic therapy. Clearly it could be some nonspecific factor common to many different kinds of therapy, such as support or warmth. The present evidence, however, suggests that the factor is indeed specific and consists of insight.

The Transference/Parent Link

The evidence given in the previous section leads naturally and inevitably to yet another question: Insight about what?

A careful study of the first series resulted in two observations:

1. The more successful therapies tended to be those in which, according to clinical judgment, the transference (i.e., the relation to the therapist) was thoroughly interpreted.

2. This relation was made much more striking if a subdivision of transference interpretations was studied, namely making the link between the transference relationship and the past, usually the relation to parents. I refer to this as the T/P link.

The question now arose whether this last observation could be checked by some more objective method. Here we can imagine the following ideal experiment:

1. Every session of these therapies had been videotaped.
2. Judges watched these tapes and made judgments on the therapist's interventions.
3. These would include judgments of whether or not each intervention was a transference interpretation, whether or not it made the T/P link, and what the impact on the patient had been at the time.
4. Some measure integrating both the quantity and impact of these interpretations could be devised and correlated with outcome.

This ideal experiment may be compared with the ideal measurement of the distance of galaxies discussed above; and, as with that experiment, it was impossible. The therapeutic work had been already carried out, without any such judgments in mind; it was conducted in the 1950s, without financial support, before even audiotapes—let alone videotapes—became generally available. All the material that we possessed consisted of accounts of each session dictated by the therapist from memory, with varying degrees of fullness and entirely unknown accuracy. One may well ask what possible scientific use could be made of such uncertain data?

The answer to this question is similar to that given by astronomers to the question of the distance of galaxies: direct measurement is impossible, the measurements that are possible are most unsatisfactory and imperfect, and in consequence all one can do is to make a number of assumptions, make the measurements, and examine the results.

The first assumption was simply that the accounts of therapy, though condensed to a greater or lesser degree, represented a reasonable approximation to what actually happened; and that where the accounts were highly condensed, then in general the crucial moments were included. There was no way of checking this assumption, but it was made more plausible by the fact that all the therapists were well trained and highly competent.

The second assumption was that there was a relation between quantity on the one hand and correctness and impact on the other. This could reasonably be assumed from the fact not only that they were well trained, but also that they all employed a technique of carefully monitoring feedback and quickly abandoning any line of interpretation to which the patient was not responding.

In order to eliminate as far as possible the effects produced by the different lengths of therapy and differences in the style and completeness of recording, I used not an absolute number but a proportion, for example, as a measure of the "importance" of transference interpretations I used the ratio of the number of transference interpretations to the total number of interpretations recorded for each therapy. Each ratio was expressed as a percentage and was referred to as the "transference ratio," "transference/parent ratio," etc.

Results of the Study of Interpretations

This method was applied to both series. The study of the second series was far more elaborate than that of the first and involved judgments made by two independent raters of the proportions of fifteen different categories of interpretation, and the correlation of these with the scores for outcome. (My collaborator was E.H. Rayner.)

The essential result was that the transference/parent ratio was the only one of these variables that gave a positive and significant correlation with outcome in both series.

Meaning of the Result on Transference/Parent Interpretations

At the end of the sections on motivation and focality I concluded that the evidence suggested an association between favorable outcome and the acquisition of insight. I then asked the question, insight about what? The evidence just presented suggests a very clear answer: insight about the way in which the relation with the therapist repeats patterns derived from relations with parents in the past.

Clinical Meaning of the Quantitative Study

I now wish to introduce a circular argument that is very similar to that used over the question of cosmological distances and the age of the universe.

1. We started with two assumptions: (a) that case notes dictated from memory bear a reasonable relation to what actually happened; and (b) that a purely quantitative measure of interpretations bears a relation to their correctness and impact.

2. We have found a significant correlation between a purely quantitative measure of transference/parent interpretations and outcome.

3. Therefore not only are both assumptions (a) and (b) correct, but there is an association between the *impact* of transference/parent interpretations and outcome.

Moreover, this result admits of a simple explanation in terms of known phenomena. Suddenly we realize that the relation between quantity of interpretations and outcome probably represents the well-known fact that a given piece of insight does not merely need to be experienced but needs to be worked through—which means reexperienced many times in different contexts. This phenomenon, recognized for many years in long-term therapy, apparently applies to short-term therapy as well. In other words, assumptions, evidence, and explanations make sense as a whole, and it is a reasonable inference to say provisionally that they are all correct.

Cause and Effect

So far, the only statements that have been made concern an association between certain factors and favorable outcome, and hardly anything has been said about cause and effect.

It has to be emphasized that this was a naturalistic study, and whether or not the patient received T/P interpretations was the result of self-selection. The inferences to be drawn from such a study need careful thought.

There are three main types of possibility, representing the three main ways in which correlations may be interpreted: (1) The first is the obvious one, that T/P interpretations cause favorable outcome, while there are also two alternative hypotheses, namely (2) that favorable outcome in some way causes the therapist to make T/P interpretations, and (3) that favorable outcome and T/P interpretations are both associated with some third factor, as yet unknown.

Those who maintain the alternative hypotheses (2) and (3) have usually not thought the situation through. They are under obligation to offer not merely alternative explanations, but more plausible ones. First, the suggestion that favorable outcome in some way causes the therapist to make T/P interpretations simply does not fit in with the facts. Every therapist knows that transference develops rapidly in many therapies and is interpreted as it arises, usually long before any therapeutic effects are manifested—many of which in any case only appear after termination.

The other explanation offers a more viable alternative. One could put up the hypothesis that these patients tend to get better because they interact with people in their life outside in a particular way; that they also show the same kind of interaction in therapy; and that this in turn causes the therapist to perceive the relation with the past and to make interpretations about it. This may even be partly true, but the argument tends to turn back on itself, since if this kind of interaction is therapeutic in life outside, why should it not be therapeutic in the relation with the therapist?

Moreover, the evidence provided by motivation and focality suggests strongly that the factor associated with favorable outcome is not the interaction itself, but insight about it. Most of these patients had been showing this kind of interaction for years, but insight about it was acquired only when they came to interact with a therapist. Therefore this line of thought, after a brief detour, leads straight back to the inference that therapy itself is causal.

Motivation and Transference/Parent Interpretations in Combination

There is a final piece of evidence which further reinforces all that has been presented hitherto. If the thirty patients in the second series are ranked for overall motivation during the first eight contacts and the rank numbers so obtained are added to the rank numbers for T/P percent, a further series of rank numbers is obtained for "motivation + T/P percent." This represents a combined rank for the two most important factors that correlate with improvement. If this variable is now plotted against outcome, the scatter diagram shown in Figure 2 is obtained. In this diagram there is an obvious trend from "below left" to "above right," but there are also certain patients who lie away from the general trend. These patients are those who lie outside the two arbitrary lines drawn on the diagram.

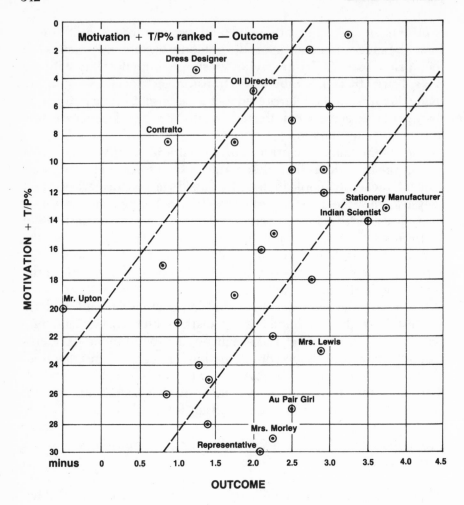

Motivation + T/P% ranked — Outcome

There are six patients lying to the right of the lower line, in whom outcome was more favorable than the combination of motivation and T/P percent would predict. Of these, the Indian Scientist was in no way exceptional on any other grounds. However, all five of the others showed unusual characteristics on purely clinical grounds, which set them apart from the main body of relatively young, purely neurotic patients in the sample as a whole. Thus the Stationery Manufacturer was a near-psychotic man of forty-six; Mrs. Morley was a woman of over sixty thought to be near a severe depressive breakdown; Mrs. Lewis and the Au Pair Girl improved long after termination in response to major life experiences (i.e., showed "spontaneous remission"); and the Representative showed major improvements after a clear "flight into health." In each of these last three patients the evidence suggests a mechanism of improvement independent of therapy.

There are four patients to the left of the upper line. These are patients in whom outcome was less favorable than the combination of motivation and T/P percent would predict. Again there is one patient, the Oil Director—and as before the one nearest to the line— who was not exceptional in any way. But the other three were all patients who turned out to be far more deeply disturbed than was seen at initial assessment. The Contralto was eventually seen to be suffering from a "false self," leading to an inability to form real relationships with anyone; the Dress Designer, originally thought to be suffering from a simple phobic illness, showed an extremely deep-seated illness involving primitive fears of loss of identity; and Mr. Upton, originally thought to be suffering from very ordinary conflicts about growing up, at follow-up showed bisexual, near-psychotic, and manic-depressive features.

Although the analogy with Mendeleyev's work should not be pushed too far—he, after all, was dealing with absolute, universal, and immutable quantities—there are interesting parallels. The features in common are the arrangements of observations in such a way as to form a pattern, followed by the inference that the pattern is so clear that the exceptions must be explainable. However, whereas it took half a century to explain the exceptions in the Periodic Table, in the present case the explanations spring to mind immediately.

Davanloo's Evidence

During the past twenty years Davanloo has been perfecting a technique of brief dynamic psychotherapy that is clearly more powerful than any discovered hitherto. He is now in process of examining his own evidence systematically. He states (personal communication) that the ability to give a meaningful T-C-P interpretation in the initial interview is an extremely important favorable prognostic sign and that the more frequently such interpretations are given in the early stages, the shorter the therapy will tend to be. Thus the conclusions presented above have now received confirmation, entirely independently, from a third series of brief therapy patients.

Evidence from Traditional Clinical Judgment

We may ask why it was that this particular hypothesis about T/P interpretations was examined at all. The answer is very clear, namely that this type of interpretation has been regarded as the most important therapeutic factor in psychoanalytic therapy for many years. This point is made by at least four separate writers on technique, Glover (1955), Alexander (1957), Menninger (1958), and Strachey (1969).

Thus we can add to the evidence already described cumulative evidence from other sources. We can now state that a particular type of interpretation, which has been shown to correlate with improvement in five separate studies of dynamic psychotherapy—two of ours and three of Davanloo's—has been considered for decades as one of the essential therapeutic factors by generations of psychoanalysts.

Can this evidence still be generally ignored? Yes, of course it can—rigid theoretical positions seem to be the rule rather than the exception in science and nowhere more than in the field of psychotherapy.

The Final Analogy with Other Sciences

Although I have mentioned parallels with the logic of cosmology and chemistry, the final analogy that I wish to make is with the logic of Darwin's work. Darwin made an exhaustive study of natural living and extinct organisms and came to the conclusion that a dispassionate appraisal of cumulative circumstantial evidence overwhelmingly supported the theory of evolution by natural selection rather than that of special creation. In our own work, cumulative circumstantial evidence can be shown to support—obviously less overwhelmingly but still powerfully—the validity of psychotherapy. However, the analogy with Darwin leads to one word of warning: these indirect methods can be used only with total objectivity.

Otherwise, of course, they can be made to lead in whatever direction anybody chooses. The marriage between polemics and truth tends to be shown, sooner or later, to be a case of incompatibility, leading inevitably to divorce.

A PSYCHOTHERAPY RESEARCHER'S DREAM

In the early part of the twentieth century a dream came true: with the aid of instruments such as the mass spectrograph it finally became possible to determine atomic weights directly with virtual certainty. Could anything like this ever occur for the validity of psychotherapy?

Let us have a dream. A new method of dynamic psychotherapy is discovered, of extraordinary power. The origins of the neurotic patterns in the past emerge with total clarity through the derepression of long buried anxiety-laden feelings. These are experienced with such intensity and completeness that therapeutic effects begin to follow soon after the beginning of therapy, and the whole neurosis dissolves after about fifteen session, leaving the patient not merely improved but recovered. The events in therapy that lead to therapeutic effects can be observed directly, and lengthy follow-up shows that these effects are permanent.

This leads to a situation in which criteria analogous to Koch's postulates can be applied, as follows:

1. Antecedent events or situations, and particularly precipitating factors, enable a strong inference to be made about the nature of the conflict underlying a neurotic symptom.

2. An examination of the symptom itself makes possible a clear-cut hypothesis about the way in which it expresses or symbolizes the underlying conflict.

3. During therapy, the conflict becomes fully conscious and is accompanied by intense and painful feeling.

4. The symptom immediately disappears.

These four criteria, if fulfilled, would virtually prove that in this particular patient the neurotic symptom had its origin in a specific conflict. Moreover, as experience increased, it would be possible to use these criteria predictively, thus performing a true scientific experiment. This would lead to the virtual proof of psychodynamic theory, something that has eluded us ever since its origins in the 1890s.

Since this is a fantasy, there is nothing to stop us from going further. This method of therapy is applicable to severe and chronic conditions: as an example, fifteen weeks of treatment result in complete recovery from symptoms that have lasted for twenty years—a ratio of about 70. Moreover, some of these conditions have failed to respond to years of psychoanalytic or behavior therapy, or both. This is the method of "duration ratio" carried to the limit. In this type of experiment, of course, the patients act as their own controls, and the result is virtual proof that it was therapy that caused the improvement. Thus psychotherapy is validated without a formal control series.

Yet mention of this possibility suddenly makes us realize that our belief that it is impossible to have a control series of untreated patients is an example of perseveration. As already mentioned, recovery is complete by the time therapy is terminated, and follow-up merely confirms that there is no subsequent relapse. At once the waiting-list control design becomes both valid and ethically and practically feasible. Control patients now only need to wait for as long as the therapy of the experimental patients lasts—not therapy plus follow-up. Changes in the experimentals at termination are then compared with changes in controls at the end of the waiting period, the passage of time in the two series being equal. As mentioned above, the method of therapy is so powerful that there is not the slightest difficulty in demonstrating the advantage of experimentals over controls. This would be the crucial experiment that we have been waiting for in vain all these years.

You may say that this is an absurd dream and may question why it should be mentioned in a serious article about the validity of psychotherapy. The dream is so utterly unbelievable that even those who have seen it come true with their own eyes on Davanloo's videotapes, as shown in many national and international symposia on Short-Term Dynamic Psychotherapy, mostly cannot take in the evident fact that it has become a reality. Clinical examples of this work are described in other chapters of the present book and have also already appeared in the Proceedings of the first two International Symposia (see Davanloo 1978); a further book, describing his work in greater detail and entitled *The Relentless Healer*, is in preparation.

An application for a research grant based on the waiting-list control design is also in preparation; if all goes according to plan, hostile counsels will be hard put to it to find fallacies in the evidence. The work described in the present essay will then become, like Berzelius's atomic weights, basically correct but of historical interest only—an outcome that would be of benefit to mental health throughout the world.

References

Alexander, F. (1957). *Psychoanalysis and Psychotherapy*. London: George Allen and Unwin.

Darwin, C. (1859). *The Origin of Species*. New York: Collier, 1962.

Davanloo, H. (1978). *Basic Principles and Techniques in Short-Term Dynamic Psychotherapy*. New York: Spectrum.

——— (in preparation). *The Relentless Healer*.

Dible, J.H., and Davie, T.B. (1945). *Pathology*. London: Churchill.

Fernie, J.D. (1969). The period-luminosity relation: a historical review. *Publications of the Astronomical Society of the Pacific* 81:707.

Glover, E. (1955). *The Technique of Psycho-Analysis*. London: Baillière, Tindall and Cox.

Ihde, A.J. (1964). *The Development of Modern Chemistry*. New York: Harper and Row.

Malan, D.H. (1963) *A Study of Brief Psychotherapy*. London: Tavistock; Philadelphia: Lippincott. Republished by Plenum Press, New York, 1975.

——— (1976). *Toward the Validation of Dynamic Psychotherapy*. New York: Plenum Press.

——— (1979). *Individual Psychotherapy and the Science of Psychodynamics*. London: Butterworths.

Menninger, K. (1958). *Theory of Psychoanalytic Technique*. New York: Basic Books.

New Frontiers in Astronomy. Readings from *Scientific American*. San Francisco: Freeman.

Strachey, J. (1969). The nature of the therapeutic action of psycho-analysis. *International Journal of Psycho-Analysis* 50:275.

19

Basic Principles and Technique of the Follow-Up Interview

David H. Malan, M.D.

THE INTERVIEWER MUST BE PREPARED

The most essential principle is that the interviewer must be carefully prepared. He needs to know as much as possible about the patient's history and state at initial interview and to have in his mind a list of the patient's original disturbances, some hypothesis about the underlying dynamics, a list of the criteria that need to be fulfilled if the patient is to be regarded as truly improved, and therefore a list of areas of the patient's life and inner feeling that need to be explored. Without this careful preparation interviews will vary from incomplete to meaningless.

The present patient came for treatment at the age of twenty-two in a state of depression, despair, and emotional confusion. His father left his mother before the patient was born. His mother remarried when he was five, and two more children were born. The mother and stepfather constantly quarreled, the position at home became intolerable, and in his early teens the patient finally gave his mother an ultimatum that either he left or his stepfather did. The mother got rid of the stepfather, but her relation with the patient was characterized by her trying to put him in the role of husband on the one hand and trying to control him on the other, which caused severe tension, constant quarrels, and hysterical scenes on her part. The patient found himself becoming depressed, withdrawn, and socially isolated. With women he was quite unable to make contact or put his feelings across. In addition he took up with a male friend who exploited him and flaunted his own success with women in the patient's face. Finally the patient took a job well below his potential as a nurse's aide in a convalescent home, in which conditions were appalling and in which his grandfather—who had provided one of the few good relationships in his life—was a patient. All these pressures came together to bring him to a state of despair and to ask for treatment.

IMPROVEMENT MEANS THAT EACH DISTURBANCE IS REPLACED BY SOMETHING POSITIVE

Clearly the dynamics are complex and probably include underlying rage against his mother, oedipal guilt about having taken his stepfather's place, difficulties in breaking free from home, and fear of losing one of the few supports in his life, namely his grandfather. This complexity does not matter. The important principle is that if the patient is to be regarded as truly improved each disturbance must be *replaced by something positive*. Specifically: depression must be replaced by reasonable hope and an ability to express what he really feels; his withdrawal must be replaced by social confidence; he must become able to deal with his mother more effectively; his passivity must be replaced by an ability to assert himself constructively; he must become effective in work that makes use of his abilities; he must become independent yet mindful of his responsibilities to his family; and finally he must become able to use his feelings effectively in his relation with women, to compete with other men if necessary, and ultimately to form a close and warm relationship with a woman in which both can enjoy love, sex, and companionship. These are ideal but not impossible criteria, and these are the areas that the interviewer needs to explore.

CHALLENGING ANSWERS AND MAKING INTERPRETATIONS

In addition to all the above, the interviewer must pay particular attention to how he gets his information. It is clearly useless just to ask a series of questions and to note down the patient's answers, as is done in structured interviews carried out for so-called scientific purposes. It is important to take account of the circumstances of the interview, the residual feelings about therapy that will bias the patient's answers, the relation with the interviewer, whether or not the patient is asking for further help, the ways in which the patient is trying to avoid or gloss over painful truths. It is essential to create an atmosphere of trust and intimacy, and it is legitimate to make interpretations where appropriate and to challenge the patient's answers in a direct or indirect way. All this must of course be done with care and circumspection since the patient is no longer able to work through the consequences of the interview in therapeutic sessions.

The circumstances of the following interview are particularly relevant since the interview was videotaped and the patient was well aware that it was being witnessed at the time by other mental health professionals in training. It is quite possible that the patient was to some degree "playing to the gallery," which needs to be taken into account in evaluating his answers. Also, the interview took place only about a month after termination, which of course is much too soon for a true evaluation of any changes that may have occurred. This follow-up interview was conducted by Dr. David Malan one month after termination.

The interviewer begins at once by trying to bring into the open the patient's feelings about the circumstances in which the interview is taking place. In doing so he offers an interpretation in the form of a question ("Do you resent it?"), and he does not immediately accept the patient's denial. The aim is of course to free the interview from tension due to unexpressed feelings and to convey to the patient that he can express what he really feels. It is possible that the interviewer missed the point here, in the sense that the patient rather enjoyed the interview rather than resenting it.

Therapist: You've been in this situation before?

Patient: Yes.

Therapist: Do you mind it?

Patient: A little bit, you know. I feel like I'm being viewed upon, and it makes me a little self-conscious. But, I mind it less than I used to.

Therapist: Yes. Your therapy was videotaped too, wasn't it?

Patient: Yeah.

Therapist: I see, yes. All right. Well, I'm sorry to put you through it. Do you resent it?

Patient: Do I resent it? (Pause.) I don't think so, no. I don't think so. I don't think I would have come if I resented it, you know.

Therapist: You could have come and resented it and not said so, couldn't you?

Patient: It's true. I don't feel I resent it, really.

Therapist: You don't. All right. Do you know the purpose of this interview?

Patient: I guess you just want to talk to me about what I've been through.

Therapist: Want you to talk to me. (Laugh.)

Patient: (Patient laughs.) Okay.

The interviewer quickly picks up the significant words of the patient ("what I've been through"). He has in mind that the patient may be referring to important feelings about therapy, which need to be brought out at once if the interview is to be open and honest and rapport is to be maintained. In fact the patient seems to be referring to what he had been through before therapy. This is valuable because it enables the interviewer to clarify some of the dynamics leading to the patient's original request for help and to help to establish a baseline of the severity of the disturbance at that time, with which the patient's present state can be compared.

Therapist: Yeah, what you've been through, that seems to suggest that you've been through quite a lot.

Patient: Yes, I have.

Therapist: You have. I think we should start with that. What have you been through?

Patient: Before or after therapy? Or during?

Therapist: Both. All three, yes.

Patient: (Patient laughs.) I guess before therapy I was . . . I guess I was very depressed and very confused about myself and my feelings. I wasn't really aware of what they were. They were all mixed up.

Therapist: Yes.

Patient: I didn't have a perspective. It just came to a point when I couldn't feel anymore. I felt like I wanted to die because I just couldn't handle situations anymore—social ones, personal ones.

At this point the interviewer follows one of the fundamental principles of the assessment of dynamic change, a principle also recognized by writers on crisis therapy: Where a patient has been brought to therapy by a phase of acute disturbance or "breakdown," it is essential to try to assess whether he is better than before his breakdown or has merely returned to the same position as before. The latter position, by inescapable logic, will contain the seeds of further breakdown under similar stress; only in the former position can he be regarded as forearmed against further breakdown, which must be the aim of all forms of dynamic psychotherapy.

Therapist: So when you say you couldn't handle them anymore, had there been a time when you had been able to handle them, and then it went?

Patient: I guess when I was much younger?

Therapist: How much younger?

Patient: I guess before thirteen, before adolescence.

Therapist: I see, yes, but since adolescence you've felt that you haven't been able to handle things. Yes, go on.

Patient: From adolescence it kind of grew, you know, this not being able to handle situations, social ones, and being confused. It started off a little bit, then it progressed, worse and worse until last year, when I just couldn't handle it anymore.

Here the interviewer takes the opportunity of trying to clarify the stresses that brought the patient to breakdown. Again a fundamental principle is that if the patient is to be regarded as truly improved, he must be able to face the same stresses as before in a new and adaptive way, without symptoms.

Therapist: I'd like to ask you a question there. In fact, you know, I know a good deal about you. I know about the first interview you had with Dr.——, so there are certain things that I don't need to ask, and we don't need to go over again, but there are certain things we do need to. One of the questions that I would like to ask you is, what do you feel set off the attack of depression that finally brought you here? Do you know that?

Patient: I'm thinking. (Pause.) I think I remember in the month——, I was . . . there was a lot of pressures on my head. I was thinking of moving out of my house because there's a lot of pressures at home and pressures with school. I started taking driving lessons, which made me very nervous, and everything built up at that time. It seemed that that was the time when everything was piling on me and I just couldn't handle things. I just . . . I just couldn't take anymore.

Therapist: What that immediately suggests to me is something about problems of becoming an independent person in your own right, leaving home, taking driving lessons—as if you felt that you weren't adequate to face this. Now is that right?

Patient: At that time I wasn't aware of it. I was just aware that I was very nervous about doing anything. I guess I didn't have enough confidence in myself, as I look back on it now. I just wasn't aware of who I was or what I felt.

Therapist: Right. Now there was another factor that I possibly understood to be there, sort of feeling into this, and that was your relation with your friend.

Patient: Yeah.

Therapist: Now, what part do you think that played?

Patient: That played a big part.

Therapist: Did it? Well, could you tell me about that?

Patient: Uh, at that time, I guess about the month of——, we were still very good friends.

Therapist: Can you give him a name?

Patient: Sidney.

Therapist: Sidney, that's right.

Patient: Sidney and I were very good friends and . . . in . . . then I started to . . . I'm trying to put it into perspective, what exactly happened. I . . . think he was drifting away from me. He was involved with a girlfriend of his and . . . he was drifting away from me. I'm not sure if I was drifting away also. It's very confusing to me to look back on exactly what happened because so many things did happen. (Pause.) I might have been becoming more aware of what he was and what he was doing to me, or what I was allowing him to do to me.

Therapist: Yes.

Patient: In terms of just walking all over me and me being afraid to be alone, so I, you know, I stuck it out with him. And I think he sensed this, and I was becoming more aware of his actions. And it also came to a point where I was kind of drifting away from any type of social situation.

Therapist: Yes.

Patient: So I was staying home a lot, and I wasn't in the mood to do anything. I just . . .I said, I just don't want to do a thing. So he kind of decided, "Well, I don't want to hang around with a guy who doesn't want to do anything." So we kind of drifted apart. That . . . was very traumatic for me . . . this kind of leaving someone I was close to.

Therapist: Well, who left whom first? It's not quite clear is it?

Patient: Uh . . . I think he left me.

Therapist: Oh.

Patient: But I also . . . it isn't quite clear, 'cause we were drifting apart at a certain time.

Therapist: All right, yes perhaps that isn't important now, the fact is that you lost him in one way or another, and this is one of the things that contributed to your state then. Is that right?

Patient: Yeah, during that transition time when I was losing him, not when I had lost him, but when we were drifting apart, it had a very great effect on me.

Therapist: All right. Now something that I'd like to ask you, to try and establish a baseline, is what you remember about your state when you were at your worst. You've said all kinds of things about staying at home, feeling depressed, but what was it like at your worst?

Patient: I would stay in my room a good part of the time. I felt black all over, like I had no real sensation of feeling. I could not cry, I could not express my feelings—I wasn't aware of them.

Therapist: Yes.

Patient: Yes, I was very sad and very angry as I look back on it now. It was just like a moroseness—a deadness, and I felt afraid of any outside associations, any personal contact. I was just very, very depressed. I had a lot of suicidal thoughts . . . I really never went to that point to try anything, but I felt that I just wanted to lie down and just pass away.

Therapist: Yes.

Patient: To die, and . . .

Therapist: And what would you do during the day when you were in your room by yourself? (The interviewer is trying to get an idea of the severity of withdrawal.)

Patient: Uh, I was working at that time.

Therapist: Yes.

Patient: Which brings back another pressure. I was working in a convalescent home.

Therapist: Yes, and you actually were able to hold yourself together enough to go to work, or were there times when you didn't?

Patient: No. I went to work, but it was . . . I was torturing myself. I was really trying just to destroy myself because the job was terrible.

Therapist: What do you mean by trying to destroy yourself? (Is this just a piece of jargon that he has picked up from therapy, or is it genuine insight?)

Patient: I was doing a job that I know I had no taste for, but for me, I guess was guilt feelings, maybe because my grandfather was sick at that time too, and he was also in the convalescent home. It was kind of substituting someone else for him and taking care of this man. The job itself was disgusting, it was terrible. Also, it was in the worst atmosphere I could possibly be in at that time because it was the last place for any human being to go.

Therapist: Yes.

Patient: So, I felt I was just torturing myself.

Therapist: You felt that you were really deliberately putting yourself through something which was unnecessary.

Patient: Yeah, because I know I would not do that now.

Therapist: No.

Patient: No, there's no way.

All this was said with sincerity and conviction and encouraged the interviewer to think both that the patient's account could be trusted and that there were quite possibly deep-seated changes.

Now, having set a baseline and established rapport with the patient, the interviewer moves forward to the patient's present state, starting with the easiest area, namely symptoms.

Therapist: All right, I think that gives me a pretty good picture of how you were then. Now, let's jump up to the present.

Patient: Okay.

Therapist: How are you feeling now as far as that aspect of you is concerned?

Patient: In terms of . . . ?

Therapist: I'm talking about the depression and isolation and all its manifestations.

Patient: I do not get depressed.

Therapist: You don't?

Patient: No, or at least what my definition is.

Therapist: Yes.

Patient: Because the way I look at depression is that I feel that it's not being aware of my feelings, being totally confused by them and going dead.

Therapist: Right, yes.

Patient: This way when I have a feeling, I'm aware of it, I react to it. I either cry or get angry or sad. So, I'm not depressed, the feeling is expressed for me.

The patient has said something of tremendous importance: not merely that he no longer gets depressed, but that he now *expresses his true feelings* and this *prevents him from being depressed.* In other words, from a position of genuine insight he both tells the interviewer—without being asked—about the dynamics of his depression and provides tangible evidence that the depression has not merely lifted but has been resolved. The way in which he said this in no way suggested that he was merely telling the interviewer what the latter wanted to hear.

Of course this needs to be gone into in detail, but before that is done there is an elementary question to ask, namely how long is it since the patient has been depressed? Obviously the longer this is the more convincing is the change, and vice versa. The interviewer therefore files away the above information for future use, and continues.

Therapist: Right. How long is it since you've been depressed?

Patient: (Pause.)

Therapist: It's only . . . I'm only trying to get you know, a few weeks or a few months.

Patient: Yes, I know. I guess there were times during my therapy in which I was depressed.

Therapist: Yes.

Patient: But since I've stopped therapy I haven't been.

Therapist: You haven't been. All right, that answers my question. Now you mentioned that nowadays you know what you feel and you feel it. You mentioned if you are upset, you cry, if you feel angry you get angry. Now can you give me examples of that? What are the kind of things that upset you for instance, and what's been your reaction?

Patient: Okay. About a week and a half after I finished therapy, I met a girl at school, and we got friendly. And I took her out on a date, and I fell for her, you know.

Therapist: Can I ask you is that the first time you've ever fallen for a girl?

Here the interviewer is mindful of another important principle of follow-up. In assessing any aspect of the patient's present state, the interviewer must always ask himself the question: Does this represent a change, or was the patient like that before he came to therapy? Failure to ask this question will leave the interviewer in ignorance of important evidence and may result in a false assessment. This interviewer had been caught this way many times before and remembers to ask the question in time.

Patient: No. No, but I was out of therapy and I felt, you know, very confident in myself, and I took her out and it just did not work out with her because I was very aware of myself and she was very unaware of herself, let's say neurotic.

Therapist: Yes.

Patient: And I just could not take her actions, her little games, but when I, you know, just broke it off there, I was very sad for a couple of days.

Therapist: Yes.

Patient: I finally broke down and cried; I just felt totally alone.

Therapist: Yes.

Patient: Uh . . .

Therapist: Can I ask you was that a different kind of crying from the crying when you were depressed?

The interviewer is once more asking the question, does this represent a change? Here the important distinction is between *depressive crying*, which is a depressive symptom and leads nowhere, and *true grieving*, which brings relief. The patient's touching answers make absolutely clear which of the two this was and show that he understands the difference between depression and grief not merely theoretically but from his own inner experience.

Patient: I didn't cry when I was depressed.
Therapist: You didn't cry.
Patient: No.
Therapist: What was the effect of the crying?
Patient: It released the sadness in me, you know, and it made me aware of certain things, like that I wasn't only crying for her, I was crying for a lot of things in my past too.
Therapist: Yes. What sort of things?
Patient: My grandfather, who died.
Therapist: Yes.
Patient: I think early moments in my childhood that I can't recollect, that my mother left me—being alone.
Therapist: Yes.
Patient: When I did have that feeling, I felt like I couldn't cope with it. For a couple of days there, I was very sad, and I even thought for a moment that I was regressing, you know, but I pulled out of it. (This rings true—the patient is not trying to pretend it was easy, which he might have if he was just trying to give the answers he thought the interviewer wanted to hear.)
Therapist: Yes. You use the word *sad* about it, you don't use *depressed*.
Patient: No.
Therapist: What's the distinction?
Patient: Because I find *depressed* so ambiguous. You know, is it really a feeling? I don't think it is. Like what does it mean to be depressed? It's everyone's choice—for me, I guess it just means being sad, or being angry, but I'm not really depressed.
Therapist: The previous depression was an *absence* of feeling, wasn't it?
Patient: Yes.
Therapist: That makes sense. Now, have there been other times when you've been sad like that since then?

Patient: Not as sad.

Therapist: No?

Patient: No. But there have been times when I would cry because of certain feelings I have.

Therapist: Such as what?

Patient: (Pause.) I think ... yeah, I was in ... I played in a big band at the Civic Center here, and my father came in, and he asked me how I was and what I was doing, and he asked me that once every month. So, I said I'm in a big band at the Center and he said, "When are you playing?" So I said to him, "In fact I'm playing this weekend." He said, "Get me some tickets." He first said two, him and his girlfriend probably, and I said, "Okay." Then he said, "Make that three, I'll take Sid and Faith." (That's my sister.) "That will be good." And that made me incredibly angry because he was saying, well now I'll be a good Daddy to him, you know?

Therapist: Right.

Patient: And I was so angry about that, and also sad about it too, because now I felt, "Now you bastard you've finally done it, but I don't want it!"

Therapist: Yes.

Patient: So I went inside the car and I started to cry, and then a couple of days later I phoned him up or he phoned me and I said, "Look, all the tickets have been sold out. I can't get you any." And that was it. I guess the two experiences in the last while that really.... I had my feelings on.

This important incident needs a good deal of discussion. First of all, it is clear that some years ago the patient was capable of asserting himself constructively with members of his family, as is shown by his ultimatum to his mother, which resulted in his father's leaving home. It is also clear, however, that in his recent crisis he had lost this capacity—for instance he was now unable to deal with his mother, and he was also unable to assert himself with his friend who exploited him. In the present incident his father was presumably trying to make reparation for his failures in the past, and the question is how we should expect the patient to react. Certainly it would be false on his part not to be angry—this would be a mere repetition of his former pattern of passivity. Probably the most constructive reaction on his part for all the parties concerned—himself, his father, and his brother and sister—would be for him to be angry but to accept his father's offer, thus allowing the possibility of undoing the vicious circle rather than perpetuating it. But of course it must be remembered that he was only a few weeks out of therapy, and this is really too much to expect. Nevertheless the painful truth is that though his reaction was assertive it was also destructive, and the interviewer feels it right to point this out. It is on such intangibles, about which each judge has to make up his own mind, that the assessment of a therapeutic result depends. They will not be made to go away by pretending they do not exist and falling back on the use of "objective" data like the MMPI.

Therapist: Yes, I can quite see how you felt, but in a way you prevented him from trying to make it up to you as well.
Patient: Because I'm too angry at him.
Therapist: Right, and you don't want to make it . . .
Patient: And I don't want to make it up because I don't feel he can really give me love, that is true. True love. And I just won't accept it because he can go and turn his back again and just shove me off again. So, I just said "No."
Therapist: Right. So that was an occasion that made you both sad and angry. What about other occasions that have made you angry, can you tell me that?
Patient: Oh, just with incidents with people in school. Just disagreements, but not really put my anger to an extreme, like in a rage, but angry feelings.
Therapist: And what did you do about them?
Patient: To one of my teachers I've expressed it.
Therapist: Can you tell me the story? What happened? (Is he perhaps able to be more constructive with his anger in situations less emotionally loaded than that with his father?)
Patient: This teacher was telling us off for not doing any work in class, in the television workshop, and I got really pissed off because most of the students in the class don't know how to put on a production. And he was telling us, "Do it by yourself," you know, and he was telling us off that we haven't done anything, and I stood up and said, "Well look, nothing has happened this term," and he was criticizing us, and I said . . . he said, "Well you could have come and talked to me about this," and I said, "You stood there a couple of

weeks ago and you said listen, this is the way I run it, if you don't like it get out. What am I supposed to say?" Anyway, it was kind of a stalemate. He says, "You do it your way, and I'll do it mine," and that was it for the . . . I'm still angry at him, but I don't feel that I have to go with it any further because I understand his position and that's all.

Therapist: So what did you do?

Patient: Well, I just talked to him in class that day. I didn't speak to him as nice as I'm speaking to you, but I was really . . . I went after him.

Therapist: Yes, and what about, you know, telling you to do it all by yourself, how did you manage?

Patient: For me, I could have done something, but the rest of the students in the class aren't motivated that way. I am; I can motivate myself to do something. I cannot run a workshop by myself, so I was kind of very angry at him for telling off the whole class because they obviously can't do it themselves. I need more than me to do something in that workshop.

Therapist: So there wasn't anything you could do?

Patient: No.

This incident is fairly encouraging since it seems to indicate that the patient is capable of assertive behavior outside his immediate family and moreover that he is capable of adjusting this behavior according to the reality of the situation—in this case making his protest but giving up when he sees there is no more he can do.

It also seems possible that this incident represented an unconscious communication about his feeling of being left on his own by his therapist; but, if it was, the interviewer failed to make the connection in his mind. In retrospect it certainly would have been worth trying to have made an interpretation about this there and then—if wrong it would have done no harm, and if correct it would have deepened rapport. Instead the interviewer leaves the incident and goes on to another area. It may well be that the patient's "playing to the gallery," which now begins to show itself, was a consequence of failing to make the above interpretation—which only goes to show how in a follow-up interview the same alertness and skill are needed as in a therapeutic session.

Therapist: So there wasn't anything you could do?

Patient: No.

Therapist: No, all right. Now there was that relation with that girl. Have there been other girls?

Patient: No, not lately.

Therapist: No. What do you feel about that, because I know that one of the difficulties that you brought to us was somehow not being able to express your feelings to a girl when you are attracted by her, is that right?

Patient: I am now.

Therapist: You are able to?

Patient: Yes, I'm smiling because *I* am able to, but *the girl* isn't able to! (This is possibly a moment when the patient started playing to the gallery.)

Therapist: The girl isn't able to?

Patient: No.

Therapist: You are talking about a particular girl, are you?

Patient: Yes.

Therapist: I thought that you finished with her, or haven't you?

Patient: Yes, I have.

Therapist: You're talking about her though?

Patient: Yes, she wasn't able to.

Therapist: She wasn't able to? How do you feel about that now, I mean if you met another girl that attracted you, you could do something about it?

Patient: Yes, I think I could, but I think I'd be more selective in who I chose.

Therapist: Yes.

Patient: Because I find myself being very aware of myself and of my feelings and who I am, that I want the same of a girl who I meet. I don't want to get involved with somebody who is confused because I know how it is. And, I'll be honest with you, there are a lot of confused girls around.

Therapist: Yes. So then with this girl that you fell for, you found yourself able to express what you felt to her at first, did you?

Patient: Uh, I'm thinking about it. Let's say we met and we hit it off right away—kind of open with each other. And I said things that I've never said to a girl before, you know, compliments. And, even when I told her off that I didn't want to see her, it was a mistake for us to get together—that was something new for me too.

Therapist: Yes.

Patient: I really said what I felt, and I feel that I can do that with any girl.

Therapist: Yes, well that's a tremendously important thing.

Patient: Oh yeah! I was kind of surprised at myself, but I know I can do it because I'm not just going to take any more crap from anyone. If something is bothering me, I'm going to say what is bothering me. (All this sounds genuine, but his next reply was playing to the gallery again.)

Therapist: How has this made you feel within yourself about yourself?

Patient: I like myself quite a deal. (Laughs.)

Therapist: Yes, I can remember at the end of the initial interview with Dr.———, he asked you, "Do you think you're a likable person?" And after some hesitation you said, yes, you thought you were.

Patient: You mean in terms of other people?

Therapist: Yes.

Patient: Um . . .

Therapist: You're talking about liking yourself.

Patient: Right.

Therapist: Well all right, is that a change? When you first came to us, did you not like yourself, or did you?

Patient: I don't think I did.

Therapist: You didn't.

Patient: I didn't. Because I wouldn't have put myself through all that crap if I did. And I like myself now. In terms of other people liking me, I don't think it bothers me as much as it did.

Therapist: No. I'm not quite clear exactly what it is you're doing currently. You've mentioned this class, is that your main work or is it . . .

Patient: No. I'm in college here, a junior college.

Therapist: Yes.

Patient: And I'm trying to complete the first year, and I'm involved in . . .

Therapist: You entered it last fall did you?

Patient: No, I've been in and out for the last three years.

Therapist: Oh, trying to do the first year?

Patient: Right.

Therapist: Okay, so please go on.

Patient: Okay, I'm completing the first year, and I hopefully will get it. I wrote in an application to a university in Toronto for television and theatre arts. So, I hope to go into that: communications, media broadcasting. And right now I'm involved in the radio station at my school. I have a show, which is, I feel is something for me, because being such a quiet person, getting up and talking to a thousand students on a radio station is quite something.

Therapist: Is that something that you didn't do before?

Patient: Oh, I could have never done it. In fact I was even nervous attempting it.

Therapist: Yes, so how did it come about that you managed it this time?

Patient: I just wanted the radio show. I was interested in radio and music. I've been into music for quite a while, and I went to a meeting and I said, "Look I'm interested in jazz and I know quite a bit." I showed them my schedule, and I got a show for two hours.

Therapist: Yes.

Patient: And, at first I was very nervous doing it.

Therapist: Well, what do you actually do? Do you play an instrument during it or do you only talk?

Patient: I spin records.

Therapist: I see, right.

Patient: I play an instrument also, but I don't play it on the show. I just got the radio show that I'm doing, and it's a lot of fun.

Therapist: That's an achievement, isn't it? *(The interviewer is very impressed with this change in the patient, and says so.)*

Patient: Yes.

Therapist: How are your studies going?

Patient: Not that well, not as well as I hoped they would. (Even if he is playing to the gallery, he still seems to be telling the truth.)

Therapist: Well, why not?

Patient: Well, there's labor problems among the teachers in school, and this is promoting a lot of study sessions and strikes, one-day strikes. This is kind of putting me off, in terms of just, you know, flowing. I feel schoolwork should just kind of flow together, and it's sort of blocking off at certain points. I just don't have the incentive anymore because there is always that thing of term may be cancelled hanging over my head.

Therapist: Who's on strike, the students or the teachers?

Patient: The teachers. They are not on strike at the moment, but they have one-day walkouts. The teachers don't seem to be into the work they are doing either, so it's a kind of apathy running around the school, and the subjects that I have to take don't really interest me. They are spread out, humanities or other subjects that I'm taking. I wish I was in university.

Therapist: Does your entry into the University of . . . depend on how well you do this year?

Patient: Well, my marks in the first term were very good, 82.5-percent average.

Therapist: The first term being when?

Patient: From September to end of December.

Therapist: Yes, I'm trying to work out . . . this was still while you were in therapy I take it?

Patient: Yes. I was still in therapy, but I had gone to a school which was a progressive type of school, where there wasn't a great emphasis on obtaining marks. It was kind of a free-form thing, so I had less pressures on my head, so I did better.

Therapist: Right, and in the last couple of months it's been not so good? (Is the withdrawal of the therapist's support responsible for this deterioration?)

Patient: Not so good. I've switched schools. At the beginning I was really into the things I was doing, but it's slackened off.

Therapist: What I'm really getting at is that if you don't do well enough, may this result in you not getting into the University of . . . ?

Patient: I won't let my marks deteriorate to the point that I won't get in because I feel my marks now, out of the exams that I've had, are okay.

Therapist: And is there a final exam at the end?

Patient: No there isn't; it's a culmination of work done during the semester.

Therapist: I see. Yes.

Patient: I feel I'll come by all right.

Therapist: And you feel your application will be accepted by . . . ?

Patient: Yes, I have a very good chance. I also had to write out a five-hundred-word statement, stating why I wanted to go into media and T.V., and it was very good, so I feel there's a very good chance with that too.

Therapist: Supposing that you don't get in? (Has the patient thought of this, or is he riding along unrealistically on the crest of the wave?)

Patient: Uh . . . I'll have to deal with that when it happens because I'm not really into staying in Montreal that much longer. I'll not stay through another year at junior college because I find it destructive for me. Most of the students there are seventeen and eighteen, and I'll be twenty-three, and I'll find there will be too great a distance. So, I will think of something about what to do.

Therapist: All right, fine. What's happened about Sidney? Have you drifted apart altogether?

Patient: Oh, I haven't spoken to him for many months.

Therapist: Have you managed to make any other friends, or not?

Patient: Well, I have my best friend, who was friends with Sidney and myself. We're very close, I still have him as a best friend.

Therapist: So Sidney wasn't really your best friend?

Patient: No, he was, but we had another close friend together with us. He is still my friend. I don't have . . . I have a lot of acquaintances, people I know in school, but as far as having friends, I term friends as very close friends. I just have one.

Therapist: All right. Do you see a good deal of each other or not?

Patient: Yes.

Therapist: What sort of things do you do together?

Patient: Oh, we go places. Go to eat, go for a drink. (Pause.) I guess we just have good times, you know.

Therapist: Can you talk to each other?

Patient: Oh yes.

Therapist: Could you before?

Patient: (Pause.) Before therapy?

Therapist: That's what I mean.

Patient: No . . . we could, but it was very surface and a lot of games between us.

Therapist: And you've been cured of games?

Patient: (Patient laughs.) Now, he looks at me differently.

Therapist: Yes.

Patient: And he's having a hard time trying to accept me as someone different than what I was before therapy because he always sees me in that old light. So, when I do something different, he says, "What are you doing?" you know?

Therapist: What sort of thing different?

Patient: Sometimes I'm walking with him in a shopping center, and I just decide . . . we're talking about something, and I say something out loud, or just jump around. He gets . . ."What are you doing?" I tell him that I'm doing what I feel like.

Therapist: It sounds like he hasn't gotten to that state himself, is that right?

Patient: No, but it is interesting because he saw the way I am looking, and he says, "Dave, where did you go for this cure?" (Patient laughs.) So, he's getting involved in this program. I think you have an interview with him. (This is important independent confirmation of the remarkable changes that the patient has undergone.)

Therapist: (Laughs.) What's his name?

Patient: Paul Hume.

Therapist: Hume, right. Well we shall see. Good.

The interviewer has deliberately left till last (1) the area where there is likely to be greatest difficulty, namely the patient's relation with his mother, and (2) the area where the patient is most likely to find it difficult to tell the truth, namely his reactions to the therapy and his feelings about the therapist.

Inquiries in the first area lead to another moment of playing to the gallery—which indeed was highly successful in that it "brought the house down" in the room next door. Because of fire regulations, the soundproofing between the two rooms leaves a great deal to be desired; the laughter was clearly audible to both therapist and patient. The playing to the gallery then became quite overt, the patient turning to the video camera and speaking directly to the audience. Although this incident was very unfortunate (and the interviewer gave the audience a good telling off afterward), it also revealed the patient as entirely equal to the occasion—an objective observation that confirmed his own account of improvement in his self-confidence.

Therapist: Good. Now then, we haven't mentioned your mother hardly at all. I know the relation with her . . . you'd had a lot of difficulties when you first came here. First question, are you still living at home?

Patient: Yes.

Therapist: You are? All right, how are things at home?
Patient: Stable.
Therapist: What exactly do you mean?
Patient: I mean that I don't talk to my mother, and she doesn't talk to me any more. (Loud laughter from next door. Patient laughs and turns to the video camera.) *Is it really that funny?*

The interviewer, both amused (which he shows) and furious (which he doesn't), waits for the situation to subside and then continues.

Therapist: When you say you don't talk to each other, now what do you mean? You literally don't talk to each other, or you don't talk to each other in the old ways, or what?
Patient: I mean that . . . we very rarely speak at all.
Therapist: How's that come about?
Patient: As I became aware of myself and projected my own personality . . . she couldn't stand for it, she wanted that old Dave back, and I just refused, so she just did not . . . I was really going through a lot of arguments about it, and I just said this is me, you don't like me, fine. This is the way I'm going to stay. She just came to my room and said, "It's better that we just don't talk." So, that was for a couple of days, then she started talking to me again. She went away for a couple of weeks, and she came back, and we haven't spoken, and that's the way it is.
Therapist: Literally haven't spoken?
Patient: I'm sure we've said a couple of words, but there's no conversation at all.
Therapist: Well, supposing you want to say, "Pass the coffee" or something like that.
Patient: Oh yeah, things like that. Courtesy.
Therapist: I mean you don't actually have to send written messages to each other?
Patient: No. No.
Therapist: What do you feel about that situation?
Patient: I'm sad in a way. I don't like it because it's every time I see her, you know, we don't talk, and there's a tension there.
Therapist: Yes, of course there is.
Patient: There's a lot of anger on my part too, but I feel it's better

than it was before the arguments. (These answers seem utterly sincere—the playing to the gallery seems to be over.)

Therapist: Yes, well of course it is, I quite see that. I think one would hope it is the transition stage to some communication on some different way from the old way.

Patient: No, she's refused to communicate with me unless it's the way she wants it.

Therapist: Is that so?

Patient: Yes, that's the way I feel. She wants it her way, because it's her house, because I'm her son, and I refuse.

Therapist: So you have little hope that it will change, is that right?

Patient: I have little hope that it will change unless she gets some kind of help.

Therapist: I see. Are you thinking of staying there?

Patient: Well, if I get accepted in Toronto . . .

Therapist: Then that solves the problem, doesn't it?

Patient: Yes. Now, if I don't get accepted, I'll have to make some serious considerations at that time because I feel my house, as it is, is not a good environment for me.

Therapist: No.

Patient: There's a lot of terrible memories there. There's sadness there, there's behavior there which I can't put up with, and I will eventually have to do something.

Therapist: I've forgotten this I'm afraid: you've got a brother and sister, is that right?

Patient: Yes.

Therapist: And you're the oldest? Well what about them? Do you get on all right with them?

Patient: Yes, we play around sometimes, you know. The age difference is great, so we're not that close. I get along with them.

Therapist: How are they affected by that situation between you and your mother?

Patient: Very affected.

Therapist: They are? In what way?

Patient: Well, between me and my mother? Or just between them and my mother?

Therapist: Between them and your mother if you like. I haven't thought of that so much.

Patient: It's very severe. I'm very worried about my brother, and I see very little that I can do right now, and I'm not that keen on getting that much involved because I feel that I have my own life right now.

Like the situation between the patient and his father, this is another situation that is extraordinarily difficult to evaluate, and yet not impossible. The basic criterion is always that the patient should take account of others' needs and his own, and act accordingly. We cannot act as God and tell him which way the decision should go, but should respect what he does as long as he does it responsibly. Here he has taken account of the potential damage to his brother, and yet has decided that there is little he can do about this and that his need to live his own life must take precedence. In other words, the basic criterion seems to be fulfilled. If he had said, "I feel I cannot abandon my brother to this situation right now; I must give up my place at . . . and try to find something that enables me to go on living at home," this also would be responsible and would be equally acceptable.

Therapist: Can I ask you, when your mother has sort of made claim that she can only communicate with you in the old way, what is the old way?

Patient: The old way is Davey doing what Mommy says, Davey staying home, helping around the house, Davey being the little husband in the house.

Therapist: Yes.

Patient: Davey not raising a word to his mother, not swearing at his mother. Not being assertive of himself and his feelings. I'm sorry, I don't do that any more.

Therapist: All right. That makes it clear to me. Let me just think if there's more things I want to ask. I've got some notes here, can I just check? (This is an important practical point for those carrying out follow-up interviews.)

Patient: Sure.

Therapist: There's always areas one's forgotten about, if one doesn't refer to these notes. (Pause.) Yes, perhaps I think the only one that I haven't fully asked about is the isolation. You gave us the impression that you were very socially isolated. I think the answer is that that has gone now, hasn't it? I mean you've talked about going out with your other friend, and you've said you've had a number of acquaintances.

Patient: Let's put it this way: I can go into a public place or bar or pub, and I won't feel that people are looking at me and talking about me. I feel socially confident, to sit somewhere by myself and just take in what's around me.

Therapist: Right.

Patient: And since I'm more assertive of myself, people know who I am. So, they have someone to relate to, they don't have someone in the background.

Therapist: Do you go to parties?

Patient: Very few parties.

Therapist: Well, they don't have them in your . . . can you relate to several people at once? I mean have you ever had a situation where there are three or four of you, you know, going out together.

Patient: Oh yeah, that's okay.

Therapist: That's okay. All right, good. Now, the other area I'd like to ask you about—no, wait a minute, one more question, and that is, how do you feel about the future? No, do you feel that there are still some areas of your life that need improvement?

Patient: Yeah.

Therapist: What are they?

Patient: There are a lot of feelings that I've had I think that I'm still relating to my past.

Therapist: Yes.

Patient: And they bother me, but they are there, and . . .

Therapist: Can you give me an example?

Patient: When I broke up with this girl.

Therapist: Yes, that's an obvious example.

Patient: And there's still a lot of hate and anger toward my father on my part.

Therapist: Yes.

The patient, with remarkable insight, has unerringly put his finger on two areas where changes are needed. This is important evidence leading toward the conclusion that however much he may at times have been playing to the gallery, his replies are basically insightful and sincere. It thus represents a situation in which the overall Gestalt can be used to verify, or cast doubt on, individual areas of the patient's replies—something that is not taken account of in most objective tests, though the "lie scale" of the MMPI is possibly an exception. The patient's sincerity is further supported by his replies to questions about his experience of therapy, which seem very balanced, containing neither resentment nor idealization.

Patient: This crops up now and then. I guess when I . . . there must be other things, but those are the things that right now I am aware of.

Therapist: Yes, obviously you can't hope for that to go completely. Your past is your past, is there . . . Whatever happens is going to be related to it in a way, isn't this right?

Patient: I kind of feel that I'd like to relate to present situations. Present feelings of sadness, that . . . things do not have to be related to the past, because the past doesn't exist.

Therapist: All right. I'll put it differently. You've got to go through a fairly long period of working that one through. You must understand that. You can't expect it to all . . . what you're saying is right, I agree with you, that you should aim to work through to the point at which you just relate to what's happening now, and that's the thing that gives you the feelings, but it must always have echoes from the past. All right, that's good. Now then, so the other area I want to ask you about is your experience with therapy, what do you feel happened?

Patient: I came into therapy in a very terrible state, and . . . with the help of Dr. ——— and myself, we went through my life and my feelings, what confused me. Just like unravelled my mind, which had been so twisted and so tangled up. And as I began to understand, my behavior changed because I was able to relate certain feelings that I have. It had to do with feelings, basically emotions, that I was so confused about. Then I held them in all the time: held in the anger, the sadness. When I began expressing them and becoming aware of them, sadness would go because I expressed it. Anger would go because I expressed it, so it wouldn't build up on the inside and cause me to do certain things, you know. And I'm now aware of myself because of the therapy.

Therapist: Can you recollect for me perhaps the most important moment of therapy to you?

Patient: (Pause.)

Therapist: It doesn't have to be the most important moment, but an important moment.

Patient: (Pause.) There were many, you know. (Pause. Patient laughs.)

Therapist: What's the difficulty?

Patient: The difficulty is in placing some, because there was one important one. (Pause.) Well one was anger. I got to a point where I went and expressed my anger to my mother of how I felt. That was a very . . . another one was, I expressed my love, which I've never done.

Therapist: To whom?

Patient: To Dr. ———.

Therapist: To Dr. ———, yes.

Patient: And that was important for me because, I was always unwilling to because when I had, I was always stamped upon for it. I was always knifed in the back. I did it this time, and that was important for me.

Therapist: Yes. Yes. So you developed quite strong feelings about Dr. ———, did you?

Patient: Yeah, because I never had a type of relationship like that, and I put in terms of father-son. It happened that way, and there's not much else that I can say about it except they were very deep feelings.

Therapist: Yes. How did you react to stopping?

Patient: Very emotionally. I was very sad because it pulled off some old hurts, but as long as I expressed it, it was okay. For a couple of days I was kind of sad, but it went away, I didn't hold it in.

Therapist: Did you get angry with Dr. ——— during the course of the therapy? (This question obviously is designed to test out the degree of idealization.)

Patient: Yeah.

Therapist: Over what sort of thing?

Patient: I didn't express my anger that much. I feel now not as much as I should have.

Therapist: No, what were the sort of things that made you angry?

Patient: His harping on me, you know, kind of attacking me. I wouldn't stand for it. It was making me tense and anxious, I was getting angry, but it was actually some other feeling. I was also angry when I had to leave. I was angry there.

Therapist: Were you?

Patient: I didn't express it to him, but I did feel anger, you know, because I felt it may have been my Daddy leaving me again.

Therapist: Yes. How was the question of stopping brought up? Did you know the number of sessions you were going to have from the beginning or not?

Patient: No. It was about toward the end, we put a date, we said how many sessions, four more, or was it three more? And we went like that.

Therapist: Three more doesn't give you very much time to get used to the idea, or was it enough?

Patient: (Pause.) I think it was enough.

Therapist: You do.

Patient: For me anyway. I really felt if I had gone on any longer it would have been a crutch for me.

Therapist: Yes.

Patient: And it would have been hard to break away.

Therapist: So how would you feel about a further interview, sometime in the future with Dr. ——— himself, rather than with someone like me?

Patient: Why would I need one?

Therapist: For his interest; it wouldn't be for your sake, not unless you asked for it, but I'm not even saying that it may happen, I just simply don't know.

Patient: How would I feel about one?

Therapist: You know, what we'd like to do is to be able to follow up patients for some time after they've stopped in order to see how they've been doing, so I was wondering how you would react to that? I'm not saying that it will happen.

Patient: I don't feel that I'd like one.

Therapist: You don't.

Patient: I wouldn't mind him phoning me up and talking for a couple of minutes, "How are you? How are things?" But I don't think I would like to go through a session with him.

Therapist: It wouldn't be a session; it would be something much more like what I'm doing with you now, you see, but what you're saying is that you wouldn't even like that, would you?

Patient: Uh, I guess it's the way I feel now.

Therapist: Why wouldn't you? Can you put that into words?

Patient: I guess it's the feelings I have that we did break away. I did break away, and it was quite emotional for me.

Therapist: What you're saying is that you don't want old wounds reopened, aren't you?

Patient: Yeah.

Therapist: Of course. What have you felt about being interviewed by me?

Patient: I feel fine about it.
Therapist: You do? It's all right?
Patient: Yeah.
Therapist: You know you've given us a lot to think about.
Patient: Yes, I'm very proud of myself.
Therapist: Yes, I should think so too. That's really all I want to ask you. Do you want to ask me anything before we stop?

This is an important question at the end of any initial or follow-up interview. The patient is very likely to be full of unexpressed feelings stirred up by the interview, and this gives him the chance to express them. In turn, his questions may lead to important moments of communication and important information which the interview itself has failed to elicit. However, in the present interview the patient declines the offer.

Patient: (Pause.) No.
Therapist: No? Are you sure?
Patient: Uh . . . (pause) . . . no, no questions.
Therapist: No, all right. Okay, well thank you very much for coming then.

REVIEW OF THE CRITERIA

A one-month follow-up is of course far too early to make any definitive judgment about the patient's improvement, but it is important to make a provisional review of the criteria.

1. Depression replaced by (a) reasonable hope and (b) ability to express feelings. According to his account both parts of this criterion are completely fulfilled. (a) He is no longer depressed and is hopeful about the future. (b) In his own words: "Sadness would go because I expressed it. Anger would go because I expressed it." Moreover, it is extremely important that he suffered a specific stress likely to lead to depression, namely the break-up with his girlfriend, and instead he reacted with the appropriate emotion of grief.
2. Withdrawal replaced by social confidence. This seems clearly fulfilled. His ability to act as a disc jockey on a radio show and to enjoy it ("it's a lot of fun") is important confirmation of this, as is his friend's question, "Dave, where did you go for this cure?"

3. *Ability to deal with his mother.* He has made plain to his mother that he is no longer willing to repeat the old patterns that she requires of him. This has resulted in a state of noncommunication between the two of them, which is a very unsatisfactory situation, but clearly not entirely of his making. It is very difficult to know whether or not he should be expected to be able to break this. Certainly at some future follow-up we would like to see that he has at least made efforts to break it, even if he has not succeeded.

4. *Passivity replaced by constructive self-assertion.* He has made considerable progress in this direction, being able to stand out against his mother and to assert himself with the teacher. His reaction in the incident with his father was destructive, though understandable, and certainly better than resentful passivity.

5. *Effectiveness at work.* He has done well in his studies and seems to have realistic plans for the future. Only time will show whether he will ultimately be able to fulfill his potential.

6. *Relation with women.* He fell for one girl, found her inadequate, left her, experienced appropriate grief, and got over it. All this seems absolutely appropriate. He feels he would now be able to express his feelings to a girl, but once more only time will show.

Summary

The progress that he has made appears absolutely genuine and is exceedingly impressive. Further follow-up is needed to see whether this can be consolidated and extended.

20

Problems of Research

Hans H. Strupp, Ph.D.

SHORT-TERM PSYCHOTHERAPY IS
THE WAVE OF THE FUTURE

The question of whether it is possible to shorten the course of
psychotherapy, preferably without loss of its effectiveness, has been
with us for some time. No sooner had Freud evolved and perfected
psychoanalysis—he was straightforward about its length and demands[1] (in those days nine months to a year!)—than innovators,

Presented at Third International Symposium on Short-Term Dynamic Psychotherapy, Los Angeles, California.

1. "To speak more plainly, psychoanalysis is always a matter of long periods of
time, of half a year or whole years (!) It is therefore our duty to tell the patient this
before he finally decides upon the treatment. I consider it altogether more honorable, and also more expedient, to draw his attention—without trying to frighten him
off, but at the very beginning—to the difficulties and sacrifices which analytic
treatment involves, and in this way to deprive him of any right to say later on that he
has been inveigled into a treatment whose extent and implications he did not realize"
(Freud 1913, p. 129).

notably Rank and Ferenczi, began to explore the possibility of shortening it. Freud was ambivalent about these attempts, and the general trend—from psychoanalysis and client-centered therapy to behavior therapy—has always been for treatment to become longer as a therapeutic system developed. Within psychoanalysis, efforts to experiment with the "standard technique" never ceased. Alexander and French's work in the 1940s (1946) was remarkably creative, and while it unleashed a flood of criticism by the establishment, it was far ahead of its time. Today short-term psychotherapy, which includes, but is by no means coextensive with, crisis intervention, is receiving renewed attention. In my judgment it is indeed the wave of the future. Let me cite some major reasons for this assertion.

1. Whether openly acknowledged or not, the vast amount of psychotherapy being done today is in fact time limited (Garfield, in press). This is particularly true of the clinical work done at outpatient clinics and community mental health centers; private practitioners, too, are becoming aware that open-ended psychotherapy, following the classical psychoanalytic model, is impractical and unfeasible in the vast majority of instances. In general, the field is overcoming the prejudice that time-limited psychotherapy is superficial therapy, that it is somehow inferior, an undesirable compromise dictated by external circumstances.

2. The search for hard evidence supporting Freud's claim that psychoanalysis, as distinguished from other forms of psychotherapy, produces radical reconstructive personality changes has not borne fruit (Fisher and Greenberg 1977). By contrast, in our cost-conscious, consumer-oriented society, which is increasingly becoming interested in making psychotherapy available to larger segments of the population, the search for economical treatments has become markedly intensified. With insurance companies and the government becoming partners in the therapeutic enterprise, there has been a new insistence on efficent modes of treatment whose results can be demonstrated and documented.

3. From the research standpoint it has become obvious that short-term therapy is the only modality that can be effectively researched. While this fact has often been seen as an unwanted limitation, we now recognize that time-limited therapy affords the researcher challenging and unmatched opportunities to learn about the process and outcome of psychotherapy regardless of its form or length.

Finally there have been some promising advances in short-term therapy which strongly suggest that we are only on the threshold of exploring its potentialities.

Despite these promising developments, there remains, as Butcher and Koss (1978) in their incisive review of short-term psychotherapy document, a lack of solid knowledge on almost every point one cares to mention: the kinds of patients for whom a particular form of time-limited psychotherapy may be suitable as well as those for whom it may be contraindicated; the kinds of therapeutic changes one may reasonably anticipate and work toward; the most appropriate techniques for reaching these goals; identification of the "active ingredients"; the training and experience a short-term therapist should possess; and the necessary procedures for bringing about an optimal match between a suitable patient and an appropriate therapist. If, as a researcher and as a clinician, one is looking for challenges, no richer ones can be found anywhere.

Consider further: There is a vast hiatus between what is taught and what is practiced. In the traditional training programs for psychiatrists and clinical psychologists, scant attention is usually paid to the realities of time-limited treatment. Instead the model that is being taught implies the availability of unlimited time and therapeutic resources. To be more specific: How many young therapists are being taught how to formulate a realistic therapeutic objective for a given patient, how to assess the patient's personality structure in relation to the presenting complaint and in relation to a reasonably specific objective, how to gear therapeutic techniques to the achievement of these objectives, and how to assess whether these goals have been reached? How does one go about identifying a "dynamic focus"? What kinds of activity should one engage in once therapy gets under way? What is the relative promise of particular techniques? What procedures and maneuvers should be avoided, either because they are potentially unproductive or possibly even harmful? These are but a few of the questions that training, practice, and research must address in the future.

What we must strive for, it seems to me, is a *new realism* in psychotherapy, a new awareness of what is feasible and practicable. This means that we must deepen and extend our knowledge of the therapeutic process and its outcome. In short, we must infuse the therapeutic enterprise, time limited or otherwise, with the best knowledge from clinical experience and research that has been accumulated over the years. We must become increasingly serious about what psychotherapy can do and what it cannot do. As this process gains momentum, we may have to abandon some cherished notions from the past and we may have to become more modest about our activities. But I venture to predict that in so doing we will evolve a profession that commands increasing respect from the public and one in which we ourselves can take greater pride.

Research Problems

But how is this to be done? In broad terms the research problems to be faced in Short-Term Dynamic Therapy (STP) are substantially identical to those of psychotherapy research in general. By this time researchers have become quite clear about the deficiencies of past efforts and the steps that must be taken in the future. A recent summary of the current situation in research on the treatment of sexual dysfunctions applies with equal force to STP:

> most of this new literature consists of case studies, uncontrolled or poorly controlled "demonstrations" of therapeutic effects, or badly confounded (and therefore uninterpretable) clinical studies. Much of this literature is further weakened by failure to clearly specify the characteristics of the patients. . . . Similarly, little attention is paid to therapist characteristics associated with good or poor outcome. It is rare that therapeutic interventions are described with sufficient clarity and detail to make it possible for others to replicate procedures. The treatment interventions are generally broad spectrum, multi-faceted combinations of a variety of procedures, with no attempt to differentiate the "active ingredients" and the "inert fillers" in the total package. In reporting the results of such treatment, formal psychometric assessment of patient functioning at a variety of levels pre and post therapy is rare. More commonly, the clinician's unsubstantiated global judgment of "success" or "failure" is simply reported. Long term follow-up data are generally not obtained. Finally, the most influential clinical literature in the field has been generated by a very small number of therapists, which creates at least the possibility that it is charismatic personality or style of these therapists, rather than the techniques themselves, which accounts for the reported success of these . . . therapies. [LoPiccolo, in press]

The message is by now loud and clear that psychotherapy research must increasingly be geared to clinical realities. In other words, research must provide practicing clinicians useful answers to the key questions: What specific outcomes may be expected when a specific form of treatment is applied to a particular patient with particular problems (Bergin and Strupp 1972, Paul 1969, Kiesler 1971)?

The strategic, technical, and methodological problems which must be confronted along this route have been discussed in considerable detail by a number of researchers and require no reiteration (Bergin and Strupp 1972, Fiske et al. 1970, Garfield and Bergin 1978, LoPiccolo in press, Kiesler 1971, Butcher and Koss 1978, Strupp 1978). Instead I shall restrict myself in the ensuing discussion to a few selected problems which impress me as being of particular relevance to research in STP.

Clinical relevance. Let me first explore some implications of the proposition that we need methodologically sophisticated research which is clinically relevant, in the sense that the goal of research is to improve clinical practice.

1. Analog studies are increasingly becoming of questionable value. Instead we must study real patients with real problems, and the treatment must serve a real function in the patients' lives, that is, it must be sought and desired by the candidates, who in turn must have a real commitment to its course and outcome. As research has progressed, there are now compelling reasons for rejecting designs involving volunteers, quasi-treatments, and many laboratory studies. Conversely the yield of "true" studies of therapy is potentially much greater than any other investment one could name.

2. The isolation of the active ingredients in STP as well as other forms remains one of the most significant research tasks, and its solution, as I have maintained over the years (Strupp 1973a, 1973b), will mark the most important advance in therapy research. Such advances will place in perspective the relative contribution of non-specific factors and cast new light on the potential utility of the many new techniques that are presented, often with great fanfare, to the public every year.

3. Furthermore, there is the growing importance of the therapeutic or working alliance, that is, the quality of the relationship between patient and therapist, which in my view determines the fate of the

therapeutic undertaking. Studied here must be those characteristics of patients that enable them to collaborate effectively with a therapist, the characteristics of therapists that make it possible to harness the forces working in favor or against therapy, and the therapeutic management of the dynamics of the patient-therapist interaction upon which treatment outcomes crucially depend (Strupp in press).

4. On the basis of my experience in the Vanderbilt Psychotherapy Research Project, I am increasingly impressed with the limited utility of traditional research designs involving group comparisons. Such comparisons undeniably represent a first step, but they are only a beginning. Clinicians' skepticism about the value of this research strategy is well taken since it typically obscures precisely those things which they most urgently need to know—the dynamic fate of the idiosyncratic patient-therapist dyad. My recommendation here is a stepwise procedure, consisting of traditional group comparisons to be followed by creative[2] analyses of the *process* of individual patient-therapist dyads. Such a combination appears to be one of the best ways for pursuing clinically meaningful research, since it takes advantage of the unique value of N=1 studies, while guarding against faulty inference.

5. Renewed and more incisive attention must be directed at patient variables and their impact upon the selection of a suitable form of therapy, its course, and outcome. A salient example is the patient's amenability, or conversely resistance, to a particular form of treatment. Categorizations in terms of phenotypical "problems" or "targets" are too crude, and it has long been known that traditional diagnostic categories are not particularly helpful. There is still too much research in which such variables as patients' motivation for therapy, expectancies, and the array of characterological variables that determine a patient's ability and willingness to enter into a therapeutic alliance, etc., are ignored. If progress is to be made in

2. The vast majority of process measures have not provided the kind of enrichment in knowledge I have in mind (Orlinsky and Howard 1978). Many of the earlier approaches have been too simplistic, and they have failed to tap those qualities in the patient-therapist interaction which determine its individual course and outcome. Another stumbling block has been the crudeness of outcome measures and related problems (see below). These shortcomings, coupled with constantly shifting patterns of human adaptation, have conspired to yield the blurred picture that is before us.

selecting the right kind of patient for the right kind of treatment—a task I consider of signal importance—we must provide the clinician with tools for accomplishing these ends. In this respect, the search for *single* variables, within patient or therapist, as powerful predictors of outcome has essentially proven futile (Garfield 1978, Parloff et al. 1978). Instead we must evolve more complex models of research which take account of idiographic factors inherent in the interaction of a particular patient with a particular therapist. Research focused on factors entering into the therapeutic alliance, in my view, is one such approach.

Let me elaborate my statement concerning the shortcomings of patient classifications in terms of "problems" or "target symptoms." In the Vanderbilt Psychotherapy Research Project (Strupp and Hadley 1979), despite serious effort to identify a homogeneous patient population through the imposition of a fairly rigorous set of criteria (male college students, single, significant elevations on MMPI scales 2, 7, and 0, presenting problems of anxiety, depression, and social withdrawal), we discovered that our samples manifested considerable diversity in terms of clinically relevant variables, which had an important bearing upon the course and outcome of their therapy (Gomes-Schwartz 1978). We reconfirmed that patient problems are not unitary (Kiesler 1966, Strupp and Bergin 1969) and that ways must be found to adequately account for this diversity. In this connection the oft-repeated argument that research dealing with highly homogeneous patient populations prevents generalizations to other groups, while literally true, is nonetheless specious since in research we must always limit our focus if precise answers of any kind are to be forthcoming.

6. Our knowledge of therapist characteristics is still woefully inadequate (Parloff et al. 1978). My own view, which first received indirect empirical support in a large analog study (Strupp 1960), has remained essentially unaltered: I consider the quality of the therapist's commitment and caring as an absolutely necessary but not suffcient condition for therapeutic change. Added to it must be technical expertise which enables the therapist, particularly in dealing with deeply engrained neurotic and characterological problems, to maximize his effectiveness. Conversely I am becoming increasingly skeptical about research on the effectiveness of therapeutic techniques in the abstract. Thus I see relatively little promise in

efforts to compare different technical approaches per se. This assertion should not be construed as synonymous with the position (Frank 1974) that common factors in all forms of psychotherapy account for the largest segment of the variance in therapeutic change; instead I propose that the amalgam of technical skills and personal qualities in a particular therapist represents the key to the "active ingredients" in psychotherapy, short term or otherwise. In this respect I continue to believe that the psychoanalytic approach, particularly the skillful analysis of transference problems in the here and now of the therapeutic relationship, has a great deal to offer. Since I am thinking here primarily of persistent neurotic patterns which in my experience typically underlie focal conflicts, I am forced to conclude that time-limited psychotherapy which has such analyses (and associated working through) as its goal cannot really be brief (to name an arbitrary figure, say, less than six months or even a year). In keeping with the foregoing, I believe that short-range therapeutic improvements capitalize to a much greater extent upon the curative effects of the common, nonspecific factors. What is needed at this point, it seems to me, is research to subject these assertions to empirical test.

The outcome problem. Apart from the study of the active ingredients in psychotherapy, no problem is of greater significance than the assessment of therapeutic change. What is the meaning of success or failure? How is improvement (or deterioration) to be assessed? While these problems have plagued the field over the years and while definitive solutions are not to be expected in the foreseeable future, significant progress has been made in identifying the issues (Bergin and Lambert 1978, Strupp 1978, Strupp, Hadley, and Gomes-Schwartz 1977, Strupp and Hadley 1977). The following points appear to be crucial:

Definitions of improvement are inseparable from and presuppose the existence of standards against which measurements are to be judged. As elaborated by Strupp and Hadley (1977), these standards embody conceptions of mental health (or in this case, notions about adequacy of sexual functioning) prevailing in our society. These conceptions, furthermore, are heavily suffused by society's values, so evaluations of improvement or deterioration always represent someone's judgment—that of the individual patient, the mental health professional, or society. We demonstrated that these three perspectives are frequently in conflict and that one cannot speak meaningfully of a treatment outcome until the perspectives and their underlying values are made explicit. For example, as researchers (or as members of society) we must decide whether we shall accept as a valid criterion of outcome an individual's self-report of improved functioning, whether we shall invoke the postulates of a particular theory of therapy and its associated value framework of mental health, or whether the individual's overt behavior, as viewed and judged by society, will constitute the yardstick. While researchers can attempt to obtain pertinent measures in all these domains, they cannot resolve the problem of underlying values. Among other things, this means that one cannot legitimately combine measures from the three perspectives (by statistical procedures or in other ways) or presume that a consensus among the interested parties exists when no prior effort has been made to achieve it. None of these problems are intrinsically insoluble; however, it is essential to spell out the rules by which the therapy outcome "game" is to be played. Unless this is done, it will remain impossible to demonstrate the effectiveness or utility of any psychosocial treatment, and therapists and researchers will continue to be vulnerable to the attacks of diverse critics.

Another problem which has still not been squarely confronted relates to the meaning and significance of an observed or measured change. Clinical significance is obviously not identical with statistical significance. Thus a decrement of ten points on the Depression Scale of the MMPT may be significantly different from chance, but it is quite another matter whether the individual patient regards it as personally significant. Furthermore, a given change may be valued highly by one patient but not by another. The difficulties alluded to in the foregoing examples are part of the growing realization among clinicians and researchers that we must seek to individualize assessments of therapeutic change (Bergin and Lambert 1978, Strupp and Bergin 1969).

Furthermore we must take more seriously the subtlety of many therapeutic changes which continues to be missed by our still primitive measuring instruments and assessment procedures. For example, a patient following STP may have shifted his or her cognitive framework and achieved a more realistic self-concept. Perhaps the patient has lowered perfectionistic standards for himself or herself and has developed greater frustration tolerance, ego strength, etc. Such changes clearly are subtle; they are intrapsychic, and they may not be reflected in overt behavior. Thus they may not be detected by most of our measuring instruments. Nonetheless for the patient they may be extraordinarily real, and they may reflect true therapeutic change regardless of numerical values derived from questionnaires, etc. Of course I cannot prove that such changes were a function of therapy and that they could not have been brought about in other ways, but I am prepared to argue that perhaps the most important therapeutic changes represent a change in "outlook," an altered view of oneself and one's place in the world. At times such changes may be reflected in responses to structured questionnaire items, but often they are more impressively demonstrated by spontaneous comments a patient may make about his therapy experience in a broader context. To the patient (as well as the therapist) such comments are extraordinarily real, irrespective of whether they can be documented by a test or scale. The lesson to be learned is that we must devise techniques appropriately sensitive to changes that are clinically and humanly significant; concomitantly we must abandon a blind faith in numbers, scores, and the statistical paraphernalia associated with them.

The following recommendations are a brief outline of some of the tasks that must be accomplished:

1. In order to make meaningful assessments of an end state (outcome), it is essential to articulate it to a beginning state (intake). That is, the success or failure of any form of psychotherapy must be assessed in relation to clear statements about the problem(s) presented by the individual patient. The problem and the associated goal may be highly limited (e.g., alleviation of a specific symptom) or they may be extensive (e.g., particular aspects of more adaptive functioning in society, greater sense of well-being); there may be single or multiple problems; the problem(s) may be stated in behavioral or psychodynamic terms, or in some combination. Crucial in any event is sufficient specificity to allow assessment of change in relation to reasonably precise anchors that have been determined in advance. In other words, greater effort must be devoted to the refinement of diagnostic procedures and the translation of diagnos-

tic formulations into meaningful indices against which therapeutic changes can be measured.

2. As pointed out earlier, the values and perspectives of the patient, the mental health professional, and society must be embodied in measures of the therapeutic problem and desired change.

3. Ideally, therapeutic operations should be maximally geared to the achievement of specific therapeutic objectives (see above). Since there is accumulating evidence that therapy generally proceeds on a relatively broad front and since a patient's presenting problem or goal may change as therapy gets under way, such precision is difficult to achieve. In clinical practice, furthermore, it is often necessary to respond flexibly to change in patients' goals and/or reformulations of the therapeutic problem in the light of new evidence. The researcher, however, must resist such changes in midstream. In other words, if one is interested in studying the effect of treatment X on, say, alleviation of a phobia or a compulsive ritual, the utility of that treatment must be assessed in relation to this problem and no other. Upon termination we cannot say: "The presenting problem is relatively unchanged, but there have been other changes in the patient's functioning, and he generally feels a lot better." On the basis of the results we might conclude that treatment X is a valuable form of psychotherapy, but one might not be able to support the claim that it is a specific form of STP or that it proves a certain theoretical position. (When all is said and done, there may be few "specific" psychosocial treatments of any kind!)

4. We must also achieve consensus on the optimal time at which a treatment is to be assessed (termination, a specified follow-up period, etc.) and the permanence of change that is expected. Follow-up is essential in any case, but what can be said about the effectiveness or value of a therapy if after two to three years the patient experiences a recurrence of his difficulties, even if his life situation has remained relatively stable (which is frequently not the case)? Therapists should not be held responsible for permanent change (if there is such a thing) any more than physicians lose face for the recurrence of a patient's illness. I have never been able to understand how the notion gained currency that psychotherapists are healers who are somehow supposed to achieve cures that no one has been able to produce in any other area.

5. Finally, and of greatest importance, concerted efforts must be

made to develop a set of standard measures consonant with and responsive to the requirements that have been delineated. Until the ideal battery is developed, we may have to settle for a carefully chosen set of existing instruments (see the recommendations set forth by Waskow and Parloff 1975). In the long run, however, it will be necessary for clinicians and researchers to join forces in developing a set of measures that embody to a fuller extent than do existing instruments the insights we have gained in recent years. This will be a major undertaking, and it will be demanding in terms of time, money, and energy. In light of society's increasing interest in evaluating the utility, cost-effectiveness, and value of all psychological treatments, as well as their safety and potential harmfulness (Strupp, Hadley and Gomes-Schwartz 1977), there is no time like the present to mount such a project. Because of its magnitude and importance, it should be spearheaded by an agency like NIMH. The end result, as I see it, will be a vastly improved set of procedures and measures that will for the first time bring diagnosis in line with treatment and outcome. These will be the tools which, in conjunction with appropriate research, will enable us to make more conclusive and authoritative statements about psychotherapy, its modus operandi, range of utility when the conditions have been specified, and its value for the individual, the mental health professions, and society. Last, but perhaps most important, we shall be developing a group of professionals whose level of sophistication and expertise far exceeds contemporary standards.

References

Alexander, F., and French, T. (1946). *Psychoanalytic Therapy*. New York: Ronald Press.

Bergin, A.E., and Lambert, M.J. (1978). The evaluation of therapeutic outcomes. In *Handbook of Psychotherapy and Behavior Change*, 2nd Edition, ed. S.L. Garfield and A.E. Bergin. New York: Wiley.

Bergin, A.E., and Strupp, H.H. (1972). *Changing Frontiers in the Science of Psychotherapy*. Chicago: Aldine-Atherton.

Butcher, J., and Koss, M. (1978). Trends in short-term psychotherapy research. In *Handbook of Psychotherapy and Behavior Change*, 2nd Edition, S.L. Garfield and A.E. Bergin. New York: Wiley.

Fisher, S., and Greenberg, R.P. (1977). *The Scientific Credibility of Freud's Theories and Therapy*. New York: Basic Books.

Fiske, D.W., Hunt, H.F., Luborsky, L., Orne, M.T., Parloff, M.B., Reiser, M.F., and Tuma, A.H. (1970). Planning of research on effectiveness of psychotherapy. *Archives of General Psychiatry* 22:22-32.

Frank, J.D. (1974). Therapeutic components of psychotherapy. *Journal of Nervous and Mental Disease* 159:325-342.

Freud, S. (1913). On beginning the treatment. *Standard Edition* 12:121-144.

Garfield, S.L. (1978). Research on client variables in psychotherapy. In *Handbook of Psychotherapy and Behavior Change*, 2nd Edition, ed. S.H. Garfield and A. E. Bergin. New York: Wiley.

Garfield, S.L., and Bergin, A.E., eds. (1978). *Handbook of Psychotherapy and Behavior Change*, 2nd Edition. New York: Wiley.

Gomes-Schwartz, B. (1978) Effective ingredients in psychotherapy: prediction of outcome from process variables. *Journal of Consulting and Clinical Psychology*, 46:1023-1035

Kiesler, D. J. (1966). Some myths of psychotherapy research and the search for a paradigm. *Psychological Bulletin* 65:110-136.

——— (1971). Experimental designs in psychotherapy research. In *Handbook of Psychotherapy and Behavior Change: An Empirical Analysis*, ed. A.E. Bergin and S.L. Garfield. New York: Wiley.

LoPiccolo, J. (in press). Methodological issues in research on treatment of sexual dysfunction.

Orlinsky, D.E., and Howard, K.I. (1978). The relation of process to outcome in psychotherapy. In *Handbook of Psychotherapy and Behavior Change*, 2nd Edition, ed. S.L. Garfield and A.E. Bergin. New York: Wiley.

Parloff, M.B., Waskow, I.E., and Wolfe, B.E. (1978). Research on therapist variables in relation to process and outcome. In *Handbook of Psychotherapy and Behavior Change*, 2nd Edition. ed. S.L. Garfield and A.E. Bergin. New York: Wiley.

Paul, G.L. (1969). Behavior modification research: design and tactics. In *Behavior Therapy: Appraisal and Status*, ed. C.M. Franks. New York: McGraw-Hill.

Strupp, H.H. (1960). *Psychotherapists in Action: Explorations of the Therapist's Contribution to the Treatment Process*. New York: Grune and Stratton.

——— (1973a). On the basic ingredients of psychotherapy. *Journal of Consulting and Clinical Psychology* 11:1-8.

——— (1973b). Toward a reformulation of the psychotherapeutic influence. *International Journal of Psychiatry* 11:347-354.

——— (1978). Psychotherapy research and practice: an overview. In *Handbook of Psychotherapy and Behavior Change*, 2nd Edition, ed. S.L. Garfield and A.E. Bergin. New York: Wiley.

Strupp, H.H., and Bergin, A.E. (1969). Some empirical and conceptual bases for coordinated research in psychotherapy. *International Journal of Psychiatry* 7:18-90.

Strupp, H.H., and Hadley, S.W. (1977). A tripartite model of mental health and therapeutic outcomes. *American Psychologist* 32:187-196.

——— (1979). Specific versus nonspecific factors in psychotherapy: a controlled study of outcome. *Archives of General Psychiatry* 36:1125-1136.

Strupp, H.H., Hadley, S.W., and Gomes-Schwartz, B. (1977). *Psychotherapy for Better or Worse: The Problem of Negative Effects.* New York: Jason Aronson.

Waskow, I.E., and Parloff, M.B., eds. (1975). *Psychotherapy Change Measures.* Rockville, Maryland: National Institute of Mental Health.

Contributors

Saul L. Brown, M.D.
Associate Clinical Professor of Psychiatry
University of California, Los Angeles
Director, Department of Psychiatry and
Thalians Community Mental Health Center
Cedars-Sinai Medical Center
Los Angeles

Habib Davanloo, M.D.
Associate Professor of Psychiatry
McGill University
Director, Institute for Teaching and Research
in Short-Term Dynamic Psychotherapy
The Montreal General Hospital
Montreal

Samuel Eisenstein, M.D.
Associate Clinical Professor of Psychiatry
University of Southern California
School of Medicine
Los Angeles

David H. Malan, M.D.
Consultant
Tavistock Clinic
London, England

Judd Marmor, M.D.
Franz Alexander Professor of Psychiatry
University of Southern California
School of Medicine
Los Angeles

Katherina Marmor, Ph.D.
Coordinator
Group Therapy Program
Suicide Prevention Center
Los Angeles

Peter Sifneos, M.D.
Professor of Psychiatry
Harvard Medical School
Associate Director
Department of Psychiatry
Beth Israel Hospital
Boston

Manuel Straker, M.D.
Professor of Psychiatry
University of California, Los Angeles
Chief, Psychiatric Services
Veterans Administration
Wadsworth Hospital Center
Los Angeles

Hans H. Strupp, Ph.D.
Distinguished Professor of Psychology
Vanderbilt University
Nashville, Tennessee

Index